The Politics of Pleasure

A Portrait of Benjamin Disraeli

WILLIAM KUHN

POCKET
BOOKS

LONDON • SYDNEY • NEW YORK • TORONTO

First published in Great Britain by The Free Press in 2006
This edition first published by Pocket Books, 2007
An imprint of Simon & Schuster UK Ltd
A CBS COMPANY

1 3 5 7 9 10 8 6 4 2

Simon & Schuster UK Ltd
Africa House
64–78 Kingsway
London WC2B 6AH

www.simonsays.co.uk

Simon & Schuster Australia
Sydney

A CIP catalogue record for this book is available
from the British Library.

ISBN-13: 978-1-4165-2601-8
ISBN-10: 1-4165-2601-3

Typeset in Bembo by M Rules
Printed and bound in Great Britain by
Cox & Wyman Ltd, Reading, Berks

for Sheila Markham

and in memory of
Carla Baumgart-Markham

Contents

Acknowledgements

Disraeli liked to say that he had been born in a library and that is where I have spent many happy hours pursuing him. I read most of his novels in the reading rooms of the British Library in St Pancras, and looked at his papers, which are on loan from the National Trust, at the Bodleian Library in Oxford. Librarians at both these places helped me write this book, as did their colleagues at the London Library in St James's Square, the Hedberg Library at Carthage and the Northwestern University Library in Evanston.

The President of Carthage, F Gregory Campbell, and the Dean of the College, Kurt Piepenburg, made this book possible by arranging a year's leave from teaching. My colleagues in the History Department at Carthage, John Neuenschwander, Thomas Noer, Steven Udry and Stephanie Mitchell, covered for me while I was away and warmly encouraged me throughout. In addition, Carthage students who spent a semester with me reading Disraeli's works helped me think about the man and his ideas. I would like to thank Kenneth Bauer, Katlyn Froslan, Kari Groff, Audrey Hansen, Casey Hart, Jeremy Johnson, Laura Narum and Daniel Perusich. Claire Rogoski was also a great help.

I have read papers on Disraeli at academic meetings and I am grateful to those who invited me to speak, as I always learned something from the discussion afterwards. In particular, I would like to mention Robert Bucholz, who invited me to speak at a Court Studies seminar at the Newberry Library in Chicago; Christopher

Lynch, who included my paper on Disraeli in a conference on empire at the University of Chicago; Walter Arnstein, who commented on my work at a meeting of the Midwest Conference on British Studies at Notre Dame, and Aileen Ribeiro, who made remarks on an early attempt to describe Disraeli's dandyism at a meeting of the Courtauld History of Dress Association.

I am equally grateful to editors who have allowed me to try out some of my ideas about Disraeli in their pages, including Sir Peter Stothard at *The Times Literary Supplement*, Elizabeth Anderson at *The Spectator* and Jeremy Musson at *Country Life*. Brian Moody took excellent photographs to accompany the article in *Country Life*, while David Gelber and Samuel Bompas cheerfully posed as nineteenth-century dandies.

Several colleagues were generous enough with their time to read either the whole or a part of my text at an earlier stage. Their comments were invaluable; I could not have written this book without them. I would like to thank Maria Carrig, Lisa Jane Graham, Albert J Kuhn, Frederick Kuhn, Jonathan Marks, Marilyn Morris, John Martin Robinson, Randolph Trumbach and James Sack. Other colleagues provided clues or information that were essential. Rosemary Baird at Goodwood helped me with the photograph albums of the Gordon-Lennox family. Michael Dewar, a classicist, once got my attention decades ago by remarking that Disraeli's novels were 'camp'. Martin Rynja, of Gibson Square Books, was the first person to take my ideas about Disraeli seriously. Richard Davenport-Hines, Sheila de Bellaigue, Helen Langley, Roberta Noe, David Parrott, Michael Silverman, Peter Stansky and Matthew Szromba all helped me too.

David and April Gladstone, descendants of Disraeli's rival, William Ewart Gladstone, put me up in London during the many months of writing this book and took an affectionate interest in its progress, even while reserving a mild disapproval of the book's subject. Disraeli slept once at their house in the country, and the Gladstones were kind enough to allow the *Country Life* shoot of nineteenth-century dandies to take place at Wotton.

This is the first book I have written while working with an agent and I do not know how I survived before being taken on by Zoë Waldie of Rogers, Coleridge and White. Andrew Gordon of Simon & Schuster in the UK commissioned the book and provided intelligent commentary at every stage, while Kerri Sharp assisted it toward publication. Christopher Phipps prepared the index.

George Dickson and Michael Holland were sceptical about my ideas as I began, while Wyger Velema and Pauline Bieringa were laughing and smoking in the next room as I wrote the final pages. They helped more than they know.

Disraeli once wrote that more than 'parks and palaces' nothing was as valuable in life as a female friend. A number of female friends stood behind me with their hands on my shoulders as I wrote this, including Emma Riva, Catherine Russell and Laura Ponsonby. Two more are mentioned in the dedication. My thanks and my love to them all.

Plates

1 Isaac D'Israeli: 'Nature had disqualified him, from his cradle, for the busy pursuits of men.' Disraeli's choice of a portrait of his father, Isaac D'Israeli, to serve as the frontispiece for *Curiosities of Literature*, with a view of the life and writings of the author by his son, 14th edn, 3 vols. (1849). *National Trust.*

2 John Gibson Lockhart: Disraeli thought him 'good for tête à têtes if he likes you, which he did me once'. Frontispiece of Marion Lochhead, *John Gibson Lockhart* (1954). *The John Murray Collection.*

3 Bradenham: the Buckinghamshire house rented by Isaac D'Israeli. Author photo.

4 Jean-Léon Gérôme, *Grand Bath at Bursa* (1885): a Frenchman's view of the same-sex pleasures of a public bath in Turkey. European travellers regarded the eastern Mediterranean as an erotic destination. *Private Collection.*

5 Jean-Léon Gérôme, *The Snake Charmer* (1880): a naked boy, embraced by a snake, watched by fully clothed men. Many Victorians believed homosexuality was commonplace in the eastern Mediterranean. Disraeli returned from the East disposed, according to one observer, 'to palliate its infamous vices'. © *Sterling and Francine Clark Art Institute, Williamstown, Massachusetts, USA.*

6 Disraeli's friend, Edward Lytton Bulwer in about 1828: they were both proud of their hair. From *The Life of Edward Bulwer, First Lord Lytton*, by his grandson, Earl of Lytton, 2 vols. (1913).

7 *Fraser's Magazine* lampooned Bulwer's vanity and narcissism by placing him in front of a mirror in their issue for August 1832. *Mary Evans Picture Library.*

8 Disraeli's friend, Count d'Orsay: *Fraser's Magazine* reminded its readers in December 1834 that Byron had been smitten with him and called him a '*Cupidon déchaîné*'. *Mary Evans Picture Library.*

9 'His little agreeable self.' Disraeli's protégé, George Smythe, 7th

Viscount Strangford. From Charles Whibley, *Lord John Manners and His Friends*, 2 vols. (1925).

10 Disraeli and his secretary, Montagu Corry: an unusual portrait from the *Vanity Fair* series because it portrays two people together, suggesting an unusual relationship between them. The image was entitled, 'Power and Place' (16 Dec. 1879). *Mary Evans Picture Library*.

11 'An exquisite young man, his pinky extended.' A 1962 paperback edition of Disraeli's best known novel, published in 1844.

12, 13 Lord Henry Lennox: in the summer of 1852 Disraeli wrote him 'I can only tell you that I love you.' *The Trustees of the Goodwood Collection*.

14 *Vanity Fair* caricatured Lennox as a fop and said he had 'a feminine gentleness of manner ... proof that he was not made of the stern stuff' necessary for statesmanship (30 July 1870). *Mary Evans Picture Library*.

15 During a ministerial crisis in 1851 when there was a chance that Disraeli and Derby might take office, *Punch* caricatured Disraeli waiting anxiously for a call from the palace. The other potential ministers are pictured in ordinary morning dress of top hats and coats, but Disraeli is in court dress with lacey jabot and breeches. The last image shows him in front of a mirror, as Lord Derby looks on with folded arms. *Mary Evans Picture Library*.

16 A cross-dressing Disraeli, once again in front of a mirror. At Oxford he had entered the debate about Darwin by declaring in favor of angels. 'Dressing for an Oxford Bal Masqué' in *Punch* (10 Dec. 1864). *Mary Evans Picture Library*.

17 The debate over making the Queen 'Empress of India' also allowed *Punch* to recast Disraeli as an oriental in a skirt. Queen Victoria here is shown as Aladdin, tricked by a wizard, Disraeli, to give up an old, valuable crown for a new, worthless one. *Punch* (15 Apr. 1876). *Mary Evans Picture Library*.

18 A stone satyr in the garden at Hughenden. Author photo.

19 A bronze Pan on the terrace at Hughenden. Author photo.

20 Hughenden: the front entrance. The Disraelis bought the house in 1848 and remodelled it in the 1860s. He told Metternich that it was 'sylvan and feudal'. *National Trust*.

21 Girodet's *Sleep of Endymion*. The name of the boy who was loved by the goddess of the moon was also nineteenth-century code for men who loved other men. Disraeli published his novel *Endymion* in 1880. *Réunion des Musées Nationaux/Art Resource, NY*.

Prologue

Benjamin Disraeli is the only man in British history to have written twelve novels in addition to having served twice as prime minister. In 1868 and again between 1874 and 1880, he achieved the summit of an Englishman's political ambition. In the same year as he retired from his second premiership, the publisher Longman paid him the highest sum ever advanced to an author during the nineteenth century for a new novel. Disraeli accepted this record advance in his seventy-sixth year, but the road to these spectacular achievements was one of dips and curves. No one but Disraeli himself would have been willing to predict such an outcome when he began his career as a young man, and sometimes even he had grave doubts. The magnetism of his personality was his openness in sharing both those heady predictions and deep misgivings with unknown readers on the printed page.

His first success as a writer came before he was out of his twenties. His novel, *Vivian Grey*, was a bestseller that quickly sold out several printings in 1826. His publisher gave him carte blanche to write a sequel. The book, however, suffered such a storm of abuse from critics who wrote for reviews he respected that he went into a tailspin of depression. He had a nervous breakdown. Afterwards he underwent a long period of sadness and lassitude. He tried to forget what he regarded as a public humiliation by travelling in the eastern Mediterranean. While living in Cairo, attended by a servant who, he told his sister, was both beautifully dressed and 'knowing', Disraeli began to feel well again for the first time in years.[1] He wanted to write again.

During the early 1830s, while rising late and living in the hot climate he loved best, he started to compose a new novel, *Contarini Fleming*, a series of autobiographical reflections on his first experience of writing fiction. The hero of the book, Contarini Fleming, is clearly Disraeli himself and Contarini remembered what it was like to compose *Vivian Grey*. He recalled that 'I took up a pen. I held it in the light. I thought to myself what will be its doom, but I said nothing.'

Contarini locked himself in his room to write this novel and would not allow any interruptions. He started before noon and his composition was frantic, almost mad. 'My thoughts, my passion, the rush of my invention, were too quick for my pen. Page followed page; as a sheet was finished I threw it on the floor; I was amazed at the rapid and prolific production, yet I could not stop to wonder.' He wrote like this for six hours. When he stopped, he 'sank back exhausted, with an aching frame'. He then paced the room and ordered some wine. 'The wine invigorated me and warmed my sinking fancy, which, however, required little fuel. I set to again, and it was midnight before I retired to my bed.' He was up again early the next morning, and 'with a bottle of wine at my side, for I was determined not to be disturbed, I dashed at it again. I was not less successful. This day I finished my first volume.' Drinking morning and evening, drunk with enthusiasm for his book, he finished it in a matter of days.

This hastily written manuscript 'was a rapid sketch of the development of the poetic character'. The story was about a young man who was 'gifted with a highly poetic temperament' and alienated from those around him because of it. He felt different from all his contemporaries. This made him lonely and miserable. He tried to be like his young schoolfellows, but he could not. He even fell in love with a school friend and Contarini confessed that 'I poured forth my own passion, when I described the fervour' of his character's love. Disraeli realized, as Contarini did too, that *Vivian Grey* was a highly autobiographical work, though he claimed that when he was writing, 'it never struck me that I was delineating my own character'. If Contarini Fleming was Disraeli, anyone who knows the bare facts of Disraeli's life will see that the hero of *Vivian Grey* was Disraeli too. What Disraeli and Contarini called 'poetic character' coincided with a dawning realization that the hero could not have his love returned as he would wish by the boy whom he loved. It was an inkling of sexual difference from his schoolfellows.

Contarini published his book and refused to be ashamed of it. When he recalled 'the heat with which this little work was written, I am convinced that, with all its errors, the spark of true creation animated its fiery page'.[2] Contarini then almost forgot his work entirely and went off to help his father settle some political business. He acquitted himself well in a series of dramatic confrontations with politicians older and more eminent than himself. His father was proud of him and told Contarini, 'My son, you will be Prime Minister' one day, 'perhaps something greater'.[3]

Here then was Disraeli as a young man, who saw with astonishingly prophetic vision his own destiny as prime minister of Great Britain. When he wrote those words he was not yet thirty years old, not even an MP, entirely without the financial backing or the social standing that it took to enter Parliament in those days. A little more than thirty years later, through a combination of indomitable will, fanatical energy and refusal to accept defeat, he became premier, just as in far off days, in a foreign country, with palm trees outside his window, he had predicted he would.

What is more incredible still, and what in fact hints at the hidden secret of his personality, is that in *Contarini Fleming*, as soon as Disraeli had accurately foretold his future, he then returned almost immediately to the recent past and the failure of *Vivian Grey*. It is as if his identity as a writer, his first failure with the critics, his sense of affectionate or even sexual alienation from the world around him, and his will to rise above it, were all intimately linked together. He narrated his feelings of agony after he had read the critical reviews. 'A film floated over my vision; my knees trembled. I felt that sickness of heart, that we experience in our first serious scrape. I was ridiculous.' He felt that he had been revealed, exposed. He had told the world something important about himself and the world not only condemned him, but laughed at him.

'I buried my face in my hands; I summoned my thoughts to their last struggle; I penetrated into my very soul; and I felt the conviction, that literary creation was necessary to my existence, and that for it I was formed.' Moreover, he refused to accept his critical defeat. 'I swore by the Nature that I adored, that, in spite of all opposition, I would be an author; ay! the greatest of authors; and that far climes and distant ages should respond to the magic of my sympathetic page.'[4] For Disraeli, the publication of his first novel, his sense of self as a person and his determination to have literary as well as political success were all wrapped up into one.

There have been many different biographies of Disraeli. The official biography was a six-volume compendium of documents and commentary written by two men who had first-hand knowledge of the era in which Disraeli lived.[5] As such it is a treasure trove of Victorian attitudes to Disraeli and narratives about him by the people who knew him best. It is an important primary source for this and every other biography that has come afterwards. Robert Blake wrote the best one-volume biography of Disraeli in 1966 and this has stood the test of time as a guide to Disraeli's political achievement.[6] Sarah Bradford's 1982 *Disraeli* paid attention to his personal life, while Jane Ridley's *Young Disraeli* (1995) made use of the first complete edition of Disraeli's correspondence that began to appear in 1987 and is still in progress.[7] Indeed, the editors' introductions to the successive volumes of these *Disraeli Letters* are masterpieces of careful scholarship on their subject.[8] There have also been two brief lives of Disraeli by first-rate political historians, as well as a Jewish Disraeli and a biography meant to mark Disraeli's bicentenary by two of the grand old men of Victorian studies.[9] Another political historian has taken a run through the territory of Disraeli's life and noticed how often Disraeli appears to prefigure the modern world of sound bites and media management.[10]

What has seldom been written about before is Disraeli the writer, Disraeli the man with pen in his hand, Disraeli the author, who is key to all the rest.[11] Rather than another political audit of Disraeli's career, this book shows how Disraeli the writer contributed to the success of Disraeli the politician. As a politician, he was always called the mystery man, the sphinx, someone who wore a puzzling mask; as a writer he confessed all. He laid himself bare. He once joked to one of his friends that in reading an unusually revealing volume of political memoirs 'the nudity of the performers' embarrassed him. In fact, Disraeli's novels were the memoirs he never wrote and if there is no actual nudity in them, there is much that is suggestive about the hidden recesses of his personality. Indeed, there is much material that, though it would have destroyed him if revealed in any other medium but fiction, he was able to make use of, to transform and to alchemize into the precious metal that made him prime minister.

This was as true of Disraeli's fiction at the end of his life as it was of the beginning. He published his last book only months after resigning his second and most successful premiership after a reverse at the polls. He was living alone at his house in Buckinghamshire, Hughenden, attended only by a few servants, including his valet, Mr Baum. Once again his servant figured in a strange story, told by Norton Longman, of the handing over of the manuscript for Disraeli's last novel. It too shows that Disraeli's sense of himself as an author, even at the end of his life, was paramount. He wanted this last book to serve not as prophecy, but as his posterity.

Longman was invited to come and stay the night at Hughenden before carrying away Disraeli's latest book. When Longman arrived he noticed that Disraeli was 'fidgety and rather excited' about 'the delivery of his precious child'. Disraeli had married, but his wife had died nearly a decade earlier. They had no children. Instead, Disraeli thought of his books as his children, his legacy, the part of himself that would live on beyond the grave.

Much to Longman's surprise, Disraeli insisted that the hand-over of the manuscript be kept a secret from Baum, the manservant. Little is known of Baum except that he helped to dress and undress Disraeli, to look after his personal needs, for nearly twenty years towards the end of his life. What we do know of Baum comes down in a comment Disraeli made to his lawyer, Sir Philip Rose. It has the faintly illicit feeling of something we might associate more with Dirk Bogarde's performance in Joseph Losey's film, *The Servant*, than with anything typical of high Victorian correctness and propriety. Disraeli told Rose of Baum that 'For the first five years he was with me I found him a most excellent servant; for the next five years he was a faithful and interesting friend; and for the last five years he has been a most indulgent master.'[12] The words 'interesting friend' are critical here because on the evidence of his novels it is clear that Disraeli always used 'friend' to mean more than meets the eye, though what precisely he did mean is difficult to say.

Longman discovered that Disraeli had secreted his manuscript in three dispatch boxes, the red leather cases used only by secretaries of state to send messages back and forth to the Queen and to one another. He was no longer prime minister, but he had hidden his manuscript in such a way as to indicate that it was a state secret. Disraeli told Longman, 'Mr. Baum knows nothing of this and we must not excite his suspicion.' Disraeli asked Longman whether he could carry two of the boxes and signalled him to follow, the older man carrying a single box. 'What was going to happen?' Longman wrote in his memoir of the incident. 'Were we going to rob a church? The air was full of mystery . . . slowly, solemnly, carefully, mysteriously I followed the ex-Premier as he trod lightly along the passage, to my apartment!' When they got to Longman's bedroom, Disraeli told him he was to take the manuscript out of the dispatch boxes and hide it in his luggage. His clothes would go on top. That way Baum would not find out.[13]

To his critics there was always something wrong in Disraeli's continuing to write novels once he had reached the highest office in the state. It was frivolous. It was undignified. It was flippant. His father had also cautioned him about this when he was a young man. Now, when he was old, he seemed to fear the disapproval of his servant too. However, his impulse to write was too strong for him to stop. He had to do it. Although he had begun to write in his twenties in order to seek fame and earn money, when he was old, and he had both, he did not stop writing. It was who he was.

This then is a portrait of Disraeli as a writer. It is a retelling of his life story with special attention to his novels, and through the lens of his written work. It examines his reflections on himself as a writer, who both remembered his own life in his fiction and rewrote what had happened to him so as to come to terms with it, and to make it better.[14]

The view of previous biographers of Disraeli has often been that his novels are not very good, that they are dull and hard to read. Very few of them are still regularly available in bookshops today. Lord Blake said that Disraeli's books were boring and unreadable.[15] Although Blake conceded that there was useful autobiographical material in the novels, and took valuable material from them as such, his view of Disraeli's fiction has influenced the Disraeli biographers who have followed him. They have read the novels and they have used them, but they have not enjoyed them. They have not seen how central the writing of the novels was to Disraeli's personality, how he flirted with his readers by both revealing and concealing things of which he was slightly ashamed, but wished to be proud.

Disraeli repeatedly denied in public that his fiction was drawn from his life. In some unpublished private reminiscences, however, he made a telling remark. One of the most important friends of his middle years was a younger man, George Smythe, an attractive figure to whom Disraeli was very much drawn, and over whom hangs something of the same romantic question mark that also hangs over his servant in Cairo and his valet, Mr Baum. Smythe appears so frequently in the reminiscences that, besides Disraeli himself, he is almost the hero. 'George Smythe,' Disraeli wrote, 'said, that, as they say, novelists always draw their own characters . . .'[16] After he had finished three full-scale novels, *Vivian Grey*, *Contarini Fleming* and *Alroy*, Disraeli admitted in a fragmentary diary, 'This Trilogy is the secret history of my feelings – I shall write no more about myself.'[17] Although he made this resolution in his diary, the following novels were in fact no less autobiographical than the early ones.

A novelist unconsciously draws on his knowledge of himself when he draws fictional characters; this was the discovery of Contarini Fleming too when he recollected the composition of his first novel. This perception has not gone unnoticed by contemporary critics, perhaps the foremost of whom, Isaiah Berlin, saw that despite Disraeli's reputation for insincerity in his politics, his novels were truthful almost in spite of their author's intention. Berlin wrote: 'A man may not be sincere in his political speeches or his letters, but his works of art are himself and tell one where his true values lie.'[18] Disraeli's art, then, is one of the richest available resources on him. There is much to consult as he wrote twelve full-scale novels (one in collaboration with his sister) as well as shorter works of fiction between the publication of *Vivian Grey* in 1826 and the appearance of his last novel, *Endymion*, in 1880.

Placing Disraeli the writer at the centre of his biography provokes a number of new questions about him. The first comes from that unfulfilled schoolboy love that took place at the gestation of *Vivian Grey* and which Disraeli remembered in *Contarini Fleming*. Was Disraeli gay? And if he was, does it matter? These are questions that have been raised before, but in a much more elliptical way than is common now. As our generation is more interested in questions of sexuality than previous ones have been, it seems time to take these questions head on. Lord Blake wrote of the schoolboy romance described in *Contarini Fleming* that 'In those pre-Freudian days it was possible to write about schoolboy romances in a way which could scarcely be imitated today.'[19] Before Freud, people did not think of sex as a central part of identity. The Victorians could speak of romantic friendship between members of the same sex without any thought of there being homosexuality involved.

Indeed, both the words 'gay' and 'homosexual' are anachronistic when considering a nineteenth-century life. 'Gay' did not become current until the 1960s and 'homosexual' was a word first coined in German by a researcher interested in the same sorts of question that attracted Freud about 1870. Before then there were different ways of referring to men who were habitually attracted to other men. In eighteenth-century London there were pubs known as 'mollie houses' where men dressed as women.[20] This derived from the Latin *molles* or 'soft' and had its origin in ancient Roman contempt for men who took the female role in sexual intercourse with other men. To take the male role, in the Roman mind, did not carry the same obloquy.

The Victorian discussion of the subject hardly rose to that level of explicitness. The newspapers reported instances of men who were caught having sex with one another. Sometimes these men were brought to trial on the charge of conspiring to commit sodomy. Sodomy was punishable by death up until 1861, but it was a crime that could scarcely be discussed in polite society. Instead, in the nineteenth century they sometimes referred to 'Greek love', familiar as they were with instances of homoeroticism in ancient Greek texts. However, when Percy Bysshe Shelley decided to translate one of Plato's dialogues, which had extensive references to homoeroticism in it, he admitted to his friend, Thomas Love Peacock, how difficult it was to address the question:

> I am proceeding to employ myself on a discourse, upon the subject of which the *Symposium* treats, considering the subject with reference to the difference of sentiments respecting it, existing between the Greeks and modern nations; a subject to

be handled with that delicate caution which either I cannot or
I will not practise in other matters, but which here I acknowledge to be necessary.[21]

So that if nineteenth-century Englishmen knew of and accepted
romantic friendship among males as not necessarily sexual, some
like Shelley were also aware that among the Greeks, and among
their own contemporaries, men could take romantic friendship
further than the spiritual stage.

Even Lord Blake, though he defended Disraeli's writing of
schoolboy romance as sexually innocent, used coded language to
say that there may have been something unusual about the adult
Disraeli's sexuality. Blake noted that Disraeli was 'a passionate
admirer of Byron'. Blake also pointed out that the Victorians
knew of the Romantic poet Lord Byron's having had 'a multitude
of sexual triumphs' as well as having practised 'what used to be
called "nameless" vices'.[22] Moreover, Blake went out of his way to
link Disraeli with Oscar Wilde.

Time and time again the stories we read about Disraeli's
demeanour, dress and conversation remind us not so much of
the grave sedate bourgeois England that he was destined to
govern as of the England which flourished ten years after his
death – the England of the *Yellow Book* and Oscar Wilde. It was
no accident that he chose the title of *Dorian Gray* for one of his
most extravagant books, and his own most famous epigrams
might well, without incongruity, have appeared in the pages of
a Disraeli novel.[23]

Blake meant that Wilde's most homoerotic novel, *The Picture of
Dorian Gray*, was indebted to Disraeli's *Vivian Grey*.[24] Blake might
have added that Wilde named his eldest son Vyvyan.

Indeed, there must have been some awareness of this even
among Disraeli's contemporaries. Vivian Grey is a character who
worries about his effeminacy throughout the novel. In those days,

there was less identification between effeminacy and homosexuality than there is today. Nevertheless, the two concepts were not divorced from one another either.[25] Two men who liked to dress up in women's clothes and paraded up and down the Burlington Arcade were arrested by the police when one of them asked to use the ladies' room at the Strand Theatre.[26] The police charged them with conspiracy to commit sodomy. Ernest Boulton and Frederick Park underwent a sensational trial in 1870 in which they were eventually found to be innocent and released.[27] It emerged from their trial that both of them had at one time or another gone under the alias of Vivian Gray or Vivien Grey.[28]

Nor do these sexual associations cluster merely around Disraeli's first novel. They are there in the last one too. Graham Robb, who has recently written an account of nineteenth-century homosexuality, says that the paintings of one of Jacques-Louis David's students, Anne-Louis Girodet, 'especially the dreamy *Sleep of Endymion* (1792), were recognized as icons of homosexual love. French novelists used his name to hint at a character's sexual proclivity.'[29] Endymion is the hero of the novel Disraeli had entrusted to Longman. He is a good-looking youth who repeatedly tells his women friends that he is not a marrying man.

Although these hints at Disraeli's homosexuality are evident in his writing and what has been written about him, few have addressed them directly. While men have generally shied away from the topic, or referred to it only obliquely, as Blake did, two women who have written about Disraeli have been bolder about the homoerotic inclination in his personality. Sarah Bradford and Jane Ridley have said explicitly that homosexuality was a part of his make-up.[30] He loved women, but he liked men too, and the younger, the more handsome and the more aristocratic these men were, the better he liked them. Both Ridley and Bradford broached a topic considered too hot to handle by their contemporaries, but neither of them made it central to her story.

If Disraeli was what today we might call 'gay', it must change the way we think not only about him but about Victorian

England as a whole. If he liked Greek love, if there was some knowledge of this among his friends, if he even flirted with revealing this in his novels, then it makes his ascent to the premiership even more surprising than it was before. We always knew it was difficult for him as the son of upper-middle-class Jews, who never went to a public school or to a university, to succeed in the exclusive world of Victorian high politics. If he were also sexually different from his fellows, this makes his feat more amazing still. Not only must this finish off once and for all the notion that the Victorians were sexually repressed and repressive, it also makes them seem more silent though no less savvy about sexual variety than we are. We pride ourselves on homosexuals living as equals with heterosexuals in modern society. Nevertheless, homosexuality is still a major problem for modern British politicians. Questions about their sexuality handicapped both Michael Portillo and Peter Mandelson, both men of considerable political talents. Would the same country that rejected them ever elect a Disraeli today? Further, what if the Victorian Disraeli not only managed to have his sexual difference from the norm accepted, but also used it in the creation of a writerly persona that was the very reason he was elected? Indeed, what if that difference from the norm was part of what made him attractive as a politician?

What made Disraeli attractive is important because the novel in the nineteenth century flourished as a female medium. The readers of novels were mainly women. This was becoming less so as the century went on, but one of the reasons his father worried about his son writing fiction was that he considered it not an adequately 'manly' pursuit for someone who had political ambitions. So when Disraeli peopled his works with androgynous characters who have troublingly romantic relations with other men as well as fulfilled romances with women, it was mainly women who were scrutinizing his texts, finding them appealing and making them sell. Victorian women apparently liked Disraeli's toying with ambiguous romances in his male characters and this corresponds to another parallel in his own biography. For, as Blake says, while

Disraeli often disturbed many men, who saw him as a young 'bounder', he often had powerful women on his side and that was how he made his way up.[31] Or, as Wilde makes Lord Illingworth, the charming reprobate, hero of his play *A Woman of No Importance*, say to his son, 'No man has any real success in this world unless he has got women to back him, and women rule society. If you have not got women on your side you are quite over. You might just as well be a barrister or a stockbroker, or a journalist at once.'[32] Long before Wilde wrote this down, Disraeli lived and experienced it as the truth.

So Disraeli's sexuality gives colour to this new portrait of his life, but there are other themes that emerge from paying close attention to his writings that also add new dimensions to the standard picture we have of Disraeli now. There is a good deal of fun in Disraeli's novels. They are often about parties and drinking and dressing up and what they had for dinner and who danced with whom. They are about duchesses and dressmakers, about politicians who rely on their tailors, about debauched guardians, innocent protégés and aloof, Jewish mystery men who seem to know the truth. They are accounts of life in country houses surrounded by deer parks written by a young man who grew up in a smoky part of London not far from Holborn. He began by craving entry to upper-class society and ended as himself the doyen of that society. Yet, as he grew older and more successful, he grew embarrassed about one of his early novels, *The Young Duke*, where, more than the others, he had romanticized the hedonistic excesses of high society. He wanted to suppress it altogether, but found that as pirated copies of it continued to circulate, he had to settle for reissuing it in a censored version. Why did he grow embarrassed about that book when some variety of social enjoyment remained one of the most vivid themes throughout his work?

One hypothesis is that social pleasure came to be a central, though hard-to-defend ingredient in his new variety of conservatism. He has long been regarded as the man who remade the

Tory party in his own image,[33] but few have seen how the pleasures of food and drink and conversation – though difficult to promise to an electorate – were central to what he most cared about in life. There is, for example, the anecdote he told in his unpublished reminiscences of the Duke of Beaufort who

> used to say, that Town life was favourable to a youthful appearance. That people who always lived in the country got to look older so much sooner than the *habitués* of London. He attributed this to selfishness, self-indulgence and not living with the desire to please. People, always living in the country, got grey and red and stout and coarse – and stooped and poked.[34]

To please and be pleased required an active life of social intercourse living in town. That social pleasure and enjoyment and going out of one's way to amuse others not only kept people looking young, it animated them, kept them alive. It was what he thought life was all about. Part of the purpose of this book, then, is to investigate how this constant theme of his books, a theme about which he sometimes had misgivings, but which kept popping up almost in spite of his intentions, is related to his politics.

A last theme that emerges from a careful attention to Disraeli's writings is his relationship to the monarchy. Disraeli is famous for having rehabilitated the Victorian monarchy by bringing Queen Victoria out of her long retirement following the death of her husband. He ushered in the era of the Queen's jubilees in 1887 and 1897 where the monarchy was revitalized as a ceremonial institution. But why was he drawn to the monarchy? What appealed to him about Queen Victoria? She was hardly the sort of stylish beauty he usually liked. And how did he contribute to the monarchy's late-Victorian renaissance, especially given that both of the jubilees occurred long after he had died? Did he have a rationale for the monarchy – something which is elusive even today, when once again, as in the 1860s, the monarchy often seems under threat?

His written work provides clues to these questions. Here too the monarchy tended to highlight aspects of his sexual ambiguity of which he was alternately proud and ashamed. In his lifetime, his opponents made fun of him as a courtier. They employed a critical rhetoric that went back as far as ancient Athens, where the Greeks, proud of their democracy, derided the Persians for being the effeminized subject of kings, tyrants and despots. Similarly, for the Victorians it was virtuous and masculine to be an independent, simple, straightforward member of a debating chamber like the House of Commons; it was effeminate and debased to be a lickspittle who bowed down before the sovereign and who understood the devious intricacies of protocol. Disraeli's enemies ignored his proficiency in the House of Commons to emphasize his dubiousness and treachery as a courtier. He knew this and capitalized on it. In his novels he said he sympathized with Alcibiades, a brilliant but untrustworthy Athenian, who switched sides and fought for Sparta in the Peloponnesian War. Plato immortalized Alcibiades in the *Symposium* as having tried also to persuade Socrates, his teacher, to become his lover. Indeed, one of the reasons Shelley wanted to translate the *Symposium* was to make his contemporaries confront Alcibiades' physical love for Socrates as central to Plato's genius. That part of the dialogue had often been censored or omitted from earlier translations, and indeed Mary Shelley had doubts about including it when deciding which of her husband's manuscripts to publish after his death.[35]

The hypothesis here too is that the novels shed unusual light on Disraeli's love of royalty and ceremony and kingship. Once again, rather than a minor quirk of his personality, this love of the monarchy is key to understanding his life as a whole. What seems apparent too is that rather than have a 'rationale' for the monarchy, its attraction was difficult for him to explain or to defend to critical audiences. Instead, through his fiction he was able to convey a sensitivity to the sort of aesthetic and imaginative appeal he also found in the crown. The medium of fiction was much more suited to making the case for the imaginative dimensions of the English constitution than lawyerly arguments in the House of Commons. You might as well put the case for a pleated skirt in a court of law. Rather, the monarchy was like love itself: it had to be romanced.

Arthur Ponsonby, son of Queen Victoria's private secretary, could remember when he was little walking behind his father and Disraeli after church at Osborne in the 1870s. Disraeli, recently created Earl of Beaconsfield, Ponsonby saw to his surprise, was 'dressed in a dark blue frock coat with a top hat partly covering his curls. He wore rings over his white gloves.'[36] Ponsonby put this recollection into a book about his father, which he showed in manuscript to Margot Asquith, the brilliant wife of another prime minister. She had known an entire generation of politicians stretching from Gladstone to Churchill. 'I never knew Disraeli,' she confessed in a letter to Ponsonby after she had read his manuscript. She suggested a nursery rhyme and a female pronoun to describe him: '"With rings on her fingers, and bells on her toes, She will have music wherever she goes." *This* describes Dizzy to me.' He was 'obviously a man of genius' she thought, but '*no* one knew him; and though many books have been written about him I have no idea what he was like. Have you?'[37]

One of the men with whom Disraeli had plotted and conspired and enjoyed himself in his younger days was a relation of Arthur Ponsonby's, a diplomat many decades Disraeli's senior. Disraeli recalled of his conversations with this man that 'After giving any account to Lord Ponsonby of any interview with a *personage*, he would say "Did he caress you?"'[38] Here is not only a joke about two political conspirators making love to one another, there is also an element of the sham intimacies and the thrilling absurdities of political life. Disraeli loved a well-turned phrase, sly innuendo, an elderly man's debonair and dry humour. It was the sort of thing of which he could paint a superb picture himself in his fiction, and the hunch here is that the artist at work in his fiction is also the active genius at work in the politician, the lover, the husband and the friend.

1

The Boys Will Laugh at Me

Several months before he died, Benjamin Disraeli unburdened himself to a confidant. Lord Barrington was the sort of man with whom Disraeli had often been comfortable, a sympathetic and admiring nobleman twenty years his junior. Barrington asked him where he was born. 'That is a thing not generally known,' Disraeli replied. 'I was born in a set of chambers in the Adelphi – I may say in a library for all my father's rooms were full of books.'[1] This was not strictly the truth. Barrington went away to write down all the great man's stories without realizing that Disraeli, even on the edge of the grave, was still spinning tales, weaving fancies and embellishing his narrative.

Many of Disraeli's biographers point out the half-truths and outright lies in Disraeli's autobiographical reminiscences. For example, among the first of these biographers was William Flavelle Monypenny, a bachelor journalist on *The Times* commissioned to write the official biography before the First World War. Monypenny wrote that with regard to his ancestry, Disraeli wished 'to escape from the sordid details of commonplace life into spacious historical atmospheres'.[2] A recent biographer, Stanley Weintraub, has dismissed Disraeli's claims to have descended from Iberian Sephardic Jews as 'little more than wistful fantasies'.[3] Even

Lord Blake felt obliged to preface his debunking of Disraeli's story of his origins with this apology: 'Throughout his life Benjamin Disraeli was addicted to romance and careless about facts.'[4]

Nevertheless, in his lies Disraeli often revealed something important about himself. In telling the myths, he was more honest, more apt to capture an essential truth about his life than if he had said what his biographers would have liked. He may not even have known the truth, the result of their intense archival digging after his death. When he did know, and altered it to suit his purposes, he became one of the greatest liars in British history: his art was in his lies and like all great artists, he captured something real and alive in the lie that a more accurate story would have lacked.[5]

The Adelphi, which Disraeli had recollected to Barrington, was a splendid series of apartments between the Strand and the River Thames of which today only a part survives. The architect Robert Adam, famous for his neoclassical country houses, built what prominent architectural historians call 'the first great Georgian riverside composition in London, a row of first-class residences forty-one bays long'.[6] Disraeli's father, Isaac D'Israeli, had lived there as a bachelor. Having inherited money from an aunt, and having had an early literary success, Isaac did not have to work. He lived in the Adelphi until he married Miriam Basevi in 1802. They moved to a town house in Bloomsbury, and it was there at five-thirty in the morning on 21 December 1804 that Benjamin, their eldest son, was born. So although Disraeli erred in placing his birth at the Adelphi, his dramatic instinct that he ought to have been born in superb Adam rooms was sure.

When Disraeli placed his birth in his father's bachelor apartments, he also edited his mother out of the picture. These choices reveal a lifetime's devotion to his father and a strange silence about his mother. They also suggest another pattern of his biography: a lifetime of independence from women, yet utter reliance on them as well. He liked to tell stories to aristocratic youths, but he craved the sympathy of women older than himself. That he chose to place his birth in a library is one final alteration of the real story that is closer to the truth than the fact itself. Libraries were the rooms where he was most comfortable all his life. He was reared and educated among his father's books. His essential identity was as a reader and a writer.

The most detailed account of his family's origins appears in Disraeli's introduction to a new edition of his father's *Curiosities of Literature* published in the year after his father's death. There Disraeli claimed that his family had been exiled from Spain at the end of the fifteenth century as a result of the Inquisition's persecution of Jews. They had settled in Venice. His grandfather, Benjamin D'Israeli, had come to England in the middle of the eighteenth century because of England's reputation for commercial and religious liberty.[7]

Disraeli's association with Sephardic Spanish Jews has never been established. In fact, his grandfather came from Cento, near Ferrara, not Venice. It is equally possible that his family came from the eastern Mediterranean rather than Spain. Here again, though, Disraeli's version of events is revealing. In England some Jews had been slaughtered and others expelled in 1290. The first substantial group of Jews to return and establish themselves, mainly in London, was Spanish and Portuguese. They were Sephardic Jews, often descended from prominent families who had fled the Spanish Inquisition and who frequently lived as 'conversos', apparently Christians, no longer following Jewish religious observances though conscious of their ancestry. These Sephardic Jews were well established from the seventeenth century in the City and east London. Many of them were involved in commerce. Jews divided themselves into two groups. The Sephardim of Iberian origins considered themselves superior to Ashkenazi Jews living in Germany, Poland and Russia. So it is not surprising that Disraeli should have chosen to represent his family as proud, distinguished, Sephardic exiles. In fact, both his grandfather Benjamin D'Israeli and his father Isaac D'Israeli were members of the oldest Jewish synagogue in London, the Spanish and Portuguese Synagogue at

Bevis Marks in the City. Completed in 1701 this was and is a handsome building with an interior evocative of Christopher Wren, whose St Paul's Cathedral was constructed at about the same time.[8] Disraeli's grandfather, Benjamin D'Israeli, married twice. His first wife was a Furtado, a family genuinely descended from Portuguese Sephardim. Thus, if Disraeli exaggerated in his account of his family's origins, it is at least true that they were part of the Sephardic Jewish community in London and that his grandfather had married into a Portuguese family. Proud Sephardic Jews, highly conscious of their Mediterranean origins and worshipping in the oldest synagogue in London, where his own birth and circumcision were recorded in Portuguese: Disraeli's account captures the high-necked spirit of these people absolutely, if in the letter he pretends to certainty where much was obscure.

Venice too was a more romantic place to come from than Cento. Here Disraeli's myth is particularly revealing. Venice had a reputation among the Victorians that was both grand and slightly dubious. Long ago it had been the gateway to the Middle East. Victorian travellers knew how the Doges' Palace and St Mark's Basilica were monuments of European architecture that also evoked the city's eastern or Byzantine and Muslim ties. They thought of the East as exotic, with political, social and sexual customs far different from their own. More than this, Venice had a reputation as a licentious place of exile from England. Disraeli's hero, Byron, had gone there and told his half-sister, Augusta Leigh, that it was quite common for Venetian married ladies to have lovers.[9] The fact that he also called it a 'Sea Sodom' suggests that not all his romantic affairs there were with married ladies. One of his critics called Venice a 'lurking place' of Byron's 'selfish and polluted exile'.[10] In the twentieth century that variety of exile was revived in Thomas Mann's *Death in Venice*, where an invalid goes to Venice for his health and falls in love with a beautiful boy. Similarly, in Evelyn Waugh's *Brideshead Revisited*, Lord Marchmain's residence in Venice is because of some vague sexual irregularity in England. Marcel Proust's biographer, George Painter, suggested that 'for Proust, too, Venice was linked with the Cities of the Plain [i.e. Sodom and Gomorrah]; and perhaps he sought and found there . . . the sinister enchantments known to Byron and John Addington Symonds, Henry James, Housman and Baron Corvo'.[11]

Disraeli did not think of Venetian enchantments as 'sinister', nor for that matter did any of the others. He thought of Venice as a louche and luxurious place to come from. Thus, to say that his grandfather's family had spent several centuries there suggests his connection to a place where sexual morality was easier going than in Victorian England. It was also to evoke a once great trading empire that looked to the East, to Constantinople and to Jerusalem, as much as to the Christian West for its historical and cultural identity.

In his memoir of his father, Disraeli emphasized dimensions of Isaac's life that remarkably resembled his own existence and concerns.[12] The engraving of his father as a young boy that he had the publisher place opposite the title page is telling. It is of Isaac D'Israeli aged eleven, with long flowing hair. [*See plate 1*.] Undoubtedly a convention of eighteenth-century portraiture emphasized the girlishness of pre-adolescent boys. Disraeli gave this portrait the most prominent place in the book. He also underlined his father's 'poetical temperament', and suggested the effeminacy of his father's preference for poetry over his grandfather's aptitude for business: 'nature had disqualified him, from his cradle, for the busy pursuits of men'.[13] Beneath his father's 'roof of worldly energy' Isaac D'Israeli emerged as a young man 'of a different order . . . timid, susceptible, lost in reverie, fond of solitude'.[14] Although both parents expected Isaac to go into business, he resisted. Isaac's mother feared for her son's 'unworldliness'. She foresaw for him a 'future of degradation' and 'inevitable doom'.[15] What did she fear? The family had money. Anti-Semitic prejudice existed in eighteenth-century England, but it was not usually the violent sort that led to Jews on the Continent being regularly harassed and even killed in pogroms. Was she worried about something other than his dying as a starving artist in a garret?

Disraeli reserved a special dislike for this grandmother who had so feared for Isaac's future. Not only had she been horrible to his father as a child, Disraeli remembered her as having been unkind to her grandchildren as well. He thought she was a 'demon'. He had unpleasant memories of going to visit her. 'I remember with horror the journeys on Sundays from Bloomsbury Square to Kensington when I was a boy. No public conveyances, no kindness, no tea, no tips – nothing.'[16] Disraeli made his grandmother the villain of the piece whereby his father was thwarted and misunderstood.[17]

Finding no sympathy from his parents, the young Isaac D'Israeli appealed to one of the literary giants of the day, Samuel Johnson. He sent Dr Johnson a poem in hopes of finding a patron. Johnson, however, was dying; the poem was returned unopened and unread. According to Disraeli, Isaac complained 'which he ever did, that he had never found a counsellor or literary friend'.[18] It may have been this failure to find a friend that led to Isaac's depression, which lasted from the middle of the 1790s until his marriage in 1802. Disraeli describes his father's depression with some feeling, as he suffered from the same symptoms at a similar age and in similarly friendless circumstances. Isaac's depression was something, his son wrote, 'to which the youth of men of sensibility, and especially literary men, is frequently subject'.[19] Marked by sadness and tiredness, Disraeli's diagnosis of his father's illness was that it resulted from 'inability to direct to a satisfactory end the intellectual power which he was very conscious of possessing'.[20] Isaac went to Exeter to recover from his illness and there met a congenial group of fellow literary men. One among them was Richard Hole, who had written an essay on the *Arabian Nights*, 'still a cherished volume of elegant and learned criticism'.[21] Recent scholarship has suggested possible connections between those who in the eighteenth and nineteenth centuries were depressed, who pined for a friend they never found and at the same time who were in some way different from the ordinary in their sexual inclinations.[22] Thus, it is interesting to find Disraeli singling out, as a colleague of his father, a critic known for his commentary of the *Arabian Nights*. This was the most famous eighteenth-century text not only for spelling out but also for romanticizing sexual practices of the East that were censured in England, including adult men's attraction to late adolescent boys.[23]

References to the *Arabian Nights* or *The Thousand and One Nights* recur in Disraeli's work. An eighteenth-century translation of popular Arab stories, the book contributed to a European fashionable interest in the East. Set in Baghdad, Cairo and Damascus, the book tells of a king who married many women, killing each one on the morning after their marriage had been consummated. When at length he marries Scheherazade, she saves herself by diverting him with her storytelling. The work was an eighteenth- and nineteenth-century source of heterosexual as well as homosexual erotica. It was Disraeli's way of both referring explicitly to and at the same time veiling his own and his father's sense of sexual difference.

Isaac had first published *Curiosities of Literature* in 1791. It is a collection of anecdotes. The book has dozens of short chapters, usually no more than a few paragraphs long, with titles such as 'The Persecuted Learned', 'Cicero's Puns' and 'Origin of Newspapers'. It is a gossipy and readable prelude to a book he never wrote, which was to be a comprehensive history of English literature. *Curiosities* was immensely popular and went through many editions. Devoted to his literary projects, Isaac lived at the Adelphi and spent his time either in his book-filled rooms or among booksellers or reading at the British Museum. It came as a surprise to his friends when in 1802, at what was then considered the late age of thirty-six, he decided to marry.[24] Her name was Miriam Basevi but she went by 'Maria'. The Basevis were a well-off family of recently arrived Jewish-Italian émigrés, not unlike the D'Israelis. Among them were barristers and businessmen. One of Disraeli's cousins on his mother's side of the family, George Basevi, was a well-known architect, the designer of Belgrave Square, who died falling off scaffolding at Ely Cathedral.

Benjamin Disraeli grew up in two substantial Georgian houses in Bloomsbury. He and his three siblings were all born at 6 King's Road, Bedford Row, now 22 Theobald's Road. It is a big house, built about 1770, on a busy street, but one which looks out on an oasis of green trees across the way in Gray's Inn.[25] Disraeli always had a feel for architectural elegance and a love of trees. It is possible to see some of the London landmarks of his life that are still standing to get a sense of his surroundings. The handsome buildings in which he grew up nurtured his taste.

His elder sister, Sarah, was born in 1802, the year his parents were married. Disraeli, often known as 'Ben' in the family, was born two years later in 1804. Naphtali, named after Maria D'Israeli's father, was born in 1807, but died in infancy. Raphael, known as Ralph, was born in 1809. The youngest, Jacobus, called James or Jem, was born in 1813. About this time Isaac began work on a book meant to rehabilitate the reputation of James I and his youngest son may well have been named after this first Stuart King of England.[26] That Isaac was particularly interested in a king known for his love of a male favourite, the Duke of Buckingham, is further evidence that his son may have been on the right track in emphasizing his father's sense of sexual, or 'poetic', difference from the rest of the world. That Isaac wrote novels and worried about his son following suit suggests father and son were alike in multiple ways.

The family moved when Disraeli was nearly thirteen to 6 Bloomsbury Square, another big town house with the graceful proportions of all the building then taking place on the Duke of Bedford's London estate. It was not an aristocratic address, but it was a more than respectable one on a beautifully designed square. These two houses, not far apart, both of them close to Isaac

D'Israeli's favourite reading rooms and booksellers, were the young Disraeli's London base.

At about the age of four Disraeli went up the road as a day boy to Miss Roper's School in Islington. Later, he went further away to board at the Reverend John Potticary's School at Eliot Place in Blackheath.[27] Potticary was a Nonconformist minister, independent of the Church of England. It was a sufficiently unusual place for the young Disraeli to be excluded from school prayers, during which he and a fellow Jewish student stood at the back of the hall. It was also sufficiently progressive for the Jewish boys to receive separate instruction in Hebrew from a teacher who visited once a week.[28] Although the exact address of Potticary's school is not known, Eliot Place in modern Blackheath still has a row of attractive Georgian buildings, the right sort of date for the school, facing the heath.[29]

The choice of Potticary's school is not explained in any of Disraeli's recollections or reminiscences. However, two of his early novels, *Vivian Grey* (1826) and *Contarini Fleming* (1832), are useful here. All his novels were to a certain degree autobiographical, as he admitted in later life.[30] The heroes of these two works, however, bear striking resemblances to their author at almost every point. As there are no authentic accounts of what happened to Disraeli at school, what happens to Vivian Grey and Contarini Fleming is probably as close as we shall ever get to finding out what happened to their author. Although these two novels will appear again in their proper chronological sequence when the story arrives at that later stage of Disraeli's life, it is necessary to look at them here first for insights on Disraeli as a boy and adolescent.

Disraeli's grandmother was the villain of the melodrama in which his father was misunderstood. So too is Mrs Grey, who corresponds to Disraeli's mother, blamed for ruining the young Vivian Grey's constitution.[31] Mrs Grey is also the first to suggest sending young Vivian Grey off to school because her son 'was getting very ugly'. Vivian's father seems not to care very much about the decision. He observes that the boy does not know his alphabet. Mrs Grey wants to send the boy to Mr Flummery's school. Mr Grey replies that she may do whatever she likes. "'I never trouble myself, you know, about these matters;" and Mr Grey refreshed himself, after this domestic attack, with a glass of claret.'[32] Disraeli obviously intended to amuse his readers with this tone of paternal insouciance, but it also connects to a lifetime of alternating solicitude and cold indifference to his mother.

His mother provokes the androgynously named Vivian when she decides to curl his hair before his departure for school. Vivian throws a tantrum. "'I won't have my hair curl, Mamma; the boys will laugh at me" rebawled the beauty . . . "Charles Appleyard told me so – *his* hair curled, and the boys called him a *girl*. Papa! give me some more claret – I won't go to school."'[33]

Several years after this initial trauma, Vivian Grey is no longer objecting to having his hair curled, but is reserving some of his allowance for curling papers and doing the curling himself.[34] He has also grown up, the reader finds, because he asks for books, loves his father's library and swears at the servants.[35] Interest in male effeminacy is a theme that runs through Disraeli's entire life. The long hair that Vivian first fears will brand him as girlish, but which he later cultivates, is also a feature of the portrait Disraeli chose of his father for the frontispiece of the posthumous edition of *Curiosities*. Disraeli himself was vain about his long, curling hair throughout his adulthood and in *Vivian Grey* he brazened out a proud place for his vanity and his slightly feminine allure.

Edward Jones, six months Disraeli's junior, had affectionate memories of Disraeli as a schoolboy. Jones, who later became a clergyman, arrived at Potticary's in Blackheath a term after Disraeli was already installed there. He recalled how

> when my father took me to school he handed me over to Ben, as he always called him. I looked up to him as a big boy, and very kind he was to me, making me sit next to him in play hours, and amusing me with stories of robbers and caves, illus-

trating them with rough pencil sketches, which he continually rubbed out to make way for fresh ones. He was a very rapid reader, was fond of romances, and would often let me sit by him and read the same book, good-naturedly waiting before turning a leaf till he knew I had reached the bottom of the page. He was very fond of playing at horses, and would often drive me and another boy as a pair with string reins. He was always full of fun; and at Midsummer, when he went home for the holidays in the basket of the Blackheath coach, fired away at the passers-by with his pea-shooter.[36]

Disraeli was at Blackheath from the age, possibly, of seven or eight, when many boys of the upper and middle classes would have gone off to school, to just before he was thirteen. In Jones's recollection he seems an unusually tender boy who was willing not only to tolerate but even to entertain a boy six months his junior. One of the first surviving Disraeli letters is an invitation to this boy, Edward Jones, to attend a party at Bloomsbury Square.[37]

The death of his grandfather in 1816, the year Disraeli turned twelve, brought about significant changes in his life. First the family moved to the bigger house in Bloomsbury Square on the strength of the property Isaac inherited from his father. Second, a controversy between Isaac and the congregation at Bevis Marks led to the D'Israelis severing their ties with the synagogue. Isaac's parents had long been associated with Bevis Marks. Isaac himself had paid dues there until 1813 when he was elected a warden of the synagogue. A fine of £40 was payable on his declining to hold this office. He refused to pay it. He was not an observant Jew. He objected that the services as conducted at Bevis Marks were offensive to him. They were orthodox and he believed Judaism needed to be reformed. He had also argued in print for greater assimilation of Jews into their local communities and denounced the irrational severity of rabbis.[38] The elders of the synagogue did not at first press him, but when they renewed their request three years later, Isaac wrote to say that his name should be withdrawn from the membership. His father's death meant that he no longer felt he needed to keep up the tie.[39]

Isaac went one step further. One of his friends from the British Museum, Sharon Turner, a solicitor and writer on the history of Anglo–Saxon England, argued that Isaac's children would be at a social disadvantage if they remained Jews all their lives. As Isaac was indifferent on questions of religion, Turner told him he should allow them to be baptized. Isaac agreed and on 31 July 1817, at the age of twelve, Benjamin Disraeli was received into the Church of England at St Andrew's, Holborn. His brothers and sister were also baptized in the same season.[40]

This baptism is probably the reason why Disraeli was sent to a new school in the autumn of 1817. The D'Israelis' choice of this new school was as quixotic as the Greys sending Vivian to Flummery's. It was run by the Reverend Eli Cogan, a Unitarian minister. Rather than confirm his eldest boy in his connection to the established Church, a tie that presumably had been brought about to give him some social advantage, Isaac once again chose a Nonconformist clergyman and one whom he met casually in a bookshop. Isaac appears to have respected the man's learned taste in books and Cogan was, in fact, a self-taught Greek scholar. When he discovered that Cogan kept a school, he decided to send his son there.[41]

Isaac had the presence of mind and the financial wherewithal to send both of his younger sons to one of the great public schools, Winchester, and this later choice may have arisen from his eldest son's having to be withdrawn from Cogan's. We do not know why Isaac sent his eldest boy to an obscure and undistinguished school near Walthamstow, but the choice goes with Disraeli's description of Mr Grey being casual and cavalier about the choice of schools for his boy, Vivian. Benjamin Disraeli, unlike his father, from an early age had political as well as literary ambitions. He may have later resented how the choice of these schools hindered rather than helped his political aspirations. The odd thing is that he blamed his mother more than his father. In *Vivian Grey* after Flummery's the hero is sent to obscure Burnsley Vicarage in Hampshire because Mrs Grey is afraid that 'boys are roasted alive' at the great public schools. Perhaps Maria D'Israeli feared that if he were at a big school, under the regime of older boys, his Jewishness and curled hair might come under attack more pointedly than if he were at a smaller school looked after by a free-thinking Unitarian clergyman.

Disraeli attended Cogan's School from 1817 to 1819 or 1820, aged thirteen to sixteen. It was in Higham Hall, an old manor house built about 1768. Humphrey Repton, the famous landscape architect who had laid out the grounds of many an English country house, designed the park.[42] There were between fifty and sixty boys there. Like Disraeli himself, they were mainly from prosperous, upper-middle-class families. In later life, the Reverend Cogan's daughter remembered that Disraeli, like Vivian Grey, 'used to keep the boys awake half the night romancing'.[43] Nor is all of Vivian Grey's time at Burnsley Vicarage unhappy. He comes to dominate the school through his verbal agility, dandyism and acting talent. Vivian persuades the boys to put on a play, even though plays are forbidden. When one of the boys protests, Vivian answers, 'Nothing is allowed in this life, and every thing is done: in town there's a thing called the French play, and that's not allowed, yet my aunt has got a private box there.'[44] There is a boy named Etherege who is blond and always blushing; he gets the female lead.[45] Vivian is the manager of the play who takes the male lead.

George Etherege, the Restoration playwright, is the first of many references in Disraeli's early novels to a period he found immensely attractive. He loved the high-spirited immorality of Restoration drama, its aristocratic rakes and fops, the cheerful, self-interested cynicism of its villains and heroes. In the Regency and under George IV, audiences would entertain these Restoration evocations with good humour; under Queen Victoria readers and playgoers grew more humourless about what they deemed to be celebrations of particularly aristocratic vice. Disraeli never ceased to think of himself as something like a cross between a rake and a fop of the era of Charles II. One of the lovable things about him was that he kept allowing this personality to bubble to the surface, even when his fellow Victorians disapproved of it.

Despite the success of the play, Vivian Grey gets into a fight with some of the other boys. The two features which had allowed him to command a following at his school – his unusually stylish clothes and his quickness with words – are the same qualities that get him into trouble. His having the 'tongue of a serpent' and being 'a dandy' are now terms of abuse rather than of admiration.[46] The fight leads to Vivian's expulsion from the school. He continues his education at home in his father's library, just as Disraeli did after he left Cogan's in Isaac's library. We do not know why Disraeli had to be withdrawn from Cogan's. Disraeli represents the change as an improvement for young Vivian Grey, but the sudden departure from Higham Hall must have come as a shock even for so apparently self-possessed a boy as Disraeli was. The fact that he returned to the same period, his early schooldays, and tried to tell the same story over again in a novel he wrote six years later shows how important his schooldays had been for him. It is to that dramatic retelling of his school story that we turn next.

2

Sublimity and Sangfroid

In *Contarini Fleming* Disraeli returned to the story of his family's origins and his own early education. Contarini Fleming as a boy is, as Disraeli himself claimed to be, partly descended from a Venetian family. Disraeli had taken the name Contarini from a real family of Venetian nobles, one of whom had been a doge and commissioned the building of St Mark's. He was asserting his family's pre-eminence. Contarini is, as Disraeli was, wholly different from the English children among whom he is raised. He is dark and Mediterranean looking, while they are pink and golden-haired. Contarini adores his father but hates his stepmother, who is cold and unsympathetic.

Contarini Fleming is also a 'sensitive child' who looks 'pretty' and loves the theatre.[1] He does not have real friends, especially boys his own age. Contarini feels that he is 'of a different order from those around me', but when he goes to school he finds that the difference is in his favour. He is able to use witty phrases and unusual sayings 'to control' his schoolfellows. He finds that he likes this mastery over schoolboys and he stops complaining about his sense of difference. 'My ambition conquered my nature.'[2] He also falls in love.

This is not a typical schoolboy romance where a younger boy

accepts the admiration and protection of an older boy. Rather, the recently arrived junior boy notices who the school star is and sets out to seduce him. The elder boy's name is Musaeus. He is the 'serene favourite of the school'. It is not just his popularity that attracts Contarini, it is what he looks like:

> It seemed to me that I never beheld so lovely and so pensive a countenance. His face was quite oval, his eyes deep blue: his rich brown curls clustered in hyacinthine grace upon the delicate rose of his downy cheek, and shaded the light blue veins of his clear white forehead.
>
> I beheld him: I loved him. My friendship was a passion.[3]

Contarini pursues this older boy. He gives up his verbal gymnastics and woos Musaeus.

> He yielded to the unaccustomed tenderness of my manner, to the unwonted refinement of my address. He could not but feel the strange conviction that my conduct to him was different from my behaviour to others, for in truth his presence ever subdued my spirit, and repressed my artificial and excited manner.[4]

There are differences between them other than their ages. Contarini's family is noble and rich. Musaeus's family is poor and undistinguished. However, the two boys get around all that. They go for long walks in the woods, their arms around one another, and talk freely about what they might be when they grow up. Contarini gives Musaeus

> all the fanciful love that I had long stored up; and the mighty passions that yet lay dormant in my obscure soul now first began to stir in their glimmering abyss. And, in conversing with this dear companion it was that I first began to catch some glimpses of my yet hidden nature . . .

Contarini's 'hidden nature' here means his future career. He knows he wants to 'be something great, and glorious, and dazzling; but what, we could not determine'.[5] There is some ambiguity about the word 'nature' though. It is as if he is talking about something at the core of his personality – his birth, or his Jewishness, or his sexuality, or his talent – that made him different from the other boys.

Musaeus is good at games. Contarini hates them, but he gets involved in a few school sports in order to please him. Musaeus gives up one or two to please Contarini. They sometimes pass each other during the course of the school day and give one another a secret look: 'there was ever a sweet, faint smile, that, unmarked by the others, interchanged our love'.[6]

Contarini has a cruel streak and he takes pleasure in making the older boy cry. This is difficult because Musaeus is the colder and Contarini the more emotional of the two. Contarini confesses:

> I was sensitive, I was jealous. I found a savage joy in harrowing his heart; I triumphed when I could draw a tear from his beautiful eye; when I could urge him to unaccustomed emotion; when I forced him to assure me, in a voice of agitation, that he loved me alone, and pray me to be pacified.[7]

When there is a misunderstanding between them and Contarini snubs Musaeus by refusing to smile at him, having detected him beginning to like another boy better, he writes a letter to Musaeus to explain himself.

> What pages of mad eloquence! . . . For the first time in my life I composed. I grew intoxicated with my own eloquence . . . I began to ponder over the music of language; I studied the collocation of sweet words, and constructed elaborate sentences in lonely walks.[8]

Contarini's love of Musaeus gives birth not only to his vocation as a writer but also to his longing for 'the Senate'. With Musaeus he also realizes that he is beginning to think and to reason in an organized way. At probably the most important autobiographical moment in all his novels Disraeli describes schoolboy love as giving rise to all his most important ambitions: as a writer, as a thinker and as a politician.

When the school holidays arrive, the two boys have to separate. They take a last walk and Contarini remembers:

> The whole way I wept, and leant upon his shoulder. With what jealous care I watched to see if he too shed a tear! One clear drop at length came quivering down his cheek, like dew upon a rose. I pardoned him for its beauty. The bell sounded. I embraced him, as if it sounded for my execution, and we parted.[9]

Contarini, who has become a hero of the school and assumed importance because of his friendship with Musaeus, finds that at home he is just a boy again. His unfeeling stepmother rebukes him for his rudeness and bad manners: 'She said all this to me, all this to one who a moment before was a Caesar, an Alcibiades.'[10] The comparison to Caesar is less surprising than to Alcibiades. References to Alcibiades crop up more than once in Disraeli's novels. He was a handsome and a brilliant orator as well as a military leader. He was able, treacherous and known in his youth to favour what the Victorians called 'Greek love', that is younger males in eroticized relations with male mentors.[11] Indeed, the choice of the name 'Musaeus' is also suggestive. He was a Greek mythological figure, usually associated with Orpheus, and sometimes called singer or bard or poet. His name suggests that Contarini loved a Greek muse of the poetic temperament.

Musaeus comes to visit Contarini at home and there the relationship begins to fall apart. Contarini is mysteriously cold to Musaeus and cannot even say why. He thinks it was perhaps because he was ashamed of the influence over him possessed 'by a fellow child'. His parents had also been snobbish within his hearing about Musaeus's family. Further, Contarini's father speaks to him for 'an unusual time upon the subject of school friendships'. Finally, and most significantly coming from the pen of a writer who had much in common with Contarini: 'in loving all this time Musaeus with such devotion, I was in truth rather enamoured of the creature of my imagination than the companion of my presence'.[12] Disraeli wrote this when he was in his late twenties, but already he was wise about the means by which longing for love and an overactive imagination could lead to disappointment.

At the end of Musaeus's visit to the Flemings Contarini gives him a handshake not a hug. Back at school, Contarini drops him. Musaeus's friends take up his cause and demand explanations for why Contarini has been so cruel to him. Contarini gets into a fight with a bigger, older boy, who challenges him in public with his mistreatment of Musaeus. Contarini, though younger and smaller, trounces his opponent. This fight virtually ends the school sequence of the novel, just as a fight ended Vivian Grey's time at Burnsley Vicarage.

It is impossible to say whether the young Disraeli, either at Potticary's or at Cogan's, ever had a Musaeus. Certainly he was able to imagine what it might have been like to have such a friend if he never had one in reality, and that may be just as important for understanding his character. Nor should we leap to the conclusion from Musaeus that Disraeli was homosexual. *Contarini Fleming* was not only published by a man who would become prime minister, but also authorized to be reprinted by him even after he had achieved political fame. Readers did not immediately jump to the conclusion that Contarini or his author was or ought to be an outcast. They were able to entertain the notion of two boys loving one another and assume both would also eventually have mature relations with women, as the author certainly did. Romantic friendships between boys were fine, if not much discussed.

Men who loved men, and older boys who loved younger boys,

did exist, but they belonged to a world that was largely unac-knowledged by most people in early nineteenth-century England. Fiona MacCarthy's biography of Byron shows how these men usually spoke in a code that they had learned from the classical curriculum at their public schools. They repeatedly referred to classical authors who openly discussed same-sex passions. Among their favourites was Plato, who had raised the love of men for boys to a high philosophical good in the *Symposium*. In the coded lan-guage of Byron's all-male circle, Hyacinth, a young man from Greek mythology who is loved by Apollo, also played an impor-tant role; they called the young men they loved 'Hyacinths'.[13] Disraeli may have been inserting Byron's code in his own early works. For example, Musaeus's hair curled around his head 'in hyacinthine grace', and the anonymous narrator of *Vivian Grey* has a greyhound named Hyacinth. At one point he tries to kiss the dog and it bites him on the lips. Disraeli edited this out of the second edition of the novel.[14]

There is a parallel too between the way Disraeli treats the schooldays of his two heroes and the way Byron refers to the schooldays of his hero in *Don Juan*. Critics have often noted the autobiographical elements in Byron's epic poem. At one stage the narrator breaks from his story of Juan's education to discuss his own time at 'college'. In verses from the first canto of the poem, Byron flirts coyly with the reader about what happened to him at boarding school. He acquired there a sort of knowledge that was both important and yet unspeakable.

> For there one learns — 'tis not for me to boast,
> Though I acquired — but I pass over *that*,
> As well as all the Greek I since have lost:
> I say that there's the place — but '*verbum sat*',[15]
> I think I pick'd up too, as well as most,
> Knowledge of matters — but no matter *what* —
> I never married — but, I think, I know
> That sons should not be educated so.[16]

At school he learned Greek and he hints at sexual knowledge he acquired as well. His never marrying might mean an adult life which is either excessively devoted to heterosexual love, or never able to recapture the rush of schoolboy romance. In the case of Byron's own autobiography, it probably means both at the same time. The ambiguity is key. Byron and Disraeli are both trying to say much by not revealing all of their heroes' late adolescent adventures. In Disraeli's case, rather than leave it at that, it is important to investigate his silence on the matter because thereby we grasp an unexplored essence of his personality.

Byron felt himself to be different from his fellows and at a disadvantage: in his sensitivity, in his sensibility, in his birth, in his deformity. Byron wrote these lines to connect his poetic ambition to his sense of difference:

> Deformity is daring
> It is its essence to o'ertake mankind
> By heart and soul, and make itself the equal –
> Aye, the superior of the rest.[17]

If Disraeli did not already know these lines, he certainly would have been moved by them, and recognized himself in them.

After Disraeli left Cogan's school, he spent the next two years, when he was sixteen and seventeen, in his father's library. There he continued reading widely in the Greek and Latin classics he had begun at school. Vivian Grey does the same and perhaps because he is reading what he wants, admittedly with his father's advice, he discovers a new love of classical texts. His first find is 'PLATO', which appears in all capital letters in the original.

He also begins to read among eighteenth-century authors that were unconceived of in the nineteenth-century public school curriculum, so severely was it devoted to classical texts and translating. He read Voltaire's criticism of *Oedipus Rex*, in which Voltaire denounced ancient superstition and reliance on priests. Disraeli made a telling comment on this, which is key to his mature philosophy. Voltaire did not understand, wrote the teenaged Disraeli, how obedience, respect and reverence were essential elements of both classical and modern culture.[18] The dominant political and intellectual ideas of his age revolved around the value of criticism, reform and doubt. Already, as a very young man, he dared to defy these trends and move in a different direction. His radical conservatism was as unconventional as his flirting with revealing unspeakable facts about himself in his early novels. He believed in himself and he had courage.

In the autumn of 1821 when Disraeli was about to be seventeen Isaac conceived a plan for his eldest son to become a lawyer and marry a lawyer's daughter. In Disraeli's later recollection, as told to his friend and secretary, Montagu Corry, created Lord Rowton, he remembered that 'My father was very warm about this business: the only time in his life in which he exerted authority, always, however, exerted with affection.'[19] The plan was for Disraeli to join one of Isaac's friends who was a partner in a firm of solicitors, Swain, Stevens, Maples, Pearse and Hunt, of 6 Fredericks Place, off a thoroughfare called Old Jewry in the City. Isaac paid £400 and Disraeli became an articled clerk. He joined the firm to learn the trade as an apprentice. Isaac's friend Maples had a daughter whom it was hoped Disraeli would eventually marry, with the idea of one day inheriting Maples's clients and share of the business. Even at that early age, Disraeli objected to this because he had his eye on entering Parliament. Isaac replied that one of the most famous solicitors of his youth was now an MP, so going to Swain, Stevens should not obstruct that ambition.

Oxford was apparently considered about this time, but decided against. There was no bar to Disraeli's attending, as there had been to Isaac, whose Jewishness would have prevented him making the oaths required to matriculate. Yet, for many ambitious Jews in this period, the road to influence over the establishment was via the City and financial success rather than via Oxford and learning.[20] Disraeli indicated in his recollections to Lord Rowton that though he regretted not having been to the university, at the time he was 'unmanageable'. He was too involved in the excitements and adventures of London to agree to months cloistered away in a university town.[21]

Disraeli spent much of his youth in ample neoclassical buildings that were suitable backdrops to his great expectations for himself. The offices of Swain, Stevens in Fredericks Place were no exception. Like the Adelphi, Fredericks Place had been designed and built by the Adam brothers. Simon Bradley and Nikolaus Pevsner, authors of the definitive guide to London's architecture, describe the building today as 'the largest and least altered' of the Adam buildings in that cul-de-sac. Upstairs is a drawing room with an Adam ceiling, an oval panel with 'relief medallions after the Antique'. Fredericks Place is off a larger street, where Jews had lived in the twelfth century and their original synagogue was close by. Installed in Adam rooms, he was a few steps away from a street that every day reminded him, if he chose to notice, of the medieval existence of English Jews. 'Old Jewry' does not come into the recollections he gave to Lord Rowton, another upper-class male, many years his junior, who copied down assiduously what Disraeli chose to tell him. He told Lord Rowton that his years at the solicitors' offices were not wasted. Disraeli acted as private secretary to one of the senior partners and was present at all the meetings when powerful clients came to call. His account possesses all the drama of a law firm where, rather than the shifting and summarizing of files that are normally the business of young men at big companies, he witnessed titanic events. Disraeli remembered 'the men of great importance – bank directors, East India directors, merchants, bankers' who came to the office. He sketched the 'often extraordinary scenes when firms in the highest credit came to announce' their bankruptcy. He remembered 'questions, too, where great amounts were at stake'. He concluded that the experience was worthwhile because 'It gave me great facility with my pen and no inconsiderable knowledge of human nature.'[22] In his old age, as in his youth, if he could not love men as perfect friends and equals, he wanted to master them, just as Vivian Grey and Contarini Fleming both aimed to master their schoolfellows. He would show them that he had had a more splendid education than Eton or Winchester, Oxford or Cambridge. At Fredericks Place he had been educated in the making and the crash of fortunes.

He was with the solicitors from 1821 to 1824. Although in later life he decided it had been a useful experience, at the time he found it boring and was impatient that it could not produce more immediate results in terms of fame or fortune. He sat in on interviews in the upstairs drawing room with its elegant Adam ceiling, but he came home at night to continue his reading in classical languages and modern literature. In the summer of 1824, there arose some worry about the health of both Disraeli and his father. Rather than take their usual holiday with the family at the seaside or in the English countryside, Disraeli and his father set off for an expedition through Belgium and Germany, leaving the others behind. Accompanying them was William Meredith, a young man of Disraeli's age, who was informally engaged to be married to his sister, Sarah.

The letters that Disraeli sent home to Sarah during the month they were away show his developing talent as a writer. They also show as strongly as *Vivian Grey* or *Contarini Fleming*, both of which were still some years in the future, that he was acquiring confidence in an aesthetic, sensual and amusingly affected persona. He also had an eye for the absurd and one of his stock figures of fun is Isaac, or 'the governor'. At the beginning of the trip, to save money on postage and stationery, Isaac would write to his wife and then leave space on the page for Disraeli to write to his sister. Disraeli savoured the ridiculousness of what was for him a comic economy.

We have been in Antwerp about 2 hours and ½, and the post goes off tomorrow morning. My father as usual emulous of saving postage, positively forbids our writing separate letters, and he has been, of course, the whole 2 hours and ½ writing his half page.[23]

A few days later he could write with affected relief on his portion of the shared letter, 'The sermones gubernatoriae are this time rather diminished.'[24] He could also paint a picture of Isaac in the presence of a more ridiculous character still. In Brussels they went to see a man

> to whom we were recommended for prints etc. We found a large collection of paintings etc. and a most original possessor of them. He talked in a loud voice, and in a most swaggering manner of himself and his fortune. He informed us that he had been a Colonel of Cavalry; that he was the richest man in the world, and the possessor of the most rare curiosities. He opened a cabinet full of jewels and cameos, exhibited a profusion of Vandykes and Rubens, paraded his wounds and dashed his bull neck into the Governors face to shew him a wound . . . My father was of course delighted and richly credulous. Vous etes un hero was his constant exclamation. After spending two hours with him in which the Colonel was indefatigable in endeavouring to persuade the Gov. to buy a 30/- work my father left without purchasing . . . [25]

Perhaps all this happened, or perhaps it did not. The genius of the portrait, however, suggests the painter discovering his sparkling talent for comic exaggeration.

Disraeli also described in detail what they ate and drank. He was developing a personality based on frank and sensual enjoyment. On their way to Antwerp they passed through the small town of St Nicholas.

> We took it into our heads to dine, perfectly extemporaneous. We ordered of course something cold, not to be detained. The hostess however seemed peculiarly desirous to give up a specimen of her cookery, and there was a mysterious delay. Enter the

waiter. A fricandeau the finest I ever tasted, perfectly admirable, a small and very delicate roast joint, veal chops dressed with a rich sauce piquant, capital roast pigeons, a large dish of peas most wonderfully fine, cheese, desert, a salad preeminent even among the salads of Flanders which are unique for their delicate crispness and silvery whiteness, bread and beer ad. lib. served up in the neatest and purest manner imaginable, silver forks etc. cost only six francks, forming one of the finest specimens of exquisite and economic cookery I ever witnessed.[26]

He adopted a mock-heroic style whereby salads were 'preeminent' and superlatives could be showered on an ordinary tavern. His habitual exaggeration begins here too. If he could make himself a Venetian by descent, he might also heighten the drama of a veal stew for the entertainment of his sister.

Yet the pleasure in food is too pronounced a theme of his letters to overlook. He made a separate journal of his dinners for himself. In Liège he 'first tasted stewed apricots [served] as a vegetable and found them excellent'. In Brussels they had a *pâté de grenouilles* at the table d'hôte. As there were fellow English guests at the table who 'had a lucky prejudice against frogs – we had it all to ourselves. I eat myself blind.'[27] Linked to his love of food was a discovery of wine. Writing from Mainz he told Sarah: 'The Governor allows us to debauch to the utmost and Hocheimer Johannisburg Rudelsheirnien Ashanhausen and a thousand other varieties are unsealed and floored with equal rapidity.'[28] His spelling of the place names was often wrong but there is no doubt that he liked what he found. Nor did he omit sweets. At Frankfurt, 'Returning home we discovered at a confiseur's "Gatteau de Pouche", something superb beyond conception, we committed an excess, and have talked of the ambrosia ever since.'[29] Committing an excess, having a debauch and eating himself blind, Disraeli delighted in the immoral implications of overconsumption. He wanted to know pleasure not within equable boundaries, but at its extremes and limits.

He was also beginning to pose as a person with artistic taste as well. He and Meredith represented themselves as connoisseurs when shown several of the Rubens treasures of Flemish cathedrals. 'We have had a perfect debauch of Rubens,' he told Sarah. 'Meredith and myself have destroyed the reputation of half the Cathedrals in Flanders by our mysterious hints of the spuriousness of their Sir Pauls.'[30] He also attended a Roman Catholic High Mass at Ghent and reported to Sarah: 'The service was sublime beyond conception and the music, one of Mozart's grandest masses was played by a full band!'[31] In a private diary he kept for himself he described elements of the same service at Ghent that he concealed from his sister. 'Clouds of incense . . . The effect inconceivably grand. The host raised, and I flung myself to the ground.'[32] This sounds a little jokey and melodramatic, but he must have been moved as well. The parallel between this and Contarini Fleming's experience is too close to be coincidental. After he breaks up with Musaeus, Contarini witnesses a Mass with bells, boys, vestments and candles. Contarini is so moved that he converts and becomes a Catholic.[33] He meets a stranger sketching Gothic ruins near the school and tells him, 'I love everything which is beautiful.'[34] He goes on to tell the strange man, 'I have ever been unhappy because I am perplexed about myself. I feel that I am not like other persons, and that which makes them happy is to me a source of no enjoyment.'[35] His aesthetic appreciation and his sense of attraction to the Roman Mass were bound up together with his sense of being fundamentally different from an ordinary boy of his age.[36]

Sometimes Disraeli delighted in being different, or at least socially elevated above the ordinary. An Irish officer 'rather grand' thought he saw in Disraeli a young man of a superior class and so invited him to a picnic at Waterloo, little realizing that Disraeli was making fun of the man's accent and social pretensions behind his back.[37] Similarly Disraeli loved the effect when they hired a carriage in Cologne. 'To our great surprise a most elegant landaulet with the coachman in military livery stopped at our gate. This we were informed was the fiacre and also nearly the only carriage in Cologne. We were almost stopped in our progress by the stares of the multitude who imagined we were Archdukes at least.'[38]

The letters home to his sister show someone who was coming into a sense of himself via a love of writing. Alliteration and stylized self-confidence flowed from his pen, as when he claimed that he and Meredith were speaking French 'with a mixture of sublimity and sangfroid perfectly inimitable . . . after having passed a long and luscious day at Bruges'.[39] He cultivated a style built on successive, silly exaggerations. Of their sightseeing at Antwerp, he wrote, 'of course we always thought each thing more wonderful than another, were exceedingly delighted and tired ourselves to death'.[40] He also began a lifetime of writerly complaints about pen and paper when he concluded one letter, 'The paper in this country is bad, the ink infamous and the pens wusser.'[41]

Disraeli later recalled his decision, as they descended the Rhine on a steamer, to leave his clerkship at Swain, Stevens. Meredith was reading for the bar at Lincoln's Inn and Disraeli decided to follow his example. He may have already alienated the solicitors when he showed up at a dinner, given by the wife of one of the partners, wearing a black velvet suit with ruffles and socks with red clocks.[42] The Maples's daughter, for whom he had been intended as a prospective spouse, told him that his genius was too great for Fredericks Place. 'It will never do.'[43] She saw that he was too exotic a creature for a firm of solicitors. He wanted to be a fashionable dandy, to imitate the seventeenth-century aristocratic libertines. Dandyism was a form of excessively refined dressing associated in Disraeli's day with Beau Brummell and Lord Byron.[44] Dandies were men who paid feminine attention to the details of dress and affected languid boredom. It was a fashionable mode that was difficult to sustain if you were trying to be a successful solicitor.

Although Disraeli began officially to read for the bar at Lincoln's Inn in the autumn of 1824 when he was about to be twenty, it did not interest him for very long. A vast financial speculation in mining shares going on in the City caught his attention and he decided to try for a piece of it. He captured this moment in *Vivian Grey* when Vivian's father is walking along the street having an earnest talk with his son about his future. 'Here dashed by the gorgeous equipage of Mrs. Ormolu, the wife of a man who was working all the gold and silver mines in Christendom.' Vivian's father sees that his son's head has been turned and he warns him of the danger of trying to make a quick fortune.[45] But Vivian is not listening to this wise advice. He has to learn the hard way.

3

Château Désir

To drive in a carriage like Mrs Ormolu's or to be taken for an archduke while riding in a fiacre in Cologne required money. His father had plenty, enough to keep his family in comfort for his lifetime, but this was because Isaac's demands were not extravagant and his spending habits cautious. His eldest son was the reverse. He knew he needed money to cut a figure in society and he was impatient to have a lot of it as quickly as possible. He had little or no money of his own. As a young man he made the most reckless promises about money he expected from Isaac but which was by no means guaranteed to come to him. Indebtedness is a major theme in Disraeli's biography until he was well into middle age. He laid the foundations for a tremendous burden of debt by entering into a get-rich-quick scheme in his early twenties.

Another theme of these early years is his love of wine. Drinking, drunkenness and knowledge of obscure recipes for wine punch crop up repeatedly in his youth. Many young men learn a love of alcoholic excess in their university years, and Disraeli's doing the same at roughly the same age is not surprising. Because he was learning to cultivate a sensual pleasure in food to match his taste in art and music and architecture, it is also unsurprising to find him learning about vintages and wine varieties. One of the early reasons he got along so well with the publisher, John Murray, was that they both loved wine. Enthusiastic descriptions of alcohol of all sorts appear so frequently in Disraeli's early works that he may have gone beyond a young man's love of drinking. He may even have had what today might be called an addictive personality. Love of excess was part of his Romantic pose, but it was also as if he could not stop himself from having excess of the things he loved. Headaches and hangovers certainly continued to dog him even in later years.

This then is the story of a young man determined to acquire the riches necessary to set himself up in style, with barouches and Burgundy to match. It is a story that has divided eminent historians. Lord Blake said of these years that Disraeli 'acquired a reputation for cynicism, double dealing, recklessness and insincerity which it took him years to live down'.[1] On the other hand, John Vincent, equally an expert on Victorian high politics, demurs. Vincent argues that Disraeli's first novel, *Vivian Grey*, lay 'the ground for all that follows', that it offered Disraeli 'salutary reflection' on his disastrous dealings with John Murray and that moreover 'it is fun'.[2] Which of the two is nearer the truth?

Disraeli met a man named John Powles, partner in a firm of merchants doing business in South America, when he was working at Swain, Stevens. The solicitors had drawn up the prospectus for several share offerings in South American mining companies that Powles was promoting. Several former Spanish colonies had recently declared their independence. George Canning, a moderate liberal in a Tory administration, had declared in favour of these fledgling republics. This had attracted a surge of investment in places like Mexico and Colombia; there was a speculative rush to make money out of South American mining shares in particular. Disraeli entered into a three-way partnership with two young men he had met via his work at Swain, Stevens to invest in these mining shares. At the end of 1824 this three-way partnership had not prospered as the partners hoped and was in debt to the tune of £400. They continued to invest even after the market in the mining shares peaked and by June 1825 the debt had ballooned to £7000.[3] For some the South American republics stood for liberty and promise. Even Byron once said he would like to live in Bolivia. For Disraeli, however, South America did not mean freedom. For him South America meant making millions in new territories that were bound to attract foreign investors. Instead, he found that in a few months his debt was bigger than he could hope to pay off in years. For a young man with no salary and no income beyond the money occasionally given to him by his father, this was a serious situation.

Disraeli made it worse when he managed to involve one of his father's most prominent friends. John Murray directed an eminent publishing business. His house in Albemarle Street was a centre of the early nineteenth-century literary and Tory political world, for he also published *The Quarterly Review*, rival of the Whig *Edinburgh Review*. In Murray's drawing room could be met Sir Walter Scott, Robert Southey and the Irish poet, Tom Moore, who would one day write Byron's biography. This was a heady environment for a young man who could not decide whether his political or literary ambitions were strongest. When he was not quite eighteen Disraeli was invited to Murray's with his father. There he heard Moore, who had recently returned from the Continent and seen Byron, discuss the man Disraeli most wished to emulate. Moore said that he was struck by the change in Byron's looks, that he was fatter and dressing in an extraordinary way. Isaac asked him whether Moore meant 'Slovenly?' Moore replied, according to a note taken down of the evening by Disraeli, 'Oh, no! no! He's very dandified, and yet not an English dandy. When I saw him he was dressed in a curious foreign cap, a frogged great coat, and had a gold chain round his neck and pushed into his waistcoat pocket.' Thinking that the chain might be attached to a magnifying glass or pair of spectacles for reading or some other useful object, Moore asked Byron about it. To his surprise he found the chain attached to 'a set of trinkets. He had also another gold chain tight round his neck, something like a collar. He had then a plan of buying a tract of land and living in South America.' At Murray's Disraeli thus found literature and writing taken seriously. In Byron, the poetic temperament was not an odd commodity, opposed to business, but itself a great source of wealth for the publisher. Best of all, Byron's dressing up and wearing gold chains that had no utilitarian object corresponded to a showy inclination Disraeli found in himself. If being a dandy did not 'do' at Fredericks Place, in Albemarle Street it was a style underwritten by talent, birth and celebrity. More than anything Disraeli wanted to be a Byron himself.

Isaac's son impressed Murray. Disraeli was a good talker and precociously well read for a young man so Murray gave him occasional work. He asked him to read some manuscripts and to do some editing. Disraeli in turn persuaded the older man to invest some money in the mining shares. As the share prices began a gradual decline in 1825, Powles, Disraeli and Murray hatched a plan to prop them up. Disraeli wrote three anonymous pamphlets, which Murray had printed and published. The pamphlets discounted the statements of officials who were warning about the instability of the South American speculation. They promoted the continuing desirability of the mining shares as investments and were intended to boost investor confidence. It was a cynical ploy to protect their own financial stake in the shares. It familiarizes us right away with Disraeli's willingness to employ secrecy, mild dishonesty and underhanded manoeuvre to protect his own interests. In his favour, it can only be said that as a young man he was being trained in this bad behaviour by the senior partner of an eminent firm of City merchants and by one of the most respectable publishers of the day.

Murray now decided to involve Powles and Disraeli, probably at the younger man's prompting, in a project of his own. He wanted to found a rival daily newspaper to *The Times*, but one that would, like the *Quarterly*, have a Tory editorial policy. Half the cash to pay for it, according to an agreement drawn up in

August 1825, was to come from Murray; Powles and Disraeli were each to put up a quarter of the amount required. On Disraeli's part this was madness. He was already deeply in debt and had no income. However, he was being treated as an equal by powerful people and that must have been a wonderful drug. Further, if he had convinced no one else, he probably believed what he himself had been writing in those pamphlets about the desirability of the mining shares. They were bound to pay off before he actually needed to produce the cash for Murray's newspaper.

Meanwhile Disraeli had so risen in the world that he was now invited to Murray's dinner table without his father. In the same month that they signed the newspaper agreement, Murray invited Disraeli to join a dinner party of travellers and explorers. Disraeli wrote to tell his father, who was away from London during the summer holidays, that at the dinner there had been 'an immense number of captain-voyageurs, and much talk about the savouriness of stewed lizard and rattlesnake ragouts'. He always noticed the food and could base some of his best jokes on questions of cuisine.

He was also attuned to the nuances of dinner party behaviour and watched his host with care. At one point Murray surprised the guests by showing them a roughly shaped ring worn in memory of Giovanni Belzoni, an Italian archaeologist who had brought back Egyptian artifacts to the British Museum and who had recently died.

> Murray did his duty both as a host and as a gentleman equally well, altho' one time in the evening he took off a course [*sic:* coarse] mourning ring and swore it was [made of] Belzoni's hair! I never heard of it till that day. Howr. it produced an effect – the company sympathised and passed the claret.[4]

Disraeli studied arresting comments and learned at Murray's table how he might shine in the spotlight himself one day.

In September 1825 Murray sent Disraeli as his envoy to recruit an editor for the new newspaper. They wanted to bring in John Gibson Lockhart, the son-in-law of the most famous novelist of the day, Sir Walter Scott. They wanted Lockhart as editor, but were willing to pay for his participation even in some reduced or advisory capacity. The task was delicate because Murray had withdrawn his support for *Blackwood's Magazine* some years earlier over controversial articles written by Lockhart. Nevertheless, Lockhart's nearness to Scott would give the fledgling newspaper project immense prestige in the publishing and literary world. Murray was either cowardly or overly confident to entrust such a thorny negotiation to someone as junior as Disraeli.

Disraeli himself set off for Scotland with immense confidence. He wrote cheerful letters back to Murray in London saying that he was enjoying Scottish breakfasts of cold grouse and marmalade. Delighting in his own deviousness, he also proposed a code to ensure the confidentiality of his future correspondence with Murray. Scott was the 'Chevalier', Lockhart was 'M' for his house at Melrose and Disraeli himself was to be 'O' or 'the political Puck'.[5] A character in Shakespeare's *A Midsummer Night's Dream*, 'Puck' was originally a goblin or sprite or malicious spirit. Thus, Disraeli chose to christen himself a sort of tricky fairy, a self-deprecating joke meant to amuse Murray and to play up to how he thought of him. The joke captures an element of truth. Spirited, crafty, unreliable though probably harmless: this was Disraeli on his trip north.

Blake has described Lockhart as a prematurely middle-aged young man. He was only ten years older than Disraeli, but formal and stiff. He was a Scottish lawyer and Tory writer, described in his *Dictionary of National Biography* entry as 'a strikingly handsome man, tall and slight, with masses of black hair'. [*See plate 2.*] He was Sir Walter Scott's protégé and had married Scott's daughter. They had three children and lived in a cottage on Scott's estate. One of Lockhart's contemporaries described him, even as a young man, as having a decided maternal or feminine interest in young

children. 'His love of children . . . was like the love of a woman.'
He was particularly attached to his eldest boy, and as this boy will
make a brief appearance at a key moment in *Vivian Grey*, it is
interesting that Lockhart's friend says he 'was never happier than
with this child in his arms'.[6] After a cold start, Lockhart and
Disraeli managed to get along, their understanding of one another
possibly assisted by Disraeli also having made friends with
Lockhart's eldest boy. Disraeli stayed with the Lockharts for more
than two weeks and was introduced to Scott.

No one knows precisely what happened when Disraeli made
the first of his two trips to Scotland that autumn. He and
Lockhart must have come to some agreement. There must even
have been some warmth between them, for the two men came to
hate each other so passionately afterwards that they must have at
least recognized in one another some fellow feeling to begin.
Nevertheless, Lockhart wrote to Murray declining the editorship
of the newspaper. Instead, Lockhart managed to obtain the position he really wanted, the editorship of the *Quarterly*. Murray
agreed to this and to pay him a handsome salary in return for also
giving editorial advice, oversight and occasional articles to the
new newspaper. Although Disraeli believed on his return that
both Scott and Lockhart had been kindly disposed to him, Scott
wrote a sneering letter after his departure. Scott called Disraeli and
his father both 'coxcombs', foolish, conceited, foppish. Thus,
even before he was well into his twenties, Disraeli was being
judged a lightweight, a professional fool, an effeminate fop by
those whom he wanted to convince of his ability and sincerity. In
later life Disraeli was always to warn against dealings with literary
men, whose intrigues he deemed especially vicious. This may
have been the in-fighting and self-hatred characteristic of a world
that was looked down upon as insufficiently vigorous and manly
by the world of commerce and politics. Certainly Disraeli had
failed to judge accurately Scott's opinion of him.

Lockhart briefly came south to settle his agreement with
Murray. Disraeli went house hunting for Lockhart in London

and kept him informed on the progress of plans for the news-paper. Lockhart and Scott had raised objections to Lockhart serving as editor of a daily newspaper because they thought it was not a position for a gentleman. Disraeli knew this, and himself fas-cinated by class distinctions, pointed out the social advantages of various houses he proposed to Lockhart. Of a house in Duke Street, St James's, he wrote to Lockhart, 'The situation, altho' not very agreeable to get at one way, is yet most genteel – many members of Parliament and people of grade residing there.'[7]

Disraeli was deep in Lockhart's personal affairs. He witnessed the agreement between Lockhart and Murray which specified Lockhart's salary. Now he was also reporting on the costs of redecoration and rental of Lockhart's prospective London house. When trouble arose in November 1825, Disraeli was the bearer of bad news to Scott and Lockhart. A group of the *Quarterly's* sup-porters and regular contributors learned of Lockhart's appointment to the editorial chair. They protested to Murray. In order to pacify them Murray sent Disraeli to Scotland again to ask Scott to write an open letter praising Lockhart's abilities. Disraeli went further than Murray had intended and also told Lockhart of the trouble. It would have been difficult to keep it a secret from the younger man with whom Disraeli was on more familiar terms than he was with the great novelist. Scott wrote the letter of rec-ommendation unwillingly, and Murray had unexpectedly to reassure an indignant Lockhart. Everyone was rather angry, at least for a while, with Disraeli. He had to try to make peace. He went so far as to write to Lockhart to tell him of everything that had gone on between Murray and himself even when he was under express orders from Murray *not* to communicate with Lockhart what had passed between them.[8]

Towards the end of November, he was still trying to conciliate Lockhart. Part of the way he did so was by beginning one letter with another self-deprecating name for himself. 'My dear Lockhart, *Ecce iterum Crispinus*! I have kept my word and am pes-tering you with communications right sufficient.'[9] The editors of the *Disraeli Letters* translate and explain as follows: "'Behold again Crispinus", or more colloquially, "Here's Crispinus again".' The reference is to the Roman poet Juvenal, in whose *Satires* 'Crispinus is portrayed . . . as the debauched intimate of the Emperor Domitian . . . Thus Disraeli may be jokingly referring to his position of intimacy with the "Emperor" Murray.'[10] Describing himself as Crispinus to Lockhart was also a way of suggesting what he suspected the upright and austere Lockhart secretly thought of him. He was making fun of himself before Lockhart could. Such jokey, disarming frankness was an element of Disraeli's considerable charm.

Crispinus was the sort of corrupt, feminized courtier Disraeli would be accused of having become later in his career. In an edition of Juvenal that would have been available to Disraeli, the editor describes Crispinus as having risen from slavery to his status as a court favourite under Nero. In the first satire Crispinus is part male and part female. He flaunts his connection with the imperial purple and loves jewellery. According to Juvenal, 'Crispinus, from his lady-shoulder throws the purple cloke which too luxuriant flows, or fans his finger, labouring with freight of a light summer ring; and, faint with heat, cries "save me from a gem of greater weight!"'[11] In the fourth satire Crispinus is described as 'Diseased, emaciate, weak in all but lust' and having deflowered one of the Vestal Virgins.[12] Juvenal's attack on Crispinus' influence over the emperor is a republican critique of the unchecked power of the emperor as well as his ability to confer wealth and status on former slaves as his favourites. Juvenal had also been used to attack another effeminate, sexually ambiguous courtier, Lord Hervey, in the eighteenth century.[13] Disraeli's affecting to be Crispinus was a light-hearted mask that also revealed something of Disraeli's real personality. He always expected more to come from coalescing secretly with powerful patrons, like Murray, than from rational debate or playing by the public rules. He also had a passion for dressing up and the colour purple. 'Diseased' or degenerate is too strong for the way he thought about his persona. Still, this joke to Lockhart hints that at the least he must have felt a degree of self-consciousness about his difference from other men. He may also have tried all this out on Lockhart as a way of saying covertly, 'You too?'

In the end Disraeli's scheming came to nothing. The South American speculation and the mining shares crashed, bringing down several banks with them, in December 1825. Neither Powles nor Disraeli was able to put up his share of the capital just as the newspaper was going to press for the first time. Disraeli's last act was to name the paper *The Representative*, which pleased both Murray and Lockhart. After December, he disappeared from the picture, and Murray cannot have been pleased that neither Disraeli, nor the man Disraeli had introduced to Murray, could live up to his promise to provide cash. Murray was not at first angry enough to break off social relations with the D'Israelis, as he certainly did later. Lockhart's hostility to Disraeli was more marked, but also more difficult to explain. Disraeli was wounded by Lockhart's change from friendliness to coldness and even in later years could never quite explain it. His dawning realization, though, was that he might turn his failure to account. The wonder of the episode with Murray, the mining shares and *The Representative* is how Disraeli was able to live it down.

The year 1826 began bleakly for Disraeli. He had no money and huge debts. His former patron was disgusted with him. He had no work and no prospects. It is his buoyancy and inventiveness that make him such an attractive figure, for now at the very bottom of his young fortunes, he began writing his first novel. This was also an astute psychological move as, in rewriting the story of his failed alliance with Murray, he was able to justify his behaviour and to relive his defeat as success.

The senior D'Israelis had rented a house in the country during 1825 from Robert Plumer Ward, a former member of the government and the author of the season's best-selling novel. *Tremaine* had been published anonymously by Henry Colburn under the auspices of Benjamin and Sara Austen, a solicitor and his wife, who had acted as Ward's agents with the publisher. The Austens were neighbours of the D'Israelis in Bloomsbury Square and Benjamin Austen had also drawn up the lease of Ward's country house for Isaac's signature. The Austens and the D'Israelis struck up an acquaintance. *Tremaine* described the manners of the upper classes and the publisher advertised that it had been written by someone who had personal knowledge of those circles. Its hero is a dandy, a rich man of fastidious temperament whose 'nice' tastes in women, politics and religion prevent him from being a man of action. The novel's success encouraged Colburn to publish more in this vein and what critics have called the 'silver fork' school was born. Silver fork novels celebrated, according to one expert, 'balls, gambling scenes, social climbers, political gossip, Almack's, the clubs, younger sons looking for heiresses, dowagers protecting their daughters from younger sons'.[14] Disraeli busily adapted this formula to some of the scenes of his own recent life and showed his manuscript to Sara Austen. She acted as his agent to Colburn, who agreed to publish Disraeli's novel, *Vivian Grey*, anonymously.

Sara Austen is usually described as Disraeli's first lover. Indeed, she fits his usual type, an older married woman who might also be of use to him as well as being a romantic object. He never saw any harm in combining the two. They may have slept together, but if he had been really attached to her, she certainly would have appeared in a recognizable way in one of his early autobiographical novels. All the people he really cared about, whether he loved them or hated them, are there. We have already seen his parents, and possibly a mystery friend from school, in *Vivian Grey* and *Contarini Fleming*. *Vivian Grey* also has vivid portraits of Murray and Lockhart, and although there is also a scheming woman in it, she is more a portrait of one side of himself rather than of Sara Austen. There is no doubt that Sara Austen grew romantically inclined to him, as her letters show, but her absence from his retrospective fictional reworking of his experience suggests she mattered less to him.

The anonymous narrator of *Vivian Grey* says that after having left school and spent some time in Horace Grey's library, 'Vivian Grey was an elegant, lively lad, with just enough of dandyism to preserve him from committing *gaucheries*, and with a devil of a tongue.'[15] The dandyism, though, is a superficial veneer of certainty and nonchalance. He has been searching for something that he cannot define, nervously unfulfilled, dissatisfied with his late adolescent relationship to the world. Rejected at his school, and prematurely retired to his father's library, he at last finds something that he thinks might be the answer, 'THE STUDY OF POLITICS'. This appears in capital letters in the original, just as had his first discovery of Plato.

> And now everything was solved! the inexplicable longings of his soul, which had so often perplexed him, were at length explained. The *want*, the indefinable *want*, which he had so constantly experienced, was at last supplied . . . He paced his chamber in agitated spirit, and panted for the Senate . . .

Vivian Grey felt he already had enough experience for a political career and did not need Oxford because he 'was already a cunning reader of human hearts'.[16]

This is another crucial moment in Disraeli's fiction. Politics for Vivian was an alternative to romantic and sexual fulfilment. The language is nearly erotic: the inexplicable longings, the indefinable *want*, which is his emphasis from the original, the agitation and the panting. He could cunningly read human hearts, but in his early twenties he had not yet found reciprocal love in another human heart. All this suggests a sublimated passion, a transformation of the overwhelming generative energies of late adolescence into the socially useful channel of politics. He found in Plato, side by side, not only frank treatment of Greek love, but also care for the training of young men destined for political leadership in the Greek *polis*. If the love part was difficult for him to achieve under the circumstances, then he would aim for political success. Given the strong autobiographical strain in the novel, it suggests that a key to the future prime minister's success was in his having changed a forbidden sexual impulse into a powerful political ambition.

Disraeli could not be as serious as that about it all. Vivian Grey meets the Marquess of Carabas at his father's dinner table. Carabas is the picture of John Murray in the novel. We learn that Vivian Grey and Carabas have in common a love of food. Horace Grey's '*cuisine*' is described as '*superbe*' and his son as an 'epicurean'. Carabas, a disappointed minister angling to work himself back into political influence, 'never made a speech without previously taking a sandwich'.[17] During the dinner Carabas is challenged by one of the other guests and gets into a muddle. Vivian Grey comes to his defence and proceeds 'with the utmost sangfroid' to invent some false quotes in the style of an author he is supposedly quoting to support Carabas's arguments. Having saved Carabas, Vivian uses 'scandal, politics, and cookery' to charm the older man in conversation. Vivian flirts with Carabas and so takes him in.[18]

They both love to drink as well. Vivian tells Carabas about 'a new Venetian liqueur' and 'taught the Marquess how to mull Moselle, an operation of which the Marquess had never heard (as who has?)'. Later Vivian goes to call on Carabas at home to give him a recipe for making Tomahawk punch, an unlikely concoction of flat champagne, a pint of Curaçao liqueur, green tea and Glenlivet whisky. Having got his attention with the punch, Vivian tells Carabas how easily he might be prime minister with a little effort and the right help from Vivian. He makes Carabas drunk with a vision of his eventual occupation of a position of enormous authority.

Disraeli often drank quite a bit too. He made a romance of the bottle, as in this praise of Bordeaux from later in the novel:

Claret, bright Claret! Solace of the soul, and the heart's best friend! how many suicides hast thou prevented! how many bruised spirits and breaking hearts has thy soft and soothing flow assuaged and made whole! Man do thy worst – and woman, do thy best – one consolation always remains ... If anyone in our chill winter clime, at any time find this liquor lie cold within its accustomed receptacle, why, after every third glass, let him warm it with one of Cognac.[19]

Drink could be a remedy for disappointment, but from an early age he also appreciated it for its sensual pleasure and the way it assisted social enjoyment.

In the midst of Vivian's first private meeting with Carabas, the older man's wife appears. 'Her ladyship had been what they style a *splendid woman*; she was now *passata*, although with the aid of cachemeres, diamonds, and turbans, her *tout ensemble* was still very striking.'[20] A rich, older woman, a little beyond her prime, treated with light mockery, sympathy and genuine admiration was a life-long motif of Disraeli's fiction.

Carabas takes on Vivian Grey as his man of business. He is invited to spend the summer at the Carabas place in the country, 'Château Desir'. The name is not only irresistible but also appropriate, because the château, like its author, is a hotbed of seductions, ambitions and desires. (Disraeli's erratic French retains the circumflex in *château* but omits the accent in *désir*.) Also staying in the house is Mrs Felix Lorraine, Carabas's sister-in-law. She is older than Vivian and for the first time in the book he is more seduced than seducing. She asks him for advice about her love affairs and then invites him back to her bedroom. Disraeli hints that they have slept together, as they are both up again early and meet before breakfast. They admire each other's dress. She tells Vivian, 'what a pretty morning gown that is! and how nice your hair curls! and that velvet stock! why I declare you've quite a taste in costume?' He replies, 'of all things in the world, what I most admire are your black velvet slippers!'[21] She accepts and admires the dandyism that caused him trouble at Burnsley Vicarage. Vivian has met his match. Here is a woman who knows how to seize upon and praise his showy dress because she also rightly suspects he is a little uncertain about it.

Vivian Grey likes women, especially those who are older, richer and more experienced than him, but he has a prematurely jaded attitude towards marriage. He decides in advance that it would be bad for a future political career to marry an attractive woman his own age.

> He looked upon marriage as a certain farce in which, sooner or later, he was, as a well-paid actor, to play his part; and could it have advanced his views one jot, he would have married the Princess Caraboo tomorrow. But of all wives in the world, a young and handsome one was that which he most dreaded; and how a statesman, who was wedded to a beautiful woman, could possibly perform his duties to the public, did most exceedingly puzzle him.[22]

Vivian wanted to put off marriage as long as possible, if he had to marry at all.

Vivian carries on several fake flirtations at Désir. His most moving and serious relationships, however, are with other men. One is with his father, Horace Grey, who leaves off his early insouciance about Vivian's schooling to give consistently good advice. Another is with John Conyers, a farmer living nearby whose farm and household goods have been repossessed for non-payment of rent. Vivian comes across Conyers at his farmhouse one day while out riding. Conyers' children and wife are upset and warn Vivian to stay away from him, as he may throw a fit of violent rage. Vivian, however, has known Conyers for some time. At one point Conyers saved Vivian when he was in difficulties with an uncontrollable horse. Now Vivian approaches Conyers in his empty farmhouse. The farmer's head is bowed and his wife is cowering in the background, beseeching Vivian to be careful. Vivian speaks to him: '"Come, come, my good Conyers, cheer up, my man!" and Vivian dared to touch him. His hand was not repulsed.'[23] This physical contact between Vivian and Conyers represents a rare moment of true feeling in the book. Vivian is not trying to pull off a stunt, or describe a silly string of events. He genuinely cares for this man. A 'big tear coursed down his hardy cheek' when Conyers recognizes Vivian's kindness to him. Conyers then has a sort of hysterical fit in which he half embraces both Vivian and his wife: Vivian could 'scarcely hold down the powerful, and convulsed, frame of Conyers on his rugged seat'. There is much clever cynicism in Vivian's relationship with attractive women, but here his touching Conyers and this awkward embrace suggest that the author found these topics too stirring to make jokes about them.

In the first part of the novel Vivian discovers the science and mechanism of charm. He calls charm 'the art of pleasing'. In *Vivian Grey* Disraeli takes a flippant and somewhat sinister view of the art of pleasing as a variety of manipulation. Underneath this, however, there are astute observations about how human beings prosper by pleasing others. In the same era that early socialists and utilitarians were trying to arrive at a calculus of human happiness, the young Disraeli approached the problem from the opposite direction. He saw that people pleased one another and were happiest not in conditions of material prosperity, nor in rational calculation of their own self-interest. Rather, they were at their best in sensitive conversation with one another. When Mrs Million, a stupendously rich woman, comes to Désir, Vivian manages to get her attention. He 'began to make his advances to Mrs. Million's feelings, by a particular art of pleasing; that is, an art which was for the particular person alone, whom he was at any time addressing, and which was founded on his particular knowledge of that person's character'.[24] Having studied her, Vivian then delivers to her 'the most brilliant apology for [her] own character, and the most triumphant defence of [her] own conduct'.[25] He is out to use her by capitalizing on what he knows about her. Looked at from a different angle, though, he is also doing what sympathetic people often do for their friends, that is to support them and to reassure them by showing that what they have done is what they most needed to do.

Certainly Vivian is one who was 'precociously convinced of the necessity of managing mankind by studying their tempers and humouring their weaknesses'.[26] When the Duke and Duchess of Juggernaut, 'the very peak of aristocracy, the wealthiest, the proudest, the most ancient, and the most pompous couple in Christendom', come to stay at Désir, 'Vivian contrived to gain the heart of her Grace, by his minute acquaintance with the Juggernaut pedigree'.[27] The conclusion to which the first part of the novel rapidly builds, however, teaches Vivian that this vision of charm as a useful tool, or a way of cosying up to the rich, is an incomplete and potentially disastrous knowledge of the science.

Armed with Carabas's instruction to approach a prominent MP who will help put together a Carabas party in the House of Commons, Vivian Grey travels to meet Disraeli's stand-in for Lockhart, whose name is Frederick Cleveland. Cleveland is initially distressed that Vivian should have become mixed up with Carabas, with whom he has had public disagreements in the past, just as had Murray with Lockhart. Cleveland is so upset that he tells Vivian, '"I could really play the woman – and weep." "Mr Cleveland," said Vivian – and the drop which glistened in his eye, responded to the tear of passion which slowly quivered down his companion's cheek.'[28] Disraeli was always able at key moments to do two apparently opposed things at once, both of them true. Here Vivian is shedding a crocodile tear in order to win Cleveland over to his side, but it is also a genuine moment of intimacy between the two young men. It recalls the moment where Vivian touches Conyers and Conyers weeps. Contarini Fleming also did his damnedest to make Musaeus cry. All this weeping by men and between men suggests a fascination with men's emotions, and with their willingness to show that weakness before another man. What is more significant still is that when the book was reprinted, rather against his wishes, in 1853, he deleted the passage.[29] Disraeli had hoped to suppress the book altogether, but his growing fame in Britain meant that he could not. So he brought out an expurgated version of the book with the later collected edition of his novels. Cleveland playing the woman and the weeping were cut. Nevertheless, the passage is an index of a complex relationship between Disraeli and Lockhart, as his later attempts to revenge himself on Lockhart will show.

Despite initial nervousness, the deal between Carabas and Cleveland is settled. However, other schemes are under way in different parts of the house. In order to understand a sudden coolness between himself and Carabas, Vivian goes to see whether Carabas's wife will tell him why. She loves her little dog and to soften her up, Vivian says he has heard that morning "'of the prettiest poodle from Paris that you can possibly conceive! waltzes like an angel, and acts *proverbes* on its hind feet." Her Ladyship's eyes glistened with imagination.'[30] She confirms that her husband is dissatisfied with him while 'settling at least a dozen bracelets' on her arm. Vivian tells her 'to alter the *order* of those bracelets, and place the blue and silver against the maroon. You may depend upon it, that's the true Vienna order – and what else does the Marquess say?'[31] By giving Lady Carabas expert fashion advice and playing on her love of little dogs, he learns, in exchange, that Mrs Felix Lorraine is plotting against him.

Without either knowing that they have been observed, Vivian witnesses Mrs Felix Lorraine's failing to seduce Cleveland. When she discovers that he has seen her romantic rejection, she tries to poison Vivian, just as she has been figuratively poisoning the mind of Carabas and Cleveland against him. He refuses to drink the poison and comes to a startling conclusion. Mrs Felix Lorraine is his double. She has 'The same wonderful knowledge of the human mind, the same sweetness of voice, the same miraculous management' that brought them together at Désir.[32] This is striking because it raises more gender ambiguity about Vivian: his twin is female. Like him, she has tried and failed to seduce Cleveland. She is addicted to secret plots, just as Vivian is, just as Disraeli was. Indeed this discovery on Vivian's part begins to make the whole first part of the book turn on a failed liaison between Cleveland and Vivian. They have wept together, come to an understanding together, and been separated by the false gossip of Mrs Felix Lorraine, Vivian's rival for Cleveland's affection.

The character who provides an utter contrast with Mrs Felix Lorraine is Horace Grey, Vivian's father. Horace writes his son a letter of useful, sensible advice. He is sad that Vivian has moved into high society, because as he will soon find,

> the scenes you live in are very moveable; the characters you associate with all are masked; and it will always be doubtful, whether you can retain that long, which has been obtained by some slippery artifice . . .
>
> When the selfish combine with the selfish, bethink you how many projects are doomed to disappointment! . . . what a mockery is their love! but how deadly are their hatreds![33]

This is one of the few good and honest people in the book speaking. Vivian ignores this advice at his peril. The passage again hints at the dazzlingly perceptive duality in Disraeli that made him able to see and do opposite things at once. He saw that the social sparkle that attracted him in upper-class society was an illusion, but it did not prevent him from writing a compelling book about it that was also his bid to enter it.

The first part of the novel ends in a series of farcical, absurd and poignant events. Mrs Felix Lorraine succeeds in permanently turning Carabas against Vivian, but she gets her comeuppance when she bursts a blood vessel and dies. Carabas breaks with Vivian, loses his minor office in the ministry and his party evaporates. Vivian, who is distraught, has a nervous breakdown in Kensington Gardens. Like Conyers before him, he is convulsed and his weeping is uncontrolled, but he cannot say why he is so upset. His life flashes before his eyes. He imagines 'the smile of his mother – he listened to the sweet tones of his father's voice'. He has no memory of what has happened to him. Then 'there came a horrible idea across his mind, that his glittering youth was gone, and wasted'.[34] His paroxysm only subsides when two beautiful children come through the hedge. He realizes that they are Cleveland's children, a boy and a girl. The boy, Cleveland's eldest child, recognizes him and rushes to greet him. This is his only comfort in what can only have been a heartfelt and realistic description of a genuine emotional collapse. Disraeli too must have felt that his youth was finished when his involvement with *The Representative* collapsed in a similarly sudden fashion. And the boy is a lightning rod of his charged emotional relations with Lockhart, which came so abruptly to an end.

Shortly thereafter Vivian happens to run into Cleveland in a club. Vivian tries to explain how Mrs Felix Lorraine had come between them, but Cleveland refuses to listen and strikes him. This leads to a duel between Cleveland and Vivian: the set piece and climactic showdown of the novel's first part. The narrator says that in a duel you should shoot to miss and then honour is satisfied. Vivian and Cleveland both miss on their first try, but Cleveland demands a second shot. This time Vivian shoots him dead. This is Disraeli's way of ending his story of what happened to him with Murray and Lockhart over *The Representative*. In retrospect the most emotionally satisfying way of bringing it to a close was to kill Lockhart.

Deeply depressed by what has happened, Vivian has a debilitating fever and his father counsels travel abroad as a way of relieving his mind. Vivian goes to Germany and there he is at the end of the first part of *Vivian Grey*, still depressed, with the author asking the reader to pray for his recovery. This is a precise and accurate depiction of Disraeli's own state of mind in the first quarter of 1826 as he was still smarting from the failure of the mining shares and the collapse of his involvement with Murray in the newspaper business. The relationship with Lockhart that had promised so fair had gone badly wrong. Murray was no longer speaking to him. All seemed bleak. But was it? He had managed to create absurd characters doing amusing things and the launch of the book gave some promise of reversing the effects of the author's depression with which he had ended the book. That he should have dared to make all his own recent history public was a hint of the author's inner genius that must ultimately guide him out of his darkened room.

4

Quite a Love of a Man

Henry Colburn was pleased with the manuscript of *Vivian Grey* which Sara Austen brought him. He used several of his magazines to publicize or 'puff' it in advance of publication. He promised that the new book was a '*Don Juan* in prose', by a man of fashion, both of which must have pleased Disraeli tremendously. He later confessed in a private diary entry that of his three most autobiographical novels, *Vivian Grey* represented his 'real ambition'. The good reviews and strong sales of the book would have given the young man who confessed to this ambition some real reassurance. It went through three editions before the end of the summer of 1826. Indeed the book was so commercially successful that in eight of Disraeli's next thirteen publications 'by the author of *Vivian Grey*' appeared on the title page. Even in the first and second edition of *Coningsby* in 1844, probably Disraeli's best-known novel, *Vivian Grey* is noticed in the publisher's postscript with excerpts from the reviews.[1] Ward, the author of *Tremaine*, told Sara Austen in May 1826 that all of society was discussing the book and several inaccurate keys were published to help readers guess the true identities of the characters.

Eventually, Disraeli's authorship of the book, which was meant to be kept a secret, leaked out. One reviewer noticed that although the author of the book was supposed to be a man of fashion, he seemed to know quite a bit about books and literary questions, topics on which fashionable men would know little and care less. The reviewers turned sour after they discovered that the book's author was merely the son of Isaac D'Israeli, and therefore someone who could not know much about machinations either in Westminster or the West End. One review in particular must have distressed him very much. A writer in the *Literary Magnet* for July 1826 claimed that Disraeli must have tipped servants to get details of high life of which he could have had no personal experience. The review continues, 'Vivian Grey is quite a love of a man; wears violet-coloured slippers, and *kisses*, or rather slobbers *Italian greyhounds until they bite his lips*.'[2] The reviewer calling him 'a love of a man' and pointing out his purple slippers is doing more than condemning him for dandyism. He is saying the author is a 'darling', perhaps what we might call 'too precious for words'. It is criticizing him for being insufficiently masculine. The reviewer had noticed the greyhound named 'Hyacinth' and in this context was suggesting that he understood Disraeli's Byronic code. The greyhound was purged from subsequent editions, but the shock of the bad reviews, the sense of being exposed, could not be got over so easily.

Contarini Fleming also publishes a first novel that gets terrible reviews. Contarini's being 'mortified' by the experience must have been similar to Disraeli's in the summer of 1826. If he had, in fact, experienced a nervous breakdown after the Murray affair, in the summer a less dramatic but longer-lasting depression set in. He was sad and unable to stir himself to do very much. He accepted an invitation from the Austens to travel with them to Italy at the end of the summer.

Of course, it is impossible to argue with a depression. Nevertheless, a calm retrospective of the past year would have had to balance the very serious indebtedness and the break with Murray against the fact that he had gained in Colburn a regular source of income. The success of *Vivian Grey* meant that Colburn was now ready to publish practically anything Disraeli proposed. This kept Disraeli's literary ambitions alive and furnished him with his only reliable source of funds. Further, if he had been derided as 'a love of a man' for his violet slippers, he had still found a market for amusing stories about himself in which the velvet slippers played an important part. He had taken the giddiest, most affected, least masculine parts of himself and shaped them into an entertaining narrative. Yes, it got him some hard knocks in the press, but more importantly, it sold. He was enabled to pay off a debt of honour to Murray for the publication of the mining pamphlets. This did not restore friendly relations between them, but it contributed to Disraeli's own sense of dignity. To use one of his own favourite formulas, in amusing others, at the very least he had been amused himself. He had rewritten the Murray disaster in a form that made him able to live with a sense of innocence about it all. Of course, Murray never entirely forgave him for being lampooned as the tipsy Carabas. Murray even broke off relations with Isaac and Maria for a time. Their son survived, battered and bruised, but with the prospect now of a little satisfying literary work.

Colburn wanted Disraeli to continue the story of Vivian Grey in several new volumes. He commissioned *Vivian Grey*, part two, which was published early in February 1827. Disraeli wrote it in the autumn of 1826 after his return with the Austens from the Continent. It reproduces some of the destinations and observations of his trip through Germany with Isaac and Meredith in 1824. It lacks the manic energy and madcap cheerfulness of part one. Its hero, like its author, is a chastened and subdued young man. He is travelling through Germany to try to relieve the grief he feels for having killed Cleveland and having been falsely accused of ruining Carabas. Despite Vivian's depression, some amusing episodes occur that further reveal the young Disraeli's character.

At Frankfurt Vivian meets a German diplomat named von Konigstein who shows him a gold snuffbox. It has a portrait of the King of Sardinia surrounded in diamonds and was given to

Konigstein in gratitude by the King for having 'settled the long agitated controversy about the right of anchovy fishing on the left bank of the Mediterranean'.[3] This is an absurdly expensive bibelot given to mark a minor treaty concerning a tiny fish. The lack of proportion and Vivian's admiration of the royalist trinket sustain the dandy tone of the first part of the novel. To place emphasis on clothing, jewellery and food at the expense of parliaments, wars and revolutions is part of the dandy sensibility. Vivian's noticing the diplomat's snuffbox shows that though he may be a little sad, he has not lost his love of the aristocratic pose or his aestheticized approach to the world. Further, this pose was not a way of avoiding politics, but of looking for the charming 'in' that will allow him back into the world of political plots, conspiracies and business.

At Konigstein's, Vivian also meets a Polish diplomat who gives his recollections of travel in the East. He has seen inside 'the chief hall of the seraglio of Constantinople. It's a most magnificent room.' This piques Vivian's interest and he wants to know more. The Pole adds, 'The women unfortunately were not there; they were at a summer palace on the Bosphorus, where they are taken regularly every year for an airing in large gold cages.'[4] Imprisoned women, sexual slavery, palaces of Muslim magnificence – all this aura of licentiousness and exoticism attracted Disraeli immensely. Lord Byron had travelled in the eastern Mediterranean. The attractiveness of the East was already in Disraeli's mind and here he hatched the idea of following in the poet's footsteps.

This is apparent too from another episode where Vivian goes to give lessons in English pronunciation to Madame Carolina, whom he has met at the court of Reisenburg, which could be roughly translated as Travel Castle. She excites Vivian by unlocking a case and taking out the manuscript of Haroun Al Raschid, Caliph of Baghdad and one of the protagonists of the *Arabian Nights*.[5] Given the raciness of the book's subject matter and the fact that Vivian is locked up with a beautiful woman as they examine it, this comes about as close to a sexual adventure as his being invited back to Mrs Felix Lorraine's bedroom in part one. A notable figure at the court of Haroun Al Raschid was Abu Nuwas, the best-known lover of handsome boys and strong drink in the *Arabian Nights*. This shows that Disraeli was continuing to use the novel to reflect on himself and his sense of being different. He was hiding and revealing at the same time: speaking to cognoscenti about a select text while confident that the majority of his readers would have no detailed knowledge of the Arab literature.

One long digression in the second part of the book concerns the English National Gallery. It had then only recently been established, in 1824, when the government had bought a collection of paintings belonging to the estate of a City insurance broker, John Julius Angerstein. Disraeli also speaks in admiration of the King, George IV, another great art patron. He said that in the King the arts have

> a steady, a sincere, and powerful advocate; one, who in spite of the disheartening opposition of vulgar clamour, and uneducated prejudice, has done more in a short reign for the patronage of the fine Arts, than all of the dynasties of all the Medicis, Roman and Florentine together.[6]

This is typical Disraelian exaggeration and flattery of the sovereign, but it is not only that. He did genuinely believe in the value of the fine arts as attributes of a civilized society and he was saying so at a time when, though George IV was still a powerful patron of the arts, he was not a popular one. In that same era Isaac was writing defences of James I (1816) and Charles I (1828). These early Stuart kings were also at a low of their historical reputation. The defenders of Britain's constitutional monarchy against the French Revolution were pointing to the Hanoverian compromise whereby Stuart despotism had been thwarted and a degree of popular representation had allowed Britain's mixed constitution to flourish. So both father and son were engaged in the defence of deeply hated sovereigns. Both of them believed that the monarchy had been unfairly attacked by Hanoverian historians and by popular orators who would have preferred to save a sixpence than to build one of London's most magnificent thoroughfares, Regent Street. Both of them were prepared to face down powerful anti-monarchical sentiment that they believed to be wrong.

Although the second part of *Vivian Grey* is less sparkling than the first one, Disraeli still advanced in it to a new understanding of himself, and thus our understanding of him, as he entered his twenty-third year. Vivian re-enters society for the first time among some English acquaintances at the German spa town of Ems. He finds that he is a different person from the Vivian Grey of part one and in this passage he describes the new Vivian in conversation with fellow English guests:

> To-day there was no false brilliancy to entrap the unwary; no splendid paradoxes to astound the weak; no poignant scandal to amuse the vile. He conversed calmly, without eagerness, and without passion; and delivering with ability his conscientious opinion upon subjects which he had studied, and which he understood, he found that while he interested others, he had also been interested himself.[7]

Here he has learned to enjoy talking calmly about what he knows, as opposed to seducing Carabas by talking excitedly about what he does not. It is not as if the excited Vivian were dead. Affectation, showing off and delight in social display were elements of Disraeli's personality. His depression was in part about the yawning gap between that excited part of him that enjoyed performing before an audience, but had been booed off stage, and the calm, bookish part of his personality that was a deep and serious student of history, literature and art. The question of how to bring these two parts of his personality back together was not answered by the publication of the second part of *Vivian Grey*, but by having captured them in print he had come at least to articulate one dimension of what was troubling him.

The period between the publication of the first part of *Vivian*

Grey in 1826 and the second part in 1827 was also filled with travel. Benjamin and Sara Austen invited him to accompany them on a pleasure trip to the Continent. Sara Austen had been useful with *Vivian Grey*. She might prove so again. She had a crush on him and he was prepared to indulge this. Benjamin Austen had his uses too, both financial and affectionate. He would eventually loan money to Disraeli and, from a surviving letter from Disraeli to Austen, it is clear the two men were on easy, jokey terms with one another. The Austens had no children and in that great child-bearing era, when women routinely bore seven, eight or nine children, this was more than a little odd. Perhaps both Austens recognized and responded to a similar oddness in Disraeli. Disraeli's letter replying to Benjamin Austen's invitation conveys something of his hedonistic love of sleep, which might also have been a cover for his depression. 'Having met many women who were *too* beautiful at the last nights danse, I slept off the memory of their loveliness by an extra three hours of oblivion, and was therefore unable to answer your note immediately.' Telling Austen about all the pretty women he had seen at a dance was also a way of reassuring him that he was not particularly attached to Sara.

Disraeli accepted Austen's invitation to join them on their tour of Italy, immediately confessing his strengths and weaknesses as a travelling companion. 'I have an ugly habit of stealing the Claret, getting drunk, and kissing the maids.' He was equally frank about what he could do well:

> You certainly could not come to any person better suited for ordering a dinner, and as to casting up accounts – if there's anything in the world which I excel in, thats the very one. And as I've got the habit of never attending to the shillings and pence because they make my head ache, I generally detect the aubergiste in a super-charge.[8]

If they could put up with his drinking, extravagance and love of food, he would be delighted to join them.

To his father, once the journey was under way, he could note a little more naturally, if also more waspishly, an observation at Austen's expense. He and Austen were both keeping journals. Austen's journal, more detailed than his, began at Guildford Street before they had even left London, 'with the incident of wheel greasing'.[9] For Disraeli to be prosaic was always a fault and his particular gift was for the satirical sting.

The further they got from London the less Disraeli played detached observer and the more he entered into full-hearted enjoyment of new, unfamiliar scenes. He was disgusted with what he saw of other English travellers, 'how much they do and how little they enjoy or understand – the excitement of idiotism I never witnessed before and it is very ludicrous'.[10] He was determined not to fall into their mistake. They thought the point of travel was keeping busy and doing as much as possible; for him the point was to observe and to experience. Foreign sensations were worth the trip. The Roman Catholic countries offered what was to Disraeli a fantastically foreign invitation to enjoy the pleasures of the table not just as a means to nourishment and refreshment as in England, but as things to be enjoyed in and of themselves. Sara Austen wrote to Sarah, Disraeli's sister, that 'The real improvement in your brother's health and looks quite surprises me . . . He seems to enjoy everything *pour ou contre*, and has just said high mass for a third bottle of burgundy.'[11] The saying 'high mass' for another bottle of wine is too good a line to be anything but Disraeli's own and it recalls not only his enjoyment of high altars in Flanders, but also the emotionalism of Contarini Fleming's post-Musaeus conversion to Catholicism. There was a structured abandon to the Roman religion, a warmer, franker and more realistic attitude to man's sensuousness than existed in cold and Protestant England.

After travelling through France via Paris and Dijon, Disraeli and the Austens went to Switzerland. They stayed at a château hotel at Sécheron, not far from Geneva. There Disraeli went rowing on the lake with Maurice, 'Lord Byron's celebrated boatman'. Byron had written about sailing on the lake at night in a storm in *Childe Harold*.[12] Now Disraeli tried re-enacting these experiences himself by going out at night on the lake with Maurice. Disraeli told his father that 'Maurice is very handsome and very vain, but he has been made so by the English of whom he is the regular pet. He talks of nothing but Lord Byron particularly if you show the least interest in the subject.'[13] Disraeli was both attracted to Maurice and anxious not to be taken in by someone eager to retell his Byron stories for a paying customer. Nevertheless, there was something irresistible about Maurice's account of his time in the boat with Byron during the storm. When Maurice warned Byron of the danger of shipwreck, 'the only answer which B. made was stripping quite naked and folding round him a great robe de chambre – so that in case of wreck he was prepared to swim immediately'.[14] There is a small sexual frisson here: the English lord stripping off before the clothed boatman, the storm howling around them, two men together *in extremis*. As it was unusual in those days for men to wear bathing suits, the following must be imagined as a continuation of the storm night. Disraeli's letter to his father continues: 'in the slightest things was Byron by Maurice's account, most ludicrously ostentatious. He gave him [Maurice] one day five napoleons for a swimming race across the lake.'[15] The *milord anglais* was overpaying his servant for a little nude competition.

Learning first-hand about Byron's extravagance underwrote Disraeli's own tendency to that habit. Maurice told Disraeli 'that he never saw a man eat so little as B. in all his life, but that he would drink three or four bottles of the richest wines for his breakfast'.[16] Disraeli liked drinking in imitation of Byron, but he liked eating too much to follow his hero in that. Any sort of physical exercise, whether naked or not, was out of the question.

Disraeli referred to his Byron obsession in the second part of *Vivian Grey*. In it he spoke semi-sneeringly of 'English youth . . . [who] travel now, it appears, to look at mountains and catch cold in spouting trash on lakes by moonlight'.[17] Having returned to England with the Austens, he was laughingly critical of an enthusiasm for Byron that would send a young man on to a Swiss lake at midnight, just as he himself had done a few months previously. He knew that he was just one of the crowd in loving Byron and he hated the fact that he was nothing special in that. In making fun of Byro-mania, he was trying to make light of his own serious enthusiasm and to render it acceptable by also looking at it from a lordly distance.

After Switzerland, Disraeli and the Austens descended from the Alps into Italy. Disraeli was unprepared for the beauty of Italy. Here, like the Englishmen in E. M. Forster's *A Room with a View* suddenly living their lives in colour once they arrive in Florence, Disraeli's eyes were opened. 'In speaking of Italy Romance has omitted for once to exaggerate,' Disraeli told his father.[18] In Milan he admired a broad street, 'the Corso'. Its great size was out of proportion 'with the population of this city, and can only be accounted for by the temper of the Italians who sacrifice everything for a box at the Opera, and a carriage on the Corso'.[19] These were people after his own heart. What he chose to describe in them is an accurate indicator of who he was at the age of twenty-one, and the journey gave life to a part of his personality that never died.

In Italy he also noted two strange men. In Milan he was attracted to a bachelor dandy who spoke in a falsetto. Though by Disraeli's standards he was old, this man kept up his trim figure as if he were still young.

> Count Ciconia is the leader of the ton at Milan. He is a dandy of genius – worthy of Brummell. He is about 45 – dresses very plainly – has been frequently in England and pays constant trips there to study. He is young in figure but his face is long and old – a bachelor with a loud shrill voice.[20]

In Florence another strange man was attracted to him. Sara Austen reported to Disraeli's mother that 'He is quite well, and making friends every day. One gentleman here, who is our great cicerone tries to persuade him to stay the winter.' This man, apparently an Englishman living abroad, had a villa 'on one of the lovely hills overlooking Florence; and about 20 times daily he says to me, "Do leave Mr. Disraeli with us for the winter. I will give him any rooms in my house that he likes best, and I am sure we shall agree in every thing."' Sara assured Maria D'Israeli that this man was 'perfectly in earnest'.[21] Disraeli was continuing to do what Vivian Grey had done so well with the Marquess of Carabas, that is to flirt with older men, to study them and by studying these odd bachelors perhaps to see what was in store for him.

Disraeli loved the architecture of Verona, evocative of the different periods in Italian history – Roman, Medieval and Renaissance. He could imagine himself back in one of these periods and 'the illusion is perfect' until he looked 'with pain on the passing citizens in their modern costumes – you look for black velvets and gold chains – white feathers and red stockings'.[22] Much as he adored fancy dress, he was also trying to educate himself in Italy. It was not all dandies and artifice, he was trying to improve his taste by exposing it to historically authentic art and architecture. 'I am sure,' he told his father in a letter, which shows his wish to improve his mind, 'there is no excuse for any reflecting man who does not come home from Italy and Switzerland with a mind more matured and a taste more correct.'[23] Although he loved outward appearances, Isaac's scholarly habits had also passed on to his son. The point of going to the Continent was to learn as well as to delight in the spectacle of it all.

The peak of the journey for Disraeli was Venice. In his letter home about it he dwelled on decoration and the aristocratic associations of Venetian palaces. Here he wrote to Isaac in his characteristic light-hearted vein, singling out objects for admiration and sending up his own exaggerated enthusiasm at the same time. His hotel was

once the proud residence of the Bernardinis a family which has given more than one doge to the old Republic – the floors of our rooms were of marble – the hangings of satin – the ceilings painted by Tintoretto and his scholars, full of Turkish Triumphs and trophies – the chairs of Satin and the gilding tho' of two hundred years duration as brightly burnished as the new mosaic invention.

He wrote of sailing down the Grand Canal 'on which most of the palaces of the High nobility' could be found. These *palazzi*, owned by the families of 'Foscari-Grimani, Barberigo, and other names which make the coldest heart thrill rise rapidly before you'.[24] His imagination manufactured the thrill, for if he was educating his taste, he was also collecting information on this continental trip that would stimulate his ability to invent and to dream. 'I never felt less inclined to quit a place than I did Venice.'[25] His tracing descent from Venetians, both for the D'Israelis and for Contarini Fleming, was a way of laying claim to the satin, the gilding and the aristocratic doges as his own.

On the travellers' return journey through Turin, Disraeli gave way to a melancholy declaration of his Englishness and his distrust of his fellow men. 'England with all her imperfections is worth all the world together, and I hope it is not misanthropy when I feel that I love lakes and mountains better than courts and cities, and trees better than men.'[26] Perhaps several continuous weeks of sightseeing, being thrown together constantly with the Austens and having insufficient time by himself were beginning to wear on him. Even so, he did not consider himself entirely Venetian, or entirely an urban sophisticate, as he now longed for a little English rustic solitude.

No doubt he was beginning to wear on his travelling companions too. Even on the last weeks of the trip he was keeping up a high standard of dress. The son of one of Benjamin Austen's relations, the future Sir Henry Layard, remembered seeing Disraeli on his way home through France. For a long time Layard retained 'a vivid recollection of his appearance, his black curly hair, his affected manner, and his somewhat fantastic dress'.[27] Sara Austen, who loved Disraeli, was willing to confide a slightly malicious story about him to his sister. 'Your brother has behaved excellently, except when there is a button, or, rather, buttons to be put on his shirt; then he is violently bad, and this happens almost daily. I said once, "They cannot have been good at first"; and now he always threatens to "tell my Mother you have abused my Linen".'[28] His bantering, blackmailing threat gives some idea of the acute psychologist he was, how he tried to play the women in his life off one another, and how tiresome he could be on a long journey. In Italy he learned a great deal about himself and the brilliant colouring of the world beyond the foggy Thames valley. He probably also had his fill of the Austens, and must have returned determined to free himself, at least as far as Sara Austen was concerned, of an entanglement that had now served its purpose.

5

A Treatise on Nonchalance

As soon as Disraeli got back from the Continent, his sadness returned as well. He had no friend to occupy his time and thoughts; he had nothing particularly that he had to do other than hang about his father's house and evade his creditors. In the summers of 1827 and 1828 he was seriously ill when his family went away first to Fyfield in Oxfordshire and next to Lyme Regis on the south coast. In a letter of March 1828 to Sharon Turner, who had persuaded Isaac to have the children baptized some years earlier, although Disraeli confessed to feeling unwell, he also displayed a rare composure. He said he could not be satisfied with moderate success and that he might not be capable of great success. 'I have ceased,' he claimed, 'to be dazzled with the glittering bubbles which float on the troubled ocean of existence.'[1] No longer drawn to social froth, he said he would calmly accept whatever fate sent him. Nevertheless, he was not rendered completely passive by his seeming resignation. He had continued to write. In the late spring of 1828 Henry Colburn published Disraeli's short novel, *The Voyage of Captain Popanilla*. It has all the sparkle of *Vivian Grey* at its best and, for the first time in his fiction, it also has a political message. The evidence of *Popanilla* and his subsequent literary production in this period is that far from preventing him from working, the depression was conducive to his particular brand of high-spirited writing. Just as *Vivian Grey* was composed among the ruins of the crash over mining shares and *The Representative*, so too did *Popanilla* appear out of what Isaac called a depressed 'blank' in his son's life.[2] Writing was for Disraeli a brilliant psychological device in which he could take the unpromising materials of a deep depression and turn them into something of which he could make a later use.

The utilitarians were a group of moral philosophers who believed that society could be improved in a rational, mathematical way. By maximizing the happiness of the greatest number of people, one could achieve the greatest good for the greatest number. This would be an improvement over early nineteenth-century society where only a small number of people enjoyed great wealth and privileges. The most important utilitarian, Jeremy Bentham, advocated an overhaul of English law and English institutions that were based on outdated traditions and irrational conventions. He wanted to evaluate laws and institutions by the standard of utility. Did for example the Corn Laws or the House of Lords promote the greatest good for the greatest number, or were they exclusive privileges designed to benefit only the few, mainly aristocratic landowners? If not, they should be abolished.

The utilitarians were the moving spirits behind some of the great political reforms of Disraeli's day, from the removal of political disabilities imposed on non-Anglican religious groups to greater representation of middle-class interests in the House of Commons. A degree of utilitarian reforming zeal runs right through the liberal politics of the era. Although he sympathized with many of their proposed reforms, Disraeli loathed the utilitarians. *Popanilla* gives his reasons why. The book is attractive because it shows up the humourlessness of the utilitarians; it shows off the author's ability to make the reader laugh. Like his defence of George IV, it also shows Disraeli's inventiveness in standing up to what rapidly became one of the nearly sacred orthodoxies of his era.

Popanilla is a young man born on the tropical island of Fantaisie. There the people are of 'an innocent and a happy, though a voluptuous and ignorant race'. For 'their slight clothing' they wear serpents' skins. To amuse themselves, they 'tell inexhaustible stories, and always laugh at each other's jokes. A natural instinct gave them the art of making wine; and it was the same benevolent Nature that blessed them also with a knowledge of the art of making love.'[3] Like all his fictional work, *Popanilla* has a strong autobiographical streak. Fantaisie is a sort of reverse Eden, dominated by the snake instead of God. Rather than this being a calamity, however, it is key to the islanders' enjoyment of sensual pleasures like wine and lovemaking. Just as Vivian Grey had a devil of a tongue, so too Disraeli was an adept at storytelling. Meredith, his sister's intended husband, said of Disraeli that 'he could make a story out of nothing'.[4] Popanilla himself is 'The favourite to all the women, the envy of all the men . . . No one was a better judge of wine – no one had a better taste for fruit – no one danced with more elegant vivacity – and no one whispered compliments in a more meaning tone.'[5] Popanilla is a delightful and cartoonish self-portrait of the author posing as a South Sea Islander. In some of its rough outlines, the book follows the story of Omai, the Polynesian who came to London with Captain Cook and was the toast of polite society there at the end of the eighteenth century.

One day after a shipwreck a trunk of books published by the Society for the Diffusion of Useful Knowledge washes up on Fantaisie. Popanilla finds the trunk, reads the books and is instantly converted to utilitarianism. Founded two years previously, in 1826, the Society meant to facilitate the publication of tracts that would spread useful knowledge, especially among those who had least access to formal education. It was a practical offshoot of utilitarianism. The Society published a wide variety of tracts and maps, on everything from *Vegetable Physiology* to *Animal Mechanics* to an *Outline of General History*.[6] Like the Society for Promoting Christian Knowledge, founded more than a century earlier, the

Society had the aim of evangelizing and converting those conceived to be less well off in this case because of their lack of practical know-how.

Convinced that Fantaisie should also benefit by acquiring useful knowledge, Popanilla appeals to the king of the island. '"Sire!" said he, in that mild tone of subdued superciliousness with which we should always address kings, and which, while it vindicates our dignity, so satisfactorily proves that we are above the vulgar passion of envy.'[7] Disraeli was always interested in those of higher rank than himself, but absolute subservience was not his style. Anyway, as Popanilla had grown convinced of the principle of utility, he could not admit that there was anything useful in a social hierarchy.

Popanilla gives a speech worthy of Bentham, in which he surveys the progress of man from the savage state to the French Revolution. He argues that 'man was born for something else besides enjoying himself', that 'pleasure could profit no one', that 'there was no utility in pleasure' and that 'therefore pleasure is not pleasant'.[8] This is Disraeli's lopsided lampoon of utilitarianism. He was trying to set up 'pleasure' as the antithesis of utility. He was arguing that enjoyment of simple pleasures like food and wine and sex in the present is preferable to the future-oriented plan of trying to reform society by improving, educating and evangelizing a rude population. Although Bentham saw the principle of utility as one able to confer happiness, meaning a predominance of pleasure over pain, on the greatest number of people, Disraeli's advocacy of pleasure was a more egotistical variety. Please yourself, he dared to say, and do not worry about calculating the costs or the benefits.

He was also out to attack what he perceived as the levelling, radical and revolutionary aims of utilitarianism. When the king appears not to take Popanilla's speech seriously, Popanilla tells him, following John Locke, that the king 'was only a chief magistrate, and he had no more right to laugh at him than a constable'. The king replies by saying he will have a cup of wine and a dance. Popanilla 'sneaked home; and consoled himself for having nobody to speak to, by reading some very amusing "Conversations on Political Economy"'.[9] Popanilla gets his revenge by converting all the young men of Fantaisie to utilitarianism. The women complain to the king that this conversion of the boys will undermine the worship of women generally. The king responds by making Popanilla a naval captain and expelling him. He is forced into a canoe and put out to sea.

Disraeli loved Voltaire's comic stories and Popanilla's journey after his expulsion from Fantaisie sounds something like the wanderings of Voltaire's *Candide*. In one catastrophe after another Voltaire's hero is irrationally confirmed in his belief that his tutor's philosophy – that everything turns out for the best in this best of all possible worlds – is correct. Against repeated evidence to the contrary, Popanilla is similarly confirmed in his belief in the wisdom of utilitarianism.

He lands in Disraeli's version of London and England: the city of Hubbabub, capital of the island of Vraibleusia. There he finds a society where a single individual owns all the corn and a law that compels inhabitants 'through force, and fear, and flattery' to buy their corn from him.[10] Here Disraeli was mocking the Corn Laws, which artificially held up the price of grain for the very small and already rich landowning classes. He was as capable and as inclined at the age of twenty-three to make fun of rich landowners as he was of the philosophic radicals who espoused utilitarianism.

A book is published in Hubbabub describing Popanilla's voyage to Vraibleusia. It includes a picture of him in which 'he looked the most dandyfied of savages, and the most savage of dandies'.[11] Daniel Maclise, a man later celebrated as the friend and sometime illustrator of Dickens, painted a watercolour of Disraeli in the year he published *Popanilla*. It shows him a dandy with curling hair, wearing a fashionable jacket with mutton-chop sleeves, a frilly shirtfront and with Napoleonic hand in waistcoat. Disraeli identified with Popanilla, and suspected that in the exclusive circles to which he aspired with his dandy dress, he would always be regarded as a bit of a savage. [*See front cover of book jacket.*]

Popanilla becomes a celebrity and is invited everywhere. He goes to a party given by Lady Spirituelle, where all of society is gathered and various scientific discoveries are being explained. Afterwards,

> Popanilla was unfashionable enough to make his acknowledgements to his hostess before he left her house . . . [H]e could not refrain from pressing her hand, in a manner which violated etiquette, and which a nativity in the Indian Ocean could alone excuse; the pressure was graciously returned . . . He did not return to his hotel quite so soon as he expected.[12]

Here is Disraeli's ironic response to the utilitarian creed: sensual enjoyment is a more sensible course than absurd scientific dabbling. Illicit sex in the present is better than social progress in the future, a reckless sentiment for a young man with political ambitions. The favourite of a Roman emperor might have got away with it, but no one with parliamentary ambitions could say such a thing without having to apologize for it at some stage. The book is a mark of his rashness, his despair at the depths of depression and of an unsinkable wit that keeps pressing to the surface.

Popanilla also has some fascinating reflections on Britain's constitution, in this his first foray into political thought. Popanilla is declared to be an ambassador from Fantaisie and is taken to meet the monarch of Vraibleusia in a palace. This is important because it is the first commentary on the crown provided by the man historians usually credit with having revived the modern monarchy in the third quarter of the nineteenth century. Rather than a living person, Popanilla finds that the monarch of Vraibleusia is a statue, composed of bits of armour and ornaments from different eras: Greek, Roman, Saxon and Gothic. 'The figure bore the appearance of great antiquity, but had evidently been often repaired and renovated since its first formation.' The statue looked old but, in fact, some of it was quite new. Popanilla is told with reference to the statue 'that ours is a mixed Government'. Popanilla also remarked that 'the Statue was held in great reverence, and viewed with great admiration by the whole Vraibleusian people'.[13] There was only disagreement about which part of the statue was most important: the gold head, or the silver body, or the iron legs.

This is an unusual metaphor for Britain's constitutional monarchy. It draws on Medieval and Renaissance ideas of the government as a body politic, with king and nobility in the head and people supporting the extremities. It also draws on Edmund Burke's image of the British constitution as an old house, often extended and renovated, not conforming to any rational plan, but founded on a core dwelling for which the population has both reverence and affection. The image of the monarch who is merely an inanimate statue, however, is no reverent Tory notion of kingship. This is an idol who is paid credulous homage and has a faintly fraudulent claim to antiquity. Those were two potent republican critiques of kingship in Britain: that it constituted a form of idolatry for an uneducated population, and that its claim to authority based on historical precedents was fake. Disraeli may have had a nature that loved deference to the highborn and royal ceremonial, but the counterpart to that was a good knowledge of republican arguments about the quackery of kingship. He was prepared to put elements of both into his satire on utilitarianism. His brilliant duality was at work once more, for he was not just the century's most famous courtier, but also one who was master of the arguments in favour of abolishing courts.

Popanilla was also a satire on what Disraeli took to be the excessive moralizing of the rising Evangelical party in the Church of England. One night Popanilla visited the theatre. During the play one of the actors addressed 'a female chorus-singer with an ardour which was more than theatrical; and every lady in the house immediately fainted'. The men in the audience insisted indignantly that the actor should be dismissed. The actor appeared on stage to apologize,

> but the most moral, and the most modest of nations was implacable, and the wretch was expelled. Having a large family dependent upon his exertions, the actor, according to a custom prevalent in Vraibleusia, went immediately and drowned himself in the nearest river. Then the ballet commenced.[14]

This was Disraeli's condemnation of middle-class morality; he preferred easy-going upper-class moral laxity. The same middle classes who were fired with utilitarian zeal for political reform were often those who wanted also a moral reform of the late-Georgian governing classes. Disraeli was not yet a member of those governing classes, but he certainly sympathized more with the manners of the old rich than with those of the puritanical classes whose wealth came from industry and the professions. 'Then the ballet commenced' is a brilliant stroke of Disraeli's black humour.

Popanilla is at its funniest when Disraeli describes social climbing, because he was a climber himself and he was good at it. A financial speculation rages as Vraibleusians prepare to make a huge profit out of trade with Fantaisie. Trading vessels sail out to Fantaisie and anticipated success of this expedition enriches speculators. The middle classes making money off this speculation are able to buy palaces, crests from the College of Arms and carriages, but they needed 'manner'.

> Accustomed to the counting-house, the factory, or the exchange, they looked queer in saloons; said "Sir!" when they addressed you; and seemed stiff, and hard, and hot. Then the solecisms they committed in more formal society, oh! they were outrageous ... it was whispered, that when they drank wine, they filled their glasses to the brim. All this delighted the

old class, who were as envious of their riches, as the new people were emulous of their style.[15]

The new millionaires decide to acquire style and they establish a Society for the Diffusion of Fashionable Knowledge. The first treatise published by the Society is on 'Nonchalance'.

> It instructed its students ever to appear inattentive in the society of men, and heartless when they conversed with women . . . Excellence was never to be recognised, but only disparaged with a look: an opinion or a sentiment, and the *nonchalant* was lost for ever. For these, he was to substitute a smile like a damp sunbeam, a moderate curl of the upper lip, and the all-speaking and perpetual shrug of the shoulders. By a skilful management of these qualities, it was shown to be easy to ruin another's reputation, and ensure your own, without ever opening your mouth.[16]

Here was Disraeli's dandy manual, his guide for acting in society as if you were Beau Brummell, the master of nonchalance in that era. Once again he was lampooning dandy manners by setting them up as the admirable epitome of an absurdly refined, really rather sinister social behaviour. Remember, though, that whatever Disraeli lampooned, he often rather liked as well.

Further treatises were announced to appear: 'On leaving cards', 'On cutting intimate friends' and 'On cravats'.

> In the meantime, the Essay on Nonchalance produced the very best effects. A ci-devant stock-broker cut a Duke dead at his club, the day after publication . . . The aristocrats got a little frightened, and when an eminent hop-merchant and his lady had asked a dozen Countesses to dinner, and forgot to be at home to receive them, the old class left off quizzing.[17]

Here was the world turned upside down by a financial

speculation. The diffusion of fashionable knowledge and new wealth upset the social hierarchy. However, the old class need not have worried too much as the newly wealthy had preposterous ideas about progress, just as they never properly understood dandies and style. The newly wealthy believed, for example, that

> when we take into consideration the nature of man, the origin of society, and a few other things, and duly consider the constant inclination and progression towards perfection which mankind evince – there was no reason why, in the course of time, the whole nation should not go to Almack's on the same night.[18]

Almack's was the most exclusive club in London of the 1820s. It had been built in the second half of the eighteenth century, a plain building in the heart of fashionable St James's, across the street from where Christie's is today. George Cruikshank drew a satirical image of Almack's in Disraeli's day, the men dancing in tight trousers, the women simpering in empire dresses. The club fell from fashion later in the nineteenth century and was replaced in the twentieth century by an office block called Almack House.

Disraeli longed to go to Almack's, though it was impossible without being known to one of the four lady patronesses who could provide an entry ticket. The impossibility of the whole nation going there was his attack on a Whig, radical and enlightened view of social progress. He is taking centuries of political thought devoted to arriving at and understanding the ideal conditions for human society and turning them upside down.

The Whig historical tradition, which connected England's history with an inevitable march towards greater political and religious liberty, gave Disraeli indigestion. Popanilla, like his author, develops 'dyspepsia . . . the national disease of Vraibleusia'. Popanilla is suffering from the loss of his native Fantaisie instinct that the pleasures of eating were not to be underestimated. In Vraibleusia, by contrast, the link between dyspepsia and

> civil and religious liberty was indissoluble; that every man, woman, and child, above fifteen, in the Island was a martyr to it; that it was occasioned by their rapid mode of dispatching their meals, which again was occasioned by the little time which the most active nation in the world could afford to bestow upon such a losing business as eating.[19]

This runs parallel to Disraeli's complaint to Isaac that English tourists did too much and enjoyed too little. Eating was one of those sensual pleasures which Disraeli regarded as central to the day, rather than as subordinate or as an impediment to business. Eating first and business later (if at all) was his creed.

In the end the trading expedition to Fantaisie is unable to find the island. The speculation collapses as rapidly as Disraeli's mining shares did. There is a run on the bank. Popanilla is arrested for high treason. He is tried in court and found guilty, though he is allowed to go free on a technicality. He ships out of Vraibleusia, destination unknown. Disraeli promises to reveal more in a second voyage of Captain Popanilla if the public demands it.

Although he was to flirt with joining political radicals before he eventually became a Tory, *Popanilla* shows that his conservatism was deeply entrenched at the age of twenty-three. He had a love of hierarchy, style, wit and taste that was fundamentally at odds with a belief in progress and rolling back historical precedents to assure greater freedom and opportunity for all classes. He infinitely preferred dandy dress and aristocratic nonchalance to granting the whole world entry to Almack's. His philosophy was based on cheerful hedonism for the few rather than on improving government for the many. The style of utilitarians was to make their points in dull, closely reasoned tracts on practical subjects to improve the lives of the uneducated. Disraeli's style was to satirize and provoke laughter as a way of enjoying the absurdities of life in the here and now.

He made fun right and left, both of dandies and Corn Laws as well as of humourless distributors of tracts to diffuse useful knowledge. Satire came naturally to him and he had yet to learn to choose his targets carefully. Poking fun and verbal dexterity were in his blood; he enjoyed himself when he could demonstrate, either in conversation or in print, his natural abilities. What begins to emerge from these years is a philosophy of enjoyment that was to underlay and underpin his later politics. Better to dance, to flirt and to drink in the present than to make overly earnest plans for the future. Better to take men as they are rather than to think, with excessive optimism, that their entire frame can be changed with improving education. Better to celebrate the snobbery and widespread interest in the activities of the upper classes than to trust in everyone's being levelled down to an ideal state of social equality. His next book was to revel in such a high-spirited fantasy about life among the upper classes that he would later be embarrassed by it. He felt compelled to issue a public apology. Although he would later expurgate and excuse these early works, the satirical spirit of *Popanilla*, and the love of nonchalance that he described there, never really left him. Having written them for publication, they were engraved on a part of his soul.

Frank enjoyment of upper-class style was something Disraeli shared with his publisher, Henry Colburn. In 1829 Colburn decided to launch *The Court Journal*, a weekly newspaper devoted to fashionable topics common in novels of the 'silver fork' school. It was satirical and aimed to provide information on what was chic in the West End and in the country; where it was not well informed, its writers invented material. It was like a modern *Hello* magazine or 'Lifestyles of the Rich and Famous', crossed with the *Tatler* and *Private Eye*.

Disraeli contributed four articles to *The Court Journal* in May and June 1829.[20] The satire here is neither as sustained nor as consistently amusing as in *Popanilla*. Nevertheless, they show Disraeli working out a defence of his interest in upper-class manners. He was well aware that reform was in the air and that it was awkward for a middle-class man with a Jewish surname to pretend to be familiar with aristocratic life. His *Court Journal* articles began to give reasons why glances towards those above you in the social scale were not pernicious.

The principal figure in these articles is Mivartinos, a foppish aristocrat who gets into a conversation with a character called 'Henry Colburn'. The first article looks like a transcription of a real dialogue, but is Disraeli's invention. It serves as a prospectus for *The Court Journal*. The name Mivartinos came from Mivarts Hotel, a place where the rich and the fashionable often stayed when they came to London. It was in a town house on Brook Street and was sold after Monsieur Mivart's death to Mr Claridge.[21] The modern Claridge's Hotel has the same reputation for luxury and exclusivity that Mivarts did in Disraeli's day. For 'Mivartinos' think of a drawling character named 'Ritzy' or 'Claridginos' and that will convey the same idea.

Mivartinos and Colburn agree 'that wealth can only be the portion of a few, but may be enjoyed by all, and that the utilitarian is a short-sighted animal.'[22] They believe that one can derive amusement from what high-ranking people do and that this amusement is itself the equivalent of great riches. They believe that 'amusement is felicity, that elegance is wealth, and that, therefore, all may be happy, and all may be rich'. The article argues that one need not be rich to adopt upper-class manners and that if one can maintain a light-hearted attitude to the world that is as good as having money in the bank. Mivartinos and Colburn 'would teach' their readers 'that gaiety is a treasure worth an equipage, and cheerfulness a brighter possession than a villa; that calmness of manner results from a well regulated mind, and not from a cold heart; and that good breeding is only the experience of amiable men'. In short, Colburn tells Mivartinos, 'Rank and Fashion, Wit and Genius, are about to amuse themselves' in the pages of *The Court Journal* and so 'delight the empire'.[23] Here Disraeli is democratizing his fascination with the aristocracy by claiming that really everyone can be calm, cheerful, amiable and well bred – just as the upper classes appear to be – by enjoying with-out envy accounts of aristocratic doings and goings-on.

In the later articles Mivartinos has a duel with a great bore and annoys all of fashionable society by failing to kill him.[24] Mivartinos is first ostracized, then goes into hiding, and then is tried on the balcony of a house in Hertford Street, Mayfair. The physical description of Mivartinos at his trial resembles that of Disraeli himself: 'his hair, which is of a dark brown, descends on his right side almost to his shoulders in long curls, which do not however, degenerate into ringlets'.[25] Mivartinos asks in his own defence: 'When was not my *nonchalance* preferable to another's enthusiasm – my sneer to another's smile – my sarcasm to another's panegyric?'[26] He threatens to turn their world upside down, as in *Popanilla*, whereby bankers will occupy their palaces and de Rothschilds will replace dukes. This terrifies fashionable society and the court acquits him.

In the last of the articles Disraeli wrote for *The Court Journal* in 1829 Mivartinos becomes Augustus Villeroy, a dandy for whom 'Mivartinos' was a sort of disguise. In 'The Levee of Augustus Villeroy' the main character is a man about town and Colburn attends his levee in the morning to watch him dress. This is as elaborate as any ritual performed by Louis XIV at Versailles. Villeroy has a Mameluke servant named Rustan, a member of a powerful Egyptian military class descended from Turkish slaves. One of the characteristics of the best dandies is to have a stylish oriental servant and Disraeli seldom omitted this detail. Villeroy spends much time adjusting the ruffles on his shirtfront and select-ing a set of pink topaz buttons for a white silk waistcoat. Villeroy defends these jewels as appropriate for masculine dress. 'There, Mr. Colburn, let your eyes rest upon their mild effulgence. Some people think that a love for jewels indicates an effeminate mind. On the contrary, I am of opinion that there is no taste more magnificent and more manly.'[27]

The use of the word 'effeminate' here is interesting. There is a long history of its association with homosexuality. Although Plato approved of spiritual love between men, in *Phaedrus* he plainly disapproved of young men behaving in an effeminate way to attract older mentors. Juvenal's Crispinus combined effeminacy with his sinister hold over the emperor. There was, however, a good deal of ambiguity surrounding male effeminacy in Disraeli's day and he appears to be exploiting that ambiguity. He could write of the king of Fantaisie that he was 'a somewhat effeminate young man', without casting doubt on his desire to make love to the nearly naked women on the island, or on his desirability to them.[28] The fops and rakes of Restoration drama, the macaronis of the eighteenth century, were upper-class men about town, who, though often silly, affected and girlish in their outward manner, were also aggressive womanizers. This may be related to a pre-Freudian understanding of the libido which still survives today in the advice coaches give their athletes before big games. To expend energy on heterosexual intercourse is to reduce one's virile abilities; excessive or extravagant heterosexual coupling leads to effeminacy in men, or, as some still think today, to athletes unable to perform on the field. This variety of effeminacy could be a sign of liking sexual relations with women too much rather than too little. It was also ordinarily associated with the aristocracy and other socially elevated men more than with any other social group. Middle-class people often charged aristocratic men with being addicted to luxury, hence effeminate.[29]

Nevertheless, if effeminacy for young Disraeli and his contemporaries was not what we could call 'gay', it was not particularly good either. It meant a lack of masculine courage, direction and willpower. When Charles Kingsley accused John Henry Newman's Christian theology of being insufficiently 'muscular' he was talking about a form of faith weakened by luxury, inactivity or dreamy contemplation. Kingsley himself thought the whole of the British aristocracy effeminate not because of their same-sex desires but because they were fastidious, enervated and no longer men of action.[30] There is also an element of Protestant chauvinism in Kingsley's attacks on Newman. He perceived Roman

Catholic sympathies in Newman even before his conversion. Newman's attraction to a Catholic doctrine of the priest's celibacy, for example, Kingsley regarded as both foreign and female, hence bad. That Newman probably was homosexual, though he may never have acted upon it, was an unexpressed dimension of Kingsley accusations of 'effeminacy' that was present, but did not quite rise to the surface, in Victorian connotations of the word. Newman left specific instructions that he was to be buried in the same grave as his best friend and we cannot know precisely what there was between them.[31]

What Disraeli hated in the utilitarians was their dogged middle-class pragmatism, their insufficient appreciation of impractical style. What he would have hated in Kingsley, if he had known him, was his unimaginative emphasis on action in the world as the sole index of a man's worth. Disraeli wanted to highlight the importance – for a man – of a feminine variety of *being*, rather than incessant, mindless *doing*. Hence he put words in Villeroy's mouth to defend male dressing up and choosing jewellery as ornamental activity which he thought unusual in a man, but more attractive than conventional male devotion to political reform or Evangelical zeal.

Villeroy, like Mivartinos, has an element of Disraelian auto-biography in him. An old school friend of Villeroy's applies to him for a loan, which Villeroy supplies. Nevertheless, Villeroy claims that he is worse off than this poor acquaintance because his is a life '*without* an object'. Villeroy is depressed, the victim of 'irremediable despair'. Disraeli was himself suffering throughout this period and what distressed him most was that he had no object towards which he was aiming, no great focused ambition he was trying to fulfil. A sense of purposelessness oppressed him. He was not so low, however, that he could not make a joke about it. Villeroy is afraid he will lose his reputation as a cold and pol-ished man if people see him being generous. He tells his old school friend to disguise himself on leaving: 'Pray, Sir, as you go out, do me the favour to look as much like a jockey as you can.'[32]

Nor was he so depressed that he lost all ambition to rise in the world. The *Court Journal* articles were all part of an attempt to mock, to praise and to make an advance to a fellow writer, Edward Lytton Bulwer (later Sir Edward Bulwer Lytton and ultimately Lord Lytton). Bulwer's novel *Pelham* had been published in 1828. It had been the sensation of that season and its dandy hero in many ways resembled Vivian Grey. Unlike Disraeli, Bulwer had an estate and connections among the landed gentry. He had not only literary success, but also, unlike Disraeli, a firm toehold in the fashionable world. It is odd that Disraeli approached Bulwer in so public yet so oblique a way, as Bulwer knew Isaac D'Israeli and a proper introduction might have been arranged. It was as if Disraeli wanted to meet Bulwer on terms entirely of his own making and without parental interference. 'Mivartinos' was also possibly a reference to Bulwer, who was known to stay at Mivarts Hotel. Bulwer had just bought a house at 36 Hertford Street and the main character from Bulwer's novel, Henry Pelham, was in the audience at Mivartinos's trial. Bulwer's house and the balcony where Disraeli placed Mivartinos's mock trial still exist today.

Pelham devoted a whole chapter to the 'science of dress' and Bulwer thought the *Court Journal* articles intended to make fun of him, or of Pelham's style.[33] In February 1829, before the publication of the *Court Journal* articles, Disraeli had written to Bulwer as a complete stranger, enclosing a second-hand copy of Bulwer's poetry he had found at a sale.[34] After the articles, in the summer of 1829, they corresponded a little more, still in a rather formal tone. Bulwer, writing in the third person, said he hoped 'to cultivate his [Disraeli's] personal acquaintance' when everyone returned to town in the winter.[35] They were like two sensitive people circling around one another. Neither one could bear the potential rejection that might come from a direct approach to the other. Yet, when it came, the friendship would provide Disraeli an important step on the social ladder and someone his own age with whom he had productive intellectual sympathy. It would take another novel to draw them closer together.

6

His Manner Was His Magic

Disraeli often had schemes on which he proposed his father should spend money. He wrote from his tour with the Austens saying that on a very modest income, like Isaac's, the whole D'Israeli family could live like princes in Italy. It was a not very subtle hint, typical of young men in their twenties without much of an income of their own, that they should all move to Italy.[1] Isaac let his son's suggestion pass. Disraeli had another scheme for Isaac to set him up as a country gentleman in England with a small estate of his own. Isaac would not agree to that either. Finally, Disraeli hit upon the idea of travelling to the eastern Mediterranean in Byron's footsteps: he wanted warm weather, oriental delights and knowledge of civilizations more ancient than Christian Europe. Disraeli had begun work on a story of the adventures of a twelfth-century Jewish hero, David Alroy, and he needed material for that as well. Isaac refused to pay for the trip, but this time, Disraeli thought he could raise the money himself by writing a new society novel for Colburn. He wrote to Benjamin Austen in December 1829:

A literary prostitute I have never yet been, tho' born in an age of general prostitution, and tho' I have more than once been subject to temptations which might have been the *ruination* of a less virtuous young woman. My muse however is still a virgin, but the mystical flower, I fear, must soon be plucked. Colburn I suppose will be the bawd. Tempting Mother Colburn![2]

His metaphor is revealing. He compares himself to a virgin because he has never written to a publisher's specifications before. He is about to lose his virginity, and his publisher is like the madam of a brothel. Once again he identifies with a female figure. He confides in a male friend about a literary project which is also a projected sexual act, a deflowering, a giving way. He goes on to say that he relies on Austen to keep this a secret as female friends cannot be relied on to keep his confidences. Having flirted and got his way with Sara Austen, who helped him with *Vivian Grey*, he was now flirting with Benjamin Austen. Austen would eventually lend Disraeli money as a sort of bridge to what he expected to receive from Colburn for this second novel and to enable the eastern adventure to occur. The underlying suggestion is that the forthcoming trip to the Islamic Mediterranean might also be a sexual adventure.

The resulting book, *The Young Duke*, is easier to read and the story is handled with more assurance than either of the two parts of *Vivian Grey*. The 'Advertisement' prefacing the book begins on the same polemical note that he had raised in *Popanilla*.

There is a partial distress, or universal – and the affairs of India must really be settled; but we must also be amused. I send over my quota; for, though absent, I am a patriot; besides, I am desirous of contributing to the diffusion of useful knowledge.[3]

Composed in 1829 and early 1830, Disraeli expected the book to be published, as it was, while he travelled in the East. He continued sniping at the utilitarians by sending them a mathematical 'quota' of amusement. He aimed to shock by saying that he really could not be bothered by unemployment in England or suffering in India. The book was to be airy persiflage and if it has a serious point, it is that amusement and affectation are more worth having than earnestness and social improvement. It is a book that unashamedly delights in what he took to be life among the upper classes. He later realized that he had got some of the details wrong, but the book is still fun and capable of amusing from the distance of more than a century and a half.

At the beginning of the novel the young Duke of St James turns twenty-one, 'an event which created as great a sensation among the aristocracy of England as the Norman Conquest, or the institution of Almack's'.[4] This is Disraeli's typical dandy strategy of comparing a small act (a young man's birthday) to a big one (the Norman Conquest), and then lampooning the big one by equating it with something trivial (a club for dancing, drinking and small talk). Exaggerating the importance of small events and pretending that big ones do not matter is imitating the blasé attitudes of exclusive circles. The critic William Hazlitt remarked that this reversal of expectations was the key to all Beau Brummell's best bons mots.[5]

The young duke's parents are dead. A neighbour and friend of his father's, Mr Dacre, has raised the boy as his guardian. The Dacres are Roman Catholics whereas the young duke is a Protestant, and one great theme of the work is the absurdity of denying civil rights to Roman Catholics, who are in every respect model English citizens. This provides a flavour of the year in which it was conceived: 1829 was the year Parliament for the first time removed disabilities that debarred Catholics from holding office.

Dacre has been a good guardian to the young duke, looking carefully after his vast financial interests and treating him as if he were a son. The young duke, however, is callous and immature. He overlooks the goodness of his father's chosen guardian and allows himself to be seduced instead by his Uncle Fitz Pompey, a man secretly annoyed that he was not selected to be the boy's guardian. Fitz Pompey wants to manipulate his rich nephew for his own purposes and secure his own family's financial fortunes by marrying him off to his daughter. The Fitz Pompeys introduce the inexperienced young man to all the delights of London society. He meets three people worth noticing.

Sir Lucius Grafton is five or six years older than the young duke and is the husband of the beautiful Lady Aphrodite Grafton, who catches the duke's eye one night at Almack's. Lucius Grafton, who goes by the name 'Lucy', is also beautiful.

> In appearance, he was an Antinous. There was, however, an expression of firmness, almost ferocity, about his mouth, which quite prevented his countenance from being effeminate, and broke the dreamy voluptuousness of the rest of his features. In mind, he was a *roué*. Devoted to pleasure, he had reached the goblet at an early age; and before he was five-and-twenty, procured for himself a reputation which made all women dread, and some men shun him.[6]

The comparison to Antinous is a reference to the handsome young man who was the homosexual favourite of the Roman emperor, Hadrian. It reinforces the aura of sexual licence and disreputability about a character to whom the author himself is clearly attracted. Disraeli would not have written of the 'dreamy voluptuousness' of a character who left him cold.

Lucius Grafton no longer loves his wife. Lady Aphrodite had adored him with a passion to begin with, but feels she is now being punished for having loved him too much. She is forced to endure a miserable existence of unreciprocated affection: 'Like the old Hebrews, she had been so chastened for her wild idolatry, that she dared not again raise an image to animate the wilderness of her existence.'[7] This is a rare reference in one of Disraeli's earliest works to Jewish history. Here, rather than taking it seriously, as he would later, he is playing with it, not unlike comparing the Norman Conquest to the institution of Almack's. The tone is of insouciant sacrilege.

If Disraeli loved his male characters with names like Vivian and

Lucy, he was also able to convey both humorously and persuasively an illicit liaison between a man and a woman. The young duke manages to begin a romantic affair with Lady Aphrodite by sending her carriage away from a charity bazaar and proposing she take his instead. She refuses to ride with him. She wants to avoid the temptation of being alone with a man who is beginning to reawaken her ability to love. He says he will save her from embarrassment. "'I shall certainly walk,' said he. "I do not think the easterly wind will make me very ill. Goodbye! Oh, what a *coup de vent!*"'[8] She relents and they ride off together. This is the young duke's first sexual liaison and it is with a married woman, just as Disraeli's was probably with Sara Austen.

The third character to make an impression on the young duke is Charles Annesley, a dandy with huge style and no visible means of support. Disraeli defends the term 'dandy' by saying that 'the muse of Byron has made it not only English, but classical'.[9] Of Annesley Disraeli wrote that

> everything connected with him was unparalleled for its elegance, its invention, and its refinement. But his manner was his magic. His natural and subdued nonchalance, so different from the assumed non-emotion of a mere dandy; his coldness of heart, which was hereditary, not acquired; his cautious courage, and his unadulterated self-love; had permitted him to mingle much with mankind without being too deeply involved in the play of their passions; while his exquisite sense of the ridiculous quickly revealed those weaknesses to him, which his delicate satire did not spare, even while it refrained from wounding.

Disraeli's description of Annesley ends by comparing him to characters from Restoration drama, gentlemen 'of our old brilliant comedy, – the Dorimants, the Bellairs, and the Mirabels'.[10] If Lady Aphrodite had been chastened because she loved too much, Annesley is perfectly preserved because, other than himself, he has never loved at all. Devoted to perfecting his dress and to commanding his coterie, who love him because he is constantly cool to them, he is a snow prince.

Disraeli's early fiction is filled with these liminal dandies, balancing delicately on the borderline between male and female. In addition to loving the gorgeousness of their dress, he likened their liminality to his own: he balanced on the borderline between Christian and Jew, having been baptized at the age when he should have been celebrating his bar mitzvah. Not only is Vivian Grey himself a dandy, but he also meets a Brummell-like character in Germany called von Aslingen. The von Aslingen character indicates another characteristic of dandies. They are creatures of courts, of hierarchical, deferential societies. His name evokes the rude words used to denounce courtiers as 'arse lickers' and recalls a story that Isaac put into *Curiosities of Literature*. A tutor of the future James I punished his charge for misbehaving. A lady-in-waiting entered the room as the boy was being spanked and he ran to her arms in tears. She remonstrated with the tutor. He replied by accusing her of an excessively courtier-like attitude to the young prince: 'Madam . . . I have whipped his a[rse], you may kiss it if you please.'[11] Von Aslingen has perfect dress and a perfect manner, but his name hints at the widespread criticism that dandies were servile for being too much in the company of kings. Brummell was famously insolent to the Prince Regent and so escaped the charge. Dandies in general, however, as habitués of high society, were likelier than most to be interested in rank and fashion, and therefore out of place in a parliamentary culture that prized independence and plain-speaking. Von Aslingen suggests Disraeli wanted it both ways, that he wanted to admire dandies, but acknowledge republican criticisms of them as well. Disraeli and his father were both fascinated with Britain's most famously homosexual king, and Disraeli at one point has the young duke dress up as James I's male favourite, the Duke of Buckingham.[12] This is one more indication of Disraeli's allied fascination with the sexual ambiguity of dandies. In exploring the delights of dressing up, he was exploring the love of courts, of elegance, and of odd sexual desire all at once.

Popanilla, Mivartinos, Augustus Villeroy and the young duke are all dandies. Although the young duke has an Italian valet, unusually he allows his Greek page, Spiridion, to dress him. This passage is suggestive of some intimacy between master and servant. After his bath, the young duke leans back on an ottoman 'while Spiridion, with a fineness of tact of which a Greek is alone susceptible, arranged the *bas de soie*, and fitted the feet into velvet shoes, fastened by buckles of mother-of-pearl. The feet would have become a woman . . .' but the duke has such special white trousers that his 'delicate extremities became in their character not merely feminine, but would have filled with envy the mistress of a Mandarin'.[13] This sustains the courtier metaphor of von Aslingen, and indeed of Crispinus as well. Dandies are not merely men who dress like women, who appear as if they were women, they are like mistresses of an oriental potentate, an attribute of the great man's power, the exquisite presence at his left hand. The courtier's role fascinated Disraeli. He wanted to be that silky mistress of the mandarin. Byron's love for a Greek boy, Loukas, was well known. So the young duke's Greek page may have been a covert reference to desire for other men that Disraeli expected certain of his readers to notice and understand.

Edward Bulwer, to whom Disraeli showed a draft of *The Young Duke*, told him to get rid of the 'ornate and showy effeminacy' of the book. He also told Disraeli: 'As a trifle not to be overlooked, I would give matured attention to the Duke's *dress*.' He went on to say that 'these are the things (strange as it may seem) that make enemies and scarcely make friends'.[14] Both authors emphasized the effeminacy in characters like the young duke and Henry Pelham, but both were a little nervous about what they were doing as well. Ellen Moers says in her study of nineteenth-century dandyism that Bulwer went through later editions of *Pelham*, and deleted references to his hero's effeminacy.[15] Only two years after the publication of *Pelham*, he was already telling Disraeli to do the same thing. Critics hated their love of liminal heroes who were attractive as women as well as men, which is why Disraeli was given a hard time over Vivian Grey's velvet slippers.

Disraeli's subtitle, 'A moral Tale though gay', is from Byron's *Don Juan*. What Disraeli, Byron and their contemporaries meant by 'gay' relates to the question of effeminacy. Their word 'gay' differs from, yet also overlaps with, the meaning of the word now. Byron meant to mock moral earnestness by telling the story of Don Juan, who has an affair with a married woman while he is still in his teens. For him gay meant 'lively', 'joyful' and 'colourful', while also retaining some of the licentious associations of the word which had been applied to female prostitutes in the seventeenth century.[16] The first part of *Don Juan* is a cheerful story about adultery, hence immoral but 'gay'.

Disraeli also equated 'gaiety' with a cheerful disposition. There is also a hint of Byronic licentiousness in Disraeli's quotation. Although the word does not mean men attracted to other men, it could mean men who were attracted to women, but who dressed to resemble women themselves, as the young duke and Lucius Grafton did. Anything likely to shock conventional middle-class morality was acceptably 'gay' for Disraeli.

Persons who were odd sports of nature, who did not at once appear to belong to a settled gender or rank, for example the jockey, fascinated Disraeli. He was not only a man who was strange because he was short. Disraeli suggested that a jockey was also odd because he crossed the line between classes. The young duke goes to the horse races at Newmarket as a part of his introduction to fashionable society. He grows popular there.

Even the jockeys were civil to him, and welcomed him with a sweet smile and gracious nod, instead of the sour grin, and malicious wink, with which those characters generally greet a stranger – those mysterious characters who, in their influence over their superiors, and their total want of sympathy with their species, are our only match for the Oriental Eunuch.[17]

Jockeys can move back and forth between the worlds of the lower and upper classes, just as eunuchs and dandies stand on the borderline between masculine and feminine. Here jockeys are also attractive to Disraeli for the hold they have on their aristocratic patrons. Disraeli was writing this book to fund his eastern adventure and one purpose of the trip was to investigate what he had heard of the oriental eunuch himself.

The young duke eventually gets into trouble. He tires of Lady Aphrodite. He has an affair with an opera singer, but he becomes disgusted with her because 'she ate so much, – and he hated your eating women'.[18] Although he loved eating himself, he seems to have disliked the sensuous physical enjoyment of eating in women. This was also one of the legends that circulated about Byron. The young duke finds a woman he really likes, May Dacre, the daughter of his guardian. She twice turns down proposals of marriage from him, partially because he has treated her father badly, partially because she senses some truth in the remark of a friend who says of the young duke, 'There is something in his eyes which tells me he is not a marrying man.'[19] The young duke also gets himself into terrible debt. He is forced to throw himself on his former guardian's mercy and confess that he has been profligate with all the riches Mr Dacre has carefully tended for him.

Both the young duke and Disraeli himself were deeply in debt; but the person in the novel who most resembles Disraeli is May Dacre's cousin, Arundel Dacre. The physical description matches Disraeli himself at this age: his complexion 'sallow, but clear, with long black curls, and a Murillo face . . . His countenance was reserved, and his manner not very easy; yet, on the whole, his face indicated intellect, and his figure blood.'[20] The Murillo reference returns so many times in Disraeli's letters and early work that it is worth attention. He must have begun by sensing a resemblance between his own appearance and the dark Mediterranean complexions of characters in Murillo's canvases. Disraeli liked wine and he would have identified with Murillo's 'Young Man Drinking' who looks sexily at the viewer over a glass of red. Disraeli first saw Murillo's paintings of boys, mainly waifs and strays, in the National Gallery in London. The 'Young Man Drinking' was in a private London collection in the early nineteenth century so Disraeli might well have seen it. Disraeli and the Austens may also have seen Murillo's 'Summer as a Young Man with a Basket of Fruit and Vegetables' when they were in Italy. It shows another handsome young man, semi-nude, with the same sallow complexion he believed he had and which he also attributed to Arundel Dacre.[21]

Arundel Dacre's personality matches Disraeli's and bears some similarities to Vivian Grey's: 'in his solitary musings, he perhaps even exaggerated his powers. He was proud, and yet worldly. He never forgot that he was a Dacre; but he desired to be the architect of his own fortune; and his very love of independence made him at an early period, meditate on the means of managing mankind.'[22] Disraeli's favourite characters, like Disraeli himself, are always hinting about how they can manipulate other men to get what they want.

Like Contarini Fleming, Arundel Dacre badly needs a friend, and the pain he suffers comes from never having found one.

> He was reserved and cold, for his imagination required much; yet he panted for a confident [*sic*: confidant], and was one of those youths with whom friendship is a passion . . . [At school and at college] he had never found that friend on whom his fancy had often busied itself, and which one whose alternations of feeling were so violent, peremptorily required.[23]

This longing for a friend is a feature of Disraeli's early biography as well. Disraeli is saying that both he and Dacre are odd because they never found a best friend at school or college.

Most interestingly of all, Arundel Dacre is in an odd religious borderland as well. The Dacres are an ancient Catholic family, but just as Disraeli was an odd Anglican among Jews, Arundel is a Protestant and this is strangely a disability for him.

To conclude, he was a Protestant among Catholics; and although this circumstance . . . was not an ungracious one, he felt that, till he was distinguished, it had lessened his consideration, since he could not count upon the sympathy of hereditary connection and ancient party . . . [H]is intense ambition sustained him, and he lived on the hope, and sometimes on the conviction, that a bright era would, some day, console him for the bitterness of his past and present life.[24]

Throughout the book Disraeli sympathizes with Roman Catholics in their ostracism from civil institutions and makes fun of anti-Catholic prejudice. He believed ostracism of the Jews was equally absurd. What is new, though, is his regarding, like Arundel Dacre, his own religious position as rather isolated. Disraeli himself was an odd Christian among proud and ancient Sephardic families, like the Basevis and friends of his D'Israeli grandfather. Since he had become a Christian, no longer could he count on Jews regarding him as one of them, nor could he count on the acceptance of John Bullish Englishmen. Like the jockey, he was odd and this sense of oddness contributed to his depression. Arundel Dacre too is a gloomy fellow.

This depression is an important autobiographical theme that runs through the whole novel. When May Dacre refuses the young duke's first proposal of marriage, he goes to the ruins of old Castle Dacre and weeps. The most bitter thing on earth, Disraeli says, 'is waking from our first delusion! For then we first feel the nothingness of self – the hell of sanguine spirits. All is dreary, bland, and cold.'[25] There are also repeated asides from the author himself. This is the egotism and 'affectation' for which he found it necessary to apologize in later editions. However, these asides provide commentary on his sadness, which he feared might be a variety of madness: 'I scribble to divert a brain, which, though weak, will struggle with strong thoughts, and lest my mind should muse itself into madness.'[26] It was part of the Romantic spirit of the day to connect a poetic muse with genius and insanity, but

Disraeli went further than that. He held himself responsible for his own mistakes and compared himself to a Babylonian king legendary for his mental imbalance.

> My life has been a blunder and a blank, and all ends by my adding one more slight ghost to the shadowy realm of fatal precocity! These are the rubs that make us feel the vanity of life – the littleness of man. Yet I do not groan, and will not murmur. My punishment is no caprice of tyranny. I brought it on myself, as greater men have done before. Prometheus is a lesson how to bear torture; but I think my case is most like Nebuchadnezzar's.[27]

The Young Duke is thus a series of reflections on Disraeli's own personality at the dawn of the year 1830 when he composed it: on his fears for his sanity, on his love of dress, on his religious oddity, on never having found a friend but on a promising acquaintance with a fellow dandy writer who told him that the 'effeminacy' had to go, on affectation and enjoyment as antidotes to earnestness and moral severity. His bravado is bracing. He was a young man of bourgeois, Bloomsbury origins affecting to know in detail the manners of aristocratic St James's. He does not always succeed, but the sweep and breadth of the gesture in the face of all the odds against him is still immensely attractive.

The Young Duke has a happy ending. The young duke is able to save May Dacre, to whom Lucius Grafton makes unwelcome advances at a party. Grafton tries to seduce May by speaking of the unhappiness of his marriage to Aphrodite. A tear 'quivered upon his fair and downy cheek. Sir Lucius Grafton was well aware of the magic of his beauty, and used his charms to betray, as if he were a woman.'[28] Disraeli was adept at painting male beauty heightened by tears streaming down cheeks. One critic, in describing Grafton's attractiveness, has noted the affinity between his name, Lucius, and 'luscious'.[29] A key to how compelled Disraeli was by the character he had created is in Grafton's fate at the end of the novel. Arundel Dacre challenges him to a duel and, though Grafton survives it, one of his legs has to be amputated. As with Frederick Cleveland, Disraeli tended to kill or to mutilate the handsome but unresponsive men he loved.

The young duke is able to satisfy Arundel Dacre's burning political ambition by nominating him for one of his pocket boroughs and thus giving him a seat in Parliament. He makes common cause with Arundel by travelling down to the House of Lords to speak in favour of Roman Catholic emancipation. This is something he knows that May Dacre and his guardian want passionately, but he does not tell them in advance that he is going to town to lend his weight to the cause. When he gets up to speak in Parliament he nearly says 'May Dacre' instead of 'My Lords'.[30] Although the pro-Catholics are in the minority, the vote is very close and Disraeli promises that this is 'the herald of future justice'.[31] The young duke returns to Castle Dacre to find May overjoyed with reports of his speech and newly softened towards him. They decide to go for a morning walk and she leaves the room. 'She ran for her bonnet, and he kissed her handkerchief, which she left behind, and, I believe, every thing else in the room which bore the slightest relation to her.'[32] At the ruins of the old Castle Dacre, where she rejected him once before, he declares his love a third time. She accepts by weeping on his chest.

One slightly sour note is the fate of Charles Annesley at the end of the novel. Even cold Annesley gives warm congratulations to the young duke after his pro-Catholic speech in the House of Lords. 'I have long observed,' Annesley tells the young duke, 'that you were formed for something better than frivolity. And, between ourselves, I am sick of it. Don't be surprised if you hear that I go to Algiers. Depend upon it, that I am on the verge of doing something dreadful.'[33] Annesley's travel to the Mediterranean, where Disraeli was shortly bound himself, suggests a banishment from cold England to a warmer, less pinched, more sensual climate. It is 'dreadful' partly because dandies habitually exaggerate, but also because it is an exile. It is like Byron's exile and his early death in

Greece. It is like Charles Ryder seeing his drunken friend, Sebastian Flyte, attended by a new German boyfriend, Kurt, in Moroccan exile in *Brideshead Revisited*. It fills Ryder with dismay. Oscar Wilde's biographer, Richard Ellmann, notes that Algiers was often a travel destination for English homosexuals. Lord Henry Wotton and Dorian Gray take a cottage there in Wilde's most famous novel.[34] Odder still, Disraeli simply kills off Annesley a little while later. Lord Fitz Pompey casually announces his death in a letter.[35] Disraeli expected delights from travel in the Mediterranean, but perhaps he feared what might happen to him there as well.

His jokey but slightly fearful tone is also evident from the beginning of a letter to Colburn in which he first mentioned *The Young Duke*. He told Colburn 'with positive Exile, probably Death, and possible Damnation hanging over me, I have been fool enough to be intent upon a novel'. Then he remembered that he had to sell this novel to the publisher and changed to a more confident register. 'But such a novel! It will astound you, draw tears from Princesses, and grins from Printers devils.' He went on that the book was 'delightfully adapted to the most corrupt taste. This immortal work which will set all Europe afire and not be forgotten till at least 3 months has only one fault – it is not written.' He concluded by saying that it was about half done, but that he was so impatient to be 'off to Greece' that he might not finish it before he left. He asked if Colburn was interested in publishing it.[36]

One can often sense the character of Disraeli's correspondents by the tone of his letters to them. He finely attuned his letter to what he judged the recipient would most enjoy hearing. As Disraeli's letters to Colburn often have camp exaggerations with capital letters, and as one of Colburn's specialities was publishing gossipy high-society novels, he must have been a fellow soul. Nevertheless, when the manuscript came in Colburn did not immediately accept Disraeli's novel. He had a reader look at it, who, Colburn told Disraeli, 'acknowledges its amusing extravagance which will cause it to be read but at the same time he adds that it is certain of being *severely criticised* for its egotism and other sins of the writer!' He offered Disraeli in May 1830 a total of £500, to be paid as follows: £100 six months afterwards, £200 after nine months, £100 after twelve months, and a further £100 after eighteen months if, and only if, there had been a second printing.[37] So Disraeli could count on £400 to fund his trip and possibly an additional £100 if the book did well. His books made him a little money, but not nearly enough to pay off the huge sums built up in the mining shares misadventure.

He wrote to his creditors in the spring of 1830 acknowledging his debts and apologizing for not having settled them before departure. In one letter he said his father would pay his obligations if he died. Despite the lugubrious tone, cheerful references to the prospective Mediterranean adventure are peppered here and there in *The Young Duke*. In one such passage, where he is defending George IV against critics of his extravagance, he gives a more spirited defence of his own philosophy of pleasure than appears in any of his previous works. He urges his readers to be contented with their current king: after all he, the author, might by an accident of birth have been their king and he would have been a tyrant.

> But what a tyrant! I would have smothered you in roses, shot you with bon-bons, and drowned you in Eau-de-Cologne. I would have banged up your parliaments, knocked up your steam engines, shut up all societies for the diffusion of any thing. I would have republished the Book of Sports, restored holidays, revived the Drama. Every parish should have had its orchestra, every village its dancing master. I would have built fountains, and burnt fireworks.
>
> But I am not a King. Bitter recollection! Yet something may turn up. Greece for instance. In the mean time, I will take a canter.[38]

It is as strong a statement of his *ancien régime*, anti-puritan, anti-industrial, anti-democratic, pro-pleasure ethic of enjoyment as appears anywhere in the book. It is a typically Disraelian paradox that the statement's silliness underlines how serious he was about it. That he tied all this together with the power of the monarch and his proposed journey suggests that he was writing purely and perfectly about his true self. It is the optimistic side of his personality seeing beyond four years of depressed English gloom and looking forward to the warmth of the Mediterranean sun.

7

This Is My Palace

William Monypenny used elliptical phrases to say why this journey to the eastern Mediterranean was important to Disraeli. The East appealed to Disraeli's 'peculiar temperament' and 'that Oriental tendency in his nature'.[1] Two of the things Monypenny may have meant which he could not quite say were that the homosexual element in Disraeli's personality and his desire to know more about his own Jewishness both spurred him to travel to Constantinople, Jerusalem and Cairo in the late spring of 1830. Monypenny's suggestion about Disraeli was also that there was something un-English about him, a comment that was common in Disraeli's lifetime. Disraeli himself sometimes felt this. It was precisely because he wanted to be in touch with those elements in his make-up – religious, racial, sexual – with which he could find little sympathy at home that he set off from Falmouth in May 1830. His contact with Muslims and Jews, the months of hot weather, his living in Constantinople and Cairo a life he could not lead in London, all these helped him overcome the depression that had plagued him in the 1820s. He had not found the friend he needed to sustain him, but what he witnessed in the eastern Mediterranean was enough to assure him that he was not alone. The trip also gave him the material to compose two novels and the determination to compete for a seat in the House of Commons.

In the autumn of 1829 he had begun a novel on a twelfth-century Jewish hero, David Alroy, a man who had for a brief time liberated the Jews of the eastern Mediterranean from their Arab rulers. Disraeli had not completed it. He needed to go to the East to be able to create the necessary geographic setting for the novel. His conversion to the Church of England had not short-circuited his desire to know what was beneath the surface of what he perceived as his racial difference from flaxen-haired Englishmen.

Byron had also travelled through Spain, Albania, Greece and Turkey, all places Disraeli intended to visit too. Byron claimed to have been interested in the East, by which he meant what we would call the Middle East or the eastern Mediterranean, since the age of ten and had read all he could find on the subject. One dimension of this interest was a belief on the part of most Englishmen of that generation that eastern sexual customs were less conventional and less restrictive than those current in Christian England. One work Byron read when he was young openly discussed Ottoman homosexuality.[2] One of the Victorian editors of the *Arabian Nights*, Sir Richard Burton, believed that homosexuality was common in a 'Sotadic zone' around the shores of the Mediterranean and that there it was held to be at worst a 'mere peccadillo'.[3] The visibility of eastern homosexuality was one of the tokens by which western Europeans judged eastern culture as morally inferior to their own, but which fascinated men like Byron and William Beckford.

Beckford was another important early influence on Disraeli. He had written an oriental novel, *Vathek*, published in 1786, where he veiled only thinly the hero's attraction to beautiful boys. Beckford got into trouble for an affair with a boy and, like Byron, had endured a long period of continental exile in order to escape rumours of illicit romance in England. This was well known. Samuel Johnson's friend, Hester Thrale, had dubbed Beckford a 'professor of pederasty' and Byron called him 'the great Apostle of pederasty'. By this, they meant his desire as an older male for adolescent boys, a relationship celebrated in Greek and Roman classical literature. On his continental wanderings, Byron even made a pilgrimage to the palace in Portugal where Beckford had spent part of his exile. He wrote about this spot in the first canto of *Childe Harold*:

> Here didst thou dwell, here schemes of pleasure plan,
> Beneath yon mountain's ever beauteous brow:
> But now, as if a thing unblest by Man,
> Thy fairy dwelling is as lone as thou![4]

Byron dwelled wistfully on Beckford's 'schemes of pleasure'. He was a rich man who in his lifetime built wonderful houses with tall towers, decorated rooms with exquisite taste and, like a precursor of Oscar Wilde, cultivated a sense of the beautiful. He had also been caught: the tutor of Kitty Courtenay, the future Earl of Devon, alleged that he had seen Beckford through a keyhole in flagrante with his charge. Beckford had to endure a lifetime thereafter of condemnation, hence his former house in Portugal was 'unblest'.

Byron had a way of seeing every place where the climate was warm as a place of forbidden sex, whether homosexual as in the case of Beckford, or heterosexual in the case of Don Juan:

> What men call gallantry, and gods adultery,
> Is much more common where the climate's sultry.[5]

Don Juan begins in 'sultry' Spain with the hero's adultery, Byron using the word 'pleasure' in an ironical tone. 'Pleasure' suggested some sort of sexual sin, which he at once wanted to liberate from religious control, yet which he wanted to reform in himself.

> Oh Pleasure! you're indeed a pleasant thing,
> Although one must be damned for you, no doubt;

> I make a resolution every Spring
> Of reformation, ere the year run out,
> But, somehow, this my vestal vow takes wing,
> Yet still, I trust, it may be kept throughout:
> I'm very sorry, very much ashamed,
> And mean, next Winter, to be quite reclaimed.[6]

Disraeli appreciated this association of sex with warm climate, and pleasure with something to be enjoyed yet of which to be somewhat ashamed. But he intended to be ashamed of nothing. It was not chance on Disraeli's part that his grand tour began where the young Don Juan started his sexual education and in the same geography where Byron had so enjoyed himself. If Beckford had 'schemes of pleasure plan[ned]' then Disraeli intended to do the same, not only by travelling, but also by writing his own new version of *Vathek*.

Sarah Disraeli's fiancé, William Meredith, was Disraeli's companion on the eastern adventure, a scholarly, serious-minded foil to Disraeli's outrageousness. They knew each other well, having also travelled together with Isaac through Flanders some years before. There is no hint Meredith and Disraeli were ever romantic friends. Meredith noted in his diary before they left London that Disraeli had come to discuss their travel plans. He was wearing such a striking costume that the crowds on Regent Street had parted before him, just like the Red Sea before Moses.[7] Meredith was amused by his friend's dandyism and cult of aristocratic extravagance. He was unjudgemental about Disraeli's chutzpah, his determination to live as if he were a young duke, but without his income. Probably Meredith also liked the serious, learned side of Disraeli underneath all the dressing up and showing off.

They sailed south from Falmouth. Disraeli was a good sailor and did not mind the rough Bay of Biscay. After several days, they debarked at Gibraltar. The young Disraeli was not a nobody. He and Meredith had letters of introduction to the highest British officials in most of the ports where they called. They met Sir

George Don, the Governor of Gibraltar, and his wife. Disraeli loved them both, the one for his *grand seigneur* style, the other because he assumed she was the sort of brilliant woman who had once corresponded with Horace Walpole. He always liked old ladies. He told his father of Lady Don:

> She is, tho' very old, without exception one of the most agreable personages that I ever met, excessively acute and piquante, with an aptitude of detecting character and a tact in assuming it, very remarkable. To listen to her, you would think you were charming away the hours with a blooming beauty in May Fair, and tho' excessively infirm, her eye is so brilliant and so full of moquerie, that you quite forget the wrinkles.[8]

He could flirt with such women without any fear of having to follow through. He could learn by example the social customs of a bygone era he had only read about in books. The old ladies liked him too: unlike many young men his age he made an effort to please, rather than cowering in horror at their age, and he was genuinely interested in what they had to say.

Of Sir George Don, he also wrote admiringly to Isaac, that he was 'courtly almost regal in his manner, paternal, almost officious in his temper . . . English in his general style, but highly polished and experienced in European Society'.[9] Here was a style that he wanted to emulate. Like all things he wanted to acquire, he paid it his highest honour by sending it up. After dinner one day, Sir George took Disraeli and Meredith on a small expedition to visit a local cave. Disraeli loved how the governor went in full state to the cave: two grooms, a carriage with four horses, the governor sitting at the window, a walking footman and an outrider. Disraeli's verb 'to lionize' denotes the governor charming his guests and the locals.

> In spite of his infirmities, he [Don] will get out to lionize, but before he disembarks, he changes his foraging cap for a full

Generals cock [hat] with a plume as big as the Otranto one, and this because the hero will never be seen in public in undress, altho' we were in a solitary cave looking over the Ocean, and inhabited only by monkeys.

Horace Walpole's novel, *The Castle of Otranto*, featured a magic helmet with sable plumes, just like the governor's. Walpole was the sort of man Disraeli wanted to be – artist, connoisseur, courtier, an effeminate man of whom it was rumoured he had male lovers, who as son of a famous prime minister also moved in the highest society.[10] Disraeli loved Sir George Don's magnificent hat, but he could not help laughing at him going in state to a cave. 'The cave is shewn, and we all get into the carriage, because he is sure we are tired, the foraging cap is again assumed and we travel back to the cottage, Meredith, myself, the Governor, and the cocked hat, each in a seat.'[11]

The dandyism of his first three novels was still an interest that he was exploring while he was abroad. He found to his delight that young British Army officers were also interested in dressing up and his outrageous costume could be a basis for laying an acquaintance. 'Tell my mother,' he wrote to Isaac,

that as it is the fashion among the dandies of this place, that is the officers, for there are no others, not to wear waistcoats in the morning, her new studs come into fine play, and maintain my reputation of being a great judge of costume to the admiration and envy of many subalterns.

His mother was evidently willing to support his love of dress by giving him studs to rival those of Mivartinos and the young duke. But what would she have thought about his affectation with canes?

I have also the fame of being the first who ever passed the Straits with two canes, a morning and an evening cane. I

change my cane as the gun fires, and hope to carry them both
to Cairo. It is wonderful the effect these magical wands produce. I owe to them even more attentions than to being the
supposed author of [*Vivian Grey*].[12]

Like a character in one of his novels, he was virtually daring the
young soldiers either to approve of him or to beat him up.

He could derive some support for ostentatious dress from the
uniform of Spanish bullfighters, which he described as 'brilliant
beyond anything I have ever seen'.[13] He was aware, however, of a
potentially more critical audience at home. He rhapsodized in a
rare letter to his mother about the beauty of Spanish ladies and
their fans. He wrote with genuine admiration and also a hint that
rather than make love to these women, he wanted to emulate
them.

A Spanish lady with her fan might shame the tactics of a troop
of horse. Now she unfurls it with the slow pomp and conscious
elegance of a peacock, now she flutters it with all the languor
of a listless beauty, now with all the liveliness of a vivacious one.
Now in the midst of a very Tornado, she closes it with a whirr
which makes you start – Pop! . . . But remember, while you
read, that here, as in England, it is not confined alone to your
delightful sex. I also have my fans, which makes my cane
extremely jealous. If you think I have grown extraordinarily
effeminate, learn that in this scorching clime, the soldier will
not mount guard without one.[14]

He was once again noticeably defensive on the subject of effeminacy. He could deploy his canes and his fans with marvellous
abandon, but he still felt the need in his letters home to put up his
guard against his mother's imagined objections.

He and Meredith decided to take a trip into the countryside.
They roughed it, camping and staying at small inns. Although this
was not usually Disraeli's style, he was thrilled that their guide was

'tall and with a dress excessively brodé and covered with brilliant buttons'.[15] They were warned about bandits preying on travellers. Disraeli was more excited by this than frightened. They heard that the robbers typically first laid their victims flat on the ground, then emptied their pockets.[16] He was also interested to know from other English travellers that the bandits had especially prized their shirts from an exclusive London shop. The Spanish bandits had actually forced these men to strip.[17] Some rich Spaniards were so afraid of this highway robbery that they hired a guard to escort them in their travels. He told Benjamin Austen that this was useless as the armed escort 'always scampers off at the first shot'.[18]

In Spain he also came across the remains of Spain's medieval Muslim past, with which he expected to have greater contact later in the journey. He was aware that with his Mediterranean complexion he resembled Arab Muslims more than pale Anglo-Saxons and he was happy to be mistaken for one of them. He and Meredith visited the Alhambra in Granada. Disraeli was bowled over by the Moorish magnificence of the palace and, according to Meredith, convinced their guide that he himself was a Moor.

> The old lady who showed us over the Alhambra, talkative and intelligent, would have it that Benjamin D. was a Moor, many of whom come to visit this palace, which they say will yet be theirs again. His southern aspect, the style in which he paced the gorgeous apartments, and sat himself in the seat of the Abencerrages, quite deceived her; she repeated the question a dozen times, and would not be convinced of the contrary. His parting speech, 'Es mi casa', 'This is my palace', quite confirmed her suspicions.[19]

A Turkish pasha whom they met later told Disraeli he did not think he was an Englishman because he walked so slowly.[20] Stateliness and grandeur always appealed to him. Rather than see Muslim and Jew as necessarily opposed to one another, Disraeli saw them as racially the same. He was convinced that he had been born to sit on a Moorish throne rather than suffer the taunts of English critics. He had imagined the young duke building an Alhambra in Regent's Park. To be taken for a Moor inside the real Alhambra, however, was a pleasure more exquisite than he had imagined in any of his fiction.

They came across a fellow English traveller named Standish, whom Disraeli thought might be a model for his own future. His letter to his father was a way of trying out this man's personality to see whether it would suit him as well. The other Englishmen thought Standish 'excessively affected', but Disraeli defended him. 'He is something more. The man of pleasure who instead of degenerating into a roué, aspires to be a philosopher, is to my mind certainly a respectable, and I think an interesting character.'[21] Affectation was the desirable opposite of a life lived according to the principle of utility. He knew how much hostility this provoked in his fellow countrymen and the trip to the Mediterranean was a way he could indulge his affectation to a degree even he had not yet dared to do in England.

He even hinted to his mother that the Spanish night was pregnant with possibilities that did not exist at home. 'Midnight clears the public walk but few Spanish families retire before two. A solitary bachelor like myself still wanders, or still lounges on a bench in the warm moonlight.'[22] He did not mention what happened among the solitary bachelors on their benches once the families had retired.

Disraeli and Meredith next went to Malta where Disraeli went to call on the governor, Sir Frederick Ponsonby. Not only was Ponsonby attractive to Disraeli because he was from one of the best-known aristocratic families of that generation, but he also had a Byron connection. Byron had a dramatic affair with Ponsonby's sister, Lady Caroline Lamb. So Disraeli was intent upon colonizing the governor, staking a claim to his acquaintance. He deployed his most formidable weapon, his sense of the ridiculous. Soon he had Ponsonby helpless on his sofa laughing and in 'convulsions'.

Disraeli sprang up and said he must be off, feeling that he had gained his point and he should not overstay his welcome.[23]

In Malta, Meredith and Disraeli acquired another travelling companion. He was James Clay, the son of a rich City merchant. Clay was also the Winchester acquaintance of one of Disraeli's younger brothers. Unlike Disraeli, Clay was good at sports, and got along unselfconsciously with the British officers they ran across in Malta. Disraeli was always trying to impress them. If wit worked with a senior officer like Ponsonby, he tried affectation with the junior officers. He dined at the officers' mess of the regiment on duty in Malta wearing Andalusian dress. He and Clay attended a game of racquets in which the ball accidentally landed in Disraeli's lap. He handed it to a subaltern seated next to him saying he had no idea how to throw it back himself. This was a brilliant line for a non-sportsman caught in an embarrassing situation. He reported the incident as a success to his father, but Clay said he had shocked the military men there.[24] In Gibraltar and Malta, English garrison communities, Disraeli had scarcely left home and he felt the eye of public disapproval still upon him. Under such circumstances he always acted in his most provocative manner, because he would be damned if he would suffer mediocrities to judge him, a genius. This was a pity, Clay thought, because on his own Disraeli was capable of being charmingly natural. Still, to be provocative was one side of his personality. Daring the subalterns to disapprove of him was also his way of courting them.

Clay was rich enough to have hired a yacht. Disraeli and Meredith decided to sail with him as paying passengers, but Disraeli was also part of the on-board entertainment. He put on a pirate outfit for their departure from Malta and remarked in a letter to his brother how he looked 'Excessively wicked!'[25] They also had with them Giovanni Battista Falcieri, a former gondolier. Clay had hired Falcieri, nicknamed 'Tita', as his valet. The Mediterranean adventure was suffused with Byron associations for Tita had also served Byron before he died. Gondoliers were famous among some Englishmen for being willing to gratify, for a fee, their sexual inclinations.[26] Byron had joked to a fellow lover of men and boys, William Bankes, that 'Tita's heart yearns for you, and may hap for your broad silver pieces.'[27] Disraeli told his brother that Byron had died in Tita's arms, and though this may have been romantic exaggeration, it was enough for Disraeli to take Tita on from Clay and bring him back to Bradenham, the Buckinghamshire estate which Isaac rented and to which he had moved the D'Israeli family from London.[28] Tita was one of those long-lasting threads that connected Disraeli to the Mediterranean voyage, to Byron and to Venice long after he had returned to England.

Disraeli was not Byronic in his politics, however. Byron had been drawn to Greece because of its association with classical civilization. He wanted to liberate Greece from its dominion by the Turks. Disraeli, on the other hand, admired the Turks. He sympathized with the Turks' recently successful military operations to put down uprisings in Albania. He preferred Turkish military order to the unruliness of Greek rebels. Lord Blake went so far as to say that Disraeli was deeply attracted to the autocracy of the Turkish sultans. 'He was not at heart a believer in liberty, or representative government ("fatal drollery", he described it) . . . [T]o him it was a game in a sense in which it was not to his rivals.'[29] Disraeli came of age during an era of enthusiasm for the reform and expansion of representative institutions in Britain, but his own conservatism and distrust of popular reform was instinctive a long time before he entered British party politics.

He thought Turkish 'dissimulation . . . the principal portion of their moral culture'. Rather than condemn them for it, he appeared to be recognizing something that came naturally to him as well. He always liked conspiracies, hiding things, not telling the entire truth. It was the key to survival in a culture where sodomy was a crime punishable by death well into his adult years. Dissimulation had also been a necessity for the first Iberian Jews in London, who had posed as Christian converts to escape persecution. On top of this, Disraeli liked the Turks because they were 'a costume loving people'.[30] He told Benjamin Austen the Turks were 'mad on the subject of dress'. He found 'the habits of this calm and luxurious people entirely agree with my preconceived opinions of propriety and enjoyment, and I detest the Greeks more than ever'.[31]

He was impressed by his first view of Athens, but it was at Constantinople and Cairo that he really enjoyed himself. He told Sarah that when he first saw Constantinople he felt 'an excitement which I thought was dead'.[32] He spent more than a month in Turkey in the winter of 1830–31. He saw there 'young Turks in uniforms which would not disgrace one of our crack cavalry regiments, and lounging with all the listlessness of royal illegitimates'.[33] It was a culture where dandy nonchalance seemed to be instinctive and he felt at home there. He told Bulwer he loved Turkish indolence, Turkish melancholy, and – a new discovery – Turkish baths. Taking a Turkish bath was a lengthy ritual that involved six attendants; these baths so impressed Disraeli that they reappeared in both novels he wrote about travel in the East. He did not say exactly what took place there, but Byron, who had been there before him, described the baths as 'marble palace[s] of sherbet and sodomy'. Byron had also told his former Harrow schoolmaster that in England the fashionable vices were 'whoring and drinking' while in Turkey they were 'sodomy and smoking'.[34] There is no explicit evidence that Disraeli socialized with sodomites in Turkey, but he certainly came back an inveterate smoker.

The French historical painter Jean-Léon Gérôme (1824–1904), roughly a contemporary of Disraeli's, captured some of the eroticized stereotypes nineteenth-century Europeans had of the 'orient'.[35] Gérôme was as fascinated as Disraeli by Turkish baths. He painted 'The Grand Bath at Bursa' (1885) [*See plate 4.*] and 'The Terrace of the Seraglio' (1886) based on his visits to baths and palaces in Turkey. Most of the figures in these two canvases are female nudes, suggesting that heterosexual men were as alive to the same-sex attractions of the baths as Disraeli was. Gérôme was suggesting lesbian sexuality for male viewers, rather than the all-male baths that Byron and Disraeli knew, but the aura of forbidden sexuality is the same. A clothed male figure reclines at the back of the 'Seraglio' and enjoys the splashing women. In the 'Bath at Bursa' a white female figure in the foreground leans on and is semi-embraced by a black servant. For nineteenth-century Europeans the orient meant not only same-sex desire, but the promise of exciting sexual contact with people of different races and classes. A third canvas, 'The Snake Charmer' (1880), captures another European view of the East. [*See plate 5.*] They believed that it was commonplace for adolescent boys to serve as the lovers of older men. Here a naked boy is embraced by a snake while watched by fully clothed men in a setting with gorgeous Arabic writing and beautiful tiles. Nothing could speak more frankly of the equation Europeans made between the East and homosexuality. Gérôme taught at the Ecole des Beaux Arts, exhibited at the Salons in Paris and received official commissions for his work. His open treatment of sexual themes appeared to attract rather than deflect popular and official approval. Gérôme's erotic themes undermine our stereotypes of repressed Victorians and hint at the Arab Middle East as a destination for sexual tourism.[36]

After a while, Meredith broke off from Clay and Disraeli to visit some ancient ruins at some distance. The explanation was that these were archaeological remains he did not want to miss. There is just a hint, though, that Meredith was Englishman enough to be a little disgusted by all the indolence and indulgence Disraeli and Clay were enjoying in Turkey. If the country entirely suited Disraeli's temperament, Meredith's breaking away to travel on his own was mildly troubling evidence that what he was doing might not entirely appeal to his family and friends at home.

From Turkey, Clay and Disraeli moved towards Jerusalem. Their journey was partly by sea and partly by land. The land portion involved travel by caravan over the Syrian desert. Disraeli's instinct when he tried to recreate this trip in print was to dwell on the food. Small, immediate pleasures of the table were always his forte. In *Contarini Fleming*, he had Contarini, on a similar journey, describe how 'We lit our fire, pounded our coffee, and smoked our pipes, while others prepared our simple meal, bread made at the instant, and on the cinders, a slice of dried meat, and a few dates.'[37] He loved luxury, but he was not unhappy living simply in the desert with Bedouin tribesmen. He believed they had discovered a successful variety of socialism. There was a mixture of all-male companionship, 'community of property' and 'equality of condition' that very much appealed to him. In his novels, Disraeli is only the most famous of English travellers who loved this combination of desert community and Arab male bonding: T. E. Lawrence 'of Arabia', Robert Byron (the travel writer, not the poet)[38] and Wilfred Thesiger were three of his twentieth-century successors who followed similar emotional if not geographical routes through the desert.

One purpose of the trip was to collect material for his novel on the Jewish hero, David Alroy. Surprisingly, then, he spent only a relatively short time in Jerusalem, the spiritual centre of the Jewish world. He stayed there a week, but was four months in Egypt.[39] In *The Wondrous Tale of Alroy*, the hero briefly visits Jerusalem and meets there the chief rabbi. He is a charming and eccentric scholar who describes the condition of the Jews living under Arab rule like this: 'Jerusalem is not Bagdad. But this has its conveniences. 'Tis safe, and we are not very rich, nor wish to seem so.'[40] The rabbi sounds like a version of Disraeli's father, Isaac. At this point in his life, he was more interested in Arab and Muslim culture than that of his Jewish ancestors. The rabbi's espousal of humble, slightly devious assimilation to Arab rule appealed to him, but it was to Cairo that he was inexorably drawn.

What did he do when he got there? While Clay and Tita rode and swam, Disraeli adopted what he took to be an Egyptian mode of life. He slept, he smoked, he reposed. In addition, he discovered that he was no longer depressed and he began to write again.

He told Sarah that 'Cairo in spite of its dinginess is a luxurious and pleasant place. The more I see of Oriental life, the more I like. There is much more enjoyment than at Constantinople.'[41] Contarini also goes to Egypt and notes that Europeans can indulge and take liberties there that they cannot at home.[42] He is silent about what precisely those indulgences are, but whenever he speaks of enjoyment, luxury and indulgence, there seem to be erotic possibilities in the background.

The Egyptian ancient ruins that he saw outside of Cairo, and to the south in Thebes, impressed him hugely.

> Italy and Greece mere toys to them . . . Conceive a feverish and tumultuous dream full of triumphal gates, processions of paint- ings, interminable walls of heroic sculpture, granite colossi of Gods and Kings, prodigious obelisks, avenues of Sphynxes and halls of a thousand columns, thirty feet in girth and of a pro- portionate height. My eyes and mind yet ache with a grandeur so little in unison with our own littleness.[43]

The whole oriental part of the trip had made him less impressed with his classical education that stressed the grandeur of ancient Greek and Roman civilizations. William Monypenny too noticed that even in Greece itself, he was turning away from ancient Greek emphasis on rationality and towards what he conceived to be an oriental love of mystery. He even thought that perhaps the whole system of English education was wrong. Arab or Persian literature might be a better source of inspiration for English schoolboys.[44] In the 1980s Martin Bernal shocked the academic establishment by arguing that ancient Greek culture was merely a weak derivative of its grand African origins.[45] Bernal's book, *Black Athena*, made an argument that would have much appealed to Disraeli a century and a half earlier. He was quite willing to believe that the Arab eastern Mediterranean and north African cultures were superior – both in the present day and in their ancient remains – to the Graeco-Roman heritage he had been brought up to revere. Most young men his age, if they went on a grand tour, visited the Christian and Graeco-Roman architectural treasures of western Europe in France, Germany and Italy. Disraeli had visited the Jewish, Arab and pre-Christian remains of the eastern Mediterranean. This travel both nurtured and strengthened his sense that he was different – better – than most of his contemporaries. It helped him adjust, to be less defensive. He was certainly no longer depressed.

8

Solitary Rides in the Desert

In Cairo Disraeli wrote substantial parts of two novels, *Contarini Fleming*, published a year later in 1832, and *The Wondrous Tale of Alroy*, published in 1833. He frankly admitted in a private diary entry that these two, along with *Vivian Grey*, made up an auto-biographical trilogy. Now the trilogy was complete, 'I shall write no more about myself.'[1] Of the three, and indeed of all his novels, *Contarini* remained his favourite. *Vivian Grey* was an 'indiscretion' and *Alroy* an idealized fantasy of what he might do with his life if he more completely embraced his Judaism. While no work of fiction need have any relationship with the life of its author, *Contarini's* life coincides more directly with Disraeli's than that of any of his other heroes. He inserted verbatim into the novel some of the travel letters he had written to his family from the Mediterranean. There are also real characters from his life who appear in the novel playing themselves, like Tita, the Venetian gondolier.

He was proud enough of this production to send it to John Murray, with whom he had not been able to restore good relations for years. Murray sent it to an expert on religion in the eastern Mediterranean, who was also poet, playwright and later Dean of St Paul's, Henry Milman. Milman encouraged Murray to publish it. On Milman's suggestion, Murray persuaded a reluctant Disraeli to change the book's subtitle from 'A Psychological Romance' to 'A Psychological Autobiography'. The romance that Disraeli had in mind was Contarini's romance with Musaeus, his romance with his eventual wife, Alceste, and the romance he has with an elder mentor named Winter. Milman and Murray rightly saw that the object of Contarini's most powerful romantic feelings was Contarini himself.

The public knew William Beckford was a rich eccentric who had written a novel of oriental fantasies, who had lived abroad for a period after the Courtenay affair, but who had returned to be a builder of great towers. One at his country house in Wiltshire, Fonthill Abbey, collapsed. Another at his house in Bath is still standing. All these elements of Beckford's known biography Disraeli worked into the character of Contarini's elder friend and mentor, Winter. He also went out of his way to meet Beckford by sending him unsolicited a copy of the book when it was published. Beckford recognized himself and was delighted.[2] These attempts to establish literary and actual ties to one of the most disgraced men of his era are some of the strongest evidence that Disraeli himself had allied inclinations.

Winter comforts Contarini in his distress at the break-up with Musaeus. They establish their mutual interest in Gothic ruins and drawings of Venice. Indeed, 'Venetian' is virtually a code for what we might call 'gay'. Winter tells Contarini, 'Like myself, you are such a strong Venetian.'[3] The advice that Winter, an older, travelling artist, gives to Contarini, the adolescent boy, sounds like what an older homosexual male might give to a younger one, where the older one has been exposed to the full force of public disapproval. 'Be patient. Cherish hope. Read more. Ponder less. Nature is more powerful than Education. Time will develop every thing. Trust not overmuch in the blessed Magdalen: learn to protect yourself.'[4] Before he met Winter, Contarini had just undergone an emotional conversion to Catholicism. Winter tells him that religion will protect him less than his own patience. He needs to trust that over time his natural talents will satisfy both his longing for love and his ambition for worldly success. In the meantime he has to be careful.

In an incident prophetic of Wilde, years before the publication of his novel, *The Picture of Dorian Gray*, Contarini goes to university and writes a prize essay upon 'the Dorian people'. He makes his first trip to Venice and there he thinks for the first time in hundreds of pages of Musaeus. He connects Venice to his schoolboy love and links them both to a love of hiding, disguising and conspiracy.

> I remembered that when a boy, sauntering with Musaeus, I believed that I had a predisposition for conspiracies, and I could not forget that, of all places in the world, Venice was the one in which I should most desire to find myself a conspirator.[5]

Loving men required hiding. Venice was the spot where he imagined that such a dual life – respectable on the surface, romantically and sexually fulfilled at night – would be most fun.

Loving men does not prevent Contarini, and did not prevent Disraeli, from loving women. Women were essential parts of Disraeli's life, though one senses that he loved women better as friends than as sexual partners. As now heterosexual men are thought to bond with other men and regard them as the fundamental though non-sexual basis of their affectionate lives, so too did Disraeli long for the company of women. Just as heterosexual men often feel awkward in social situations when surrounded by women, Disraeli was never entirely happy in all-male company.

The woman that Contarini marries in Venice, Alceste, is problematical, however. Like her mythological namesake, Alcestis, she has the aura of doom about her even before the romance with Contarini starts. The mythological Alcestis planned to sacrifice herself and die in her husband's place, until Hercules stepped in and rescued her. Disraeli's Alceste is a close cousin of Contarini, so her name also suggests 'incest'. As often, there is a Byronic angle here. Byron's affair with his half-sister Augusta Leigh had become known. Contarini is attracted to Alceste not because she is a living, breathing, fleshy woman, but because of her wealth and high birth. She and Contarini are wed and leave Venice. On this day that should be the happiest of his life, Contarini feels only sadness at leaving the one place in his existence he has felt truly at home.[6]

He and Alceste go to Crete where Alceste dies almost immediately in childbirth. Contarini is once again plunged into the deepest depression. He leaves Crete resolved to travel, taking as his companion and 'page' a Greek boy named Spiro. Contarini now meets Winter again, who tells him that his depression is as a result not of mourning his wife, but of 'quarrelling with his nature'. Contarini begs Winter not to leave him. Contarini does not love Winter in a 'flaming June' sort of way, but coolly as one might an elder and teacher. Contarini promises Winter he will stay out of his way if overcome by one of his depressive passions. Winter replies flirtatiously, 'Oh! I should like to see you in one of your fits.' He also gives Contarini more sober advice. 'Put yourself in a new world. Go to Egypt. It will suit you. I look upon you as Oriental.'[7]

In Egypt Contarini recovers, just as Disraeli did. He ceases to be depressed and finds that 'during solitary rides in the Desart [*sic*] of Cairo' he wants to write again. In Egypt Contarini also experiences the last major romance of the novel, with his father. Disraeli acknowledged unashamedly a tremendous intellectual debt to his father. In many ways Isaac had been his most important teacher. The evidence of *Contarini Fleming* is that he also suspected Isaac to have experienced identical failure to find a suitable romantic friend and sexual frustration that led to depression. Like Disraeli, Contarini learns much about what he wants to do in his career from his father. Contarini also receives a letter when his father is dying including a history of his emotional life that runs directly parallel to his son's. On the verge of the grave, Contarini's father 'comes out' to his son.

Throughout the book Contarini's most significant reflections about his future arise in interviews with his father. When asked by his father why he has run away from school, Contarini complains that all he learned there were useless words. His father replies simply, 'But with words we govern men.'[8] This was an important moment in Disraeli's sense of who he was and what he might become. Sitting in Egypt, aged twenty-six, Disraeli saw that his talent lay in his command over language. Whether in the writing of fiction or in the mastery of oratory, with words his own future career must lie. Contarini's interview with his father comes to a climax when his father asks him why he is so unhappy. With tears of rage streaming down his cheeks, Contarini says, 'Because I have no one I love, because there is no one who loves me, because I hate this country, because I hate everything and everybody, because I hate myself.'[9] This expression of self-loathing comes directly after the failure of his friendship with Musaeus. He seeks in his father some crevice in a cold exterior, some comfort for not having found in Musaeus the love he wanted. 'Only tell me that you love me,' Contarini says to his father, 'and I will always do everything.'[10]

After following his father's suggestions for reading, and writing a novel called *Manstein*, that is identical to *Vivian Grey*, Contarini returns and tells his father in another significant interview that he wants influence over men. This begins a phase of political apprenticeship to his father, who is an influential minister in a northern European court. Contarini's and Disraeli's growing ambition to dominate either the world of politics or the world of literature – or both – thus derived in part from an unfulfilled need to find an adolescent male friend. The failure to find a single romantic friend drove him forward to demand the adulation of many. His father appears to understand this because he has experienced similar feelings himself.

Contarini is impatient and impulsive. He cannot stick to one thing. Though he is successful acting as his father's private secretary, and his father wants him to go to Paris to train as a diplomat, Contarini rejects his advice. He disappears without warning and travels, ends up in Venice, and marries Alceste without telling his father. He is in Egypt when he receives a letter from his father. He decides to return home. 'I felt an irresistible desire to hasten to him without a moment's delay. I longed to receive his blessing and his embrace.'[11] Before he can reach home, however, his father writes another letter saying that he is dying. 'Yet I would not die,' writes Contarini's father,

> without expressing to you my love, without yielding to feelings which I have too long suppressed . . . You think me cold; you think me callous; you think me a hollow-hearted worldling. Oh! my Contarini, recall the doubt and misery of your early years, and all your wild thoughts, and dark misgivings, and vain efforts – recall all these, and behold the boyhood of your father! . . . The passions of my heart were not less violent than yours, and not less ardent was my impetuous love.
>
> Woe! woe! the father and the son have been alike stricken. I know all, my Contarini; I know all, my sweet, sweet child. I would have saved you from the bitter lot – I would have borne the deep despair.[12]

His father knows Contarini's sexual secrets because he shares them.

Contarini's father tells of his first wife, Contarini's mother, who died in childbirth. His father too was depressed at this until he found a friend in Vienna and there started his political career. 'Friend' in the year 1831 when this was composed could be a romantic friend or a political friend who helps one on the career ladder.[13] Neither of these was thought then to include a sexual dimension, but that was the one missing element in Disraeli's London life that he had hoped to find in the East. Some fulfilment of that need may well have occurred by the time he got to Egypt and he was composing *Contarini Fleming*. Disraeli has Contarini settling down with the Beckford character, Winter, in Naples at the end of the novel. He starts to construct a house on the model of the homosexual emperor Hadrian's villa and, like Beckford, to build a tall tower. Winter, he says, is his only friend and together they are devoted to cultivating 'the Beautiful', though, Contarini adds, he is willing to participate in Europe's political regeneration if the opportunity arises. This then was Disraeli in Egypt acknowledging via Contarini his love for his father. In coming to terms with the love of his male parent, he was also coming to terms with one enduringly problematic, but also enduringly fruitful and creative, part of himself. He also imagined a world where living in Hadrian's villa with a Beckford lookalike might well be the launching pad for a career in European politics. And although many of Disraeli's contemporaries would have found this fantasy laughably unlikely to come true, Disraeli's having imagined it so was the first stage in making it happen.

In addition to *Contarini*, while living in Egypt Disraeli had recommenced work on his Jewish novel, begun almost two years previously. He returned to England late in 1831 with much of it completed. The novel takes place in the twelfth century when Jews living in modern-day Israel had been conquered and were ruled from Baghdad, but were allowed their own local governors, called 'Princes of the Captivity'. Not only does the book complete Disraeli's autobiographical trilogy, and thus make compelling reading as he shares more of his secrets with the reader; but it is also his first treatment of Jewishness in print and remarkable because he seems to be more in love with Muslim Baghdad than Jewish Jerusalem.

The uncle of David Alroy is one of the Princes of the Captivity. As the novel opens, he describes the condition of twelfth-century Jews, which Disraeli clearly meant to evoke the condition of some nineteenth-century English Jews: 'the age of power has past; it is by prudence now that we must flourish. The gibe and jest, the curse, perchance the blow, Israel now must bear, and with a calm, or even smiling visage.'[14] This resembles what the chief rabbi tells Alroy in Jerusalem. We are not rich nor do we wish to seem so. This is one strategy for Jewish survival: patience, endurance of insults, lying low.

The novel tells the story of a young man who rejects this survival strategy. Through abundant courage and clever military manoeuvre, David Alroy releases the Jews from subjection to their Arab rulers. He marries the Muslim daughter, Schirene, of the Caliph of Baghdad. He establishes a brief period of Jewish liberty and reconciliation with their Muslim oppressors. This collapses at the end of the novel and the hero dies. However, the boldness of Disraeli's vision for peace in the Middle East is braver, more romantic and more breathtaking than any settlement of the Arab-Jewish conflict proposed in the last hundred years. The novel reaffirms his belief that Jews and Arabs were in race and ethnicity more similar than they were different. He was later to call Arabs merely 'Jews on horseback'. The hero's marriage to a Muslim also shows his characteristic attraction to mixtures, whether architectural, marital or personal, of the great religions. He loved St Mark's Basilica in Venice because it looked like a 'Christian Mosque'. He himself was such a mixture, a converted Christian with Jewish parents and a surname that spoke of Mediterranean origins.

Alroy and *Contarini Fleming* are much more serious novels than *Vivian Grey*, *Popanilla*, or *The Young Duke*. There is very little of the bubbly silliness of the early novels in these two works. In Egypt he had begun to take himself a great deal more seriously as a writer as if to counteract the tone of what he believed were adolescent errors. He sometimes goes too far the other way and overdoes the gravity of these two later novels. However, there are still amusing reminders of his abiding interests and passions. David Alroy, for example, is an attractive boy who looks like a girl. He has a 'girlish face' that conceals 'dark passions' and 'dangerous fancies'.[15] He has a sister, Miriam, who is the hero's true love in the novel. She is a constant, familial source of affection. When she dresses up as her brother, no one can tell the difference between them.

The novel has interesting descriptions of attractive males. David Alroy says he is not attracted to Jewish women: 'The daughters of my tribe, they please me not, though they are passing fair. Were our sons as brave as they are beautiful, we still might dance on Sion.'[16] It is those 'beautiful' Jewish men that he wants to lead into a dance by stirring up their courage.

There is also an erotic dimension of David Alroy's relationship to his teacher, Jabaster. Jabaster, 'the Cabalist', is an expert on Hebrew religious mysteries as well as a master of cabals and secret rituals. He looks upon David when he is sleeping and reflects, 'How solemn is his visage in the moonlight! And yet not Solomon, upon his youthful throne, could look more beautiful.' The female adjective, 'beautiful', rather than the masculine 'handsome', indicates how aware Jabaster is of his pupil's physical presence. David too adores his teacher. When they part from one another, it is like the separation of lovers. They embrace weeping and Jabaster tells David, 'Ah! that I could be thy mate! 'Twould be nothing then. At the worst, to die together. Such a fate seems sweeter now than parting.'[17] David entirely reciprocates his teacher's love and even awakens from a dream of his future greatness in his tutor's arms.[18] For Disraeli in his twenties, the questions of finding true love in a male friend and satisfying his ambition for worldly success were closely linked.

The book's one dandy moment comes when David Alroy disguises himself in order to gain access to the apartment of the caliph's daughter, Schirene. David plays upon his girlish appearance: ''Tis lucky I am beardless. I shall make a capital eunuch. So! a very handsome robe. One dagger for a pinch, slippers powdered with pearls, a caftan of cloth of gold, a Kashmere girdle, and a pelisse of sables. One glance in the mirror. Good! I begin to look like the conqueror of the world.'[19] Both Disraeli and Bulwer had argued before that dandyism was a way of achieving mastery over one's fellow men. Here Disraeli made his hero into a crossdressing woman wooer of the first order. It was his comic defence of effeminacy to sceptical critics.

The backdrop to Disraeli's composition of *Alroy* was the sudden occurrence of one of the great tragedies of his life. In old age, he often revisited the scene of it in conversation with Sir Philip Rose, his lawyer and trusted adviser.[20] Meredith rejoined Clay and Disraeli at Cairo, having not seen them since Constantinople. There he came down with smallpox. Before Disraeli realized the seriousness of the illness, Meredith died. Disraeli then had the task of writing to his father and sister with the dreadful news. The death took Disraeli's mind off his own problems and he wrote emotionally to his sister rededicating his life to her happiness. *Alroy* is dedicated to Sarah Disraeli and David Alroy's sister, Miriam, is as powerful a female character in the book as his wife, Schirene. In fact, Schirene proves disloyal to him and contributes to his downfall. At the end of the novel, his reign having collapsed, defeated, imprisoned, awaiting his death, David Alroy considers himself a failure, just as Disraeli was still ashamed of the years of depression and publishing books he did not like. Miriam comforts her brother. His sister is a truer love than his wife.

The final pages of the novel are filled with a renewed tribute to Beckford and fear-fantasies of impalement. David's Arab captors accuse him of having succeeded by conspiring with the black-magical force, Eblis. Eblis is nowhere treated at greater length than in Beckford's *Vathek*. It is a sort of Muslim variety of hell, dominated by a fallen angel, like Satan. No one believes David's denial of any knowledge of Eblis and he is condemned to be impaled, the most humiliating and painful death his captors can devise for him. The king of Karasmé, who is responsible for bringing Alroy to justice, offers him a way out. 'Is it not better to be my slipper bearer than to be impaled?'[21] He is offering David the chance to be his homosexual slave. The slipper is significant, because it is the same item of apparel that got Vivian Grey into trouble with the critics and which David used earlier to disguise himself as a eunuch. He is saved from being impaled by answering the king rudely. The king in a flash of anger cuts off David's head, thus giving him the painless, dignified death deserved by an equal. By alluding to the torture of impalement Disraeli tempts the reader to conclude that the masculinity of his handsome hero is up for grabs.[22] He toys with these handsome young men – Vivian Grey, the young duke, David Alroy – dressing them up, introducing them to unsuitable companions, dwelling upon their androgyny, threatening to hurt them, before restoring them to a fate a conventional English public might comfortably understand.

Disraeli returned home via slow stages in 1831. He had to spend a considerable time at the quarantine station in Malta, a practice of that era intended to stop the spread of infectious diseases. Therefore, although he set out almost immediately after Meredith's death in July 1831, he did not reach Bradenham until the very end of October that year. For some reason he had almost no baggage with him and claimed to his father that he had 'literally not a shirt to my back – and nothing but Turkish Slippers and a single coat'.[23] It was a great contrast to the dandy costume with which he had cut such a figure in Spain; the one significant dandy item he retained was his pair of oriental slippers. But what of his mental baggage? What had he acquired on his eastern trip to outfit his intellectual apparatus, to suit his psychology?

First of all he had regained his ability to write. He returned home with two novels substantially completed in his portfolio. With these two new works he would 'assail' the reading public, convinced that he had weightier and more compelling material in them than in either *Vivian Grey* or *The Young Duke*.[24] On the voyage home he had also met the son of one of the most powerful political dynasties in the country, the Stanley Earls of Derby. They had discussed the passing of the First Reform Bill and both concluded that it was going to throw the doors of Parliament open to men of talent. This had convinced him that he ought to try for a seat in Parliament himself. Like Contarini, he did not know whether his future greatness lay in politics or literature, but he came home determined to take a shot at both of them.

Secondly, he came home knowing himself better. The twin poles of his existence were ambition and repose. Repose had been imposed on him by his depression, but he had also found in the East cultures he believed celebrated repose in a way that was impossible in busy, frantic England. He said in his preface to _Alroy_ that the East made possible an 'existence of blended splendour and repose'.[25] This appealed to him tremendously and it is what kept him in Cairo for so long. Meredith's death brought that phase to an end. The pendulum now swung back away from repose to the ambitious side of his personality.

Finally what he brought back from the East was a greater sense of peace about his ambiguous sexuality. He told both Sarah and Isaac that now that he knew himself better, he did not intend to marry. He would try to increase the happiness of his existing family without starting one of his own.[26] We do not know for certain whether he consummated his desires for other men. On the other hand, we do not know for certain that he did not. We have only the evidence of his letters home and his novels. These dwell so lovingly on Greek pages, Spanish nights and solitary bachelors, Turkish baths, eunuchs and beautiful, girlish boys that homoeroticism begins to emerge as one of the most persistent themes of the written work. His ability and willingness to explore such a forbidden subject in letters home and in novels he hoped would sell must change our thinking about Disraeli and the age in which he lived. In early nineteenth-century Britain men were still hanged, or died after being pelted with stones in the stocks, or were forced into unwilling exile if they were suspected, let alone convicted, of having committed sodomy and other sexual acts with other men. Beckford, Byron and the celebrated collector of oriental antiquities, William Bankes, all went into exile under these sorts of circumstances. In this climate it took bravery verging on recklessness to deal so openly with homoeroticism.

On the other hand, it suggests a greater openness at least among the literate upper classes and the novel-reading public than we have come to expect from the nineteenth century. They were willing to entertain Disraeli's long disquisitions on romantic friendship in _Contarini Fleming_. They did not object to his repeated passes at Beckford and homage to _Vathek_. They consumed his paeans of praise to the sensual delights of Turkish baths without batting an eyelid. They had no difficulty putting his love of beardless pages together with his heroes' heterosexual romances. Perhaps so long as the outward forms of conventional marriage were respected, and so long as nothing definitive was actually observed through the keyhole, they were willing to recognize the homoerotic as a classical, an oriental and therefore an acknowledged source of human pleasure, not just for some sexually identified minority, but for everyone.

9

An Awful Ambition and Fiery Passions

Disraeli returned from Cairo resolved to conquer either the world of literature or of politics. He acted on his intentions with great energy and over the next several years engaged in a frenzy of literary composition. He either contested parliamentary seats or manoeuvred to be involved in contests three times at High Wycombe, as well as once each at Marylebone, Taunton and Maidstone. He also made the first of his tries to sit in Parliament for the county of Buckinghamshire. The burning issue in England on his return from the Mediterranean was the controversy aroused by debate over the First Reform Bill, passed in 1832. He believed, as did many others, that this bill would break the stranglehold of the *ancien régime* on Westminster, and that it would create opportunities for middle-class men like him to come into the House of Commons. He was composing *Contarini* about that time and the book shows that he wanted to be in Parliament for the influence over men and social position it would give him, rather than for his commitment to any particular issue.

Becoming an MP took a lot longer than he thought it would. For the next several years he shaped his political message to the demands of different political parties, whether Radical or Whig or Tory, as he stood for different interests in different constituencies.

What was essential for him was to be a Member of Parliament; how he got there and what issues he espoused mattered less. This ambition left him open to charges of being unprincipled, but he had an airy confidence in the power of his pen to explain away his political shifts and an overwhelming urge to be in Parliament whatever the cost.

He collaborated with his sister, Sarah, in writing a novel about his first election contest, at High Wycombe, which they published as *A Year at Hartlebury, or The Election*. He also published an epic poem about the Napoleonic era. In a single twelve-month period he wrote two full-scale, three-volume novels, *Henrietta Temple* and *Venetia*. He also wrote on contemporary political issues, including a pamphlet insisting on his political consistency entitled *What Is He?*, a defence of the House of Lords in *A Vindication of the English Constitution* and a series of letters to the editor of *The Times* attacking the Whig government, later published separately as *The Letters of Runnymede*. This was in addition to miscellaneous journalism and stories. He liked to picture himself as lazy, indolent and in perpetual need of repose, a dandy who could not bear to do anything but get dressed and lift his cane. This was one side of his personality, but the other side of him was devoured by ambition. He was determined to advance his career and achieve renown, or as he put it, 'to astonish mankind'.

His father worried that some of this energy was at cross-purposes. Isaac gave money to assist his eldest son's election expenses. This was a help, though it was merely a drop in the bucket of Disraeli's debt. With the money came advice. Isaac was worried that his son was still writing novels and not devoting himself to the more serious, sober and businesslike activity of winning a seat in Parliament. 'How . . . will the fictionist assort with the politician?' Isaac asked.[1] If nowadays it is uncommon for writers of fiction to be politicians, then it was rarer still. Throughout much of the eighteenth and early nineteenth centuries, the reading of novels was conceived as mainly a female pastime. Although this did not entirely feminize the writers of novels, authors knew they were writing for largely a female audience. This is what separated them from the parliamentary world of hard facts, lawyerly legislation, property rights and taxation. That was most definitely a man's world. A great writer of fiction, like Sir Walter Scott, might be assuredly masculine, but his identity as a writer, if it did not entirely disqualify him from politics, rendered him above and beyond the sordid world of Westminster and Whitehall. The case was worse for a writer of ephemeral society novels like Disraeli. This is what Isaac was objecting to when Disraeli, for the urgent purpose of clearing off some debt Isaac knew nothing about, devoted himself once again to novel writing.

Disraeli refused to be bound by conventional ideas about what was appropriate for a politician or for a writer. He considered himself a genius, a dandy, above and beyond worldly considerations such as his father's. However, he also had an unusual perception about the worlds of literature and politics that offers an insight into his personality, his success, and the era in which he was to become such a celebrated man. He thought of these two worlds that everyone else saw as separate, as uniquely bound together. This came from a critical view of his father's work that even his father had failed to grasp. He told a friend that Isaac's ongoing work on his history of English literature was 'full of new views of the history of our language, and indeed of our country, for the history of a State is necessarily mixed up with the history of its literature'.[2] He understood that language and literature on the one side were intimately mixed up with history and politics on the other side. How did he know that? How was he able, contrary to the expectations of Isaac and all his critics, to make this mixture of literature and politics work?

Disraeli had returned from Egypt telling Sarah and Isaac that he had no intention of marrying. The unexpected death of William Meredith made him dedicate himself to relieving his bereaved sister's sadness, to try to be to her what Meredith might have been. She was his main correspondent throughout these years. His letters to her are chatty, unaffected, newsy, sometimes peremptory as those from brothers sometimes are, but also more natural and affectionate than those to his other correspondents. On 7 April 1832 he wrote to her, 'My dearest, I write only to say I love you.'[3] In many ways his sister Sarah was the love of his life.

The nineteenth century was less on the qui vive than we are for signs of sexual idiosyncrasy. Nevertheless, there is still something peculiar about the way Disraeli and his sister persisted in talking of marriage to one another. The novel they wrote together in the autumn of 1833, *Hartlebury*, appeared in 1834 under the pseudonyms 'Cherry and Fair Star'. They wrote in the preface: 'Our honeymoon being over, we have amused ourselves during the autumn by writing a novel. All we hope is that the Public will deem our literary union as felicitous as we find our personal one.'[4] This is partly a good joke to conceal the identity of the authors, but it also suggests that brother and sister liked the idea of being married to one another. The plot of the novel reinforces this suggestion of a forbidden marriage, because incest and homosexuality are just beneath the surface of events, and bigamy is the novel's big revelation. That Disraeli was an aspiring MP and a writer of novels at the same time was odd, but to be a politician and a writer of fictions imbued with such sexual strangeness is more surprising still.

The principal characters in the novel are Aubrey Bohun, the Disraeli alter ego, who returns from travel in the East and contests the parliamentary seat at Hartlebury, for which read High Wycombe, and Helen Molesworth, Sarah Disraeli's other self, an unmarried young woman who looks after her scholarly father in a country house remarkably like Bradenham. The third principal character is George Gainsborough, a young man of the same age who has met Aubrey Bohun in the East and lives in a large house nearby. He is a more purely fictional character who does not correspond to anyone in the D'Israeli family's Buckinghamshire circle, although he sometimes seems to be another partly Disraelian, partly Byronic persona. He had 'travelled over Germany and Italy, had visited Constantinople', an itinerary identical to Disraeli's, 'and had finally taken an active part in favour of the Greeks' as Byron had.[5]

Disraeli and his sister were able to keep the secret of their authorship of *Hartlebury* for a long time. It was discovered only comparatively recently by the editors of the *Benjamin Disraeli Letters*. They have shown how Sarah wrote the majority of the first half of the novel, while her brother wrote most of the second half, on the election itself. Sarah's loving and sisterly descriptions of Aubrey Bohun add a dry and sometimes even satirical twist to what we already know of Disraeli. She says of Bohun that 'His delicately moulded features would have perhaps been effeminate, but for the intelligence and passion which beamed in his deep grey eye.'[6] Her brother's particular interest in effeminacy must have been the subject of explicit conversation between them and she went out of her way to say something openly that still bothered him.

Sarah took a more critical view of pleasure and enjoyment than her brother did. She says in her part of the novel: 'It is mortifying to observe how very intense are all physical pleasures. A glass of champagne has more effect upon the mind than the finest apothegm of the deepest sage.'[7] She also took a dimmer view of Disraeli's youthful drunkenness and his trip to the East when she observed that:

> it is rarely that the cup of pleasure is in vain presented to a youth. Handsome and headstrong, Aubrey Bohun seized it with avidity, and drained it to the lees, and just before he attained his majority, an aching head and a dissatisfied heart sent him to other countries, to seek that health and happiness he had wasted in his own.[8]

Like Disraeli, Bohun had travelled abroad because of a failure to find love, or a 'dissatisfied heart'. He too had returned from the East 'resolved against matrimony'.[9] In fact, as one of the modern editors of the novel has remarked, both Bohun and Gainsborough have returned from the East somehow 'tainted' by their experience.[10] Sarah also worried about her brother's drinking and was less pleased than he was by the changes the East had brought about in him.

Bohun and Gainsborough both fall in love with Helen Molesworth and wish to marry her. Bohun's decision to contest Hartlebury, aided by Helen Molesworth and George Gainsborough, intensifies the romantic conflict between the three. It emerges that Bohun and Gainsborough had once fallen in love with the same young woman before, that they duelled over her, that Gainsborough injured Bohun in the duel, but ultimately lost. Bohun married the young woman, then abandoned her. As a way of preventing Helen Molesworth marrying Aubrey Bohun, Gainsborough discloses to her that his friend has married before and that this wife may still be living. At the end of the novel Bohun is discovered dead in a ditch, his murderer a complete mystery.

The most passionate relationship here is between the two men. They are always falling in love with the same women, as if they needed a woman present to express their love for one another.[11] They know dark secrets about one another: Gainsborough about his friend's secret previous marriage, Bohun about Gainsborough's debts which he has generously discharged even though his friend lost the duel. Aubrey Bohun, who is supposed to be the hero of the novel and who wins the election with Helen Molesworth's help, is rather a darker figure in reality. His being killed off so brutally in the end might even suggest some latent hostility between Sarah Disraeli and her brother. Certainly the whole question of marriage is fraught with difficulties. Disraeli's determination not to marry and to dedicate himself to his sister is reproduced in *Hartlebury* as bigamy, murder, and young men who have been in some way spoiled by their travels in the eastern Mediterranean. The innocent-sounding decision not to marry appears in the novel as a rather guilty hiding of dark secrets. Novel writing for Disraeli was seldom purely imaginative work. It was a way of transforming recent experience, recasting it in fictional characters, working through what it all meant with pen on paper. The advantage of *Hartlebury* is seeing Disraeli's recent experience in the East through the eyes of a concerned and intimate observer. Sarah was clearly a little troubled not only by her own single state following the surprising death of her fiancé, but also by what the East had done to her brother.

Disraeli's attitude to marriage changed after he met and had an affair with Henrietta Sykes. She was the wife of Sir Francis Sykes, a frequently absent husband, who was older than her and with whom she had had several children. She, in turn, was older than Disraeli and certainly had lovers after him, possibly before him as well. A contemporary portrait, which Disraeli loved, is also key, as Jane Ridley has pointed out, to her personality. The painting shows her a 'bare-shouldered, rather heavy woman, ripe and expensive; her wide long-lashed eyes glance sideways, but modest she is not; an English Madame Bovary, she is tempestuous, moody, voluptuous'.[12] Disraeli had had affairs before, possibly with Sara Austen, and the wife of one of his doctors, Mrs Bolton, but they do not compare to his relationship with Henrietta, which lasted for several years and about which he wrote more warmly in both a diary entry and a new novel. In September 1833, he used an unusual superlative to describe the past eight months, which included the beginning of his affair with Henrietta:

> one incident has indeed made this year the happiest of my life. How long will these feelings last? They have stood a great test, and now absence, perhaps the most fatal of all [illegible]
>
> My life has not been a happy one. Nature has given me an awful ambition and fiery passions. My life has been a struggle, with moments of rapture – a storm with dashes of moon-light.[13]

He rarely described his love life in this diary, this entry proof that something new and good had happened to him. He remained in the pose of a Romantic hero, however, and was convinced that suffering was more characteristic of his life than emotional fulfilment.

If he rarely described his love life in the diaries, the novels describe nothing else. In his novel, *Henrietta Temple*, he did not even bother to disguise the heroine's Christian name. As usual, though, the most compelling character in the book is the one modelled on himself, in this case, Ferdinand Armine. Ferdinand is from an old Catholic family. He will inherit a great Gothic house and an estate encumbered by debts. He has added to these burdens by living a life of dissipation. His debts compel him to marry his rich cousin, but he declares his love for her in a way that suggests he does not love any woman much: 'I love her – at least I suppose I love her. I love her at any rate as much as I love, or ever did love, woman.'[14] This is hardly a ringing endorsement of marriage.

However, before he can marry his cousin he falls head over heels in love with Henrietta Temple, a young woman recently moved into the neighbourhood. He sees her and immediately remarks upon the 'startling symmetry of her superb figure', one of the few ways available in the nineteenth century to describe remarkable breasts. He also gives a defence of 'love at first sight. This is the transcendent and surpassing offspring of sheer and unpolluted sympathy.' It seems a little odd for him to be putting in a suggestion of pollution so near to a transcendent emotion. Still, he continues: 'All other [love] is the illegitimate result of observation, of reflection, of compromise, of comparison, of expediency. The passions that endure flash like the lightning: they scorch the soul, but it is warmed for ever.' His use of the same storm metaphor earlier in his 1833 diary entry indicates that his love for Henrietta Sykes was unlike any he had experienced before. He must have been immediately struck by her, forced almost in spite of himself to drop his affected indifference to the sexual and physical charms of women, or at least of this particular woman.

Henrietta Temple has one or two racy references that suggest Disraeli's relationship with Henrietta Sykes was sexually enjoyable. In the first flush of his love for her, we find the hero of the story naked. In his room at night, Ferdinand Armine takes off all his clothes, removes a flower Henrietta has given him from its vase and 'deposited it in his bosom. "Beautiful, beloved flower," exclaimed he; "thus, thus will I win and wear your mistress!"'[15]

We do not see Henrietta naked. Indeed, traces of Disraeli's recent adventures in the Mediterranean survive in this description of her appearance. She dresses up to go outdoors on a moonlit night, putting a scarf over her head: '"There," she said, "I look like the portrait of the Turkish page in Armine Gallery; don't I?"'[16] Those Turkish pages and eunuchs were among Disraeli's favourite androgynous figures, so to imagine his first real girlfriend dressed as an eastern boy was also to say that he found her appearance arousing. Those who were in the know about the sorts of pleasures Byron and Disraeli had enjoyed in the East would have smiled at the double entendre.

Still, his relationship to Henrietta was serious and tapped into deep feelings he had about his relations to other women, notably his mother. Many of Disraeli's biographers have commented on his apparent longing for his mother's love.[17] It is significant then that Henrietta's term of endearment for Ferdinand is 'My child'.[18] The depth of Disraeli's feeling for Henrietta also emerges from the extent of his bitterness when the relationship ended. He wrote the novel in the autumn of 1836 as the relationship was well past its peak. They had finally broken up by January 1837. Therefore, although the novel has a happy ending to please his readers, there is much heartfelt description of people falling out of love with one another. In the following passage, he compares the close of a love affair to the destruction of an ancient civilization.

It is not so much ruined cities, that were once the capital glories of the world, or mouldering temples breathing with oracles no more believed, or arches of triumph that have forgotten the heroic name they were piled up to celebrate, that fill my mind with half so mournful an impression of the instability of human fortunes, as these sad spectacles of exhausted affections, and, as it were, traditionary fragments of expired passion.[19]

He was impressed with the impermanence and changeability of even the grandest passion. Disraeli was good at dramatizing his own sorrows and it made him feel better to think of his expired love for Henrietta as a spectacle on the scale of the ruined Roman Forum or the fragments of the Acropolis.

The affair with Henrietta changed his attitude towards marriage in the years after he returned from the East. When in June 1833 Sarah urged him to consider Ellen Meredith, the sister of William Meredith, as someone he might marry for love, he replied:

As for 'Love', all my friends who married for Love and beauty either beat their wives or live apart from them. This is literally the case. I may commit many follies in life, but I never intend to marry for 'love', which I am sure is a guarantee of infelicity.

As for 'companionship', the phrase is so vague I do not know what it means. I shall always be with my wife at proper times and in proper places.[20]

His tone is of cynical impatience with his sister's suggestion, but it does seem that he has already moved on from the notion that he would not marry at all. He appears to be saying that he will keep up proper appearances with whomever he marries, but that he intends to go on suiting himself. *Henrietta Temple* is evidence of a dawning recognition that his debts were now becoming so pressing that marriage to a rich young woman was one of the few ways out of his trouble. Luckily for Ferdinand Armine, both of the women whom he might marry are rich enough to extract him from pressing debts. Disraeli occasionally wrote about meeting rich heiresses to his sister, gaily reporting how much they were worth; but, while Henrietta was on the scene, he had no interest in courting actively some suitable young woman of his own age. Rather, he spent his time compiling a wish list. He has a rich cousin, who knows Ferdinand well, say in _Henrietta Temple_: he 'must marry some one whom he looks up to, somebody brilliant like himself, some one who can sympathize with all his fancies'.[21] Disraeli wanted someone who was not only rich, but also a match for his intellect, someone who could cope with his unconventional likes and dislikes. He thought this marriage, when it came, was likely to be a maturely considered partnership, rather than a grand passion. What was coming with his increased experience of the world was recognition that such a partnership might advance his career rather than simply add to his domestic afflictions. Part of his learning how to achieve a career that combined the novelist's imagination with the politician's tactical skill was his beginning to admit that he might be better off married than not.

While the relationship with Henrietta was a crucial event in his life, his more long-term emotional energies were invested in his friendships with other men. The chief of these were friendships with Edward Lytton Bulwer and with Alfred, Count d'Orsay. Although there are occasional erotic flashes, Disraeli's friendships with Bulwer and d'Orsay do not seem to have involved a strong sexual element. Recent biographies have shown that an aura of sexual ambiguity did surround both Bulwer and d'Orsay. Disraeli's friendship with them might have been based on a common sense of sexual difference, but the attraction to one another was not primarily a physical one.

Disraeli had got to know Bulwer well enough before he left England to share his manuscript of _The Young Duke_ with him, not something a writer does lightly. On his return, Bulwer introduced Disraeli to fashionable London, to which Bulwer as a landowner, the author of _Pelham_ and Member of Parliament had greater access, at first, than Disraeli did. His friendship with Bulwer was not all social glitter, however. Disraeli recorded in his diary for 1833 that Bulwer, along with a man he had met in the

East, Emile Botta, and John Gibson Lockhart, had been the three great intellectual influences on his life so far.[22] They were all men whose minds he respected and with whom he had had conversation that helped him clarify his own ideas.

In the early 1830s Disraeli and Bulwer went to Bath together, where they both spent their days writing. Disraeli produced a short story, *The Rise of Iskander*, to accompany *Alroy* and in it he provided interesting autobiographical commentary on his relationship with Bulwer. He and Bulwer had both written dandy novels with dandy heroes and both had been accused of effeminacy. They both wore their hair in elaborate curls and ringlets. [*See plate 6.*] Both were said to be great egotists. It was said of Bulwer that he had such a narcissistic love of his own image that he sat and composed in front of an enormous mirror. *Fraser's Magazine* underlined Bulwer's vanity by placing him in front of a mirror. [*See plate 7.*]

In *Iskander*, the hero is an apparent Muslim who is in fact a Christian, one of Disraeli's wonderful meldings of world religions. He is also a dandy, who dresses in velvets, but with a belt full of sabres and knives. He also wears a diamond aigrette, a sort of jewelled comb or tiara. Disraeli's male heroes in this period are always wearing jewels one might expect in the hair of duchesses rather than on the battlefields of eastern adventures.[23] While Iskander is a powerful figure, like Byron, who wants to liberate Greece from Turkish domination, his best friend, Nicaeus, is a reader and not a man of action. They fall in love with the same girl: this is the same male bonding that takes place between Aubrey Bohun and George Gainsborough in *Hartlebury*. Rather than suggesting erotic longings for one another, however, the overwhelming impression in the story is of jealousy and envy on Nicaeus's part for Iskander's superior skill, manliness and energy. Iskander gets the girl they both want in the end, while Nicaeus redeems himself for his jealousy, and various attempts to doublecross his friend, by dying honourably in battle.

There is no strict relationship between Disraeli and Iskander or

Bulwer and Nicaeus. Rather, what is most autobiographical is the strong feeling of envy that Disraeli felt for Bulwer. Bulwer had a seat in Parliament, which still eluded Disraeli in 1833 when he wrote this work. He went to hear Bulwer speak in the House of Commons and was critical of both Bulwer and the other speakers he heard. He told his sister, 'between ourselves, I could floor them all'.[24] Repeated defeats in High Wycombe kept him out of the House of Commons, and he was thus frustratingly unable to show them who was boss. That Bulwer should already have a place there was rather galling in a best friend.

Nevertheless they had a good time together and sampled the sides of London that only two freewheeling bachelors could enjoy. Bulwer's most recent biographer, Leslie Mitchell, mentions that Bulwer and Disraeli went 'to "the Naughty House" together, and expressed pleasure in being "shampooed and vapour-bathed"'.[25] Bulwer was briefly married to a young woman named Rosina, with whom his relationship was tempestuous and from whom his separation was more tempestuous still. Rosina used her husband's friendship with Disraeli to attack him. Mitchell is a careful and learned scholar, the author of eleven works on eighteenth- and nineteenth-century political history. It is worth paying attention to his point that all Bulwer's relatively small number of friends, after the separation, were attacked by Rosina. The

> virulence with which she attacked Disraeli may be taken as good evidence of just how strong their association was . . . Above all, she persistently and repeatedly accused him of being homosexual, annotating a book in the library at Knebworth with the words "I like Dizzy signing as if he were a Peer when he was only a Queer" . . . Since Lytton was occasionally subjected to the same innuendoes, being compared to the homosexual Henry III of France, it was easy for Rosina to construct unpleasant assumptions about their friendship.[26]

Rosina's accusations culminated in 1858 when she arrived to denounce her former husband at his election in Hertford. This was just following his first appointment to the cabinet led by the Earl of Derby and Disraeli. Her speech was so wild that her former husband had her committed to a mental asylum in Brentford. She told officials in Brentford

> the matter that was 'generally uppermost' in her mind was that he [Bulwer] had committed sodomy with Disraeli, and that this was the reason why he had been offered a Cabinet post. Having had the run of the London brothels before he was thirteen years old, he was now anxious to take Disraeli's advice to travel in the east where 'seraglios of boys' awaited him.'[27]

She also wrote a letter to Queen Victoria saying that 'in making the two men Ministers, "she might as well have chosen two of the inhabitants of Sodom and Gomorrah"'.[28] Mitchell concedes that much of Rosina's behaviour was outrageous and indicative of mental instability; but there may have been something to her charges. Mad people are often astute judges of character. In 1864 both men were trying to buy up letters that had reference to Rosina from a man named John Birch.[29] Were they being blackmailed? What did they have to hide? The sense of Disraeli's fiction, letters and diary is that Bulwer's intellectual influence was stronger on Disraeli than any passing physical attraction between the two young men. If there had been a real romance, Bulwer certainly would have made a more powerful appearance in the fiction than the briefest of allusions to him as Nicaeus in *Iskander*.

Another important friendship of this era was with Alfred, Count d'Orsay. D'Orsay was a young Frenchman, who had literally been 'picked up' on a continental tour by the Earl and Countess of Blessington. The Blessingtons were themselves an unusual couple. He was a rich elderly man with an enormous income from Irish property where he never lived. She was many years his junior. She had been born Margaret Powers, the daughter of an Irish alcoholic, who had married her off against her will to a man who beat her. She left him, lived unmarried with an officer named Jenkins in Hampshire, and was literally bought by Blessington, whom she later married. She changed her name to Marguerite. Lord and Lady Blessington were both attracted to d'Orsay, who was charming, talented, strikingly good-looking and liked to please. He was the younger son of French nobility. When Byron met d'Orsay travelling with the Blessingtons in Genoa, he wrote a flirtatious letter to him. Byron admired the younger man's 'figure' and called himself 'the Devil'.[30] In later years, d'Orsay became a permanent member of the Blessingtons' ménage. Lord Blessington even arranged for d'Orsay to marry his daughter Harriet. D'Orsay's most recent biographer suggests that there 'are reasonable grounds' to conclude that d'Orsay had been the sexual partner of Lord Blessington, his wife and his daughter.[31] Theirs was a close family.

Blessington soon died. The widowed Lady Blessington set herself up in great style at Gore House in Kensington where she wrote novels, kept a literary salon and installed d'Orsay next door 'in a villa which is a bijou'. D'Orsay had a talent for interior decoration. Lady Blessington allowed him to decorate both houses in the most sumptuous style: 'long galleries, crimson saloons, libraries green as spring, boudoirs blazing with reflected lights, cabinets without end and colossal tripods'.[32] Harriet soon fell out with d'Orsay and chose to live apart from him. D'Orsay now was the most famous dandy of the 1830s and 1840s in London, a latter-day Beau Brummell, maker of male fashion. The Blessington and d'Orsay household suited Disraeli down to the ground. It was semi-intellectual and the food was perfect. The clothes and curtains in swags could not have been more gorgeous. It was the sort of place where respectable women could not call; Lady Blessington's being the supposed mistress of d'Orsay was thought then to spread a sort of infectious moral taint. This moral taint, however, did not affect men. For men like Disraeli, it was a definite plus. Therefore, when he was introduced to d'Orsay at a party and d'Orsay actually remembered him when they met soon thereafter in the street, he wrote exulting to Sarah: 'D'Orsay attacked me yesterday in Bond St. attired with a splendour I cannot describe, so dishevelled were his curls, so brilliant his bijouteries and the shifting tints of his party-coloured costume. He knows who I am, and has I suppose been crammed by Lady Blessington.'[33] The success of his novels and the friendship with Bulwer had begun to give Disraeli some of the social éclat he had always wanted. To be recognized by d'Orsay was a sign that he had truly arrived.

Disraeli and d'Orsay became fast friends. They went to parties together. They dressed up together. Here is Disraeli exclaiming about d'Orsay's waistcoat as he arrived late at a party where d'Orsay was already present: '"What a beautiful pattern! Where did you find it my lord?" Upon this a general excitement prevailed, and all the guests simultaneously threw back their coats to allow a freer inspection of that portion of their dress beneath.'[34] *Fraser's Magazine* joined in the fun and depicted d'Orsay as a cock with a puffed-out chest and jacket thrown back to reveal his waistcoat. [*See plate 8.*] Disraeli and d'Orsay lived together for a few weeks at d'Orsay's house in Kensington while Disraeli was writing a new novel, *Venetia*. He and d'Orsay took vapour baths together. He told his sister this was to keep off the flu.[35]

Of course, it is possible for two young men to sit naked in a steam room together and not be lovers, but a degree of erotic interest often circulates with the steam, even among men who love women. The impression from Disraeli's fiction and letters is that he and d'Orsay were not lovers. However, d'Orsay appeared as a character in *Henrietta Temple*, always an important sign with Disraeli that the person had made a big impression. Disraeli dedicated the novel to him and signed himself d'Orsay's 'affectionate friend'.

What Disraeli learned from d'Orsay was a philosophy of life that matched his own growing experience, and d'Orsay was an effective antidote to his periodic fits of melancholy. In *Henrietta*

Temple d'Orsay is Count Alcibiades de Mirabel, 'a child of impulse', who

> through a native grace, and an intuitive knowledge of mankind, made every word pleasing and every act appropriate . . . The Count Mirabel was gay, careless, generous . . . It seemed that the Count Mirabel's feelings grew daily more fresh, and his faculty of enjoyment more keen and relishing.[36]

Mirabel, again a name from Restoration drama, is someone who lives to please, to make people happy, to enjoy himself. He urges the Disraeli character, Ferdinand Armine, to be more cheerful, and to cultivate his pleasure in everyday life:

> Existence is a pleasure, and the greatest. The world cannot rob us of that, and if it be better to live than to die, it is better to live in a good humour than a bad one . . . Feel slightly, think little, never plan, never brood. Every thing depends upon the circulation; take care of it. Take the world as you find it, enjoy every thing. Vive la bagatelle![37]

Mirabel is convinced this can be accomplished by taking a comewhat-may attitude and looking after the circulation of the blood. Although he is a light-hearted butterfly of a man in the novel, his philosophy spoke to something in Disraeli's own feeling that hedonism and repose, the sensual enjoyment of food and fabric, were what life was all about. Or, if they were not completely what life was about, it was worth paying more attention to them than ordinary Englishmen did.

Two more male friendships, in this case fictional friends, are worth noticing because they show the extent to which Disraeli cared and wrote about unusual intimacy between men. In *Henrietta Temple* Ferdinand Armine's father, Ratcliffe Armine, has a good friend named Adrian Glastonbury. Like the Beckford character named Winter in *Contarini Fleming*, 'Glastonbury was most remarkable for his taste'.[38] He sketches Gothic churches and never marries. Soon after his own marriage, Ratcliffe moves his friend Glastonbury into one of the gatehouses at Armine Castle and he becomes the tutor to Ratcliffe's only child, Ferdinand. When Glastonbury speaks to Ratcliffe about Ferdinand, he calls him 'our child . . . for thus, when speaking to the father alone, he would often style the son'.[39] It is as if the two friends have got married and had a child. The two men leave Ferdinand's mother out of the picture, and Glastonbury does not use the term 'our child' in front of her.

Disraeli's second big novel of this period was *Venetia*, published in 1837. It describes two poets recently dead, Lord Byron and Percy Shelley, whom Disraeli recreated as Lord Cadurcis and Marmion Herbert. He incorporated non-fictional elements of their works and their personalities in a fictional story, where the daughter of Herbert, named Venetia, spends the story falling in love with Cadurcis. She nearly marries him at the end, but before she can Disraeli kills him off, not in Greece where Byron died, but in a shipwreck off the Italian coast like the one that killed Shelley. Before they die, Cadurcis and Herbert, who have read and admired one another's poetry, meet and become friends. At one point they discuss Plato's *Symposium*. In the *Symposium* Plato argues that sexual attraction is an early step on the ladder of love. Ideally, erotic or physical attraction should lead on to a spiritual love which is a higher, more fulfilling, even immortal variety of love. This is also a dialogue in which Plato openly discusses both sexual and spiritual love between adult men and adolescent boys, between teachers and their pupils, and between pairs of males of similar ages.

Disraeli pointed to a part of the *Symposium* popular with later readers in which one of the participants in the party speaks of human beings having been split into two by the gods, and spending their lives searching for their other halves. According to this story, sometimes a male finds his other half in a female, sometimes a male finds his other half in another male, sometimes a female finds her other half in another female. Disraeli translates this as a human being's search for his 'spiritual antetype'. He has Marmion Herbert say on the subject of sexual love:

> Plato believed, and I believe with him, in the existence of a spiritual antetype, so that when we are born, there is something within us, which, from the instant we live and move, thirsts after its likeness. The propensity develops itself with the development of our nature. The gratification of the senses soon becomes a very small part of that profound and complicated sentiment, which we call love.[40]

Cadurcis replies that he believes he has found his spiritual antetype in Venetia. It is clear that the two men also have a sort of intellectual love for one another. There may perhaps even be some element of sexual attraction in their love. Disraeli says that Herbert in his early portraits looked 'effeminate' and that his chin had 'the impassioned tenderness of the shape of Antinous', two ways of hinting a man could be attracted to another man.[41] At the end, though, their friendship is a spiritual one. They agree not only on the importance of Plato but, following d'Orsay, of the ancient philosopher, Epicurus, 'who maintained the rights of man to pleasure and happiness'.[42]

These friendships suggest Disraeli's struggle to take his sexual attraction to other men and to make it something higher, something socially acceptable, something intellectually useful, an ideal. He did this by forming friendships with Bulwer and d'Orsay that may have had an element of sexual attraction in them, but who were essentially men who shared some of the enthusiasms for which he had been censured by critics. In *Henrietta Temple* he imagined male characters who establish unusual bonds to one another, and even pretend to have children together, a bond Plato thought was the surest way to immortality in a heterosexual couple. Disraeli turned to Plato in *Vivian Grey* more than a decade previously, as the great idealist, who inspired universal respect, who had advocated a love between men that could barely be spoken of in Victorian England. Mainly it was spoken of in classical allusions, as in Antinous, Alcibiades, Crispinus and Hyacinth. Plato tamed and rendered philosophically acceptable Disraeli's homoerotic impulse. To dwell on the theme of male friendship in fiction was also one way of casting about for a bridge between the female world of society novels, in which he had already had some success, and the male world of Parliament, which had so far been beyond his grasp.

10

A Singular Blending of
the Daring and the Soft

Bulwer and d'Orsay were good friends. Disraeli also experienced friendships that soured in the 1830s. He was a colourful *bon vivant*; but he was also willing to contemplate dishonesty and piling up levels of debt which one doubts whether he ever had any intention of paying back. With insobriety came hangovers. With debt and towering ambition came treachery. One can love the man, yet clear-sightedly keep in mind the lies he told to keep himself afloat.

We have already seen how Disraeli's friendship with John Gibson Lockhart came to an end in the debacle over *The Representative*. Disraeli did not quickly forget the injury which, as he thought, had been unfairly done to him in that affair. When *The Quarterly Review*, which Lockhart edited, published some criticism of *The Young Duke* in 1832, Disraeli wrote him a letter calling him a sidewinding snake. 'You have,' Disraeli wrote, 'by one of those sidewind sneers for which I have been often indebted to you held me up to ridicule.' The offending passage, which the critic in *The Quarterly Review* claimed was from *The Young Duke*, had actually appeared in *Vivian Grey*, so Disraeli was on shaky ground in objecting to it. The slap he got in reply from Lockhart disavowed either an intention to ridicule, or indeed to remember any former affection between the two, which was at the base of Disraeli's original complaint. 'As to myself,' Lockhart wrote, 'I disclaim entirely the feelings with respect to yourself which your letter seems to impute to me.'[1] Disraeli was unduly sensitive to slights, especially from other men. The real story of his sensitivity to Lockhart is his disappointment at their friendship ending. He said in his diary, when speaking of the intellectual influence on him of his closest friends, 'Lockhart is good for tete á tetes [sic] if he like [sic] you, which he did me once.'[2] He decided when he wrote this in 1833 that Lockhart was overrated by the world. Disraeli's persistent admiration, however, showed in him taking a story Lockhart had translated from the Spanish and making it into a play as *The Tragedy of Count Alarcos* in 1839. The rather sad reflection that Lockhart had liked him once suggests that Disraeli never quite got over him.

Disraeli was himself a treacherous friend to Benjamin Austen. Not only had he had an affair with Austen's wife, but he also continually evaded repaying his debts to the older man. When in 1833 Austen wrote to Disraeli asking him to repay a £300 loan that had been outstanding for some time, Disraeli replied asking for another £1200. Even the imperturbable modern editors of the Disraeli letters, who rarely pass comment on his doings, are roused to remark 'Surely only D' could get away with a thing like this.'[3] When Austen refused this further request, Disraeli, like a beggar on the street who says 'Have a nice day and God bless' after being refused money, employed emotional blackmail with Austen. 'For these eight years,' Disraeli wrote, 'I have considered you my friend, with me no idle word, whatever you may think.' Disraeli's letter to Austen went on, 'I am too shrewd an observer not to feel that [our relation] is all now over, and that as far as friendship is concerned, I am now alone in the world, and always shall be.'[4] He did not get the additional money, but the emotional ploy worked. Austen protested that they were still friends and Disraeli managed to string him along without having to repay him for several more years. It required more letters to do this and throughout the 1830s his letters to Austen are filled with excuses for not being able to repay him. He is either busy, or he cannot trouble his father for the money in his father's precarious state of health, or he is expecting a big deal to come through at any moment, or he has been disappointed by someone else, or he is just leaving town so he will have to write again in a few days.[5]

None of this shows Disraeli in his best light. His debts were one of the principal sources of his bad behaviour and the indebtedness was very pressing in these years. *Henrietta Temple* has in it a long meditation on the way in which debt drives people to do bad things. The narrator says of Ferdinand Armine:

> He was in debt. If youth but knew the fatal misery that they are entailing on themselves the moment they accept a pecuniary credit to which they are not entitled, how they would start in their career! how pale they would turn! how they would tremble, and clasp their hands in agony at the precipice on which they are disporting! Debt is the prolific mother of folly and of crime; it taints the course of life in all its streams. Hence so many unhappy marriages, so many prostituted pens, and venal politicians! It hath a small beginning, but a giant's growth and strength. When we make the monster, we make our master, who haunts us at all hours, and shakes his whip of scorpions for ever in our sight.

Here he described his own sense of desperation in 1836 as he wrote the novel. Throughout this period he was always only a step away from being arrested for non-payment of debts and he seriously considered going abroad to evade his creditors. He believed he had 'prostituted' his pen. He seems to have foreseen that he would need to contract a future marriage in order to get clear of the debts. Even his future political career might be up for sale until he got clear of debt. How would future electors regard him if they knew this passage described his own predicament? Still, as with what appears the incredible recklessness of references to his sexuality, he seemed to have a confidence with a pen in his hand, writing a novel, that he believed would carry him through all difficulties. He was at his best describing his own experience and 'doubters be damned' he appeared to be saying.

He also refused to apologize or to affect regret for having collected a mountain of debt. 'When we are young,' the passage continues,

> we must enjoy ourselves. True; and there are few things more gloomy than the recollection of a youth that has not been enjoyed. What prosperity of manhood, what splendour of old age, can compensate for it? Wealth is power; and in youth, of all seasons of life, we require power, because we can enjoy everything that we can command. What, then, is to be done? I leave the question to the schoolmen, because I am convinced that to moralise with the inexperienced availeth nothing.[6]

You cannot get young people to listen to you, so you may as well let them contract debts so they may enjoy the sensory organs of their youthful frames. He refused to apologize for his own youthful enjoyment of gambling and investing, wine and clothes, travelling and electioneering. Youth and enjoyment were key; financial care and self-denial were for puritans and utilitarians.

Debt led him into a kind of treachery against fellow Jews, with whom his identification in this period was only passing and fitful. Unless they were select Sephardim from old Iberian families, or heroic boys like David Alroy, he did not much identify with them. In *Henrietta Temple* there is a Jewish moneylender named Levison. He is a coal merchant to whom Ferdinand Armine is already in debt at the extortionate rate of 10 per cent. He lives in richly furnished rooms decorated in the poorest taste. Levison refuses to lend Ferdinand more money unless he will help sell coal to all his friends. He is at least a canny businessman, which Disraeli was not. Although greedy Jewish moneylenders were clichés of European literature, it is a little tawdry for someone with the surname Disraeli to be painting this unflattering portrait that merely caters to his readers' prejudices. The only plausible explanation is that he was living in Bulwer's and Lady Blessington's and d'Orsay's world now, a world which was as far away as could be from his grandparents' commercial success in the East End and their long-standing affiliation with Bevis Marks. He did not always think of himself as a Jew and it would require all the energies of his next phase as a writer to live down the stereotype into which he had himself breathed life in *Henrietta Temple*.

The debt made him treacherous. It also coarsened him. It made a man with a big heart and a deep vein of sentimentality rather cynical. 'As men advance in life,' he wrote in the last volume of *Henrietta Temple*, 'all passions resolve themselves into money. Love, ambition, even poetry, end in this.'[7] This is partly explained by the bitterness of his break-up with Henrietta Sykes, which was happening as he wrote the novel. Recent commentators have even suggested that what had begun as a first true love, had degenerated into a scheme whereby Disraeli was keeping his creditors at bay by using sums made available as an allowance to Henrietta by her husband, Sir Francis Sykes. The debt had clearly driven him to desperate measures.

As always, however, his sense of humour and some native instinct of self-preservation stopped him from taking things too far. At last he approached Isaac for help. Isaac came up with a considerable amount of money to discharge his son's most pressing debts, although Disraeli kept the extent of his remaining indebtedness a secret. He put in a cheerful exchange towards the end of *Venetia* where Cadurcis/Byron and Herbert/Shelley are talking about indebtedness being reduced as one grows older. Here Disraeli is clearly more worried about losing his youth than he is about paying off his debts. He returns to his favourite topic, pleasure. 'I fancy every period of life has its pleasures,' remarks Cadurcis, 'and as we advance in life the exercise of power and the possession of wealth must be great consolations to the majority; we bully our children and hoard our cash.'

'Two most noble occupations!' replies Herbert, 'but I think in this world there is just as good a chance of being bullied by our children first, and paying their debts afterwards.'[8] This must reflect Isaac, whom Disraeli regarded as a hoarder of cash, being made to pay his swaggering son's debts. Disraeli did not like growing old. He did not like his lovely black hair going grey. At least he looked forward hopefully to middle age as a time when he might not be forced into the expedient of siphoning money off his mistress's allowance, or writing two novels at speed in twelve months.

At some level, however, Disraeli believed there was something treacherous in his soul, that a capacity for disloyalty, for changing colours like a chameleon to suit his environment, would be with him for his whole life. Rather than regard this as a disadvantage, his repeated return to the figure of Alcibiades shows that it might be an aspect of his genius. Alcibiades, the student of Socrates, aimed to seduce his teacher, but was rejected, or so said Plato, at the end of the *Symposium*. Socrates shows by his actions that though he may be attracted to beautiful young men, he is above their physical charms. Alcibiades's having switched sides in the Peloponnesian War was nevertheless blamed on Socrates when the Athenian *polis* indicted him for corrupting their youth.

Alcibiades has been regarded as 'the patriarch of dandies'.[9] A famous French dandy, Disraeli's contemporary, Jules Barbey d'Aurevilly, wrote that dandies have double and multiple natures; they are 'Of undecided intellectual sexuality . . . They are the Hermaphrodites of History, not of Fable, of whom Alcibiades was the supreme example in the most beautiful of nations.'[10] D'Orsay is Count Alcibiades de Mirabel in *Henrietta Temple*. The Disraeli figure, Aubrey Bohun, describes himself as Alcibiades in *Hartlebury*.[11] In *Venetia*, Cadurcis/Byron says that 'of the ancients . . . Alcibiades and Alexander the Great are my favourites.

They were young, beautiful, and conquerors: a great combination.'[12] He might have added that both Alcibiades and Alexander were also bisexual. Graham Robb, in his recent book on nineteenth-century homosexuality, has pointed out how references to figures like Alexander the Great were secret ways Victorian homosexuals had of referring to a forbidden topic; Robb might have added Alcibiades to his list.[13]

If the world condemned Alcibiades for disloyalty to the Athenians, Disraeli admired him for being young, and beautiful, and ambidextrous. What was treachery seen from one point of view, was actually an endlessly plastic ability to sympathize with both sides of an apparent division at once. To marry the history of literature to the history of the state, one had to be both male and female at a glance. With his uncanny knack for prophecy mixed with a kind of giddy bravado, the indebted Disraeli, in his early thirties, offered Alcibiades as the excuse for what he was, and the prediction of what he might become.

What fun it was too. What astonishing costumes one could wear into the fashionable drawing rooms of London with one's entrée as a well-known novelist. What wise old ladies there were to applaud one's progress, defend one's latest outrage and offer advice about the next step.

The three daughters of the playwright Richard Brinsley Sheridan were among the leaders of fashion in London of the 1830s. Here is one of them, Lady Dufferin, describing Disraeli's dress at her sister's dinner party in 1833:

> a black velvet coat lined with satin, purple trousers with a gold band running down the outside seam, a scarlet waistcoat, long lace ruffles, falling down to the tips of his fingers, white gloves with several brilliant rings outside them, and long black ringlets rippling down upon his shoulders.[14]

This was not just a matter of London salons, where he could expect a certain amount of dandy company and where people were unperturbed by languid exoticism among men. Disraeli also dressed this way when he was addressing electors and the rowdy crowds on election platforms. There his dress was considered an aspect of his Jewishness. An eyewitness account of his appearance when he contested Taunton in 1835 reads:

> His physiognomy was strictly Jewish. Over a broad, high fore-head were ringlets of coal-black, glossy hair, which combed away from his right temple, fell in luxuriant clusters or bunches over his left cheek and ear, which it entirely con-cealed from view. There was a sort of half smile, half sneer playing about his beautifully-formed mouth, the upper lip of which was curved as we see it in portraits of Byron . . . He was very showily attired in a dark bottle-green frock-coat, a waist-coat of the most extravagant pattern, the front of which was almost covered with glittering chains, and in fancy-pattern pantaloons. He wore a plain black stock, but no collar was vis-ible. Altogether he was the most intellectual-looking exquisite I had ever seen.[15]

He lost at Taunton, but when the election was over, and he addressed the local Conservatives (as Tories increasingly called themselves in the 1830s, though Disraeli liked the older term), something was there underneath the dandyism that the outside observer had not noticed before. Although Disraeli began 'in a lisping, lackadaisical tone of voice', gesturing with his hands to show off his rings, 'as he proceeded all traces of dandyism and affectation were lost . . . The dandy was transformed into the man of mind.'[16] Political passion appeared to overcome his effem-inacy; or, rather, desire to make himself clear, and to persuade an audience, emerged from his pose as dandy aristocrat, his act as Restoration fop. The two were as inextricably linked in Disraeli's personality as, in his view, the history of English literature con-nected with the history of the government.

When he appeared on the election platform in Maidstone in

1837, the mob was more interested in attacking him for his Jewishness than for his fancy dress.

> They offered him bacon, ham, etc., and repeatedly suggested that he was a Jew; but he was very ready in replying to them. His appearance was very remarkable – long black hair in curls – and he was dressed in what appeared to be an extraordinary way, the extreme, it may be supposed, of fashion. Nothing like it had been seen in Maidstone before.[17]

Yet, it was for Maidstone that he was at last elected. He used dress to get himself noticed, to affect belonging to a higher class than he did, to pretend as if he belonged to the Prince Regent's circle of two decades earlier and because he simply enjoyed dressing up. The 'man of mind' in Taunton, and the man who could so stoutly defend himself against the anti-Semitic catcalls of the crowd, clearly had mental qualities to proceed with beyond his curls and jewelled fingers.

There were risks associated with the self-advertisement of the dandyism. *Fraser's Magazine* published a cartoon image of Disraeli as a dandy in 1833. It captures the curls, the jewels on the fingers, the frilled shirt, the tiny feminine shoes. It associated this unusual dress with Disraeli's trip to the East: in the image there are also Turkish slippers, a Turkish pipe, elaborate eastern swords hanging on the wall and a divan with great cushions for what Englishmen regarded as Turkish indolence. For those in the know, all these Turkish references would have been also markers of Disraeli's unusual sexuality, something on which the painter Benjamin Haydon commented in his diary. Haydon was shocked when Disraeli, at a dinner party, showed a letter from his friend Emile Botta, which had explicit descriptions of sexual practices in the East. According to Jane Ridley, Haydon said that Disraeli 'talked much of the East, and seemed tinged with a disposition to palliate its infamous vices . . . I meant to ask him if he preferred Aegypt, where Sodomy was *preferment*, to England, where it very properly was Death.' A week later, Haydon learned that a man had been 'charged with indecency with a policeman the very night of Disraeli's extraordinary behaviour' at the dinner party where he and Haydon had both been present. 'I think no man would go on in that odd manner . . . wear green velvet trousers and ruffles, without having odd feelings. He ought to be kicked. I hate the look of the fellow.'[18] The dandyism got him noticed in social circles, but it tended to be the women who loved him for it, who did not much mind whether he had slept with men or not; perhaps it even made him more attractive to them if he had. Some men, on the other hand, like Haydon, felt viscerally affronted.

One of Disraeli's great patrons in this period, a society hostess who took him up, promoted him, defended him, and told him what to do next, was Lady Cork. She was the widow of the seventh Earl of Cork. In 1834, when Disraeli reported this conversation overheard by Henrietta Sykes at a party of Lady Cork's, she was eighty-eight and full of fire. Lord Carrington, a Buckinghamshire magnate, described Disraeli as a troublesome agitator, whom he believed had gone abroad again. Lady Cork replied,

> You old fool! Why, he sent me this book this morning. You need not look at it; you can't understand it. It is the finest book ever written. Gone abroad indeed! Why, he is the best *ton* in London! There is not a party that goes down without him. The Duchess of Hamilton says there is nothing like. Lady Lonsdale would give her head and shoulders for him. He would not dine at your house if you were to ask him. He does not care for people because they are lords; he must have fashion, or beauty, or wit, or something; and you are a very good sort of person, but you are nothing more.[19]

Lady Cork also ratified and encouraged Disraeli's choice of Henrietta Sykes. This is Disraeli's report of what she said of

Henrietta when she sat next to him at dinner. 'She is my favourite of all the young women in London and I have left her my china. I have left it her because she has got a heart, and she is very beautiful too.'[20] In fact, Lady Cork made a more regular appearance in letters home to Sarah than anyone else he met at London parties.

Disraeli paid her the ultimate compliment of casting her as Lady Bellair in *Henrietta Temple*. 'Bellair' was another of his tributes to Restoration drama, but he drew the character from the living person. She was 'of child-like stature, and quite erect, though ninety years of age'. She had a 'keen sarcastic grey eye', a brilliantly absurd sense of humour and, like him, a fondness for pageboys. Here she is getting out of her carriage and exclaiming about her page as she arrives at Henrietta Temple's house in the country:

> There was no room for him behind, and I told him to lie under the seat. Poor dear boy! He must be smothered. I hope he is not dead. Oh! there he is. Has Miss Temple got a page? Does her page wear a feather? My page has not got a feather, but he shall have one, because he was not smothered. Here! woman, who are you? The housemaid. I thought so. I always know a housemaid. You shall take care of my page. Take him at once, and give him some milk and water; and, page, be very good, and never leave this good young woman, unless I send for you. And, woman, good young woman, perhaps you may find an old feather of Miss Temple's page. Give it to this good little boy, because he was not smothered.[21]

Disraeli says that Lady Bellair has been on the social scene for seventy years, and although she has reached ninety, she is

> still restless for novelty, still eager for amusement; still anxiously watching the entrance on the stage of some new stream of characters, and indefatigable in attracting the notice of every

one whose talents might contribute to her entertainment, or whose attention might gratify her vanity.[22]

Lady Bellair likes talented people first, beautiful people second, and aristocratic people third. 'As for mere wealth, she really despised it, though she liked her favourites to be rich.'[23] Disraeli had learned via Lady Cork that addressing the upper classes as if you were their equal worked better than bowing down to them; if you treated Lady Bellair with 'servility, she absolutely loathed you'.[24] He was also charmed by the fact that, like him, she was a user. When Lady Bellair went to Bath every year after her London season, she picked up some nouveaux riches who could transport her up and down the country on visits to friends so she did not have to pay for carriages herself.[25] Above all, Lady Bellair liked having fashionable young men at her parties, because they caused the stir and created the sexual tension that made an evening go. At Henrietta Temple's she discovers someone who has a connection to the latest Italian opera singer named Pasta:

Oh! you know her, do you? . . . Very well; you shall bring her to my house. She shall sing at all my parties: I love music at my evenings, but I never pay for it, never. If she will not come in the evening, I will try to ask her to dinner, once at least. I do not like singers and tumblers at dinner – but she is very fashionable, and young men like her; and what I want at my dinners are young men, young men of very great fashion. I rather want young men at my dinners. I have some – Lord Languid always comes to me, and he is very fine, you know, very fine indeed. He goes to very few places, but he always comes to me.[26]

Significantly, Lady Bellair tells the Disraeli alter ego that it is time he was married. This is not in spite of his sexual ambiguity, as if she has not noticed it, but because marriage is about getting on in the world, advancing one's career, not about sexual fulfilment.

Also, he is getting too old to continue traipsing around as a young dandy: 'You should marry. I hate a *cidevant jeune homme*.'[27] Lady Bellair also is the first to say out loud what has been secretly and silently apparent to Disraeli throughout the 1830s as his debts pressed and his parliamentary ambitions remained stymied. When Ferdinand Armine is arrested for debt, Lady Bellair says she needs money to free him: 'Why is not he in Parliament; and then they could not take him up?'[28] She says the unutterable: an MP's immunity from arrest for debt will hold off his creditors. She saw and sympathized with Disraeli's predicament and his ambition at the same time. Isaac did not know the whole of Disraeli's financial problem and saw more novels as a way of taking him further away from, rather than closer to, Parliament. Lady Cork saw that the young novelist who had been the life of her parties literally now must be in Parliament or else go to gaol. She was a patron who gave Disraeli a push in London society and boosted his self-confidence by saying precisely what he should do next. By writing novels he had gained power among the women who ruled the drawing rooms, Lady Cork the foremost among them. The women launched him then into the world of men.

Disraeli began by acquiring male patrons. He had learned something from the disaster with Murray; he was more assiduous, deferential and circumspect this time. Through Henrietta he met Lord Lyndhurst. Lyndhurst had been lord chancellor under the Duke of Wellington until 1830. He was thirty years older than Disraeli, but the two recognized in one another fellow sensualists. Disraeli was having an adulterous liaison with Henrietta. Lyndhurst too was well known for moral laxness and a general susceptibility to women. The scandalous rumour current at the time was that Disraeli even encouraged Henrietta to have an affair with Lyndhurst. He thought this would help promote him, via Lyndhurst's influence, for some safe Tory seat. Disraeli also went out of his way to compliment Lyndhurst by dedicating *Venetia* to him.

Lyndhurst did indeed like and begin to see Henrietta, but he had a more practical and prosaic need of Disraeli's pen. He needed an adept writer to defend Toryism in the face of the repeated Whig victories at the time of the First Reform Bill. Lyndhurst encouraged Disraeli to write on his party's behalf. The younger man was eager to do so. He defended Lyndhurst's power base, the House of Lords, in his *Vindication of the English Constitution* (1835). He also attacked the Whig government in anonymous letters to *The Times*, later published as the *Letters of Runnymede* (1836). Disraeli, like Isaac, already had conservative instincts, but to have Lyndhurst as a patron meant that his attack on the Whigs, and defence of the Tories, had a more specific, urgent focus.[29] In later years Disraeli would say that he acted as Lyndhurst's private secretary, though the arrangement between the two was probably more informal than that.

Disraeli's other patron in the early 1830s was Lord Chandos, heir to the Duke of Buckingham. Isaac had been renting Bradenham since 1829 and Disraeli's younger brother, James, eventually farmed there. The D'Israelis were minor members of an elite of Buckinghamshire families who lived in substantial country houses. Bradenham was a big brick manor house. Even today it is an imposing building and serves as a country retreat for a major London firm of accountants. [*See plate 3.*] It is not far from Wotton, an elegant house, rebuilt after a fire by Sir John Soane, where Chandos lived. The two families knew of each other. Chandos saw in Disraeli a potential ally when Disraeli approached him to speak about local agricultural interests. To have the backing of a man who lived at Wotton, and who would one day be the ducal proprietor of Stowe, was real stature in that world of country-house power.

Chandos also supported Disraeli's candidature for the Tories' club, the Carlton, where he became a member in 1836. Disraeli had been a candidate for many of the principal clubs in St James's. He dreamed in *The Young Duke* of being able to come and go at Almack's, but though he went once or twice, he was certainly not a regular ticket-holder from one of the lady patronesses, through whom one gained admission. He had been turned down at the Travellers Club. He had been blackballed at the Athenaeum, even though Isaac was a member. The Carlton Club was different in that it was primarily a political rather than a social club, but Disraeli had at least succeeded in gaining entrance into one corner of the British establishment.

This patronage was important, but it would have got him nowhere if he had not had genuine talent. One of his discoveries in the 1830s was a new and long-lasting source of pleasure: the pleasure of speaking, of addressing an audience, of delighting a crowd with his peculiarly sarcastic oratory. In *Hartlebury* where Disraeli described his first election contest at High Wycombe, he said the crowd was 'equally astonished' at Aubrey Bohun's 'fluency and fun'.[30] It was not simply that the crowd enjoyed him, he enjoyed them as well. When Bohun mounted the portico of a pub to address an election crowd, just as Disraeli had done at High Wycombe in 1832,

> It was quite evident that the speaker was himself in a state of almost ecstatic enjoyment. He seemed almost intoxicated with his inexhaustible sarcasm. His teeming fancy fired with the maddening shouts of the populace. There is nothing like a good thundering cheer to prompt a man's imagination.[31]

Wherever Disraeli put 'enjoyment' and 'intoxication' in the same passage, you can be sure that he had discovered something that he found almost addictively fun. However, he had also stumbled on one of the keys to his success: when he enjoyed himself addressing an audience, the audience enjoyed him. It gave him a sense of power over people he never knew he had before. It was of a different order from the pleasure he derived from dressing up, or impressing a drawing room, or romantic friendship, but the personality he had created for all those other purposes now went into the making of his platform oratory.

Others were aware of this too. The eyewitness report of one of his election appearances at Taunton, after he had failed to be elected at High Wycombe, had described him as facing his audience with 'half smile, half sneer'. Contemptuousness was part of his stage persona, and it seemed to go down well with those he addressed. In 1836 he wrote to Sarah quoting from a review in *The Spectator* where his performance at a dinner of the Buckinghamshire Conservative Association had been noticed. The writer said the speaking 'was as stupid as usual, except Mr. Disraeli'. After a little of his usual boasting about the House of Lords, which the writer found annoying, Disraeli had grown 'abusive and amusing'. Disraeli was obviously pleased with the assessment of his speech.[32] In sarcasm he had found an authentic voice.

In those days the death of the sovereign brought about an automatic dissolution of Parliament and new elections. When William IV died and Queen Victoria came to the throne in May 1837, Disraeli was offered the chance to stand for a fairly safe Conservative seat at Maidstone. He had the backing of the Conservative party and the support of the senior member for the constituency, Wyndham Lewis. At last he was successful and in July he was elected for the first time as a Member of Parliament for Maidstone. Afterwards, he declared to Sarah: 'I am very well and begin to enjoy my new career. I find that it makes a sensible difference in the opinion of one's friends. I can scarcely keep my countenance.'[33] For him this was an unusual declaration of happiness. The first sight of Athens and Constantinople, falling in love with Henrietta, and now election for Maidstone, these were among his landmark moments of transcendent pleasure. He knew them and wrote them down.

He came into Parliament at the accession of the new queen. Her magnificence was indelibly associated in his mind with his own success and his first taking his seat in the House of Commons. He attended the State Opening of Parliament in November and described it as 'a magnificent spectacle. The Queen looked admirably, no feathers but a diamond tiara; the peers in robes, the peeresses, and the sumptuous groups of courtiers, rendered the affair glittering and imposing.' Later that day he had the wonderful experience of the police intervening to protect him as a Member of Parliament when he was struggling through the crowds to get to the Carlton Club for lunch. Afterwards, he heard his chief, the Tory leader of the opposition, Sir Robert Peel, speak well on the Queen's speech. He voted for the first time and walked back to the Carlton for supper. 'Thus ended,' he told Sarah, 'the most remarkable day hitherto of my life.'[34]

Having been in the House for only a few weeks, he made his maiden speech in December 1837. It was an utter failure. He was howled down. He stood up to oppose the views on Irish elections of the Irish radical, Daniel O'Connell. A group of Irish members were most effective in drowning him out, but others joined in the general derision. Before he sat down, his voice rising above the din, he said: 'I sit down now, but the time will come when you will hear me.'[35]

It would take him some time before he understood what would work and what would not in that all-male assembly. Monypenny's conclusion was that 'With his un-English appearance, dandified dress, affected manner, and elaborated style, Disraeli was hardly likely to win the favour of the House of Commons.'[36] His father probably came as close as any to putting his finger on what the problem was: 'I am always fearful that "theatrical games" will not do for the English Commons.'[37] The difference between father and son was that the son was never, or never admitted to being, 'fearful'. He told another correspondent, to whom he frankly admitted the failure, that 'I rather like a row, and never succeed in anything unless I am opposed.'[38] That was a just assessment of his own psychology. His business of the next several years would be to study those who had howled him down, to listen to what worked in the House of Commons and what did not, to find some way of astonishing them. Trying to pacify them or to placate them was not his style. Ever since *Contarini*, dominating men had been what he had in mind.

1. Isaac D'Israeli: 'Nature had disqualified him, from his cradle, for the busy pursuits of men.' *National Trust*

2. John Gibson Lockhart: 'Good for tête à têtes if he likes you, which he did me once.' *The John Murray Collection*

3. Bradenham: the Buckinghamshire house rented by Isaac D'Israeli.

4. Jean-Léon Gérôme, *Grand Bath at Bursa* (1885). Europeans regarded the eastern Mediterranean as an erotic destination. *Private Collection*

5. Jean-Léon Gérôme, *The Snake Charmer* (1880). Disraeli returned from the east disposed 'to palliate its infamous vices'. © *Sterling and Francine Clark Art Institute, Williamstown, Massachusetts, USA*

6. Disraeli's friend, Edward Bulwer. They were both proud of their hair.

8. Disraeli's friend, Count d'Orsay. *Fraser's* told its readers that Byron had been smitten with him. *Mary Evans Picture Library*

AUTHOR OF 'THE SIAMESE TWINS'.

7. *Fraser's* lampooned Bulwer's narcissism by placing him in front of a mirror.
Mary Evans Picture Library

9. 'His little agreeable self.' Disraeli's protégé George Smythe.

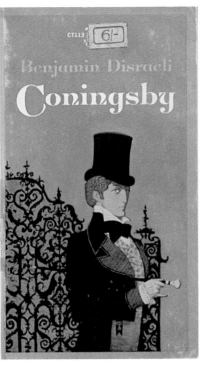

11. 'An exquisite young man, his pinky extended.' A 1962 cover of Disraeli's best-known novel.

10. Disraeli and his secretary, Montagu Corry. An unusual portrait from the *Vanity Fair* series. *Mary Evans Picture Library*

12. & 13. *Above & below:* Lord Henry Lennox.
Disraeli wrote him 'I can only tell you that I love you.'
The Trustees of the Goodwood Collection

14. *Vanity Fair* caricatured
Lennox as a fop. *Mary Evans
Picture Library*

MR. DISRAELI, on hearing of the Ministerial crisis, immediately waited upon Fortune, but was not favoured with an interview.

On hearing that LORD STANLEY had gone a second time to the Palace, MR. DISRAELI took his seat—and the oaths—as "gentleman in waiting," before the fire.

Such was the confusion of the ministerial movements and political promenades, that everybody went to call upon everybody. The hall porters were never known to have had such a time of it, but though knocking and ringing at doors continued throughout the whole day, nothing seemed to answer.

During the whole of the day, MR. DISRAELI was understood to be so particularly engaged, that, with the exception of LORD STANLEY, he could see nobody. So important were MR. DISRAELI's interviews with himself during the Ministerial Crisis, that it appears to have had the effect of shutting him up in the most extraordinary manner.

15.
Punch made fun of Disraeli as a courtier,
as a cross-dressing angel and as an oriental wizard in a skirt.

Mary Evans Picture Library

PUNCH, OR THE LONDON CHARIVARI—December 10, 1864.

DRESSING FOR AN OXFORD BAL MASQUÉ.

PUNCH, OR THE LONDON CHARIVARI—April 15, 1876.

"NEW CROWNS FOR OLD ONES!"

16.   17.

18. A stone satyr in the garden at Hughenden.

19. A bronze Pan on the terrace at Hughenden.

20. Hughenden Manor. The Disraelis bought the house in 1848 and remodelled it in the 1860s. He told Metternich that it was 'sylvan and feudal.' © *NTPL/Matthew Antrobus*

21. Anne-Louis Girodet, *The Sleep of Endymion* (1793): the name of the boy who was loved by the goddess of the moon was also nineteenth-century code for men who loved other men. Disraeli published his novel, *Endymion*, in 1880.

In another insightful moment of autobiographical reflection, Disraeli had written of Ferdinand Armine in *Henrietta Temple* that he was 'in truth, a singular blending of the daring and the soft'.[39] He knew his own recklessness and his own soft-heartedness. In the right mood he could be cavalier in the face of danger and risk. At quieter moments, he was defensive and self-conscious about his effeminacy. He had found a way of entertaining crowds outside the House of Commons, but in it he still had to find a rhetoric that would work.

He had discovered that the same autobiographical vein that he drew on for his fiction could be put to use for his political writing. The *Letters of Runnymede*, for example, were filled with the same sarcastic invective that he had used to entertain election mobs, but his best hits were those that had a personal flavour. He attacked the Whig premier Lord Melbourne for 'saunter[ing] over the destinies of a nation, and loung[ing] away the glory of an empire. Yet the swift shadows of coming events are assuredly sufficiently dark and ominous to startle from its indolence even "The sleekest swine in Epicurus' sty".'[40] He and the characters of his own novels had aimed at a lounging, sauntering Epicureanism for the last decade; if then the portrait of Melbourne was entertaining, it left its author vulnerable once again to the charge of hypocrisy.

Disraeli also assailed the Whig minister, Lord John Russell. Russell's book, *Memoirs of the Affairs of Europe*, Disraeli wrote was 'Busied with the tattle of valets and waiting-maids', just what the critics had also said of *Vivian Grey* and *The Young Duke*. Disraeli continued, 'This luckless production closed your literary career; you flung down your futile pen in incapable despair; and, your feeble intellect having failed in literature, your strong ambition took refuge in politics.'[41] Some would say the same of Disraeli himself. The risk of developing this sarcastic and satirical invective was that it might end in a bitter and self-destructive meditation on his own career. Was there any point in developing one's talent for sarcasm if it were always going to feed off one's own life, one's own failures and one's own self-consciousness? How was Disraeli to sustain himself in politics, to portray himself to himself and to the rest of the world as a confident success? That was the problem that faced him as he settled down in his new parliamentary career.

11

I Love Fame

Having had his first drubbing at the hands of the Irish, it was nice that he got excellent advice from a senior member, the Irish playwright Richard Sheil, about how to improve his chances of being heard in the House of Commons. Sheil told him to start by getting back on his horse. He could not show himself intimidated by the reversal of his first efforts. He must speak shortly and on matters of detail. 'Quote figures, dates, calculations. And in a short time,' Sheil told him, 'the House will sigh for the wit and eloquence, which they all know are in you; they will encourage you to pour them forth, and then you will have the ear of the House and be a favourite.'[1] Disraeli, hardly knowing how prophetic these words would be, took note of this advice and acted upon it.

His problem was partly curbing the giddy love of language that inspired his speaking. He told his sister that while speaking to constituents in Maidstone in 1838 he began his talks never knowing how his sentences would end.[2] This is the admission of someone who is used to speaking well, who knows his own ability to please and amuse. One can only launch into that sort of high-spirited extempore speaking with the confidence that comes from repeated successes around crowded and critical dinner tables.

The following year he told Sarah that members had rushed into an empty House in order to hear him speak.[3] He always exaggerated in his own favour, but there was evidence that he was already getting a reputation as an orator. This reputation rested, at first, on his amusement value, his ability to entertain. Sometimes, he was able on short notice to come up with a startling simile that got a good laugh. He replied to the Whig chancellor of the exchequer's criticism of his support of the Chartists by casting doubt on the Whigs' suitability to govern. He said that they were like flies in amber, it was difficult to know how the Whigs had got stuck into government in the first place.[4] In oratory he had begun to discover the link he knew existed but had never quite been able to find before: the link between the novelist's expertise in language and the politician's necessity to command the attention of colleagues and electors. The peculiar oratorical style he would develop was a link too between the society world of sardonic humour and the political necessity of effectively criticizing the policy of opponents.

However, it took him some time, and preparation, to find a topic on which he could speak as an expert and in detail. Moreover, he harmed his chances of gaining a hearing by desperate measures outside the House. In 1841 he decided to abandon Maidstone, after a dispute over unpaid election bills, in fact unpaid election bribery, a practice then common, and to stand for Shrewsbury instead. The question of his debts came up during the contest. His opponents collected reliable information on his creditors who had been forced to go through the courts to get their loans repaid. Even Monypenny concedes that Disraeli lied to the electors of Shrewsbury over the extent of his indebtedness. Later that year, when Sir Robert Peel was forming his first government, and Disraeli appealed to him for office on the basis of the attacks he had withstood at Shrewsbury on behalf of the party, Peel coldly turned him down. In the first several years of his parliamentary career, Disraeli was considered a brilliant liability rather than a steady asset.

Mortified by Peel's rejection and his having banked too early on his own indispensability, Disraeli determined that Peel should be sorry for having turned him down. For the first several years of Peel's government, Disraeli gave the prime minister his support from the backbenches. He also began to cultivate his potential as a speaker. He gave a long speech of two hours and twenty minutes advocating reform of the consular service in March 1842. He recounted facts and figures entirely from memory. Like a conductor who conducts without a score, this impressed his audience. Disraeli had combined a businesslike command of data with the dandy mannerism of not bothering about notes or papers.

Lord Palmerston, one of the most prominent Whig statesmen, gave the official reply to Disraeli and made cutting remarks about Disraeli having been disappointed when he sought office under Peel. He finished ironically by hoping for Disraeli's promotion another time. Here Disraeli could deploy his talent for off-the-cuff remarks as well as his courage in the face of a much bigger gun like Palmerston. He said in his reply:

> I must in the first place return my thanks to the noble Lord for his warm aspirations for my political preferment. Coming from such a quarter, I consider them auspicious. The noble Viscount is a consummate master of the subject, & if to assist my advancement, he will only impart to me the secret of his own unprecedented rise, & by what means he has continued to enjoy power under seven successive administrations, I shall have at least gained a valuable result by this discussion.[5]

The House loved that kind of mild but clever personal attack. They even respected the chutzpah that it took to reply in the face of Palmerston's putting into words the damaging gossip about Disraeli's disappointment under Peel.

Another example of his brilliance in speech came in 1844 when he combined surprising categories in his analysis of the Irish problem. You could not find a consistent answer, he said, to what the Irish question actually was when you approached different experts. 'One says it is a physical question; another a spiritual. Now it is the absence of the aristocracy, then the absence of railroads. It is the Pope one day, potatoes the next.'[6] By putting 'Pope' and 'potatoes' into the same sentence he had managed to trivialize an important religious official, and to make important the most ordinary, commonplace item of consumption. This reversal of expectations was a rhetorical gesture typical of dandies. The House roared with delight.

His official biographer claimed that even by 1844 Disraeli had still won no great standing in the House because of the 'element of pretentiousness and presumption in his speeches'.[7] Monypenny may have been right about the slowness of Disraeli's progress. What he missed is that the element of pretentiousness and presumption was Disraeli's genius, his métier, what made him amusing. Along with the pretentiousness went a candour and self-mockery that neutralized and compensated for it. For example, he spoke at Shrewsbury to his new constituents after he had ceased to represent Maidstone and defended some criticism he had made of his leader, Sir Robert Peel. He told them frankly what his motives were: 'I love fame; I love public reputation; I love to live in the eyes of the country; and it is a glorious thing for a man to do who has had my difficulties to contend against.'[8] What modern politician would confess so much? This kind of frankness would feel different and refreshing even today. Disraeli's appeal was that he could combine dandy nonchalance with strategic honesty about why he had sought a political career. Underlying both was a sense that he might have slightly been pulling his audience's leg and inviting them to join him in a smile or even a laugh at his own expense. His clothes began to change from dandy ostentation to a more sober costume at this period, but his speaking retained entertaining and engagingly candid reminders of his success in ballrooms.[9]

The decade of the 1840s was in many ways the most dramatic of Disraeli's political career. He went from being a backbench nobody to a position on the front bench leading one of the two major parties in a matter of a very few years. Although there was open hostility to him in all parts of the House, he managed to gain a hearing because of his undeniable and developing talent as an amusing speaker. There were other factors too that contributed to his rise – his heading a tiny group of attention-getting youths helped, as did his marriage to a rich widow who was as ambitious of success as he was, and, above all, his next two novels. The remainder of this and the subsequent two chapters consider how he used his writerly persona to romance the House of Commons. His growing standing in the House brought him increased contact with royalty and his pleasure in this helped sustain him through what were still tough times for him in Parliament.

Disraeli's provocative speaking attracted some of the young Tory members to him in the early 1840s. They were a stylish group, descended from prominent families and determined to make a mark on the House even though they were all still in their twenties. Although the group they formed was not large, their attachment to Disraeli was one of the features of his rise to renown in the 1840s. The most important of this group of young men was George Smythe, son of the sixth Viscount Strangford, a former diplomat whom Disraeli had known socially when he was younger. The Strangfords were nineteenth-century Turcophiles. George Smythe's father had served as ambassador in Constantinople and collected antiquities. He sold a magnificent male nude, 'the Strangford Apollo', to the British Museum in order to raise cash, as the Strangfords were always short of money.[10] George Smythe's younger brother, Percy, eventually the eighth Lord Strangford, also served in an official capacity in Turkey. He was for many years a confirmed bachelor and even kept his bachelor habits after he married. He surprised the people at an important diplomatic reception at the time of the Crimean War by showing up dressed as a woman. It was not a fancy-dress party. A recent commentator says that he wrote in an elegant, Oscar Wildean, epigrammatic vein.[11] Love of the East, collecting of male nudes, showing up in women's clothes – all this is circumstantial evidence to suggest that the Victorian Strangfords had a colourful, homoerotic vein.

George Smythe appears frequently in Disraeli's unpublished 'Reminiscences', which were probably written in the early 1860s. One of the reasons why the manuscript was unpublishable as he left it was because it included rude jokes, including one of Smythe's which turned on the similarity between 'Bulgaria' and 'buggery'. 'George Smythe, apropos of the Bulgarians, said of the Sclavonians [Slavs] "What an unfortunate race, that they have given names to the two most infamous conditions of humanity – Slaves & —."'[12]

George Smythe was born in 1818. He went to Eton, where he was nearly expelled, and to Cambridge. The biographer of one of Smythe's closest friends, Lord John Manners, describes Smythe in his youth as 'handsome and gay and debonair', 'careless' with his friends, 'a sinner' much influenced by Byron, and like the poet melancholy on the subject of friendship.[13] One surviving portrait of him suggests he was an attractive young man. [*See plate 9.*] According to his sister-in-law, he had an 'erratic and restless disposition'. He was also 'sensitive and highly-strung'.[14] He liked women and had numerous affairs. He also had romantic friendships from his schooldays and he remained extravagantly attached to this small band of men his own age. Though only in his twenties, he contested a parliamentary seat for Canterbury. His father had some property in the area and this recommended him to the constituents, but he was elected as a Tory MP mainly on borrowed money.

When Disraeli first noticed George Smythe, in 1842, he was twenty-four, or fourteen years Disraeli's junior, and a new member of the House of Commons. Disraeli wrote a letter about Smythe's maiden speech that is decidedly interested and alert. 'George Smythe made a most elaborate speech; very Radical indeed, and unprincipled as his little agreeable self, but too elaborate – his manner affected and his tone artificial, and pronunciation too; but still ability though puerile.'[15] These were the same criticisms often made of Disraeli's own speeches. Indeed, when Smythe came to congratulate Disraeli on his consular service speech later in 1842, Smythe paid similar attention, though in more positive terms, to Disraeli's manner, telling him that his delivery had not been 'stilted . . . [his] manner easy, a little nonchalant, and always tinged with sarcasm'.[16] One fairly recent biographer says that Disraeli saw in Smythe a fellow 'wit, rake and cynic'. Another observes that Smythe came to replace Bulwer and d'Orsay in the 1840s as Disraeli's most important friendship.[17] Disraeli's phrase to describe Smythe – 'his little agreeable self' – suggests a whiff of romantic attraction in the air.

Disraeli felt the warmth of Smythe's attention and the thrill of new disciples as early as the spring of 1842. By the autumn, Smythe and his friend, Alexander Baillie-Cochrane, had approached Disraeli in Paris, where he had gone to spend the recess. They proposed formalizing their party under his leadership. They would sit and vote together in the House of Commons, though they would not all insist on being given office if a post were offered to one of them. The group was never very big. Its only other regular member was a younger son of the Duke of Rutland, Lord John Manners. Nevertheless, they were noticed for several brief seasons in the press. What they wanted was a more principled, inspiring variety of Toryism than was on offer from Sir Robert Peel. They did not like Conservatism if it meant merely hanging on to wealth and possessions. Inspired by Romanticism, by Walter Scott, and by the religious revival of High Church Anglicanism called the Oxford Movement, they wanted a nobility more aware of its duties than its privileges. They wanted industrial and agricultural workers protected by old money rather than exploited by new capitalists. They loathed the utilitarians. They loved the Stuarts. They were called 'Young England'.

Disraeli had not overcome the distrust of most members of his own party. He was considered an entertaining speaker and not a great deal more at first. But it was precisely his slightly shady character that made him attractive to Smythe. Like many talented young men, he wanted to flout the opinion of backbenchers, not to court it, and in Disraeli he thought he had found a fellow soul.

Several commentators have noticed that there was a certain homoerotic bond that attached the principal members of the Oxford Movement to one another. This was true of Young England too, which drew some of its enthusiasm from the religious revival.[18] Perhaps this was nothing more than the sentimentality and emotionalism often to be found at English public schools and universities. The young men dedicated books and wrote romantic verse to one another. There was something between Smythe and Disraeli, though, that did not include the others. Smythe was one of the few who addressed him as 'Diz', a diminutive then used by few people. Monypenny, writing in 1912, admitted that Disraeli was attracted by Smythe's 'fascinating manners'. Long after the cooperation of Young England had come to an end, Disraeli was still intimate with Smythe and trying to help him find a rich wife. Smythe drank too much and was deeply in debt. It was as if Disraeli had found a younger version of himself to guide and protect. Smythe's father was unhappy about Disraeli's hold over his son. In a biographical retrospect, Emily Strangford, George Smythe's sister-in-law, was to say that Disraeli's influence over Smythe was 'unwholesome'.[19]

Like Disraeli, Smythe appears to have had an unusual relationship with his father. They disagreed over debts and politics and which women could be considered eligible matches. In 1844 Smythe wrote to his father saying: 'The misfortune of my life has been that I have not loved you only as a son, but with a jealous passion, which is always getting me into scrapes.'[20] This has a hint of the incestuous that adds to the general picture of Smythe being an excessively passionate young man. Smythe lived abroad after leaving Parliament and trying to make money in journalism. He sought out places renowned for dissipation like Venice and Egypt. He married a few weeks before he died at the age of thirty-nine. This was young to die, but it was also late to marry.

In his last year he wrote to Disraeli to say that he had heard that 'I was the only man who had never bored you'.[21]

All this is indicative that if he had now entered Parliament, Disraeli did not give up on the side of his nature that was drawn to attractive young men. In discipleship, he found a ready, perhaps less satisfying, but nevertheless an effective substitute for friendship between young equals. He could even use such disciples for more attention-getting ploys that advanced his own career without too much fear of embarrassment. The submerged erotic and affectionate bonds that tied Young England together proved that one could sustain and profit from one's writerly and dandy persona even when one shed the dandy clothes. But Disraeli now planned a further assault on Peel's leadership and the House's affections by writing anew.

12

He Interests Me

One recent historian has remarked that Disraeli's fiction always started from hopelessness.[1] The suggestion is that Disraeli's next two novels, *Coningsby* (1844) and *Sybil* (1845), both owed their origins to Disraeli's disappointment at being passed over for office by Sir Robert Peel. One of the best political historians now writing in Britain has also described Disraeli's writing as a 'retreat' into literature.[2] There is an element of truth in both these comments, but equally both miss how these next two novels were essential to Disraeli's rise to a position where he would not only be considered eligible for cabinet office, but also able to come within striking distance of the leadership of Peel's own party. 'After writing a book, my mind always makes a great spring,' Disraeli once said.[3] As he composed *Coningsby* late in the summer of 1843, he was not just licking his wounds, but preparing the ground for a principled attack on the leader of his own party. One of his greatest objections to Peel was his lack of imagination and his inability to inspire. *Coningsby* showed that Disraeli had imagination to spare and that he could still enjoy himself on the printed page, as the finished result makes clear. That enjoyment also gave him title to inspire. MPs might still be suspicious of ambitious novelists, as they were of Disraeli, but it was hard ultimately to resist someone who had so much racy self-confidence in orchestrating his characters.

Disraeli's first novel since entering Parliament is one of his best. Its hero, Harry Coningsby, has often been said to be modelled on George Smythe, but as in all of Disraeli's books the author himself is the real star. It is set in the period just after the passing of the 1832 Reform Bill. Lord Monmouth is a corrupt English marquess who lives abroad much of the year. He is bitter about having lost all his rotten boroughs in the recent Whig legislation and determined to be a duke. At the opening of the novel, he is set to meet his orphaned grandson, Harry Coningsby, for the first time. Although Monmouth is meant to represent the old, 'bad' aristocracy that Young England wanted to reform, Disraeli clearly loved Monmouth's old-style corruption. He is a most attractive villain.

The decoration of Monmouth's house, in St James's Square, lovingly described by the author, suggests indolence, luxury and indecency.

> The walls of the saloon, which were covered with light blue satin, held in silver panels portraits of beautiful women painted by Boucher. Couches and easy chairs of every shape invited in every quarter to luxurious repose, while amusement was afforded by tables covered with caricatures, French novels, and endless miniatures of foreign dancers, princesses, and Sovereigns.[4]

The French novels and the Bouchers on the wall indicate Monmouth's immorality, as does the fact that he has living with him Prince and Princess Paul Colonna. Colonna is an ageing dandy, his wife a beautiful courtesan. Their daughter, the sullen, adolescent and beautiful Lucretia, also lives there. The suggestion is that Monmouth has slept with both of the Colonnas, just as Lord Blessington did with both his wife and d'Orsay. Monmouth will later shock his most unshockable servant, Mr Rigby, by marrying Lucretia.

Another index of Monmouth's attractiveness to Disraeli is the fact that he holds a morning levée. He performed 'this ceremony in the high style of the old court, and welcomed his visitors in his bed'. Monmouth House is a mini-Versailles surviving and prospering in England despite the passage of the revolutionary Reform Bill. Disraeli wanted to live in that house on St James's Square himself.

Harry Coningsby's parents have both died prematurely, banished to a life of poverty and obscurity by wicked Monmouth. He is only twelve years old and newly arrived at Eton when summoned to meet the grandfather he has never known in London. Monmouth's valet calls him to enter his grandfather's room and Coningsby

> sprang forward with that desperation which the scaffold requires. His face was pale; his hand was moist; his heart beat with tumult . . . Music, artillery, the roar of cannon, and the blare of trumpets, may urge a man on to a forlorn hope; ambition, one's constituents, the hell of a previous failure, may prevail on us to do a more desperate thing – speak in the House of Commons; but there are some situations in life, such for instance as entering the room of a dentist, when the prostration of the nervous system is absolute.[5]

Disraeli is always at his funniest when he inserts large portions of autobiography and this passage is no exception. In the writing of *Coningsby* he was still recovering from the 'hell of a previous failure', his maiden speech.

Monmouth rose 'when his grandson entered, and leaning with his left hand on his ivory cane, he made Coningsby such a bow as Louis Quatorze might have bestowed on the ambassador of the United Provinces'.[6] Monmouth asked him how he liked Eton. Coningsby, frightened by this polished old man, asked himself: 'Where was the intervening link of blood between him and this superb and icy being?' He then sank 'into the chair which had been placed for him, and leaning on the table burst into tears'.

Monmouth is horrified. He is afraid that Coningsby is 'tender-hearted like his father. Another tender-hearted Coningsby! Unfortunate family! Degenerate race! He decided in his mind that Coningsby must be provided for in the Church.'[7] 'Tender-hearted' and destined for the Church are meant to suggest that Coningsby has the typical problem of Disraelian heroes: he is not manly enough. Disraeli's novels are frequently about the anxieties of effeminacy as well as the special powers, exploits and adventures of girly men. The fact that Monmouth recognized a strain of effeminacy in the Coningsbys indicates that long before genetic research, Victorians believed such conditions ran in the family.

There have been many keys to *Coningsby*, but it is generally agreed that Monmouth is Disraeli's portrait of Lord Hertford, a rich marquess recently died of extravagant living. There are certainly parallels between many characters and real people. The more remarkable fact is that Disraeli is himself all the characters at once. He is certainly Monmouth in his love of ceremony and sensual pleasures. Although Coningsby's Eton adventures recall those of George Smythe, they also recall Disraeli and Contarini's schoolboy fantasies. There are also paeans of praise to schoolboy friendship in the novel.[8] The climax of the Eton portion of the novel comes when Oswald Millbank, the son of a rich industrialist, is swimming naked, as schoolboys did then, in the Thames near a lock. He gets into trouble and slips under the water. Coningsby sees Millbank's distress, throws off his own clothes, jumps in the water and pulls him up on the riverbank. After this rescue in the buff, the two then become best friends.

Mr Rigby, the Tory MP and agent of Lord Monmouth, is usually identified as John Wilson Croker, agent of the real Lord Hertford and an enemy of Disraeli since he had been mixed up in the failure of Murray's newspaper, *The Representative*. Rigby writes 'slashing articles' in favour of aristocracy. One such article shows how the new penny post will be the ruin of the old nobility. This is clearly Disraeli making fun of himself as well. No one had written more slashing articles on behalf of the House of Lords than he in his old guise as secretary to Lord Lyndhurst. In Rigby he could attack an old literary enemy and send up his own partisan journalism at the same time.

Two female characters also evoke elements of Disraeli's own personality. Lady Everingham is the married sister of one of Coningsby's school friends and is supposed to correspond to a daughter of the Duke of Rutland. However, with her great expertise at conversation, at both talking and listening, she is Disraeli as well.[9] Mrs Guy Flouncey is an 'adroit flatterer' who insinuates herself in Lord Monmouth's favour.[10] No one was a more adroit flatterer than Disraeli himself. Her wonderful name, suggestive of flouncing in and out of grand rooms, must give a hint of how Disraeli saw himself.

Disraeli is also Prince Paul Colonna, 'a man still young; slender, not tall, very handsome, but worn; a haggard Antinous; his beautiful hair daily thinning; his dress rich and effeminate; many jewels, much lace; he seldom spoke, but was polished though moody'.[11] Disraeli had worried about his hair showing signs of age as long ago as 1830 when he set off for the Mediterranean. He dubbed Contarini, like Colonna, with the name of a prominent Italian aristocratic family. The continuities between *Coningsby* and his early years were still strong.

Above all and most importantly Disraeli is Sidonia, a dark, handsome stranger, whom Harry Coningsby meets in a wood just before a storm. Sidonia is Jewish and has Rothschild-style wealth, but he is unmistakably Disraeli too. A 'spirit of mockery' plays over what Sidonia says and believes in most passionately. You can never tell whether he is serious or not. Sidonia's conversation with Coningsby has in it a

repose amounting almost to nonchalance. If his address had a fault in it, it was rather a deficiency of earnestness. A slight spirit of mockery played over his speech even when you deemed him most serious; you were startled by his sudden transitions from profound thought to poignant sarcasm.[12]

This was the sort of thing said about Disraeli even in the prime of his political power. Henry Ponsonby, the Queen's private secretary, and an accurate judge of character, told his wife three decades later that he could never tell when Disraeli was telling the truth and when he was pulling his leg. Disraeli knew very well what the outside world's picture of him was and he put that into the character of Sidonia in the novel.

Disraeli writes of Sidonia that he was an expert on the court of the homosexual King of France, Henry III. 'It was of course well-known that Sidonia was not a marrying man.'[13] The possibility of finding a female loving partner in marriage 'Nature had denied to Sidonia'.[14] Disraeli adds that

> Such a temperament, though rare, is peculiar to the East. It inspired the founders of the great monarchies of antiquity, the prophets that the Desart has sent forth, the Tartar chiefs who have overrun the world; it might be observed in the great Corsican, who, like most of the inhabitants of the Mediterranean isles, had probably Arab blood in his veins. It is a temperament that befits conquerors and legislators, but in ordinary times and ordinary situations, entails on its possessor only eccentric aberrations or profound melancholy.

The passage is ambiguous, as any discussion of homosexuality had to be in an age when it was forbidden and sodomy was punishable by death. There are signs though that this is precisely what it was about. The fact that the Victorians regarded homosexuality as commonplace in Arab countries or eastern geography is the first clue. The other is Disraeli's 'Commonplace Book' for 1842, where he composed several lists: 'eunuchs', 'Heroes impotent, or averse to women' and men who had romantic feelings for other men. In the last of these lists Disraeli put Napoleon, the 'great Corsican' in the passage above. More controversial, the list also includes the name of Jesus, with a curious 'x' next to it, which may correspond to a prophet 'that the Desart sent forth'.

This list is an unusual record of men who can be grouped together on the basis of their reputation for having loved other men. One scholar of gay literature has pointed out that gay writers in the past have often made lists of fellow gay men in history so as to reassure and ground themselves in a glorious history as well as to offset the hatred of their contemporaries.[15] Composed in the years roughly contemporary with the gestation and composition of *Coningsby* Disraeli's list is as follows:

Alexander the Great
Julius Caesar
Hadrian
Socrates
Lord Bacon
x Shakespeare
Ld. Londonderry
Ld. George Sackville
Count Rousford [?]
x Gray
Byron
Anacreon
Marlowe
x Jesus
Alcibiades
Critias
Napoleon
Leo 10.
Euripides
Pope Julius II
Julius III
Cobbett

H. Walpole
Frederick
Cleveland
Salt
Bankes
Beckford
x F. Douce
Canning
Epaminondas[16]

Aside from the ambiguous 'x's and question mark, most of these figures had romantic or sexual contact with other men at some point in their lives. For example, to follow roughly in the same order as Disraeli's list, Alexander the Great was legendary for boy lovers. Suetonius speaks in his lives of the *Twelve Caesars* of rumours that Julius Caesar had slept with an eastern king. Hadrian loved Antinous. Both Socrates and Alcibiades speak warmly of men loving younger men or boys in Plato's *Symposium*, as do Anacreon and Critias in fragments of surviving love poetry. Shakespeare wrote many of his sonnets to men. Lord Castlereagh had become Marquess of Londonderry just before he committed suicide, having told the King he was about to be charged with an attempt to commit sodomy. Lord George Sackville resigned his command in the Army after a reverse at the battle of Minden and having been accused in the press of cowardice and sodomy. King James I had defended his male favourite, the Duke of Buckingham, by saying that Christ too 'had his John', and Christopher Marlowe had also suggested that Jesus and the apostle John were lovers. Frederick the Great was forced to watch his male lover executed in front of his eyes by a father who wanted to cure him of his proclivity for persons of his own sex. Byron and his friend William Bankes traded salacious gossip about loving men, while Bankes was actually caught twice, deciding after the second time to live in exile in Venice. Horace Walpole and William Beckford both loved other men. Epaminondas, the last on the list, with his friend Pelopidas, was part of the Theban Band or Sacred Band, a group of 150 pairs of male lovers that helped defeat Sparta in the fourth century before the Christian era.[17] The mixture of classical heroes and contemporary figures from the recent past is striking. It was a way of saying that, contrary to popular prejudice, those who had homoerotic passions were likely to be great men.

Sidonia makes direct reference to two of these, Frederick the Great and Epaminondas, in his first conversation with Harry Coningsby.[18] Coningsby is so impressed by Sidonia's manner of speaking and erudition that he develops a crush on the dark stranger. '"You seem to me a hero"' Coningsby says to Sidonia 'in a tone of real feeling, which, half ashamed of his emotion, he tried to turn into playfulness'.[19] Other people notice that Coningsby has romantic feelings for Sidonia. When he tells the party at a country house where he is staying that he has met 'a most extraordinary man' in the woods, Lady Everingham teases him, 'It should have been a heroine!'[20] Sidonia, for his part, when he re-encounters Coningsby at Lord Monmouth's asks 'rather earnestly' of one of his fellow guests: 'Who is that? . . . I met him once before, by chance; he interests me.'[21] There is warmth on both sides of this relationship, as there was between Disraeli and Smythe.

Sidonia underlines an important truth so far unexamined in the many volumes of Disraeli scholarship: for Disraeli his Jewishness and his sexuality were mixed together. They had a common eastern geography as the 'orient' was not only a way of referring to the Arabs, but also to the Jews for Victorians. We have already seen too how Turkey and Egypt and the rest of the eastern Mediterranean were places regarded by the Victorians as sites for what they thought of as homosexual 'vice'. Disraeli was defensive about both traits, as both generated prejudice among the Christian and conventional majority. It was true too that contemporary commentators regarded his showy effeminacy in dress and mannerism as partly 'Jewish' showiness and partly the sort of effeminacy associated with what they thought of as 'vicious' practices like sodomy. These two traits come together in the character of Sidonia, who has a militant pride in his Judaism, and speaks of its superiority to all other world religions, at the same time as he acquires a warmly romantic though evidently Platonic disciple in Coningsby.

At the end of the novel Coningsby marries his school friend Millbank's sister in one of those triangular relationships where the two men seem to need the intervening woman to express their love. Sidonia is left aloof and alone. In the novel, Disraeli nevertheless made great strides towards transforming himself from a dandy novelist who controlled drawing rooms to an adept satirical orator in the House of Commons. He gained a certain respect in the House of Commons by having written a bestseller, his first since *Vivian Grey*. Even men who were legendary lovers of women liked reading the book. Lord Lyndhurst told Disraeli that *Coningsby* was enjoyable because it was 'spicy' and 'malignant'.[22] In that era, men who had been at public schools and universities, though they might be devoted womanizers in their adulthood, still remembered the same-sex romanticism of their youth with affection. It was considered a normal phase of upper-class growing up. Men also liked a good gossip just as much as a rational argument or an earnest sermon or a businesslike statement of accounts, which were the rhetorical strategies of Disraeli's parliamentary rivals. Women bought and read the novel too. Even in the twentieth century, paperback versions of the novel appeared picturing an exquisite young man, his pinky extended and ivory-headed cane under his arm, to suggest the attractiveness to both men and women of a sexually ambiguous dandy. [*See plate 11.*]

Coningsby put forward Young England's argument for the revival of a dutiful aristocracy looking after the interests of ye olde peasantry, but Disraeli himself was sometimes sceptical about all this. When Coningsby made the Young England argument to his grandfather, Monmouth dismissed it as 'fantastical puerilities'.[23] Monmouth may be corrupt, but he speaks rough common sense. What Disraeli was really proposing in *Coningsby* was a new kind of conservatism where his own literary imaginativeness trumped Peel's boring legislative pragmatism. The medium was his message. The reading of a novel was about pleasure, enjoying Disraeli's scenes of upper-class life, schoolboy romances and parliamentary intrigues. Yes, there were long episodes in praise of the Jews and attacking the Whigs, but really the novel's purpose was to divert and amuse. These were the basis of Disraeli's conservatism. He was taking the dandy life devoted excessively to pleasure and boiling it down to an essential sauce: the point of his politics was to preserve as much amusement as possible for himself and his friends. The object of his novel was to aim for power. He did like the notion of an enlightened aristocracy and updated paternalism, but this should not obscure that the novel was both Disraelian fireworks meant to gain general attention and a 'heads up' rocket sent to startle Peel.

What Disraeli did not anticipate was that the discipline and experience of collaborating with parliamentary colleagues would begin to reshape him as much as he aimed to dominate them. This is evident in his next novel, *Sybil*, where he continued adapting the world of Beau Brummell to the England of the Chartists; and was in turn moulded by a political ethos in which he had never showed much interest before, as his was now a parliamentary world where poverty and the aftereffects of industrialism were uppermost concerns. Disraeli's response was to create one of his first working-class characters, 'Dandy Mick'. Before we see him at work making characters in this new fictional world, we must consider several women who began to have decisive influence in making his character.

13

I Poured into the Fictitious Scene
My Actual Sensations

Another of the features of Disraeli's rising stock in the political world during the 1840s was his marriage to a woman whom, ironically, many of his friends regarded as a liability. Disraeli had met Mary Anne Wyndham Lewis at a party of Bulwer's in 1832. He described her as 'a rattle and a flirt'. She was the daughter of an obscure naval lieutenant who died when she was young. Her husband, Wyndham Lewis, was Disraeli's first parliamentary colleague when he was elected for Maidstone in the summer of 1837. He was older than she was and they had no children. She also loved flashy clothes, had a capacity for making odd remarks and aspired to move up the social ladder, although she did not really fit into upper-class society. So she was able to meet Disraeli on common ground at several levels. When Wyndham Lewis died in March 1838, she inherited a substantial income of about £5000 per annum and a house in Grosvenor Gate, off Park Lane, the centre of fashionable London. Even before the death of her husband, Disraeli had begun to pay her special attention as the wife of a man to whom he was in debt for several thousand pounds over the election. He returned her flirtation, as he was accustomed to do with married women. The Lewises were both invited to Bradenham over the Christmas holiday. These sorts of invitation were Disraeli's way of manipulating his father's comfortable country house to impress his friends. Lyndhurst, Henrietta Sykes and d'Orsay had also been invited there in the early stages of his friendship with them. That Christmas Wyndham Lewis was otherwise engaged and only Mary Anne was able to come. When she left, Disraeli wrote her a letter in January 1838 saying that everyone at Bradenham missed her very much, and that everyone was 'dull and dispirited, almost as dull and dispirited as you think me'.[1] It was his racy assumption of intimacy that charmed Mary Anne at once.

Monypenny said the friendship between them was 'cordial from the first, and gradually became tinged with a sort of mock devotion'.[2] Wherever Disraeli mocked, he was at his most serious and most characteristic. He loved playing upon the line between mockery and sincerity. This is clear from their correspondence after her husband died in March 1838. They exchanged confidences from the start, even though she warned him she wanted a year to elapse from her husband's death before any public romance between them. Nevertheless, she teased him jealously about spending so much of his time with Lady Londonderry, one of London's great hostesses who had taken him up and invited him to all her parties once he had some success as a novelist. He replied defending himself, and mocking his own devotion to aristocratic ladies at the same time. 'I do not know what you mean by passing "*so much*" of my time with Lady Londonderry: I do not pass any more time with her than with Lady anybody else.' He concluded by taking a swipe of his own at her: 'I hope you are amused at Clifton. You do not appear to have any time to write; at least not to me.'[3]

By November 1838 in a letter to her he was using an affectionate formula similar to that he used with his sister: 'I can tell you nothing but I love you.'[4] Throughout that autumn at Bradenham, he was writing a tragedy for the stage, *Count Alarcos*. Never one to be modest, he also said he hoped the play would revive Shakespearean drama in England. In October he told Mary Anne he was working on the play regularly from nine to two every day. These were very early hours for him, as he usually did not get up before noon. He wrote her name in large letters on a card and set it up in front of him on his desk. He also told her that

> I poured into the fictitious scene my actual sensations, and the pages teem with passages which you will not read without emotion, for they came from my heart and commemorate my love, my doubt, my misery . . . I believe in [Mary Anne's promised visit to Bradenham] as men believe in the millennium.[5]

If she had only been able to read then what he was writing, she might have had her doubts.[6] It is possible that because of what Rosina Bulwer had told her about Disraeli and her husband, with whom Rosina was by that time in acrimonious dispute, Mary Anne had doubts enough already.[7]

Count Alarcos is about loveless marriage, murder and mayhem. The story is certainly about love, but it was about Disraeli's inability to exorcise his love for his former friend, John Gibson Lockhart. Lockhart's story about a Spanish nobleman had appeared more than a decade previously in *Ancient Spanish Ballads, Historical and Romantic*.[8] The story's hero, Count Alarcos, has been forced into a tactical marriage during his exile from the Spanish court of Burgos. Alarcos returns to Burgos to find his first and true love, the king's daughter, still committed to him. The king tells Alarcos he must murder his wife in order to marry his daughter and eventually inherit the throne. Alarcos does kill his wife, but the king's daughter dies struck by lightning. Alarcos kills himself. The end.

As usual there is a good deal of autobiography here. The king's daughter explains to Alarcos why his exile was harder on her, kept to the palace in Burgos, than it was on him far away: 'A wounded heart beats freer in the desart; 'tis the air of palaces that chokes it.'[9] This refers to Disraeli's own desert exile from London in 1830–1, where he eventually recovered from broken-hearted melancholia and depressed perplexity about his sexuality.

Similarly, Alarcos explains his tactical marriage in exile by saying that he had wanted 'to fix a bar betwixt me and defeat'.[10] Disraeli looked upon his position with Mary Anne in a similarly tactical way: he wanted to marry Mary Anne for her money in order to avoid financial disaster. He had finally made it into Parliament, but his debts were so crushing and his position in the world so tenuous without an income that it must have still felt sometimes like defeat.

Perhaps Mary Anne read this and did not see the clear parallels to Disraeli's own experience. Or, perhaps she saw exactly what he was saying. Early in 1839 he and Mary Anne had a confrontation. He wanted a clear understanding that they would marry and marry as soon as possible. She wanted the year's public mourning after Wyndham Lewis's death respected. He wrote her a letter in February saying all of London regarded him as a gigolo and she could no longer keep him in this humiliating position. He admitted that he had begun to court her for her money, but said he now knew she had a great deal less than he thought. The fact that, under Wyndham Lewis's will, the money was only hers for her lifetime was no added incentive to marry her. He ended his high drama letter with a line similar to the impromptu remark with which he had closed his disastrous maiden speech: 'But the time will come when you will sigh for any heart that could be fond, and despair of one that can be faithful.'[11] That slightly hysterical ultimatum − 'the time will come when . . .' − which he had also addressed to a hostile House of Commons suggests a parallel in Disraeli's unconscious mind between political and romantic success. The writer and the orator, the lover and the friend, the prospective parliamentary hero and the aspiring husband were alike ambitious of worldly recognition. He would be damned if he would accept defeat, so he menaced Mary Anne, just as he had menaced the House, with the prediction that she would regret it if she rejected him.

It worked. She gave in. She agreed to marry him, though in the end, they had to wait as there were deaths in her family and he needed to finish the parliamentary session. They married in August 1839 and their letters home from their honeymoon suggest their happiness together was not feigned. He genuinely liked women's company, knew how women thought and could play up to Mary Anne's romantic sensibilities through inventive declarations of his affection. He also blossomed in the company of people who genuinely liked him. She looked after him, made sure he was well fed and well clothed. As she was without formal education of her own, his bookish knowledge made her respect and rely on him. She was just as ambitious of social recognition as he was, so quite willing to assist him in his conquest of the political world. He told his mother in a rare letter to her after his marriage, 'I am the happiest of men.' To Isaac, Mary Anne reported from their honeymoon journey that she too was happy. She had already thoroughly entered into her new husband's cheerful hedonism: 'We exemplify life's finest tale – to eat – to drink – to sleep – love and be loved.'[12]

At the beginning of their marriage, they enjoyed sexual contact with one another. He told her that when arriving at Bradenham in December 1838 with her mother she should leave her hand ungloved so he could touch her.[13] When he had the flu, he told her he wished she were in bed with him, though perhaps that was more of a longing for maternal comfort than for sexual contact.[14] When they were parted from one another in 1842, he told her he missed her when he woke up and found her pillow was empty.[15] Perhaps he had even renounced for a time his younger enthusiasm for sexual contact with men. He told Beckford while he was wooing Mary Anne that his 'youthful feelings of poetical enthusiasm' were now a dream that was past.[16] As 'poetical enthusiasm' was one of those ambiguous phrases that for Disraeli could mean love of young men as well as love of poetry, it is possible he meant that marriage would 'fix a bar' between him and the world he had formerly enjoyed along with Beckford.

As soon as they got back from their honeymoon on the Continent in 1839, Mary Anne began to be a most useful wife. She helped him give political dinners for Members of Parliament in February 1840. He told Sarah proudly that he had asked nearly sixty MPs and forty had come. Mary Anne was making it possible for him to entertain at his own table and thus to court MPs socially as well as in the House of Commons. Her house was in Mayfair, facing Hyde Park, and he was able to attract prominent colleagues to their lighted windows on grey evenings with the promise of a sumptuous dinner. She was also essential, as he readily admitted, to his political victory at Shrewsbury in the summer of 1841.[17] The shopkeepers and tradesmen who were among his most important constituents seemed to like Mary Anne almost better than they did him and one of them told him that his 'domestic character' did him much good in the town.[18] He was not above milking this for all it was worth. When he had to be separated from Mary Anne on their anniversary in August 1844, he found that telling his constituents of this separation produced a great sentimental effect.[19] Two years later, he told a man who was considering divorcing his wife that it would be a mistake. You may live a wild life when young, he wrote, but as you get older your wife helps you enjoy society and achieve promotion.[20] Thus, Disraeli was very much alive to the worldly and career benefits that Mary Anne brought him. That he also loved her and enjoyed her company were added attractions. Theirs was a successful alliance not in spite of his sexual ambiguity, his dandyism or his wild youth, but because he now realized that marriage was essential to the achievement of the ambitions he had conceived in that wild youth. He still liked grand parties and female companionship as well as he sympathized with how women viewed the world. This made theirs a gay marriage in many senses of the word.

As an MP Disraeli had official contact for the first time with the Queen. Historians have often written about Disraeli's devotion to the monarchy as if it were a weakness. This is to miss how one of the attractions of parliamentary prominence for him was the promise it carried of access to the court. His personality cannot be understood properly or sympathetically unless we take seriously the magnetic pull of the court on his personal compass. In these years he was mainly a privileged spectator at royal events. His commentary on these events is especially sparkling. From an early stage of his career he had an eye for ceremony and understood the attractions of state spectacle. The coronation of Queen Victoria took place in June 1838. Disraeli began by telling his sister that he would not go as he did not have the right dress. He did not want to get up at eight o'clock in the morning, dress like a 'flunky', sit in Westminster Abbey all day, and hear a sermon by the Bishop of London anyway.[21] His excuse for not going is telling: if he could not dress properly himself, and be a part of the show, he did not want to go.

Then at two o'clock in the morning on the day of the coronation itself, someone loaned him the proper court costume for a Member of Parliament and he was delighted to go. His description of the ceremony in a letter to Sarah employed three superlatives.

> The pageant within the Abbey was without exception the most splendid, various, and interesting affair at which I ever was present . . . [I]t far exceeded my expectations. The Queen looked very well, and performed her part with great grace and completeness, which cannot in general be said of the other performers; they were always in doubt as to what came next, and you saw the want of rehearsal. The Duke [of Wellington] was loudly cheered when he made his homage. Melbourne looked very awkward and uncouth, with his coronet cocked over his nose, his robes under his feet, and holding the great sword of state like a butcher.[22]

The Whig premier, Lord Melbourne, was the object of all Disraeli's political scorn at that moment, so it is not surprising that he should be critical of his performance. The two also had far-reaching differences in their attitudes towards ceremony. Contrast, for example, Disraeli's enthusiasm for the event in this letter to his sister with Melbourne's defence in the House of Lords of the government's deciding to spend as little as possible on the Queen's crowning. He made the typical Whig references to royal cere-mony as regrettable window-dressing for the more important parts of the constitution. Coronations, he said, were 'mere shades and mere shadows . . . mere vain pageants, useless and idle'.[23]

A fellow young Tory MP, William Ewart Gladstone, on the other hand, made a religious critique of the ceremony. He thought the religious part should have been longer, even though, as it was, he was in the Abbey for almost eight hours. He also wanted chanting and more High Church practices put into the ceremony. For the coronation to be improved, Gladstone thought it needed more religious earnestness and historical associations.[24] Disraeli's criticism, however, was that the procession was a failure because there was 'not enough music or troops'.[25] Better than Melbourne or Gladstone, Disraeli understood this was a colour-ful display, a theatrical event. Yes, it had to be historically accurate and religion was not to be overlooked, but more than anything it had to be enjoyable, if not thrilling, for everyone involved. More brass bands, more men in uniform, fewer premiers pretending to be butchers were what he wanted. Of the three, Disraeli's instincts for royal spectacle were the most attuned to popular demands. If he understood what the people wanted from royal ceremony, it was because Disraeli himself was an unashamed enjoyer of such spectacles.

Disraeli admired his friend Lady Londonderry who swept up the nave of the Abbey at the coronation looking like 'an Empress' in all her jewels. He also identified with the Duchess of Sutherland who 'walked, or rather stalked, up the Abbey like Juno; she was full of her situation'.[26] Though slightly malicious in his description of her manner, more than anything he wanted to be her in that procession up the centre of the Abbey. His colleagues caught this whiff of envy in his attitude. Lord Norreys teased Disraeli and his Maidstone colleague about their fancy-dress-on-loan when they emerged from the Abbey and waited for their carriage. He affected to mistake them for provincial officials, notorious for their overly dressy and fanciful uniforms: 'Make way for the Maidstone Sheriffs!' Norreys cried. Disraeli admitted to his sister that it was a good joke, 'tho' rather annoying'.[27]

A few weeks after the coronation, the Londonderrys gave a memorable party at their new house in Park Lane. Disraeli was delighted to have been invited. His friendship with Frances Anne Londonderry got him in the door. She was about his age and an heiress in her own right to vast coal-rich estates in the north of England. She always affected great superiority and wore twice as many jewels as every other lady of her rank. Disraeli adored that icy manner and those liquid jewels. Once he arrived at her coronation party, he enjoyed it to the hilt. The Londonderrys had made up in bands and military men what the coronation processions lacked.

> It was the finest thing of the season. Londonderry's regiment being reviewed, we had the band of the 10th [Hussars] playing on the staircase. The whole of the said staircase (a double one) being crowded with the most splendid orange trees, and cape Jessamine [*sic:* Jasmine] . . . The banquet was in the gallery of Sculpture; it was so magnificent that everybody lost their presence of mind. Sir James Graham said to me, that he had never in his life seen anything so gorgeous. 'This is the grand seigneur indeed' he added. I think it was the kindest thing possible of Fanny asking me, as it was not to be expected in any way. The splendor of the uniforms was remarkable.[28]

That everyone 'lost their presence of mind' in the blasts of music and jasmine on the staircase was what Disraeli loved best: the capacity of a well-staged party to break up social conventions, to overwhelm people's social frigidity with the warmth of unusual sights, sounds and smells.

In the year after Disraeli married Mary Anne, the Queen married her German cousin, Prince Albert. Disraeli went up to Buckingham Palace with the rest of the House of Commons to congratulate her. Once again he had on his borrowed court costume. His friend Lord Ossulston, who had a collection of Sèvres and invited Disraeli to select dinners, was the opposite of Lord Norreys. Ossulston pleased him by saying that he must always wear court dress, as he looked 'a very Charles II' in it. Late seventeenth-century moral easiness combined with formality in deportment was always attractive to him. The difference between him and others like him was that in that era of Evangelical earnestness, where stiff middle-class morality ruled all, Disraeli was franker in flouting it than others. To love being taken for a Restoration courtier in the Victorian era was a little like espousing eighteenth-century nepotism in a twentieth century of meritocracy and egalitarianism. Disraeli did love the glamour of the Restoration, but he also liked the shock value of saying so in an era when Restoration manners were considered morally reprehensible.

He was also franker in admitting his admiration for the monarchy than his contemporaries. He thought pretty much everyone was interested in royalty, but everyone refused to talk about it. As the Queen's marriage approached, he sent off an ironic letter to Sarah in which he referred to a rude song, supposedly sung by the Queen's fiancé.

> Everything is very dull: nothing is thought of but the Queen's marriage, and nobody ever mentions it, unless the balladsingers, who may be heard in every quarter chaunting:
>
> They say I'm a ninny
> and not worth a ginny [guinea]
> But Vic, she declares I'm a trump . . .
> So much for the spirit of loyalty in 1840.[29]

That everyone was thinking of the coming ceremony, but nobody was talking about it, street singers excepted, made him think there was something wrong with loyalty in his era. There was a sort of national hypocrisy in everyone thinking of the marriage and no one mentioning it.

This hypocrisy manifested itself in off-colour humour. When in 1841 Disraeli was mentioned as a possible candidate for office in Sir Robert Peel's government, *The Satirist*, a periodical that was often critical of Disraeli, said he was good for nothing except to be groom of the stole.[30] In the medieval past this was a nobleman who took away the king's chamber pot, or stool, or 'stole' in the morning. *The Satirist* was calling Disraeli a brown-noser, a flatterer, someone who was too interested in courts and kings. This detracted, they would have suggested, from his status as citizen or public servant. They were making the old republican critique of courtiers as bending servants of despots rather than as upstanding, masculine citizens of the state. He thought it was only human to like kings and colour, and that there was nothing wrong with living for power in the House of Commons at the same time. The monarchy was the dignified or the 'dressy' part of the constitution and his youthful love of dressing up now prepared him to think about the part that royalty might play in his own political fortunes. His evident love of royalty, like his Jewishness, exposed him to taunts and teases. This was a condition he had been learning to accept and if possible to accentuate for his own benefit.

14

So Many Gentlemen, So Little Gentleness

While Disraeli had made a good and politically useful marriage, while he enjoyed an MP's invitation to royal
occasions, he grew restive in the later 1840s that neither Peel nor
other senior members of the House of Commons were giving
him the recognition he wanted. He decided to follow *Coningsby*
with a new novel that was openly critical of the aristocratic establishment that was being slow to mark his genius. In truth, Disraeli
always had a love-hate relationship with the British aristocracy and
in these years 'hate' was in the ascendant. George Buckle, a
former editor of *The Times*, took over the six-volume official
biography of Disraeli when William Monypenny died, having
completed only the first two volumes. Buckle observed that
Disraeli's satire of high society became more bitter as his trilogy of
novels went on: Disraeli enjoyed society in *Coningsby*, made fun of
it in *Sybil*, while he really 'flout[ed] and trample[d] upon it' in
Tancred.[1] The change of tone becomes evident on the first page of
Sybil where he has inserted a quote from the Tudor bishop, Hugh
Latimer, known for his interest in the poor, saying 'There never
were so many Gentlemen, and so little Gentleness.' The novel is
about English gentlemen behaving badly.

The novel opens on the eve of the Derby in 1837. He describes a gentlemen's club where bets on the horse race are being taken and the men are sitting down to dinner. 'The seats on each side of the table were occupied by persons consuming, with a heedless air, delicacies for which they had no appetite.'[2] Here is another difference from the earlier fiction. It was seldom that Disraeli did not enjoy a dinner, but in *Sybil* aristocratic surfeit is more his theme than hunger for their company.

The different tone continues when Disraeli describes a young man 'of very tender years, and whose fair visage was as downy and blooming as the peach from which with a languid air he withdrew his lips'. Another man asks this youth why he was not at a party. '"I never go anywhere," replied the melancholy cupid, "everything bores me so."' A little while later, the same young man, Alfred Mountchesney, says 'in a tone of elegant anguish', 'I feel so cursed blasé!' He has a friend, who is his 'companion and brother in listlessness. Both had exhausted life in their teens, and all that remained for them was to mourn, amid the ruins of their reminiscences, over the extinction of excitement.'[3] Even the hero of the novel, Charles Egremont, has acquired at Eton a somewhat repellent philosophy from his schoolfellows: 'To do nothing and get something formed a boy's ideal of a *manly* career.'[4] The dandies and Old Etonians whose style Disraeli used to love to emulate are now wastrels. They are not painted in such a way that one wants to slide on to the sofa next to them, as they certainly were in *The Young Duke* or *Coningsby*. The fact that he has fallen into the critical mode of his usual opponents by suggesting that these boys are not 'manly' alerts us to the fact that, like Alcibiades, he has switched sides.

There are two aristocratic families who dominate the book, the Marneys and the de Mowbrays. In both cases the humble, even criminal origins of the family contrast with the pretensions and grandeur of the current incumbents. Charles Egremont's brother is the Earl of Marney. The Marney peerage originated in a canny servant who bribed King Henry VIII with baubles and accumulated valuable church property after Henry's dissolution of the monasteries. The Marneys got a barony in the seventeenth century and persuaded the College of Arms to certify the fiction that they were actually a Norman family who had come over with William the Conqueror. They supported the Stuarts during the Civil War but changed sides and supported William of Orange when they thought James II might take back their property that had once belonged to the Church. William made them earls. Disraeli concludes his indictment by remarking that

> from that time until the period of our history, though the Marney family had never produced one individual eminent for civil or military abilities, though the country was not indebted to them for a single statesman, orator, successful warrior, great lawyer, learned divine, eminent author, illustrious man of science, they had contrived, if not to engross any great share of public admiration and love, at least to monopolize no contemptible portion of public money and public dignities.[5]

Although the Marneys made their money from monastic lands once devoted to holy and charitable purposes, the current earl is greedy, grasping and ungenerous. He is the antithesis of a life devoted to prayer and poverty.

The de Mowbray family is just as bad. Their peerage derived from a waiter in a St James's club. The waiter impressed a member who was going out to serve as an official in Madras. He took on the young waiter as a sort of page or valet. During the six-month voyage there, the waiter transformed himself from valet to private secretary. He made money through a rice monopoly in a time of famine, inherited in addition the estate of the official he originally went out to serve and returned to England immensely rich. He bought another estate, purchased seats in the House of Commons, voted with the King's ministers in Parliament and was eventually rewarded with a peerage. The venal heralds once again 'discovered' that the club waiter, whose name was John Warren, descended from a Norman family; using their authority he changed the family name to Fitz-Warene. He became Earl de Mowbray for supporting the government of the day through two mismanaged catastrophes: first in their prosecution of the King's divorce from Queen Caroline, and second in their violent repression of a peaceful demonstration of workers at St Peter's Fields in Manchester, later known as Peterloo. If this were not bad enough, the waiter's son, who became the second earl, 'was the most aristocratic of breathing beings'. In his fake Gothic castle 'his coat of arms was emblazoned on every window, embroidered on every chair, carved in every corner'.[6]

Disraeli may have loved a lord, but he was also one of the most pitiless anatomists of aristocratic corruption there ever was. He saw himself as a latter-day Edmund Burke, who famously turned on his grandee patrons and reminded them of their humble origins when they treated him badly in the late eighteenth century.[7] Disraeli was conscious of the parallel between what he was doing in *Sybil* and the attack Burke had made on his aristocratic patrons. It is evidence of Disraeli's confidence in his own genius that he should compare himself at the age of forty-one and without apology to someone of Burke's stature, a great of the previous century's political thinkers.

Sybil, like *Coningsby*, is a call to the aristocracy to remember that they have duties as well as privileges. Here, however, for the first time he shows how bad conditions are for the working classes. He describes rural hovels, urban slums and the injustice of having to buy goods at the factory shop. The best of his working-class characters is a young man called Dandy Mick.

He was about sixteen, with a lithe figure, and a handsome, faded, impudent face. His long, loose white trousers gave him height; he had no waistcoat, but a pink silk handkerchief was twisted carelessly round his neck, and fastened with a very large pin, which, whatever were its materials, had unquestionably a very gorgeous appearance.[8]

Dandy Mick also has 'a mischievous blue eye'. He is attractive and a flirt, who teases a butcher woman in Mowbray market. His 'movements were as nimble as his words' and the butcher woman retorts to his tease, 'It's very well known you're no Christian, and who'll believe what you say?'[9] In short, Dandy Mick is a lot like Disraeli himself: a fancy dresser, who has a way with words, is not entirely to be believed and, as a Christianized Jew, rather difficult to make out from a religious point of view. He completes the picture by telling the reader that Dandy Mick has a best friend whose name is Devilsdust.

The novel is centrally about the enlightenment of Charles Egremont, who sees that the aristocracy must change its way. The climax is a showdown of the dandies. Dandy Mick leads a mob of angry agitators and workers on a march to Mowbray Castle. There, languid Alfred Mountchesney, who has married one of the Fitz-Warene daughters for her money, tries in vain to hold them off. Disraeli imagined the revolutionary scene that all Victorian middle- and upper-class readers feared: a violent confrontation between the rich and the poor. Here it is nearly a rape scene as the rich women are in a grand but defenceless country house in the midst of its rural park with only a man of fashion to protect them. There is immense prescience in this too, as the revolutionary year of 1848 when workers and nationalists allied in violent confrontations with the upper classes on the Continent was still several years in the future.

Mowbray Castle burns. The Marney peerage goes to a newly enlightened Charles Egremont. The Mowbray lands go by an obscure legal deed to the heroine of the title, Sybil, a nun-like figure who is always breaking into religious song. She marries Egremont, thus uniting the Marney and de Mowbray estates. Egremont's first act as the new Lord Marney is to bring two deserving boys together. He establishes Dandy Mick and

Devilsdust together in business; both marry their sweethearts from the local pub.

This novel is not Disraeli at his best. His sense of grievance or hurt, his playing the part of an injured Burke, make the novel less fun than some of his previous works. Nor is he very good at adopting a tone which is half Karl Marx and half Charles Dickens to examine the relations between rich and poor. Somewhere lurking in the background of the novel is Lord Stanley's comment to Sir Robert Peel in 1841 when Peel was considering putting Disraeli into his government. According to one report Stanley had said to Peel, 'if that scoundrel were taken in he [Stanley] would not remain himself'.[10] This or something like it must have been reported back to Disraeli. He believed that his oratorical abilities entitled him to a place on the Conservative front benches of the House of Commons, but that the prejudice of the aristocracy and country gentlemen kept him out.

Following the publication of *Sybil* in May 1845, and its successful sale, he told his sister that he and Mary Anne were being invited to all sorts of smart parties. The great hostess Lady Jersey was 'in a stupor of malice and astonishment' to see them everywhere, while his old friend Lady Londonderry, who disliked Mary Anne, was nevertheless being 'sufficiently courteous' to her.[11] He had less interest in going out now, though, than he once had. He remarked in a later novel that after bachelorhood was over, going out had fewer charms and was more of a bore.[12] There are also fewer comments in the letters of this period about hangovers, and going out less probably helped him drink less. *Sybil* won him more attention, and kept the disciples of Young England admiringly pleased with him, but the social success did not satisfy him. He had taken the pulse of the zeitgeist and seen that he could no longer simply celebrate upper-class society, but his success in doing something different gave him little pleasure.

Less interest in society meant more time for politics, bad news for Sir Robert Peel. Disraeli had been generally loyal to Peel from the Conservative backbenches, even though he had been disappointed in his ambition for office. Disraeli's natural tendency, however, was to criticize. To ask him to be loyal to a leader who had shown no particular affection for him personally was to ask a lot from him. Further, two new successful novels under his belt gave him a new confidence in his abilities and a willingness to aim at targets even he would not have dared to oppose so openly before now. When Peel broke with his natural supporters among the owners of agricultural property in 1845, and decided to repeal the legislation called the Corn Laws that artificially propped up grain prices, he offered Disraeli an irresistible opportunity. There had long been a middle-class and urban Anti-Corn Law League that argued the Corn Laws were unfair. These were men who generally supported Peel's opposition. So it was a surprise for Peel to change his mind and side with them against the upper-class owners of property who formed the usual mainstay of his own Conservative party. Peel's cabinet refused to back him. After a Whig attempt to form a ministry failed, Peel came back into office, but without one of the most prominent men from his own side, Lord Stanley, the future Earl of Derby. Stanley represented a small but powerful, largely inarticulate group of MPs who were called Protectionists, because they deemed the economic protection of agriculture to be fundamental to the wellbeing not just of property owners, but of all who lived and worked on the land. In that era people in the countryside who fitted that description were only just ceasing to be a majority of the population and they were still a considerable group.

Disraeli had a field day. He stood up in the House of Commons and made the comparison between what Peel was doing in 1845, and what he had done in 1828, when he had once before decided against the bulk of opinion in his own party that the civil disabilities imposed on Roman Catholics could no longer be sustained. The result was the legislation in 1829 that allowed Catholics to sit in Parliament. Disraeli had been sympathetic to the repeal of the Roman Catholic disabilities, but he abandoned political consistency in a bid to get the ear of the Conservative members of the House of Commons. Disraeli declared on learning of Peel's intentions towards the Corn Laws that Protectionism was in the same state as Protestantism in 1828. He meant that both were under attack. He said a Conservative government, meaning Peel's reforming ministry, was an 'organized hypocrisy' because it was doing just the opposite of conserving what Peel had pledged at the outset of his government to support. He recalled both of these phrases in a memoir he wrote five years after the event. Nevertheless, the words were good and produced an excellent effect. They generated support for him among the Protectionist ranks. They are more evidence of how with a sneer or a surprising alliteration he was converting a love of fancy dress into a love of showy speech. He even converted Peel's defence of the repeal of the Corn Laws into an ironic juxtaposition of an unimaginative speaker, Peel, and an apprehensive, Protectionist audience. In one of Peel's characteristic speeches defending abolition of the Corn Laws 'he entered into a dissertation on the duties of foreign brandy and foreign sugar; while visions of deserted villages and reduced rentals tortured his neighbours'.[13] Disraeli's oratory worked because he could both amuse himself and others with such writerly fancies.

Peel knew how to fight back. When he reconstructed the government following Stanley's departure, he offered a desirable undersecretaryship at the Foreign Office to Disraeli's friend and Young England colleague, George Smythe. Smythe accepted. Years later Disraeli confessed to Prince Metternich, living in exile in England following the 1848 revolutions that had toppled him from power in Vienna, that the loss of Smythe contributed to the violence of his attack on Peel. Disraeli wrote in an exceptionally frank manner to Metternich about his relationship to Smythe.

He is a young man of brilliant abilities, and once my aid-de-camp; but Sir Robert bought him away from me. He is still a great favourite of mine; if no longer a confidential friend, and

I am not very angry now about his defection, as he only
enjoyed his office for five months, at the end of which time, I
turned out both himself and his new patron. I think his loss
rather sharpened my lance.[14]

In his greatest assault on Peel's policy he spoke for three hours
with lance so effectively sharpened that Peel had to rely on the
Whig and Radical opposition to pass repeal, rather than on the
bulk of his own Conservative supporters. Peel was so stung by
Disraeli's attack that he stood up and wondered aloud why, if
Disraeli had always been such a consistent opponent of his policy,
as Disraeli had claimed, he had applied for office in 1841. Disraeli
replied that this was untrue. He had never been an applicant for
office.

Disraeli's attack on the leader of his own party was reckless, but
denying that he had applied for office was sheer foolhardiness, as
Peel could have proved easily that Disraeli was not telling the
truth. Lord Rosebery, a future prime minister and another disciple of Disraeli's, tells the story in his life of Peel that Peel had
stayed up all night looking through his papers trying to find
Disraeli's begging letter. If he had found it, Disraeli would have
been destroyed. Either he never found it, or, as Lord Blake
believed, he decided not to use it.

As it was, the repeal of the Corn Laws passed but the
Conservative party was divided into two impotent halves. A
reforming, modernist wing clung to Peel; a reactionary
Protectionist wing, stirred up by Disraeli, but generally loyal to no
one but themselves, remained behind. When Peel lost a key vote
on Irish legislation and resigned, Disraeli was left as one of the
natural leaders of this Protectionist rump. Even so, Stanley, who
led the Protectionists from the Lords, though willing to acknowledge Disraeli's talent, was not prepared to give him full leadership
in the House of Commons for some years. In addition Disraeli
was now lumbered with a policy that was a sure-fire vote-loser,
and condemned, apart from brief periods, for nearly twenty years

to opposition. Repeal of the Corn Laws was popular, and though Disraeli had raised his value with the silent majority of landowners and farmers, he had espoused a policy that would get him nowhere with the vast majority of the country. He had gambled on oratorical brilliance and short-term applause. He had won a brief spell in the limelight and a dubious place in parliamentary history for bringing down the leader of his own party. The longer-term prospects were bleak indeed.

15

Recklessness as a Principle of Action

Having destroyed his leader, and having gained only equivocal advantage in the quasi-leadership of a seemingly doomed party in the House of Commons, Disraeli began composition of the last in his trilogy of political novels. Buckle described *Tancred* as a 'final fling' before he settled down to the greater gravity that leadership in the House of Commons would impose on him.[1] Although there were continuities between *Coningsby*, *Sybil* and *Tancred*, the political purpose of the trilogy had disappeared as the Young England group of young men had dissolved along with Peel's government.

> And *Tancred* strikes the reader less as the accomplishment of a political purpose, than as a sudden revolt of the author against the routine and hollowness of politics, against its prejudice and narrowness; and as an assertion of his detachment and superiority to it all by the glorification of his race and by the proclamation of the mystic ideas, inherited from the Jews, which marked him out from the commonplace mediocrities around him.[2]

The novel seems to have been born of a post-Peel despair about his future. He began it in a frame of mind, very much like failure, with which he also began novels like *Vivian Grey*, following the disaster with *The Representative*, or *Henrietta Temple*, following the break-up of his affair with Henrietta Sykes. From this feeling of failure, he was once more able to extricate himself with his pen.

In a recent novel where a fictional Henry James reflects on his work, Colm Tóibín has his hero contemplate writing an auto-biographical short story. 'No one reading the story,' the Henry James character thinks, 'would guess that he was playing with such vital elements, masking and unmasking himself.'[3] This is what Disraeli was doing in *Tancred*, and to a certain extent in all his fiction. In this last of his 'eastern' novels even more than he had done so recently he found something stirring or reviving in writing about himself. Politics was dead to him for the time being; fiction and autobiography were 'vital'. By returning to the themes and topics that had animated him in the past, particularly male friendship and Middle Eastern geography, he took new risks. He was revealing both his sexuality and his arrogance to a poten-tially unforgiving audience. Unlike in the episode with Peel, however, these were bold risks, bravely worth taking.

The book opens with a celebrity chef named Leander. This is a good sign. He has left off playing Engels to Marx and he is back to some inspired silliness. The chef is wearing green braided trousers, French boots, a velvet waistcoat, primrose-coloured gloves, and a silk hat 'placed rather on one side of his head'.[4] He is in the most exclusive part of London, Mayfair, calling on his father, who is another well-known cook. Leander usually works for Mr Coningsby, but the Duke of Bellamont has hired him to cook for the coming-of-age festivities of his son, Tancred, Marquess of Montacute. The party is to have an Arabian theme, 'the thousand and one nights; the whole county to be feasted'. Leander's father agrees that his son will have to hire helpers. They discuss great cooks as if they were great generals, mustering their forces in the kitchen. Leander also wants help in table decoration, which he says, 'demands an artist of a high calibre'. His father agrees and proposes Monsieur Vanillette. 'Vanilla' was one of

Disraeli's favourite comic names. In *Sybil* he introduced a minor character, Lady Vanilla, who accidentally got into a railway compartment with a felon. This was an excuse for Lord de Mowbray to remark on the levelling influence of the new railways. He says with that mock gravity, where you do not know whether Disraeli is serious or means you to laugh out loud: 'but believe me, my dear Lady Marney, in these times especially, a countess has something else to do than be amusing'.[5] The proposal that Monsieur Vanillette should be brought over from Belgium for the sole purpose of setting the tables is evidence that Disraeli was enjoying himself tremendously.

Leander is also probably a nod from Disraeli in the direction of Christopher Marlowe's erotic poem, 'Hero and Leander'. Leander swims the Hellespont to visit his love Hero, but before he gets there he attracts an amorous advance from the sea god, Neptune. Byron reproduced Leander's mythical feat when he travelled in Turkey by also swimming the Hellespont. When asked why he did it, he replied that it was so he might enjoy Neptune's pull on his manhood. Stanley Wells, an expert on the literature of Shakespeare's era, who is generally sceptical of overly 'sexual' readings of works of that period, nevertheless regards 'Hero and Leander' as quite explicitly homoerotic.[6] Leander refuses Neptune's advance, but Disraeli is asking his literate readers to remember that he was a handsome youth who inspired an advance from a god in the first place.

When Leander cooks up banquet after magnificent banquet for the Bellamonts and receives no word of thanks or appreciation, he is hurt. This is a slightly defensive, autobiographical reflection. A wise and imperturbable neighbour of the Bellamonts tells Leander that he has not been called in to receive the applause of the guests, but 'to form their taste'.[7] The author then comments, 'If anything can save the aristocracy in this levelling age, it is an appreciation of genius.'[8] Disraeli felt he and Leander were in the same boat. He too felt that the nobility for whom he had sacrificed so much in the House of Commons did not adequately appreciate him. He was imagining himself as a brilliant, dandy chef, forming the taste of rich simpletons, and that thought must have made him more cheerful.

The novel reintroduces several characters from *Coningsby*. Coningsby's wife, the former Edith Millbank, now has a baby. Coningsby is absorbed in politics, while she looks after the social world for him. She notices that her baby has 'a debauched look' like that of her husband's grandfather, Lord Monmouth. Sarah Disraeli protested at this, telling her brother, 'I am so sorry that the beautiful and pure Edith should have turned out what she is . . . We were very much in love with her; but I cannot forgive her for saying her child has a debauched look.'[9] But the pure and the innocent never much interested Disraeli.

Mrs Guy Flouncey also reappears, winning the favour of a countess by not seducing the countess's husband. She becomes friends with the wife instead. She achieves thereby a great social victory and the countess introduces her to the best parties. Disraeli uses a naval metaphor and makes Mrs Flouncey into an absurd Nelson of the drawing room. 'This friendship,' Disraeli says, 'was the incident for which Mrs. Guy Flouncey had been cruising for years.'[10]

The principal characters of *Tancred* are two handsome young men, a British marquess and a Lebanese emir. We meet Tancred, Marquess of Montacute, at his coming-of-age party. He is

above the middle height and of a frame completely and grace-fully formed. His dark brown hair, in those hyacinthine curls which Grecian poets have celebrated, and which Grecian sculptors have immortalized, clustered over his brow, which however they only partially concealed. It was pale, as was his whole countenance, but the liquid richness of the dark brown eye, and the colour of the lip, denoted anything but a languid circula-tion. The features were regular, and inclined rather to a refinement, which might have imparted to the countenance a character of too much delicacy, had it not been for the deep meditation of the brow, and for the lower part of the visage, which intimated indomitable will and an iron resolution.[11]

This is the first young man since Contarini's Musaeus who is described as having 'hyacinthine' hair. Reference to the Greek mythology around Hyacinth was one way of hinting at 'Greek love'.[12] This is too persistent a motif in Disraeli's fiction to be mere chance: the boy Ganymede, beloved of Zeus, who figures as a character in Disraeli's short story, 'Ixion in Heaven', is another example. The Greek poets who immortalized male beauty did so in verses addressed to other men. Greek sculpture was the subject of learned but also homoerotic commentary from the critic Joachim Winckelmann in the late eighteenth century to Walter Pater, Disraeli's contemporary. This suggests that Disraeli was working in an approved tradition.[13] He could dwell on the physical beauty of a young man by appealing to a classical tradition; this both veiled the homoeroticism from readers who were not classicists themselves, and communicated in code to those in the know that this young man was seriously good-looking.

Tancred shows in his very face that he has the problem of many Disraeli heroes. He combines effeminacy or 'too much delicacy' with 'indomitable will' or too much strength of purpose. Tancred throws a fit and collapses weeping on his father's chest when he declares that he does not want to stand for Parliament as his parents wish him to do. He has not been able to find a satisfactory religious faith, and he wants to go to Jerusalem to seek one. He pleads with his father to save him from the surrounding 'corruption' and wishes that 'an angel would but visit our house as he visited the house of Lot!'[14] This refers to angels visiting Lot's house in Sodom, warning him to flee because the city was about to be destroyed as punishment for the wickedness of the inhabitants. Part of their wickedness, according to the Bible, derives from men lying together with other men as if they were women. Tancred's problem, thus, is not only his religious but also his sexual confusion.

Tancred's parents chide his tutor for not telling them that Tancred has hatched such an outlandish plan to make a pilgrimage to the Holy Land. The tutor replies that Tancred has always been 'inscrutable. He has formed himself in solitude, and has ever repelled any advance to intimacy, either from those who were his inferior or his equals in station. He has never had a companion.'[15] Thus, the old Disraeli theme returns. Tancred is not only looking for a god, he is also looking for a friend. 'I require a Comforter,' he says later.[16]

Meanwhile, at an assembly of Arab and Hebrew merchants smoking pipes in Jerusalem, there appears a different character. At first he is no more than a pile of coloured clothes. He

> might have been mistaken for a mass of brilliant garments huddled together, had not the gurgling sound of the nargilly [water pipe] occasionally assured the spectator that it was animated by human breath. This person was apparently lying on his back, his face hid, his form not to be traced, a wild confusion of shawls and cushions, out of which, like some wily and dangerous reptile glided the spiral involutions of his pipe.[17]

The pipe imagery is interesting, because for Disraeli reptiles and devils are never pure evil, but wily creatures he admires. Hence Popanilla, the clever, natural young man, wore nothing but a snakeskin, and Dandy Mick's best friend is called Devilsdust. Disraeli often sounds as if he is siding with the wicked dwellers in Sodom and friends of Satan against the boringly good Christian god and his judgemental angels.

This character who is smoking at the end of a snake-like pipe is the most autobiographical of all Disraeli's characters. Perhaps it would be more accurate to say that he represents Disraeli's middle-aged reflections on what he could remember of his 20-year-old self. Even more than Tancred, his features recall those of the opposite sex. He has 'a youthful countenance; fair, almost effeminate, no beard, a slight moustache, his features too delicate, but his brow finely arched, and his blue eye glittering with fire'. When he asks Besso, the host of the smoking party, for a loan, he has the 'coaxing voice and wheedling manner of a girl'.[18] Like the author, the character, whose name is Fakredeen, is deeply in debt. He is also a strange religious mixture: he is called 'most noble Emir', which means an Arab prince or a lord descended from Mohammed. Elsewhere he is referred to as a Christian prince of Lebanon, but he has been brought up in the Jewish family of Besso. He adopts Christian, or Jewish, or Muslim faith and manners as the occasion requires and as it suits him. He is described as

> vain, susceptible, endowed with a brilliant though frothy imagination, and a love of action so unrestrained that restlessness deprived it of energy, with so fine a taste that he was always capricious, and so ingenious that he seemed ever inconsistent. His ambition was as high as his appreciation was quick. He saw everything and understood everybody in a flash.[19]

The self-analysis, even the confessional quality, of Disraeli's description of Fakredeen goes on at a length not accorded to any other character. We find that Fakredeen loved to 'dissemble and simulate'. He was 'ready to adopt any opinion and to possess none' and 'to look upon every man as a tool'. 'Though he intended to make a person his tool and often succeeded, such was his susceptibility, and so strong were his sympathetic qualities, that he was perpetually, without being aware of it, showing his cards.' 'To be the centre of a maze of manoeuvres was his empyrean.' He 'had no principle of any kind'. He was an aesthete who loved 'beauty and the beautiful'. Above all, 'Recklessness with him was a principle of action.'[20]

We know too that Fakredeen's 'restless, intriguing, imaginative spirit revelled in the incognito. He was perpetually in masquerade.'[21] Even his name suggests 'faker', or Winston Churchill's derisive name for Gandhi a century later, 'that half-naked fakir'. A character of a similar name was a Lebanese hero of the seventeenth century and also appears in Beckford's *Vathek*. Disraeli was recalling the orientalism and the homoeroticism of his master. 'Tancred' on the other hand was the name of a twelfth-century Christian crusader. The nineteenth-century English crusader and the nineteenth-century Lebanese hero are fated to meet, to become friends, even perhaps lovers.

Once Fakredeen hears of the arrival of a rich Englishman, Tancred, in the Holy Land, the emir arranges to have him taken captive as a way of extorting money from him. When he first meets him and sees how handsome he is, however, Fakredeen wants to become Tancred's friend instead. The feeling is mutual. Tancred was wounded during his capture and is sitting in the desert camp of his captors. The young Englishman sees Fakredeen for the first time, unaware that he is responsible for his captivity, and immediately becomes a little less sulky. 'Tancred, while he was struck by his earnest gaze, was attracted by his physiognomy, which indeed, from its refined beauty and cast of impassioned intelligence, was highly interesting.'[22]

Fakredeen too feels something very close to love at first sight. He is 'captivated' by Tancred and

> seemed at length to have found the friend for whom he had often sighed, the stedfast and commanding spirit whose control, he felt conscious, was often required by his quick but whimsical temperament. And in what relation did he stand to this being whom he longed to press to his heart, and then go forth with him and conquer the world? It would not bear contemplation.[23]

The situation is both awkward and promising. What could be more desirable than to have a handsome young man captive? Now, how to keep it a secret from the young man that his capture is owing to one's own devious plot?

Disraeli also signals that both young men have similar temperaments. The word 'morbid' was one way possible in the nineteenth century to refer to what we would call homosexuality. The morbidity in both cases arises from desires that are not procreative and generative, but inward turning, melancholy, narcissistic. Tancred is depressed about his capture and asks himself: 'Was it a morbid curiosity, or the proverbial restlessness of a satiated aristocrat, that had drawn him to these wilds?'[24] Fakredeen too has a 'morbid sensibility', but he is less troubled by it than Tancred. His solution is to go off to the baths for six hours to think about how he can placate an Egyptian creditor.[25]

Tancred gets a fever and lies in Fakredeen's tent. Fakredeen tells his foster sister, Eva, that he has no wish to live if Tancred dies. She sends people to find a flower that may cure Tancred. While everyone departs to search for the plant, 'Fakredeen remained behind, and passed his time partly in watching Tancred, partly in weeping, and partly in calculating the amount of his debts. This latter was a frequent, and to him, inexhaustible source of interest and excitement.'[26] Someone finds the necessary flower and Eva mixes the potion. Tancred takes the remedy, sleeps and feels better. He emerges from the tent wearing 'a Bedoueen cloak'. By putting the English aristocrat into a Bedouin cloak, Disraeli was recalling a high point of his youth as a way of regenerating his own high spirits in the midst of a funk.

Disraeli was also trying to serve as spokesman for the East in this novel and to reverse anti-eastern prejudices in England by claiming that the laws of Moses are 'Arabian laws' that dominate Christendom. The central irony of English anti-Semitism, Disraeli argued, is that

The life and property of England are protected by the laws of Sinai. The hard-working people of England are secured in every seven days a day of rest by the laws of Sinai. And yet they persecute the Jews, and hold up to odium the race to whom they are indebted for the sublime legislation which alleviates the inevitable lot of the labouring multitude.[27]

The laws of Christian England originated in the Jewish Old Testament and in the Arab geography of Sinai. In the East, however, rather than persecuting one another, at least in Disraeli's novels, Muslim, Christian and Jew tend to rub along together: they smoke together, in *Alroy* they marry one another, and in *Tancred* they become best friends.

At the end of volume II, Fakredeen takes Tancred to his Lebanese mountain castle. On their journey Fakredeen watches over the not-quite-healed Tancred 'with a delicate solicitude which would have almost become a woman'.[28] When they arrive, Fakredeen shows him to his rooms, and leaves him in the bathroom, where he calls in attendants to help Tancred undress.[29] That interesting prospect would persuade readers to go on to the next volume.

Disraeli begins volume III with reflections on friendship. In the old days, he claims, he would have compared Tancred and Fakredeen to the Roman fable of Damon and Pythias, a pair of male friends who lived together and shared their goods in common. When one was condemned to death and allowed to return home to settle his affairs before his execution, the other stood in his place, guaranteeing his friend's return under the pain of being executed himself. When the other returned in time to face his execution, the tyrant who had originally condemned him was so moved by the mutual loyalty of the two friends that he pardoned the man who was about to die. It was a story written down in the first century of the Christian era by a Roman. Nowadays, Disraeli says, we do not understand this sort of story.

Of all the differences between the ancients and ourselves, none more striking than our respective ideas of friendship. Grecian friendship was indeed so ethereal, that it is difficult to define its essential qualities. They must be sought rather in the pages of Plato or the moral essays of Plutarch perhaps, and in some other books not quite as well known, but not less interesting and curious. As for modern friendship, it will be found in clubs. It is violent at a house dinner, fervent in a cigar shop, full of devotion at a cricket or a pigeon match, or in the gathering of a steeple chase. The nineteenth century is not entirely sceptical on the head of friendship, but fears 'tis rare. A man may have friends, but then are they sincere ones? Do not they abuse you behind your back, and blackball you at societies where they have had the honour to propose you? . . . Generally speaking, among sensible persons, it would seem that a rich man deems that friend a sincere one who does not want to borrow his money; while, among the less favoured with fortune's gifts, the sincere friend is generally esteemed to be the individual who is ready to lend it.[30]

Not since *Vivian Grey* and *Venetia* had Disraeli recurred to Plato as a way of hinting that male friendship in his imagined world often had a homoerotic element in it. Plutarch too had written a work, *Eroticus*, comparing married heterosexual love to love between men, allowing that the latter could be more enriching than the former.[31] Disraeli's mocking of Victorian friendship, that it is at its most 'fervent in a cigar shop', is his usual trick of making fun of what he cares about most. He is also returning to a theme, male intimacy and its coming rupture, that is treated at length not only in *Vivian Grey*, but also in *Contarini Fleming* and *Coningsby*.

Disraeli continues,

As we must not compare Tancred and Fakredeen to Damon and Pythias, and as we cannot easily find in Pall Mall or Park Lane a parallel more modish, we must be content to say that youth, sympathy, and occasion, combined to create between them that intimacy which each was prompt to recognise as one of the principal sources of his happiness, and which the young Emir, at any rate, was persuaded must be as lasting as it was fervent and profound.[32]

It is Fakredeen, the more Disraelian of the two, who fails to see that nothing this good lasts. The two go off on a mission to assert Asian world supremacy and 'utterly extinguish the grovelling tyranny of self government' in a Kurdish mountain region.[33] There they meet a queen whose subjects are the last living people to worship the Greek gods of the classical period. She creates jealousy between the young men. There are more captures and releases. Christian Tancred declares his love for Jewish Eva, thus creating another interdenominational love affair; but, wait, his parents have arrived in Jerusalem. The end.

Disraeli confessed to his friend, Lady Londonderry, that the novel had given him much trouble. It must have been difficult to arrive at a conclusion to a work that had so many explosive ideas, not the least of which is the heroes' going to war against the system of 'self government', of which Disraeli himself was supposed to be an elected champion in Parliament. Victorian commentators more often noticed and objected to Disraeli's assertions of Jewish superiority. For example, Eva tells Tancred that as half Christendom worships a Jewess, by which she means Catholics worshipping the Virgin Mary, and the other half a Jew, by which she means Protestants worshipping Christ, Jews should be considered 'the superior race'.[34]

It is no coincidence that Disraeli's reflections on Jewishness appear in the same place as one of his most extended stories about men being attracted to other men. It was a common Victorian myth that Europeans could find less guilt-ridden, more libertine sex in the East than they could at home.[35] Note, for example, the casual remark made in a pamphlet on a homosexual scandal in England, published in 1813, that says Arabs typically make light of homosexuality and 'Mahometans, also, are much addicted to this crime.'[36] Or, compare Disraeli's orientalism to that of an American novelist of the 1870s who wrote of a night he spent in Paris with another man: 'that night was Arabian, and no mistake!'[37]

A recent commentator on the *Arabian Nights* remarks on the

semi-pornographic nature of many of the stories. As one of the most popular works of literature about the Arab world in Europe since the eighteenth century, it contributed much to the European mythology about the East. It is also relevant that the *Arabian Nights* treats sexual attraction between males in a way which is not always approving, but not always disapproving either. Other than works of ancient Greek and Roman literature, it was one of the few available texts that referred to homosexuality at all. It is no surprise, then, that Disraeli at one point had plans for bringing out a new edition of the *Arabian Nights*, with an original story of his own appended.[38] Although Disraeli never brought out this edition of the *Arabian Nights*, *Tancred* is a near equivalent.

What all this means is that for Disraeli his Jewishness and his homosexuality were linked. They both shared an eastern geography. They both were the subject of Christian and European disapproval. In *Tancred* Disraeli is an unusually aggressive advocate of both male friendship and the Jewish faith, or 'race', as he preferred to think of it. Other historians have noticed something similar to this, as when, for example, John Vincent remarks that Disraeli loved Islam 'for its sense of fraternity'.[39] Vincent is speaking in Disraeli's own code to say that Disraeli's love of eastern religion went along with his love of other men.[40]

Disraeli was so reckless with the code in this novel that he threatened to destroy his political future, or at least to unsettle the mid-Victorian compromise that homoerotic flirtation might exist, especially in upper-class circles, as long as it never led to the crime of sodomy. Or, as long as one was never caught. Having destroyed Peel and his party, Disraeli looked set to destroy himself by revealing the extent of his own sympathy with sexual practices punishable by death in England. His recklessness must have come from some sense of the force of prejudice set against him in the House of Commons. On the one side Liberals and Peelites would never forgive him for having brought down a man whom they regarded as a courageous politician. On the other, the Conservatives and Protectionists, though temporarily voting with him against Peel, were more bitterly hostile than the other side to Disraeli's Jewishness and his ambition. The impossibility of making his way against such people must have been behind some of the more outrageous scenes and ideas of *Tancred*. Yet, writing it down, setting out a long story of romantic male friendship, along with assertions of Jewish superiority, tended to exorcise his sense of grievance. Having declared himself in an unusually frank way, he somehow freed up his emotional energy for more constructive, less introspective tasks. His old friend and publisher, Henry Colburn, brought out the book; he was back to politics the following month.

In January 1847 Disraeli took his place for the first time on the front benches of the House of Commons, sitting a few places down from Peel, his vanquished leader, and opposing the Whig government led by Lord John Russell and Lord Palmerston across the way. The two halves of the Conservative party sat together on the opposition benches of the House of Commons, though they hated each other more than they did the Whig ministers opposite them. There was still so much hostility towards Disraeli that he was not formally recognized as leader of the Protectionist Conservatives until two years later. Even then, he had to serve in an unusual leadership committee of three, so much did members of his party distrust him. Buckle says that his dandyism, along with his 'Bohemianism', his Jewishness and being a literary man, were all reasons for the party's reluctance to acknowledge his superior abilities.[41] One of the senior figures in the party, Lord Malmesbury, said that Conservatives were slow to acknowledge him as leader because of his 'mask', his seeming to be a foreigner and his 'mysterious manner'.[42] The novelist Anthony Trollope 'made a system of ethics out of condemnation of Disraeli's unmanly, or Jewish qualities'.[43] Thus, some Victorians equated Jewishness, or even being 'foreign', with effeminacy. Perhaps it was not only in Disraeli's own mind, but also in the minds of his parliamentary colleagues, that his odd religion went with his dubious masculinity. And what about the mask? What was he hiding from them?

Buckle also noted that Disraeli's clothes and his oratory now became graver, duller, less colourful than before, so as not to frighten the Protectionist remainder of the Conservative party away.[44] This was not the impression of *Fraser's Magazine*, who carried an article in February 1847 saying that he still reminded them of a 'ballroom exquisite'.

> With his supercilious expression of countenance, slightly dashed with pomposity, and a dilettante affectation, he stands with his hands on his hips, or his thumbs in the armholes of his waist-coat, while there is a slight, very slight, gyratory movement of the upper part of his body, such as you will see ballroom exquisites adopt when they condescend to prattle a flirtation . . . . [H]is words are not so much delivered as that they flow from the mouth, as if it were really too much trouble for so clever, so intellectual – in a word so literary a man to speak at all.[45]

Fraser's Magazine had flayed Edward Bulwer's dandyism and they were known for being intolerant of affectation. It could be that, if he were still a dandy at the beginning of 1847, *Fraser's Magazine* was among the influences that finally hurried Disraeli into all black. Or, it could also have been that the fashion was changing. The colourful style-setter d'Orsay went abroad in 1849 and died in 1852. Disraeli's black may well have been the new stylish sub-stitute for fancy waistcoats, rather than a retreat before the disapproval of the House.

The writer in *Fraser's Magazine* was not entirely critical of Disraeli's oratory, however. The dandy style of speaking had something to be said for it. *Fraser's Magazine* thought Disraeli was at his best with sarcasm and irony.

> In conveying an innuendo, an ironical sneer, or a suggestion of contempt, which courtesy forbids him to translate into words – in conveying such masked enmities by means of a glance, a

shrug, an altered tone of voice, or a transient expression of face, he is unrivalled. Not only is the shaft envenomed, but it is aimed with deadly precision by a cool hand and a keen eye, with a courage fearless of retaliation.[46]

They were ready to concede that there was bravery in the ball-room exquisite. The truth is too that if his dress began to get more sober in this period, his dandyism with words remained the great draw for his own backbenchers and men on the other side of the House as well.

In August 1848 he made a long speech summarizing the session, mainly as a way of attacking the poor record of the government. Thirty years later he recalled it as 'the speech that made me leader'. *The Times* said that the best thing about the government's proposals during the session 'was that "Mr. Disraeli was able to elicit out of them matter enough to keep the house in one long laugh for the greater part of his brilliant speech yesterday"'.[47] Laughter or amusement remained an important part of his rhetoric, perhaps the essential part, even as he gave up amusing dress. Disraeli's rival on the Peelite side of the Conservative party, W. E. Gladstone, admitted that Disraeli had a talent 'for summing up with brilliancy, buoyancy, and comprehensiveness, at the close of a debate'.[48] This was one rising orator's appreciation of another. It is also a reminder that sobriety and earnestness are misleading stereotypes of the Victorians, which miss the whimsical or comical elements that the Victorians loved; Disraeli exploited this trait in his speeches. Charles Dickens's novels of that era, *Pickwick Papers* (1836), *Oliver Twist* (1837), *Nicholas Nickleby* (1839), *The Old Curiosity Shop* (1841) and *Dombey and Son* (1848) all employed a comic voice that the Victorians found irresistible. *Punch* was a bestselling satirical magazine in the 1840s. That Disraeli also had a talent to amuse, along with one to annoy, certainly appealed to a mid-Victorian love of laughter. The man who could make serious Victorian legislators laugh was the one they were finally willing to make their leader.

Laughter was not the only weapon in Disraeli's rhetorical arsenal. During 1851 he wrote a very dull book, his own parliamentary history of the three years that led up to the fall of Peel's administration. Disraeli had become friends with Lord George Bentinck during the assault on Peel. A younger son of the Duke of Portland, Bentinck was a sportsman who enjoyed racing horses. He had been stung into political activity by Peel's desertion of landed proprietors. He became an ally of Disraeli. There is even some circumstantial evidence that he may have been homosexual as well. He was still a bachelor in his mid-forties and never married. Bentinck had also served a political apprenticeship as private secretary to George Canning for three years. Canning appears on the list in Disraeli's 1842 'Commonplace Book' of men like Byron, Beckford and Bankes, who shared an appreciation for the homoerotic. However, the surviving correspondence between Bentinck and Disraeli bears no trace of the warmth Disraeli sometimes allowed into his letters to younger men, or the flippant gallantry he used with an older man like Beckford. It should also be said that Disraeli's correspondence was heavily 'weeded' after his death, with several of his executors deciding what should and should not be preserved for posterity. It is curious that so little of Disraeli's correspondence with George Smythe should have survived, when the letters of more minor figures in his emotional life were so carefully preserved. Warmer letters between Bentinck and Disraeli might well have been destroyed.

Disraeli's father died in 1848. Sarah cared for their father as he died. Disraeli's absence from the scene, though accounted for by his involvement in politics, was emotionally a little strange, given the great affinity to Isaac he had acknowledged in his novels. Disraeli began negotiations about this time to purchase a manor house and its estate called Hughenden, close to Bradenham. Even with the money that came to him from his father's will, he still had to borrow heavily. The purchase would not have been possible without a loan from the Bentincks first negotiated by Disraeli's friend, Lord George. With the purchase of Hughenden his total indebtedness increased to something like £40,000, a sum comparable to £4 million today. He had virtually no income to repay this debt other than Mary Anne's annual income of several thousands, which was already tied up with the expense of their house in London and his other debts. The Bentincks took over the income yielded by the Hughenden estate. 'The whole business must be pronounced, from a financial point of view,' said Buckle, ordinarily circumspect about criticizing his subject, 'to have been very imprudent.'[49]

Worse still, Lord George suddenly died of a heart attack before the deal was done. He walked out from his father's house at Welbeck to visit a neighbour several miles distant at Thoresby and never returned. A servant found him lying dead near a stile. He was only forty-seven. Disraeli had to complete the negotiation with a brother, Lord Henry Bentinck, whom he did not know nearly as well. This may explain some, though not all, of his despair, as he wrote from Scotland, where he was staying with Mary Anne, to his Young England friend, Lord John Manners: 'I shrink from exposing what I feel to any one here; it was no ordinary tie of political or social friendship that bound us together, and to no one but you would I say so much.'[50] This may be simply the sentimentality the Victorians attached to death and friendship, but on the other hand it may not.

Disraeli managed to convince Lord Henry Bentinck to continue the loan arranged by his brother, but it took some delicate talking. When it was over, Disraeli reported to Mary Anne that he had had to be frank with Lord Henry. Disraeli had told him 'it would be no object to them [the Bentincks] and no pleasure to me, unless I played the high game in public life; and that I could not do that without being on a rock'.[51] If the Bentincks wanted him as their hired gun to continue speaking in favour of agricultural proprietors in the House of Commons, they needed to establish him in an unassailable position: in his own country house, with a landed estate, so he could continue to sit for one of the fairly safe county seats of Buckinghamshire, where he had been elected for the first time in 1847. It is of a piece with his dandy rhetoric that he used the phrase 'high game' to describe political life. It was cynical. It was fun. It was a wonderfully knowing, eighteenth-century style of referring to service in Parliament, completely at odds with the usual view of prosperous Victorians that service in Parliament was a duty, an almost religious calling.

Disraeli was extremely pleased with his new house. Mary Anne immediately began improving the grounds and he reported to Sarah, 'The alterations here seem very successful. It is quite another place, and of far more pretension and effect.'[52] To the Austrian statesman in exile, Prince Metternich, he reported that he was writing from his lonely 'Bucks château. This is a singular province without a large town. Its towns are only villages. It is sylvan and feudal.'[53] It was like him to approve of 'pretension' and to pretend to one of the grandfathers of European conservatism that he lived in a feudal castle. Pretension was never anything to be ashamed of for Disraeli; he regarded it as a species of imaginative or artistic genius. [*See plate 20.*]

Disraeli next asked for permission from the duke of Portland to look through his son Lord George's papers in order to write a biography. This was not only an act of *pietas* in memorializing a dead friend, but an attempt to justify his own extraordinary behaviour in attacking Peel, and probably also an effort to shore up the loan from the Bentincks that made the purchase of Hughenden possible. The book took the form of a narrow parliamentary history of the three years leading up to Peel's resignation. Its highlights are the quotations from Disraeli's own best speeches. Portions of it employed the ballroom style for which his speeches had been noticed. Of Peel's premiership his lines reversing expectations were a mark of the style: Peel had relied upon 'the servility of Parliament', but had himself 'reeled under the favour of the Court'.[54] Disraeli meant the lines to raise a dry laugh through reference to Peel's well-known authoritarian style and the fact that Prince Albert admired him.

The book may have helped him for a short time with the

Bentincks, who were grateful for it. On the other hand, the book may have injured him with the man with whom he now had to work closely if he was ever to establish his leadership on a sound footing in the lower house. Lord Stanley had become Earl of Derby in 1851. By his rank, his wealth, his experience and his abilities, he was the top Conservative in Parliament. If the Conservatives were ever to regain political office, he and Disraeli had to be able to agree and to trust one another. On the publication of *Lord George Bentinck*, however, William Beresford, a whip in the lower house and confidant of Derby's, told Derby that the real hero of the book was Disraeli himself. The book, Beresford said, was 'untrue and unjust' in its omission of Derby's role in putting the Protectionist case.[55]

If the book harmed him with Derby, it may have helped him with a new young man. Disraeli liked being friends with the younger sons of dukes. He had been a friend and political ally of Lord John Manners, a younger son of the Duke of Rutland, since the earliest of the Young England days. Manners was really too religious for Disraeli's taste. Disraeli could not get as excited about the medieval Christian Church that inspired Manners as he could about the mixture of races and faiths in modern Jerusalem. Their relationship was mainly political, judging from the tone of their letters to one another, but he did occasionally try on a diminutive, 'Johnny', in referring to Manners.[56] For some reason, Manners was shy about revealing to Disraeli in 1851 that he had decided to get married. Although they had been sitting together night after night in the House of Commons, Manners delayed telling him in person, and almost apologized for his decision in a letter.[57]

Lord Henry Lennox was a younger son of the Duke of Richmond. He wrote to say in December 1851 how pleased his father was with Disraeli's new book, *Lord George Bentinck*. Disraeli replied in a friendly vein, and signed himself in what was for those days an exceedingly friendly way: 'Ever, my dear Henry, Yours, D.'[58] It was the dawn of a new friendship, a crush that would bring him some pleasure, and quite a long drawn-out period of embarrassment and pain. It coincides with his first spell of office under the premiership of Lord Derby, by no means 'the top of the greasy pole', but definitely higher than he had reached so far.

Disraeli's forty-seventh birthday was 21 December 1851. Before leaving him there, it is worthwhile to reflect on the alternating successes and feelings of despair that plagued him when he was in his forties. He was still deeply in debt and the editors of the *Disraeli Letters* say that financial worries became more acute in this period. It may have been that, as with Fakredeen, his debts and his impending sense of ruin were the principal spurs to what seemed one reckless act after another. Desperate measures seemed to be required and Disraeli always liked 'to astonish mankind'.

There was, however, some sense in his seeming madness. He told Derby at a moment when one would have thought the utmost tact and delicacy were required from a younger man seeking the trust of a more powerful elder, 'I am Disraeli "the adventurer".' He had a way of shocking people with his utter frankness and his perfect knowledge of what was being said behind his back. It required them to deal with him as he was.

Seen from this angle, his attack on Peel and the destruction of his party still appears a rather egotistical manoeuvre that won him short-term applause, but decades of headaches and immense effort at painful reconstruction. What does not seem so reckless in retrospect is his conscious antagonizing of members of his party with his arguments about Jewish superiority and his long narratives romanticizing male friendship. He seemed to be throwing down Leander's primrose-coloured gauntlet, or for a moment to be removing his mask. This is what I am: take it or leave it. That appears less like foolhardiness and more like fearlessness. It may well have been, too, the secret of a generally happy middle age.

16

That Fine Tall Room

The period after 1846 was one of shifting and unstable political alliances. Disraeli's destruction of Peel over the repeal of the Corn Laws had split the Conservative party into two. Disraeli no longer stood alone as an attention-getting orator. He had gained prominent allies in Bentinck and Derby. Although Bentinck's early death was the loss of a friend, it also meant that Disraeli's was the only voice with any weight possessed by a significant portion of Sir Robert Peel's former party. The larger, landed, Protectionist wing of that party reluctantly stuck with Disraeli as the coming man and Lord Derby as the one they could trust.

The Peelites ordinarily voted with the aristocratic Whigs, and their middle-class allies who called themselves Liberals. Disraeli and Derby themselves were only in uneasy alliance with one another. Disraeli wanted to abandon their policy of agricultural protection; although he had been quick to jump upon Peel's inconsistency, he was not in love with the policy of protection itself, as he saw that it would win the Tories no votes with the majority of the country. Derby was slower to come around to this point of view. They only agreed with one another about discarding the protectionist policy late in their first spell of office in 1852. Together they had to make do without much parliamentary talent, and with very little commitment to any constructive policy.

The Whigs, on the other hand, led by Lord John Russell and Lord Palmerston, were the normal party of government in this period. The difficulty was that Russell and Palmerston often disagreed with one another. Queen Victoria and Prince Albert disliked Palmerston and were always angling to get rid of him. There was also tension between the Whigs, who liked the status quo, and some increasingly restive Liberals, who wanted to carry forward the programme of electoral and administrative reform begun in the 1830s. The Peelites often sided with the Whigs and Liberals, but the Conservatives were always trying to win them back. In addition, there were the Irish representatives, who usually, but not always, sided with the Whigs and Liberals.

The statutory length of any given Parliament, and therefore of any cabinet, was seven years. In practice, however, the governments of this period were much shorter than that. Under these circumstances, in the eight years between 1851 and 1859, Disraeli had a chance of taking office four times. He and Derby were only successful in their attempts to form a government and to kiss the hand of the Queen in exchange for their official seals of office on two brief occasions: in 1852, and between 1858 and 1859. These were both minority governments in which they held office on the sufferance of the opposition, or on the inability of the opposition, for a short time, to agree with one another.

Early in 1852 a disagreement between Russell and Palmerston led to the resignation of the Whigs. The Queen asked Derby to form a government and Disraeli, as his principal lieutenant, took office as chancellor of the exchequer. For the first time he was a servant of the Queen and a privy councillor. Although Members of Parliament were in those days unpaid, members of the cabinet and subordinate office holders did receive salaries from the state. So it was the first time he received official pay and also the first time he occupied 11 Downing Street, one step away from the prime minister's residence at number 10. His letters, instead of the sparkling, dandyish personality of old, are those of a practical person, much occupied with the settling of business in the House of Commons, with the details of administration or legislation, with the politics of acquiring or holding on to office. He wrote no autobiographically inspired novels in the 1850s. He drank less. There were no adulterous affairs. Even his indebtedness, though pressing, bothered him less. Where then is the pleasure in this period? Where is the enjoyment? Why was he willing to devote himself so completely, so obsessively to political business?

It may have been that he made a discovery in this period that he never committed to print: that power was the greatest pleasure of all, that it eclipsed the joys of dressing up, going out, or thinking about the Queen. This possibility can only be examined, or illustrated, by approaching his life in this period from an odd angle. Politics occupied most of his time in the 1850s, but several episodes in what, from the surviving documents, would appear to be less central parts of his life shed an oblique but revealing light on the whole man. His friendships with a trio of young men and two ageing ladies, his sense of wonder and fun at his still small, but expanding relations with the Queen – these are the sideshows which help to make sense of the main-stage performance of his life in the 1850s. In May 1852 his sister Sarah went for the first time to his office in Downing Street. She remarked: 'I enjoyed very much my visit to you and all the actual manifestations of your power. I can think of nothing else since but that fine tall room, and you so calm and composed at that great official desk.'[1] To look a little beneath his calm and composure, it may be well at first to establish the outline of what was happening in his political career in the early 1850s.

He may have looked composed, but he had much to do. Disraeli believed it was necessary to move the party towards accepting that protection was now largely dead. Nevertheless, Derby had yet to be convinced this was true and the Protectionist backbenchers were more intransigent still. He also had to manage government business from the front bench without a parliamentary majority. Although a large section of the party hated him for now embracing the policy for which he had attacked Peel, there was a growing sentiment in the months of 1852 that he was doing rather well against the odds. Indeed, although he introduced a budget at the end of 1852 that was the subject of a famous attack by Gladstone, and which led to the government's collapse, the brief time in office in 1852 made him famous in a way that was new. He was put into Madame Tussaud's, while Gladstone did not appear in the waxwork museum until 1870. Moreover, he was able to make that fame pay by bringing out a cheap edition of his novels. The edition sold 300,000 copies in a year, a hundred times the initial sale of *Coningsby* or *Sybil*, both of them considered successful books at the time of their publication.[2]

In the later 1850s and afterward, really until the 1870s, Disraeli's normal place was opposite the government front benches. He was an official critic, attacking official policy sometimes constructively, sometimes with an eye on keeping his party unified behind him. He was always angling for office himself, looking for potential weaknesses or gaps in the unified front of the cabinet. He traded and listened to gossip; he had semi-official friends in embassies abroad who sent him information he might use in attacking the government. He was involved with a newspaper which for a short and rather expensive time put the Disraelian spin on current events, when he felt the existing papers were not giving the Conservatives the breaks they needed.

George Buckle called these long years of opposition the 'tragic' side of Disraeli's career. For someone with so strong a creative side, it was sad that he should be so long condemned to criticism.[3] Were they tragic though? Disraeli's enjoyment of the brief spells of office suggests that they were worth the wait, and that they sustained his patience through the long spells of opposition. He told the foreign secretary, Lord Malmesbury, that when he first held the seals of office in 1852 he felt like a young girl going to her first ball.[4] He loved playing up to the worst possible images of himself that circulated among his critics. He had supreme self-confidence which he masked here with a giddy image.

Even before he left his first spell of office at the end of 1852, he found that power brought him perquisites that perhaps he had anticipated, but which were nonetheless sources of real pleasure when they arrived. The Duke of Richmond was a Tory grandee who owned estates in Scotland and West Sussex. Several of his sons held seats in Parliament which even then, long after the First Reform Bill, were virtually pocket boroughs in which the duke could guarantee the election of practically any man he chose. Lord Henry Lennox, his third son, was thirty-one years old in 1852. Educated at Westminster and Christ Church, he had been a Member of Parliament since 1846 for one of the seats allied to his father's west Sussex property, Chichester. He was seventeen years younger than Disraeli, but they became close friends during the early 1850s. Disraeli persuaded Derby to give Lennox office in 1852 as a junior lord of the Treasury, a move that gratified his powerful father, but also suited Disraeli. Lennox appreciated the proximity to power that Disraeli brought him; Disraeli liked being with the good-looking bachelor sons of dukes.

Many of Disraeli's biographers go out of their way to dismiss Lennox, though to acknowledge in roundabout language that there was an unusual bond between him and Disraeli. Blake was rather exasperated with the friendship, calling Lennox 'feather-headed' and twice a 'flibbertigibbet', a word that emphasizes Lennox's effeminacy and his character as a gossip. Blake noted that Disraeli told Lennox that he loved him. He argued that 'The language must be discounted as the hyperbole of the time. But it remains something of a mystery that Disraeli should have been as fond as he was of such an essentially trivial personality.'[5] The editors of the *Disraeli Letters* write Lennox off as a 'mere dalliance'; they concede, however, that Disraeli uses 'more romantic terminology' with Lennox in this period than he does with his wife, Mary Anne.[6] Sarah Bradford is more at ease describing Disraeli's relationship with Lennox as drawing upon homosexual inclinations, though she too thinks it 'unfair' to emphasize this. She believes he liked 'youth' and 'vitality' more than young men as sexual objects.[7] But why not both?

Buckle, writing in the era just before the First World War, said frankly that 'Disraeli was obviously much attracted by [Lennox], as he was wont to be attracted by a combination of youth, birth, smartness, and intelligence.'[8] Buckle would hardly have reprinted Disraeli's letters to Lennox beginning 'My Dearest' and 'My Beloved' if he suspected there had been a homosexual relationship. Rather, he expected his readers to interpret these words as Blake did, the typical Victorian excesses of sentimental friendship between members of the same sex. I think it probable, however, that both Buckle and Blake fully intended to invest the friendship with some ambiguity. They may well have been employing Disraeli's own strategy of revealing and concealing at the same time. For the initiated few, who perhaps remembered their own days at an all-male school, there would have been some unsaid acknowledgement that Disraeli's feelings for Lennox were not entirely sentimental.

There is no surviving evidence that the relationship ever had a sexual dimension. Indeed, the tone of letters Disraeli sent Lennox is often wistful or somewhat melancholy rather than sexually suggestive, as if he imagined something that might have been had he himself been younger. We may be misled by the 'sexual' in the word homosexual to assume that the distinctive feature of such a relationship is its erotic character, but it may be just as or an even more important characteristic of homosexual men to have an affectionate or romantic orientation to the same sex. Just as sex is not necessarily the most important element in a marriage between a man and a woman, so too may two men be drawn together because of a love of companionship, or physical appearance, or emotional magnetism. Disraeli was deeply interested in Lennox, but fraternal or paternal pride and protectiveness also characterized many of his relationships with younger men.

Photographs of Lennox survive from the 1860s and 1870s in the family albums of the Dukes of Richmond at Goodwood. [*See plates 12 and 13.*] Another image of Lennox is a caricature of him as a fop, delicately putting on a pair of white gloves. The text that accompanies this cartoon in an issue of *Vanity Fair* from 1870 says Lennox is not man enough to be a serious politician: 'Favoured by Nature with a graceful figure and presence, and a feminine gentleness of manner, and suspected of literary ability, the pleasing qualities he has disclosed have been received as proof that he was not made of the stern stuff that it is assumed must go to form a statesman.'[9] [*See plate 14.*] An image of affectation comes through in one of the letters Lennox wrote to Disraeli in the summer of 1852. He wrote in the midst of that summer's elections when he heard some of the counties were going against the party. 'I am quite *effete* without good news! without the Chancellor [Disraeli]!! and without Champagne Cup!!!'

Disraeli frankly liked having disciples and he was not ashamed to reply to such a letter from Lennox. He gave him some political gossip, and told him to read *Coningsby*. He was less self-deprecating among his younger friends than he was among his contemporaries. He ended the letter semi-flirtatiously: 'I am glad you are dull in my absence. I also feel lonely . . .'[10] To which Lennox immediately replied, 'Dearest D! How could you suppose I should *not be dull* without you?' Lennox may have been exploiting Disraeli's weakness for him, in order to keep up the flow of insider gossip, and whatever favours, monetary or otherwise, might be on offer. Although the son of a duke, Lennox was not rich, and his office at the Treasury was lucrative. He may have wanted to use Disraeli's affection to ensure continued good times for himself, an attitude Disraeli himself had many times adopted and ought to have recognized. Blake certainly believed that Lennox's goal was to use Disraeli for some permanent office in the gift of his patron that would not expire at the change of governments and could guarantee him an adequate salary.[11]

The summer of 1852 was the peak of the good times between them. After the election was over, Lennox invited Disraeli to come with him 'to see the Melodrame at the Princess' theatre with the famous husband-and-wife actors, the Keans. 'You would see no one but me and a very clever, agreeable creature, the new

Member for Beverley.'[12] Even then it would have been camp to call any new MP a 'creature'. Lennox may be referring to Frank Lawley, Gladstone's former private secretary, who was about to be charged with corruption in his service at the Treasury. Or it might have been William Wells, the other member for Beverley in Yorkshire; they were both young men and both bachelors according to *Dod's Parliamentary Companion*.

In early August Disraeli wrote to Lennox, 'I think very often of my young companion, and miss him sadly, for his presence to me is always a charm, and often a consolation.' Why did he need to be consoled? He was at last in office, a privy councillor and sitting in the seat of power. Was it a mock pathetic means of ensuring Lennox's devotion? Still, he was not afraid to introduce a slight chastisement in the same letter for Lennox's overenthusiasm concerning a newspaper matter, but softening the rebuke with 'my beloved'.[13]

Then apparently Lennox proposed to leave London for a few days at a moment when Disraeli thought he had a right, for all the gifts he had showered on his subordinate, to demand his presence. 'Excuse my frankness,' Disraeli wrote with cold majesty, 'but I do not wish, too hastily, to look upon our friendship as the last of my illusions.' Then he summoned Lennox to a *dîner à deux* at his club: 'I apprehend that my morning will be very much engaged, but I hope we may dine together, alone, at the Coventry.'[14] The Coventry Club was a purely Disraelian place to go in the summertime. He remembered it in his reminiscences as a 'very exclusive club of fine gentlemen', opposite Green Park. He placed the beginning of *Sybil* with its bored youths drinking elaborate alcoholic concoctions at the Coventry. His knowledge of celebrity chefs in *Tancred* also came from there, as he remembered that the club 'had the famous Francatelli for their cook, who had been expelled [from] the royal household because he had attempted to assassinate one of his marmitons. But the Coventry was indulgent to the irritability of men of genius.'[15]

Lennox had to learn about the irritability of men of genius the hard way. He replied to Disraeli's letter, 'My dearest D., I am aghast at your letter. Our Friendship dissolved. God Forbid. I shall not *now* leave London.'[16] A few days later, Lennox never-theless felt compelled to leave London for his father's house, Gordon Castle, in Scotland. In order to avoid another rebuke from Disraeli, he went to the length of writing him a letter from the train. 'I am so determined that you shall not write a second letter, like your last, that, at the risk of its being quite illegible, I have commenced an Epistle, in the Railway Carriage!' He also knew how to flatter Disraeli's vanity in order to assist in smooth-ing over the crisis in their relationship. He said he was reading *Coningsby* for the first time and loving it, marvelling at the author's genius. He concluded 'Write to me Dearest D when you have time! a *nice*! kind, affectionate, letter! amusing! it *must* be.'[17]

This did the trick. Disraeli wrote back saying he was busy, but calm. 'I cannot let another day close without thanking you for your letter, but I am so tired that I can only tell you that I love you.' The latter part of this was a formula with Disraeli, but one he only used with his greatest intimates. Before now, he had only used it with his sister Sarah, or with Mary Anne. Still, Lennox's letter had put him in an expansive mood. 'I am amused about *Coningsby*, and am rather surprised that you never read it before.' He told him anecdotes of Sir Robert Peel being so taken with the book that he 'shut himself up a whole day in his dressing-room, and locked up the book when he went out, lest his family should get it'. Then he teasingly told Lennox some unpleasant truths about himself, while suggesting some more of his own books. 'If you ever have inclination or power to read another book – for reading, I suspect, is not your forte – you must manage to read *Sybil*, and especially *Tancred*.'[18] Why 'especially' *Tancred*? Did he want him to read about the friendship between Tancred, who was like Lennox the son of a duke, and Fakredeen, the character most clearly modelled on himself?

That autumn, Lennox came to stay at Hughenden, probably at a time when Mary Anne was not there, as Disraeli reported that Lennox had done a drawing of the house for her, and that he was bringing it up to London with him.[19] In that season Lennox was almost an officially recognized friend. When Disraeli made his big speech of several hours' length introducing the budget in December 1852, certainly the climax of that government and of his recent parliamentary career, Derby wrote to congratulate him. Derby got his news of Disraeli's health after the ordeal from Henry Lennox, 'who tells me you are well'.[20] A rather more insinuating report on their relationship appeared in a journal called *The Leader*, which was often a critic of Disraeli. The paper professed to give an account of Disraeli's appearance in the House of Commons to someone visiting to hear him speak. The account begins with the usual summary of Disraeli's dandified appearance:

> His body is half thrown across the table, one hand resting behind him, flirting with a laced cambric [handkerchief], the other white hand tapping gently a red box . . . Mr. Disraeli has a most exquisite voice, and he is using only its gentlest modulations. He is quite colloquial, and his tone is friendly and familiar – especially when he comes to a bitter innuendo, when he turns his head to the country gentlemen, that they may hear it and laugh – a low simmering chuckle, that just agitates the surface for a moment only, Lord John [Russell] and the Whigs and the Radicals smiling, too, as though the sarcasm were a good-natured joke.

But *The Leader* was capable of its own innuendo, especially in their account of the climax of Disraeli's speech:

> having got the cheer at the right spot, the great orator, concluding, sinks into his seat, as nonchalant as though he had been answering a question about Fahrenheit, and immediately . . . turns to ask Lord Henry Lennox whether Grisi was in good voice that night![21]

Grisi was a prima donna of the opera in those years and Lennox must have been by Disraeli's side rather frequently in that season to be mentioned in the papers. His hand 'flirting' with a feminine handkerchief, his 'exquisite' voice, his 'nonchalant' manner – these were all dandy traits, but the implication is that they might be also those of someone addicted to an unmentionable, foreign vice. *The Leader* was using Disraelian innuendo to say that Lennox might be his partner in crime.

The brief 1852 government ended in December, but Disraeli's friendship with Lennox continued. In January 1853 Lennox made a pilgrimage to Byron's villa at Genoa. 'How I wish you had been with me, the other day,' Lennox wrote from Italy, 'when I landed at that lovely place; and strolled in a glorious hot sun and under an *intensely* blue sky, to Byron's villa! It was gorgeous and lovely! and I only wanted a *kindred soul* to sympathize with my feelings!'[22] As Lennox was no great reader, he had probably got to know of Byron via Disraeli. Reference to Byron may well have been a secret code between them.[23]

Later in 1853 Lennox experienced a financial crisis and wrote to Disraeli that he was coming down to Hughenden to talk it over.[24] After some suspense, his father and his eldest brother extricated him from the crisis and paid his debts. He wrote to Disraeli that there was now 'but *one thing* left for me and that is, to sell my rank and position for such a sum as will enable me to keep it up; I must not be squeamish as to the birth or appearance of the young Lady but really try to find such a sum'.[25] Lennox is surprisingly cynical and brutal about marrying for money, but ducal children, other than the heir, are often like that. Brought up with immense privileges and immense wealth, the system of primogeniture means that the eldest son takes most of the inheritance, and if the younger children do not marry well, the privileges and wealth to which they have been accustomed vanish. Nor would Lennox's story have surprised Disraeli. He was used to extravagance and improvident spending. He had been in exactly the same situation with George Smythe, who also asked for help finding a wife.

Smythe and Lennox met each other that autumn at

Hughenden. Disraeli told a sympathetic female friend of his two visitors.

> Lord Henry Lennox, one of my aide-de-camps, and whom I had the pleasure of making a Lord of the Treasury for ten months; and Mr. Smythe, the eldest son of Lord Strangford, and who both, as to ability and acquirement, is perhaps the most brilliant man of the day; tho' more adapted to social and literary pursuits than the stern business of politics. It was his first visit to Hughenden, tho' not Lord Henry's.[26]

The visit came as something of a shock to Smythe. Though his friendship with Disraeli had cooled, he was still surprised to see how much he ranked beneath Lennox in Disraeli's current affections. Smythe wrote to Manners to say it was curious to see Lennox's 'almost tyrannical influence over so great a man, as Disraeli has proved'. Smythe confessed: 'I see now how vain an ass I must have been in our Young England days, when I attributed to my intellect the favour which I see, he must have accorded, to his personal friendship only for myself.'[27] Smythe thought the great man had loved him for his brains, but concluded from how Disraeli behaved with Lennox that it had been more a question of his beauty.

The relationship between Lennox and Disraeli cooled too in the mid-1850s. Their letters were never quite as intense again as they were in 1852 and 1853. Lennox still merited a salutation rare in the Disraeli correspondence, 'My dearest Henry'. Lennox could also still make a teasing reference to Disraeli as if he were a Catholic cardinal and address him 'Your Eminence'.[28] Their letters tend to be filled with more routine political gossip. Lennox, however, had made an impression on Disraeli somewhere down deep in his personality, as he was still the subject of speculation in Disraeli's letters to other friends even in the later 1870s.

In the nearer term, Lennox proved an embarrassment for Disraeli. When he took office under Derby again in 1858, Disraeli had to tussle with a trusted colleague, Sir William Jolliffe, about putting Lennox back into his old place at the Treasury. Disraeli told Jolliffe, the party whip, who was making lists of who among the party's supporters deserved office and who thought Lennox not worth such a plum appointment,

> *It is quite impossible* that Henry Lennox can be thrown over. The family must be represented in the Government, and it can't be done at a cheaper rate – but, besides this, Henry Lennox, during the last five years, has been of great service to the party, and though his labours, from their nature, have been known only to myself, they have, on some occasions, as could be shown, been of critical advantage.[29]

Jolliffe gave in and Lennox went back to the Treasury.

Before many months had elapsed, however, there were already plans to move Lennox abroad, possibly into a permanent diplomatic post that would secure him a salary, and free up valuable political patronage in the Treasury. Disraeli's private secretary, Ralph Earle, thought that while Lord Derby would probably consent to this, Lord Malmesbury at the Foreign Office might object. Moreover, the Duke of Richmond was 'warmly' interested in his son's appointment.[30] Disraeli had to tangle with the most formidable figures on his side to find his friend a job. In September, however, the diplomatic appointment had fallen through as Lennox had refused whatever had been proposed to him as beneath his dignity. Disraeli had to write to Malmesbury, 'Henry Lennox will take nothing under a mission, or a Sec[retaryship] of [an] *Embassy*: therefore, I conclude, he remains at the Treasury.' On top of this, Lennox was annoyed that he had even been asked to consider a position abroad 'so very much inferior' to the post and salary he enjoyed as a lord of the Treasury. There was an acrimonious exchange between them where Lennox accused Disraeli of angling to reward his brother with a more important job than he had offered to him, as well as declarations of wounded feelings.[31]

In December 1858 Disraeli tried to get Lennox into a permanent seat on the Privy Council, but was turned down by his
colleague, Lord Salisbury.[32] Then in March 1859, as Disraeli was
preparing to introduce the reform bill that would make or break
the government, Lennox resigned in protest over the measure.
Disraeli could scarcely believe it, writing to him: 'My dearest
Henry, What is all this about? And what have you to complain of?'
Lennox replied rather lamely that he had the 'Stigma of Stupidity'
for being so silent in the House of Commons and that he could
better serve Disraeli as a 'Policeman in plain Clothes, a detective so
to speak' who would report on the feelings of ordinary members.
Both of them had a passion for secrecy and intrigue, but what
makes little sense is that only the day before Lennox had written to
Mary Anne to remind Disraeli of 'his kind promise to let me take
him into the Hall and House' before his speech introducing the
reform bill. In other words, Lennox wanted to remain as Disraeli's
spy, but he also wanted to keep up his official position of publicly
escorting Disraeli to his place in the House of Commons. Lennox
ended his strange explanation for his resignation with a postscript
'Do not speak to me at the Levee for my heart will be too full.'[33]

Lennox out of office was no less trouble to Disraeli than when
he was in it. Disraeli heard via his lawyer, Philip Rose, who was
also acting as an agent for the Conservative party, that Lennox was
gossiping and being indiscreet with his inside knowledge of the
government's transactions. Ralph Earle, said 'I cannot tell you
how much anxiety it causes me, to know that a man of H[enry]'s
infirmities and shortcomings is in so important a position. Your
reputation as an administrator may be seriously compromised by
his ignorance and indiscretion.'[34]

This caused Disraeli to write a letter rebuking Lennox, but
also gently psychoanalysing the cause of his spreading information
that could harm his former chief.

I am vexed at what I hear of your sayings and doings. If they
could now, or eventually, lead to any advantage to yourself, I

should be more reconciled to your course, however mortifying to myself: but I see, in its results, nothing for you but permanent discomfort.

You have many enemies, but you have one devoted friend; and, believe me, that is a possession in life, not to be despised.

You are betrayed by those in whom you now precipitately confide. This is always the case.

What really makes you uneasy and unhappy is, that you are dissatisfied with what you have done. But the proper remedy for such a position is sympathy, and the counsel of experience and affection, which in time, and with opportunity, may put you, in all respects, right – and especially with yourself.

Think over these lines, my dearest Henry, and let me see you, when you like.

Yours ever, D.

Lennox was unrepentant. He replied saying that he had not confided in anybody and that he had never been happier than in the three months since his resignation.[35] George Buckle said that Disraeli thought that Lennox's resignation in the spring of 1859 was so 'capricious' that their friendship was never on the same terms again.[36] Disraeli had seldom taken so much trouble over any other individual and that he was willing to expose himself to all the difficulties that friendship with Lennox entailed, suggests that this relationship was a landmark for him. Power brought increased opportunities for intimacies with young men such as Lennox which he had only imagined in his novels; but relationships with these younger men exposed him to greater risks than ever before too.

Two other young men from the 1850s, with whom Disraeli's feelings were somewhat less involved, yet to whom he responded with similarly quick offers of friendship and patronage, were Ralph Earle and Edward Stanley. Earle came from a prominent Whig family in Liverpool, had been educated at Harrow and, when Disraeli met him for the first time, was serving as an attaché to the British Embassy in Paris. Earle was in his early twenties, Disraeli more than thirty years older. Blake said that Earle 'like Manners, Smythe and Lennox, fell under the spell which the magician could always cast over youth'. Although Disraeli was in some ways a magician, and liked to cultivate an aura of mystery, he was himself equally under the spell of the young men. Earle was particularly ambitious and may have seen his opportunity for promotion in the particular indulgence Disraeli was willing to grant well-spoken men in their twenties. When Disraeli visited Paris with Mary Anne on a trip lasting from late 1856 to early 1857, he and Earle came to an agreement, possibly even an 'unspoken' agreement according to Blake, that Earle would provide Disraeli confidential information from the embassy in exchange for Disraeli's advancement of Earle's career.[37]

The Victorians were much more formal than we are. It took them a long time to be on a first-name basis with one another and they almost never signed their letters 'love' except to family members, sometimes not even then. It is surprising, therefore, to find Earle writing with unusual familiarity to someone much senior to him in the official hierarchy whom he had only just met. When the Disraelis left Paris, Earle wrote 'I cannot tell you how I miss my conversations with you' and that the older man should believe in his 'affectionate devotion'.[38] A few months later Earle wrote that he was 'dying for further news'. He claimed Disraeli knew 'how little bureaucratic distinctions excite my ambition' and offered himself as Disraeli's private secretary should he become foreign secretary the next time the Tories were in office.[39] Disraeli did not forget him. Earle became his private secretary in 1858 when he came into office for a second time as chancellor of the exchequer. Lennox was somehow mixed up with Earle in keeping the secret intelligence flowing from Paris, but the two disliked one another, probably because Earle had replaced Lennox in Disraeli's affections.[40] Buckle observed that 'Earle attracted Disraeli in the same sort of way that Lennox had attracted him.'[41] Jealousy was in the air. In a large correspondence between Earle and Disraeli, Lennox is one of the only people referred to by his Christian name, and sometimes only as '*H*'. This might have been to keep their spying secret; but they may have also all belonged to an informal freemasonry of homosexual men who knew of and acknowledged one another without committing the nature of what they had in common to print. Disraeli described Earle to an elderly female friend, along with the man from the Treasury who was helping him, C. L. Ryan, like this:

> I have two excellent private Secretaries: both young men and very good-looking and clever. The first Secretary, Mr Earle, has been returned to Parliament though he is only 23 – but a man in matured thought and power of observation. Without his assistance I could not get through my work. I can trust him with interviews. He can see men and manage them.[42]

Earle would remain with Disraeli as his private secretary until 1866. Even Blake, who disliked Earle for his disloyalty to the Foreign Service in leaking confidential material to Disraeli, admitted that Earle 'must have had some power of pleasing, or Disraeli, who was fastidious about personalities, would not have employed him so long'.[43] There were risks and dangers in courting these young men, but there were also pleasures and rewards. To be aware of Disraeli's attraction to Earle is to notice a dimension of enjoyment that power brought to him that he had not experienced quite so abundantly before.

A third young man in Disraeli's orbit during the 1850s was Lord Derby's eldest son, Edward Stanley. His relations with Stanley were much less emotionally charged than those with Lennox or Earle. Nevertheless, he enjoyed serving as a mentor to all three. Stanley was elected to succeed Lord George Bentinck in the constituency of King's Lynn after Bentinck's death in 1848. He quickly became friends with Disraeli and spent much time at Hughenden talking over politics and affairs. Like Disraeli he was allied with Conservative Protectionists, but in his willingness to entertain reform questions he often had more affinities with Liberals than with those in his father's party. Stanley's abilities, and the fact that he would one day inherit substantial estates, marked him early as destined for office and power. His intimacy with Disraeli was a cause of 'mortification' to his father, according to the celebrated diarist, Charles Greville, as Lord Derby was slower to overcome his distrust of Disraeli than his son was.[44] But then, the fathers of Smythe and Manners were equally disgusted at their sons being mixed up with Disraeli. Did they fear something more than his political ideas?

Stanley has left behind charming images of Disraeli in the library at Hughenden taking down and consulting books as they talked. Disraeli may have even raised with Stanley a story connected with Lord Canning's homosexuality. Canning appears in the list Disraeli made in his 1842 'Commonplace Book' of men who had had intimate relations with other men. Stanley remembered that Disraeli told him a story in the early 1850s of the politics of setting up a newspaper in 1826–7. Stanley's recollection of Disraeli's story was that 'G. Dawson[,] Peel's agent in politics, proposed to attack C[anning] on the ground of certain practices well known.' The editor of the newspaper Dawson and Peel were organizing told Peel:

'If you ask me to fire upon a political enemy I will do it: but I will not pelt him with a turd.' [O]f this G. Bentinck heard for the first time in '46 or 7. and believing Peel to have had a hand in the matter, wanted to make it all public. This wd have ruined C[anning]! D[israeli] deterred him.

Stanley does not say what, according to Disraeli's story, the 'imputations against Canning' were, but it was routine in that era for men accused of sodomy to be put into stocks and pelted by the public with raw sewage. George Bentinck would have had an interest in protecting Canning's reputation, having served him as private secretary when he was a young man.[45] Stanley and Disraeli were both interested in the workings of political newspapers, as they were both involved in the running of *The Press*, a newspaper for which he and Disraeli both wrote in the 1850s. The episode is significant because, although sodomy was an unspeakable crime in the Victorian period, it still played a role in men's attempts to blacken one another's reputations. They were like little boys calling one another 'fag' and 'queer' and 'poof'. In Disraeli's case, however, he may have brought up this story to see whether Stanley was sound or shocked.

Stanley was not an uncritical disciple. He disliked Disraeli's exploiting his talent for satire at the expense of the party's reputation for prudence.[46] Equally, Disraeli resented his own dependence on the Stanley family and attacked them in the most damning way he knew how, for having bad interior decoration. When Disraeli first went to Knowsley, their big house in Lancashire, he described it as 'wretched', and 'the ugliest house in England, were it not for . . . [the] "family mansion" in St. James's Square. That is furnished like a second-rate lodging house, and is in itself essentially mean: all this not from stinginess, but from sheer want of taste.'[47] Disraeli was critical of Derby *père* for going to the races at Doncaster when he was needed in London,[48] and of Derby *fils* for turning down a dinner invitation at Disraeli's house when a show of party unity was essential. It is interesting that in the latter case, Disraeli used the same sort of emotional blackmail on the younger Stanley that he had once tried on Benjamin Austen when Austen tried to compel Disraeli to pay a debt. 'I cannot conceal,' Disraeli wrote to Stanley, 'that my feelings are deeply wounded. My friendships, though I have to deal with many men, are rare, I counted yours among my chief and most enduring possessions.'[49] Yet, just as Disraeli could make fun and be serious at the same time, so too could he be emotionally manipulative and in earnest at the same time. He wanted to make sure Stanley came to the dinner, which in the end Stanley did, but he did value the younger man's friendship. Stanley might in some way have served as the imaginary son Disraeli never had.

This is clear from Disraeli's report to Derby of the young man's performance at a critical juncture in the House of Commons. Stanley, who at the young age of thirty-four had been appointed to the cabinet as colonial secretary in the 1858–9 government, had defended the principles by which the government was proceeding towards legislation to deal with the Indian Mutiny of 1857. Disraeli told Derby,

> It will make you happy to hear, that Stanley has *greatly* distinguished himself; indeed, I hardly know a parliamentary effort, that, both on the House, and his own party, ever produced a better effect.
>
> And quite unstudied: it occurred to me, that it would be wise, that he should rise after Palmerston: instead of myself: I thought it was a great occasion, and that he *might* be equal to it. He WAS.
>
> I never was so nervous in my life, and I never was so pleased. Except yourself, I do not know anyone who is so content.[50]

Disraeli is surely not the first middle-aged man to have mixed up pride and paternal affection in his attitude to a protégé.

Those relationships of friendship and protection could be sources of trouble, long after the initial intimacy had been replaced by cooler affections. We have seen this with Lennox, but it happened with the others too. George Smythe came back to help Disraeli as a researcher in the 1850s, and through some carelessness led Disraeli into plagiarizing part of his speech paying tribute to the Duke of Wellington after he died in autumn 1852.

More embarrassingly still, Disraeli's friendship with Edward Bulwer, now Sir Edward Bulwer Lytton, came back to haunt him during the 1858–9 government. Bulwer Lytton reluctantly agreed to be secretary at the colonial office in 1858 when he would have preferred to be a peer. Derby refused to ennoble him and Bulwer Lytton had to face re-election in Hertfordshire. It was now that his former wife, Rosina, accused him publicly of having had a homosexual past. As Disraeli was named in Rosina's accusations, it was awkward for him too. He wrote his old friend:

> I thought you had tamed the tigress of Taunton [Rosina] – but, unhappily, this is not the case.
>
> She is writing letters to your colleagues, and friends, of an atrocious description, such as, I thought, no woman could have penned, accusing you of nameless crimes, at least which only can be named by her, and threatening aggravated hostilities.
>
> This is not very pleasant to your friends: I should think, hardly, to yourself.
>
> What can be the explanation? Is it possible, that your agent has been so negligent, or so imprudent, as to leave her allowance in arrear?[51]

'Nameless crimes' were virtually synonymous in the nineteenth century with a charge of an unnatural offence or sodomy. Bulwer Lytton had reduced his wife's allowance in order to cover his expense in suppressing some of her novels. The upshot of this episode was that he had her committed to an insane asylum in Brentford, but a newspaper outcry compelled him to release her and then one of her children took her abroad for the summer. Her allowance, once £400 a year, had been reduced to £180, but was now increased to £500 a year. It looks from the last paragraph of Disraeli's letter as if Bulwer Lytton was paying her to be quiet.

Bulwer Lytton had an international reputation as a novelist and had served many years in the House of Commons. He lent some weight to the 1858–9 government, but he also caused endless trouble to Disraeli and Derby by repeatedly threatening to resign due to ill health. In January 1859 Disraeli told Derby dryly that he had averted Lytton's resignation: 'He expects to die before Easter, but, if so, I have promised him a public funeral.' That worked for a few months, but when Lytton tried to resign in the spring citing his health again, Derby told Disraeli '*Ecce iterum Crispinus*' or 'Here's Crispinus again', the same phrase Disraeli had once used to describe himself to Lockhart.[52] Derby was underlining Lytton's reputation for being a lily-livered man of letters rather than the robust man of action they needed on the front bench. Doubtless Derby knew too of what Rosina had said. The throwaway line emphasizes the degree Disraeli's later reputation for being a capable statesman was occasionally compromised by his early friendship with Bulwer Lytton.

To do him credit, Disraeli defended his old friend. Even in a letter to Queen Victoria, who had reputedly received one of Rosina's letters accusing her husband of unnatural practices, he went out of his way to show Bulwer Lytton's best qualities despite the popular tendency to make fun of him. In his official letter to the Queen as leader of the House of Commons, Disraeli reported on the debates about the Tories' proposed reform bill in March 1859. He said it had been 'A night of immense power and excitement.' Sir Edward Bulwer Lytton's had been one 'of the greatest speeches ever delivered in Parliament'. He described his old friend in vivid terms:

Deaf, fantastic, modulating his voice with difficulty, sometimes painful – at first almost an object of ridicule to the superficial – Lytton occasionally almost reached the sublime, and perfectly enchained his audience. His description of the English Constitution, his analysis of democracy – as rich and more powerful than Burke.[53]

Disraeli may have been exaggerating, but he certainly was not abandoning Bulwer Lytton, even though he had proved to be something of a liability.

Disraeli had longed for friendship with an equal in his early novels. Power brought a kind of fulfilment to those earlier longings that had never been satisfied and often been troubled. Whether it was deference from the men in the House of Commons who had once derided him, or the attendance of chic young men like Henry Lennox, or the attentions of genuinely talented ones like Earle and Stanley, power brought Disraeli newly intensified relations with other men. These relations also had liabilities, as not only Smythe and Bulwer Lytton, but also Lennox, Earle and Stanley were capable of embarrassing him in later life because of the special favour he had extended them. Nevertheless, there was something compulsive in Disraeli's relationships with these men that he was not able to stop. Even though his pattern was to grant quick intimacy to a younger man and then be burned, that did not stop him from continuing to repeat his errors. His close relationships with several women in the same period were a good deal less fraught and, in the long term, more fulfilling as well.

17

More Valuable than Parks and Palaces

Someone once remarked maliciously that all Disraeli's girl-friends were grandmothers. Blake too noticed how Disraeli preferred his women either to be married, or to be older than him, or both. Both of these are sly although possibly unintentional ways of undermining his masculinity, of suggesting that he was never really up to a 'normal' relationship with an attractive woman his own age. But, in fact, these relationships with women were one of the most untroubled parts of Disraeli's biography and one of the best features of his personality. That women responded to him as deeply and as warmly as they did is a tribute to the sort of man he was, and a truer test of his masculinity than the 'sidewind sneers' of those who wanted to attack him.

Mary Anne was a constant presence in his life during the 1850s, but as they were often together, there are few surviving letters that testify to the quality of their relationship. In the first years of their marriage, she had been envious of his closeness to Sarah. That passed. That she now tolerated and assisted, even encouraged, his relationship with two other women shows how wise and generous she was. Her lack of jealousy or possessiveness indicates how firmly she felt rooted in his affections.

Sarah Brydges Willyams was already an elderly lady when out

of the blue and unintroduced she first wrote Disraeli an admiring letter. She was, like Disraeli himself, born Jewish but had married a Christian, in her case an officer of the Cornish militia who had died long ago. She was proud of her heritage, and was one of the few people who responded warmly to his defence of the Jews in Parliament as there were repeated attempts from the late 1840s onwards to lift the civil disabilities imposed on them. Although her first letter to him went unanswered, he could not ignore a letter she wrote in 1851 asking him whether when she died he would serve as an executor of her will. The bonus was that the executor would also be a residuary legatee and stand to inherit a considerable sum. To this Disraeli responded with alacrity, though he and Mary Anne were not able to arrange a visit to Mrs Brydges Willyams in Torquay until 1853. The visit was a great success for all three and afterwards there grew up a correspondence between Disraeli and his prospective benefactor that is fun to read and as revealing as any of his novels.

When she died ten years later in 1863, Disraeli inherited something near £30,000; the equivalent sum today would have to be counted in seven figures. Disraeli was using her for her money, being kind to her in gratitude for what she had done for him and would do after her death; but their relationship was also much more than that. He talked to her about his work and reflected on his own character in a vein that would ordinarily have gone into his fiction. He was so busy with politics that he wrote no novel during the twenty-three years after *Tancred*, published in 1847. Instead, he told Sarah Brydges Willyams about himself: 'difficulty and care are what I thrive on'.[1] In fact, he had been absolutely crushed by Lord Derby's refusal to take office earlier in 1855. Disraeli believed, as it turned out rightly, that the party would not be offered a similar opportunity for years. Sarah Brydges Willyams was one of the few people with whom he could find a sympathetic ear, and an audience allowing him to reconstruct his hopes. Similarly, when he was in office in the spring of 1859 and facing a hostile House with a reform bill that did not have much prospect of passing, he could write to her, 'Labor, anxiety, and responsibility seem to act on me as tonics.'[2] He was reflecting on what he was like, and helping himself to cope with the daunting odds by telling himself that uneven odds were what he enjoyed. Few of us will find many in life who can serve as a willing ear for such self-indulgent but also self-sustaining and ultimately productive egotism.

He also talked to her of Hughenden. He and Mary Anne went to visit her at her house, Mount Braddon, on the south coast, once a year, staying in a hotel, but having meals and walks and playing cards with their hostess. Although she was invited many times to Hughenden, Mrs Brydges Willyams never made the journey there, so Disraeli drew her amusing pictures of the place. He could talk quite openly of noticing the local boys in their unusual military manoeuvres when the local militia was quartered there. 'I have got the militia quartered here, and am obliged to give, what Lord Londonderry would call, "great military banquets". I want you on my arm to help me. You would be quite at home.' He also told her that 'It is astonishing how quickly the ploughboys turn into martinets.'[3]

Ever since he posed for a picture at his father's house with his hand in his waistcoat, Napoleon-style, Disraeli had loved posing in the imperial purple. He could usually make a good story out of his pose, though, and manage to send himself up at the same time. He told Mrs Brydges Willyams in April 1854:

> We have been here, some ten days, after an absence of five months – agitated and agitating months. We left so suddenly on the 19th. November last, that, when we returned, I found my book open on my table, and my pen, as it were, still full of ink. It was like the flight of Louis 18th. on the return from Elba [in 1814], when Napoleon eat [sic] the dinner which the King had ordered, and read the royal letters, tho' he did not answer them.[4]

Disraeli never liked the Irish and never went to Ireland, one of the strange features of a life, typical of many of his political contemporaries, where a disproportionate time was spent debating about a country they had never visited. Irish grievances left him cold. He told Mrs Brydges Willyams that he and Mary Anne had been in the country during days of 'almost unceasing rain. Hughenden is so green, that I should fancy I was in the "emerald isle", only my tenants do not, as yet, fire at me from behind the trees.'

The two of them were warmly interested in the Jews and family history. According to Weintraub, he was first intrigued that she had been born a Miss Mendez da Costa, from a prominent Sephardic family he had mentioned in his memoir of his father in 1849. He liked to make fun of the College of Arms in his novels, but he had heraldic instincts himself and he loved helping her with her coat of arms. He had to negotiate with the heralds in establishing a correct coat of arms for her.

> They were anxious to know how you had obtained them [elements of the Mendez da Costa arms], as nothing is more difficult than correct emblazonments of ancient Spanish arms. I told them that they had been copied from the Queen of Spain's own golden book, which was kept under her own key, which seemed to make their mouths water.[5]

Frankly, both of them liked questions of rank, hierarchy and distinction. So he could joke with her when he and Mary Anne sent her a gift of trout and she sent them turbot: 'We thank you very much for your kind recollection. Turbots visiting trout are patricians noticing country cousins.'[6]

His relationship with Frances Anne, Lady Londonderry, was equally warm. She was closer in age, and knew many of the personalities he saw in Parliament and in society, so he could gossip with her about their mutual friends. He had met her as long ago as 1835. There had been a brief estrangement between them after his marriage in 1839, but in the 1850s their letters to one another were those of friends who had a deep understanding and long-standing affection for one another. If Mary Anne had once, at the beginning of their relationship, been jealous of Lady Londonderry, now there was no sign of it. Whenever Lady Londonderry wrote, she pressed them both to visit her; and he never passed to her a disloyal word about his wife, as he sometimes had, for example to Sarah, at the start of his marriage to Mary Anne.

Sarah Bradford has said of the Londonderrys that they were 'universally disliked for their pride and ostentation', precisely the reason Disraeli did like them. Although his friendship with them had been an early 'social *coup*' for him,[7] by the 1850s he had in Lady Londonderry a mellow, reliable friend. In 1854 he complained to her, in a fairly rare outburst of petulance, that he had never been adequately backed in life, and that his chief Lord Derby had a large income but contributed to none of the funds or charities or newspapers that would help the party. She replied with soothing words. His 'Magic of the Mind' must at last 'command mankind'. It was as if she had taken her balm out of the pages of *Contarini Fleming*, which she quoted back to him in order to reassure him. She was one of those crucial women in Disraeli's life who saw that the genius of the written page would at last draw together the fragments of the old Conservative party, give it a coherent argument and make it once more into a force in the House of Commons. However, if he were hinting that she should subscribe where Derby had not, she ignored the hint. She said she needed about a half million herself for all her projects. Instead, she said he and Mary Anne must come and visit her at her country house in Northern Ireland 'and we will sit on the battlements and moon and dream and look into the future – and although I urge this selfishly as of course it would be a great charm to me I really and truly believe it would benefit you and you want some sort of *relache* and a little *dolce far niente*'.[8] What could be better than such imaginative sympathy, and from a marchioness to boot?

He knew how to enter into her feelings as well. She said a

month later that she was suffering still from the death of her husband, as well as anxiety from the possibility of her son being sent to the war in the Crimea. She apologized for writing solely of herself. Disraeli replied:

> What you suffer from, is want of sympathy. It is not merely the emotions of the heart, that are the source of happiness, but also that identity of sentiment and taste on all the pursuits and objects of life, which similarity of disposition may give, but which only the friendship, and confidence, and habit, of long years can maturely and completely develop.[9]

He was talking about married love and his letter was as much a tribute to his love of Mary Anne, as it was a reflection on what she was missing in the absence of her husband.

He could also tell stories of high society to Lady Londonderry, finding in her another outlet for the sort of narratives that would ordinarily have gone into his novels. For example he wrote to her in 1855 that the Duke of Somerset had died leaving a will in which he tried to disinherit his eldest son, the new duke, and leave everything to his second wife, the dowager duchess.

> [T]he Dowager Duchess has got everything – an immense jointure, £200,000 savings in cash, 'family mansion', as it was always called at the dinners, a crown of jewels, that belonged to Jane Seymour, and Heaven knows what besides! In the meantime, Seymour [the new duke], who is yachting . . . had not, when I heard all this, himself even been heard of. 'If he were only here' says 'the young Duchess' 'something might be saved – but now this dreadful old woman is pillaging everything.'[10]

He and Lady Londonderry had a mutual friend in the society hostess, Lady Jersey. In the summer of 1857 there were many parties where both domestic and foreign princes attended. Of one garden party at Twickenham he wrote, 'So much Royalty, that our friend, Lady Jersey, seemed to be rushing about the gardens in perplexed ecstasy.'[11] Disraeli may have gone out less to parties in the 1850s and worked on political problems more, but he saved his novelist's ability to comment on aristocratic absurdities for Lady Londonderry.

Or he could tell the light-hearted story of the son of his colleague, Sir William Jolliffe, who proposed marriage to a young lady during a ball at Hatfield. '[T]he future bride and bridegroom were so taken by surprise themselves and so enraptured, that they circulated the news themselves, and continued to receive the congratulations throughout the endless polkas.' Sir William heard about the engagement through Lord Derby, who told him the next morning at Downing Street. What better than beautiful young people announcing their engagement during endless polkas?

Early in 1858 Disraeli wrote to her that a new man had been appointed to the cabinet through being the protégé of the prime minister's wife, Lady Palmerston. 'There is nothing like female friendship – the only thing worth having.'[12] This might almost be read with a certain degree of cynicism in it, were it not so perfect an echo of what he had written twenty-one years before in *Henrietta Temple*: 'a female friend, amiable, clever, and devoted, is a possession more valuable than parks and palaces; and without such a muse, few men can succeed in life, none be content'.[13] What he had written in the 1830s about Henrietta Sykes, applied also to his sister Sarah; he felt something similar for Lady Londonderry and Sarah Brydges Willyams in the 1850s. Indeed, he probably felt it most warmly of all for Mary Anne.

One of the best results of the two brief periods of power in the 1850s was greater intimacy with Windsor Castle, or as he called it in 1854, 'the Château'.[14] He might even have said Château Désir, as Windsor was in many ways the peak of the aspirational register of the man who had written *Vivian Grey*. He was a natural courtier and loved reading the memoirs of Comte Ségur, French ambassador at the court of Catherine the Great, especially as the Russians in that era underwent a Crimean adventure similar to the one the

British suffered in the 1850s.[15] People knew this and used it to make fun of him. *Punch* pictured him as a child prematurely in court dress and impatiently waiting for the call to enter the cabinet during a failed attempt by Lord Derby to take office in 1851. [*See plate 15.*] It was the usual British embarrassment and ambivalence about the monarchy. True, it was a constitutional monarchy and members of the cabinet were servants of the Queen. But this was a formality, and to take too great an interest in the monarchy was just not done. It was unparliamentary. It was womanish. It smacked of servility and despotism. Disraeli was not prepared to observe this convention and swept it off the table with a clatter. He loved court dress and the satirists be damned.

What he loved in the monarchy was not simply the grandeur of it all, but the grandeur mixed with different varieties of human absurdity. He was like an adolescent boy who discovers that a picture of a naked woman is good, but even better if the model is wearing silly white socks. For example, he told Lady Londonderry in June 1852:

> The great foreigner of the season is Said Pasha, a prince of Egypt. He weighs 24 stone, and the Queen burst out a-laughing when His Highness was presented to her. He is, however, a somewhat enlightened man, speaks French with facility, and is travelling for his health, that is to say, has leave of absence for having failed in getting up a rebellion against his sovereign.[16]

Which was better? The Queen laughing because he was so fat, or the fact that the Egyptian prince was on a 'leave of absence' because of his failed rebellion?

He also loved telling a story of the self-denial and almost puritan self-mortification involved in the Queen's daily ritual. He told Mrs Brydges Willyams in 1856:

> Our Sovereign is very well. We had the honor of dining at the Palace a short time back, when she said, that she never had

been better, and that from the life she led, rising early, taking cold shower baths every day, and being frequently in the air, she had almost come to defy *catching cold*.[17]

Disraeli never got up early if he did not have to. He might have denied himself wine or dining out on rich meals in middle age, but he was certainly not about to take cold showers. The image of 'Our Sovereign' doing so was irresistibly ridiculous.

Disraeli was also a minute observer of the state visit of the French emperor and his wife to England in 1855. First of all there was much bowing, which Disraeli loved. In the reception line in addition to the Queen, Prince Albert, the French emperor, Napoleon III, and his wife Eugénie, were the Queen's mother, the Duchess of Kent, the Queen's aunt, the Duchess of Cambridge, and Princess Mary, the Queen's cousin: 'so one had to make seven reverences!' His letter to Mrs Brydges Willyams continues with a little gossip. He noticed that the Queen and the emperor appeared to have a small crush on one another.

> I understand [the emperor] enjoyed his visit very much, and greatly captivated Her Majesty, once so much prejudiced against him. There was immense embracing at the departure and many tears. When the carriage door was at length closed and all seemed over, the Emperor re-opened it himself, jumped out, pressed Victoria to his heart, and kissed her, on each cheek, with streaming eyes. What do you think of that?

Disraeli did not mind the Queen having an innocent extra-marital passion. What he did mind was royalties not acting worthy of the grand roles assigned to them.

> I was greatly disappointed with the Empress [Eugénie]. For me she had not a charm. She has Chinese eyes, and a perpetual smile or simper which I detest. I understand she is very

natural – too natural for a sovereign . . . and was sometimes found sitting on the edge of a table! What do you think of that? The courtiers were horrified.[18]

He was never quite satisfied with the dignity of the different French dynasties he got to know during his time in politics. He liked the Orléans King Louis Philippe, who had been forced to abdicate in 1848, but he always thought him a bit too casual for a king. Of the revived Bonaparte empire, he was sometimes inclined to agree with Karl Marx, who observed that if the revolution that brought in the first Napoleon was a tragedy, the Bonapartes a second time around were a little comic.

The Prussian royal family was a different matter. No lack of dignity there, but when they came over in 1858 for the wedding of Queen Victoria's eldest daughter to the young man who would one day become German emperor, the royalties were bored because they did not mix enough with the other guests at the bridal ball. Disraeli told Lady Londonderry with as much excitement as if he were writing in the persona of Lady Jersey:

> There were as many princes as at the Congress of Vienna. The Royal party did nothing but dance with each other, and I thought, perhaps in consequence, looked bored. I saw the Princess of Prussia [groom's mother and future empress] cram her pocket handkerchief into her mouth to stifle a yawn. The Princess Royal, however, looked bright and gay, though I understand she is continually crying about leaving home, but then, they say, she is very childish and always cries.
>
> The Queen rather expands too much in form, but she danced with the Prince of Prussia, and some others.

He was a great connoisseur of male beauty, especially in princes, and wherever he decided to send up a young man's appearance, he must also have been interested as well. 'One of the Princes,' his letter to Lady Londonderry continues,

> the Duke of Brabant, a tall, and otherwise, good looking young man, has so long a nose, that it startles every one, who meets him, and makes the women almost scream. It is such a nose as a young Prince has in a fairy tale, who has been banned by a malignant fairy, or as you see in the first scenes of a Pantomime, or in the initial letter of a column of 'Punch'.[19]

Because Disraeli was the ranking official or 'leader' in the House of Commons, as well as chancellor of the exchequer, during the 1852 and 1858–9 governments, it was his duty to write a letter to the Queen reporting on each night's parliamentary debate in the lower house. Here is where he combined the excellences of his two careers, in literature and in politics, in a way never seen before. Queen Victoria noticed the difference. She first wrote to her Uncle Leopold using Disraeli's nickname to indicate her detachment, 'Mr. Disraeli (alias Dizzy) writes very curious reports to me of the House of Commons proceedings – much in the style of his books.'[20] But she soon was hooked.

The custom was to write dry, colourless accounts of debates that were merely shorter and more authentic reports than the verbatim accounts that appeared in the newspapers. Disraeli saw his chance to add colour and spice, to arouse his sovereign's appetite for news, to liven up her hours spent reading the dull contents of dispatch boxes with accounts of real characters and indications of atmosphere. Here, for example, are his descriptions of two opposition speeches, one of the Peelite, Sir James Graham, as 'elaborate, malignant, mischievous'; the other of Lord Palmerston, 'mild and graceful, with a sarcastic touch'.[21]

He also liked to try to capture a mood for her, as for instance in 1858 when he wrote, 'The House is wild and capricious at this moment.' He added:

Your Majesty once deigned to say that your Majesty wished in these remarks to have the temper of the House placed before your Majesty, and to find what your Majesty could not meet in the newspapers. This is the Chancellor of the Exchequer's excuse for these rough notes, written on the field of battle, which he humbly offers to your Majesty.[22]

In other words, he pictured himself as military commander, as if he were Wellington writing his dispatch on horseback after Waterloo.

If a good anecdote could be made out of a dull debate it got a prominent place in his letter to her. In the discussions connected with transferring authority away from the East India Company after the Indian Mutiny of 1857, there had arisen a question of whether Singapore and the Straits Settlement should or should not be transferred to the colonial secretary. He told the Queen:

the speech of Sir [James] Elphinstone, master of the subject, and full of striking details, produced a great effect. His vindication of the Convict population of Sincapore [sic], as the moral element of that strange society, might have been considered as the richest humor, had it not been for its unmistakable simplicity.

His [Elphinstone's] enquiry of the Governor's Lady, who never hired any servant but a convict, whether she employed in her nursery 'Thieves or Murderers?'

and the answer,

'Always Murderers'

was very effective.[23]

Nor did he suppress his pride in serving her. A year later when he reported that her fifth Parliament since her having come to the throne in 1837 was on that day prorogued, he wrote, 'The Chancellor of the Exchequer has sat in all these five Parliaments, having entered public life at Your Majesty's happy accession.'[24] He was writing in the formal, correct, third person a version of what he wanted to say, but could not, or at least not yet, which was, 'You and I, my dear, have been through all this together.'

Power helped him realize some of the pleasures he had only dreamed of or longed for in his novels, new and more exciting varieties of friendship with both men and women, vistas of access and influence among diplomats and at court. But power could not protect him from the first real pangs of grief that he experienced at the end of the 1850s. His sister, Sarah, died prematurely in December 1859 of a bowel complaint. Although both his parents had died in the later 1840s, nothing survives in his letters up to this date that is anything like the pain he experienced at the death of his sister. On first learning that his sister's illness was serious, he wrote to his brother, Ralph, 'I have had a sleepless night, and so have you. Language cannot describe what this sudden, and by me never contemplated, catastrophe has produced on me. She was the harbor of refuge in all the storms of my life, and I had hoped she would have closed my eyes.'[25] To his colleague, Jolliffe, the next day he said, 'I cannot express to you, how unhappy, and over-whelmed, I am; I feel as if I could work no more.'[26] He was thrown back on the sympathy of two old friends, John Manners and Henry Lennox, with whom his former intimacy had diminished. But he needed them now, and was grateful for both their letters of sympathy to him. To Henry Lennox, on Christmas Day, a key day in most people's emotional calendar, and for Disraeli too despite all his pride in his Jewish heritage, he wrote, 'It was like you, dearest Henry, to remember me in my great grief . . . I am very sorry, that I have seen you so little of late; but I always think of you with unchanged affection.'[27]

18

Pearls Are Like Girls, My Lord

A popular pastime of the Victorian upper classes was to write a sketch, or 'character', of a friend or a fellow guest staying in a country house. It was meant to be a brief, elegant, but ruthlessly truthful account of the person's strengths and weaknesses. Lord Stanley, the eldest son of Disraeli's chief, Lord Derby, wrote such a character of Disraeli in the 1850s. Stanley remarked that 'politics constitute his chief, almost his sole pleasure'.[1] The trouble for Disraeli as the 1850s came to a close was that the prospects were bleak. Not only had he lost his sister Sarah, but the Conservatives had decisively lost an election to Lord Palmerston in 1859 that promised to keep them out of office for a good long time. Stanley also perceived another of Disraeli's vulnerabilities in the fickleness of his friend, Henry Lennox.

> D. has not been successful in forming and retaining personal friends. By none of his colleagues in office and opposition is he personally beloved: and his principal confidant, a young man of rank, whom I will not name, wrote to consult me only a few days ago, on the expediency of quitting [Disraeli's] flag for that of some other leader.[2]

How then was Disraeli to seek and satisfy his main pleasure when the political and the emotional forecasts were gloomy?

One clue comes from *Lothair*, published in 1870. This was the first book he had written since the publication of *Lord George Bentinck* in 1852, and the first novel since *Tancred* in 1847. In it the hero has a conversation with a Bond Street jeweller about the Duchess of Havant's splendid pearl necklace. Pearls 'want both air and exercise,' says the jeweller. '[T]hey must be worn frequently; you cannot lock them up.' The jeweller recounts what he has told the duchess, 'Wear them whenever you can, wear them at breakfast.' He adds:

> I go down to Havant Castle every year to see her Grace's pearls, and I wipe every one of them myself, and let them lie on a sunny bank in the garden, in a westerly wind, for hours and days together. Their complexion would have been ruined had it not been for this treatment. Pearls are like girls, my Lord, they require quite as much attention.[3]

This runs parallel to a story Disraeli once told of laying Mary Anne's pearls out in the morning sunshine to warm them for her at Hughenden. Disraeli loved jewellery. He loved women. He loved women who wore their pearls to breakfast. They were as sure a source of pleasure for him throughout the 1860s as politics ever were, and sometimes a good deal more reliable. They were his best friends and he was good to them in return.

No one has ever been able to calculate Mrs Brydges Willyams's exact age, but she was probably more than thirty years his senior. He could confess to her what did not come easily with a male equal. He knew that the political situation was rather desperate in the 1860s: a long prospect of opposition along with distrust of their leader among the Conservative backbenchers. He wrote to her in February 1861 of his party in the House of Commons in the new session:

I think I have got everything now in good order, and have brought the troops into the field in ample numbers and in fine condition.

The difficulty is to keep them in: but forbearance and patience are clearly our game.[4]

Although the military metaphor was common with reference to parliamentary contest, it is revealing in the context of Disraeli's biography. When Contarini Fleming arrives at his public school, though he has in the past been worried about his difference from other boys, he finds that his 'ambition' conquers his 'nature'.[5] Contarini Fleming first feels in his heady conversations with Musaeus that he is 'to be something great, and glorious, and dazzling'.[6] For Disraeli this combination between *eros* and parliamentary battle was essential, even though it seldom rose to the surface quite so explicitly after he was finished with his first trilogy of autobiographical novels. Succeeding in parliamentary battle was a way of fulfilling the ambition he had first recognized with Musaeus. When he could make Musaeus cry, he experienced for the first time a new kind of power. When he could make the House of Commons shout and murmur and laugh, he experienced the thrill not only of a general, but also of a lover.

It says something of his intimacy with Sarah Brydges Willyams that he could return so frequently to this metaphor. To her, he could tell of his defeats with his troops, his men, his boys. He wrote of a sizeable section of his party refusing to vote with him during a crucial contest with the government in June 1861:

In the very hour of victory, when the signal for the last charge was given, I had the mortification, great for a general indeed, to see a division of my own troops march from the field of contest. One bears this, however, as one bears many things, when the heat of youth is over, and one has experienced, in one's time, what is the surest, perhaps the only, support under discomfiture – the memory of former success.[7]

He knew better now than Contarini ever did how to be philosophical about defeat.

Sadly, though, Sarah Brydges Willyams died in November 1863. Disraeli wrote his last letter to her six days before she died, probably unaware that it was his last. 'Adieu!' he said, 'we shall soon meet.'[8] But they were never to meet again. Cynics have often said Disraeli was using her. He was the executor of her estate and she left him a portion of her considerable fortune. He used this to pay off lingering debts that still survived from his wild youth. He wanted her buried in the church at Hughenden, but when he found this was impossible, he arranged for her to be buried next to himself and Mary Anne, in the churchyard at the eastern end of the church. All three of them can still be seen there today. This unusual graveyard arrangement is emblematic of the complexity of the relations between them in their lifetimes. He certainly used her for her money and pursued her when he found she was rich; but he also grew to rely on her. He wrote some of his best letters to her. He loved her too. Nor are these mutually contradictory impulses.

The mark of Disraeli's unusual self-confidence with the women he loved was that he would sing their praises to each other. Although his wife had once been passionately jealous of Disraeli's friendship with Lady Londonderry, he rashly gambled that he could tell Mrs Brydges Willyams how much he admired Frances Anne. When he and Mary Anne went to stay with Lady Londonderry at Seaham Hall in December 1861 he wrote Mrs Brydges Willyams an amusing set piece about the lady he had once known in golden drawing rooms, now at home near her blast furnaces.

This is a remarkable place, and our hostess is a remarkable woman. Twenty miles hence she has a palace (Wynyard) in a

vast park, with forest rides and antlered deer, and all the splendid accessories of feudal life. But she prefers living in a hall on
the shores of the German Ocean, surrounded by her collieries,
and her blast-furnaces, and her railroads, and unceasing
telegraphs, with a port hewn out of the solid rock, screw
steamers and four thousand pitmen under her control. One day
she dined the whole 4,000 in one of the factories. In the town
of Seaham Harbour, a mile off, she has a regular office, a fine
stone building with her name and arms in front, and her flag
flying above; and here she transacts, with innumerable agents,
immense business – and I remember her five-and-twenty years
ago, a mere fine lady; nay, the finest in London! But one must
find excitement, if one has brains.[9]

As with all the best characters in his fiction, this is a good portrait
because he found something in Lady Londonderry that was like
himself. He too was someone who had 'brains' and this had sent
him off in search of excitement.

Lady Londonderry was soon off on a stranger journey still.
She died aged only sixty-five in 1865. When in the 1870s he was
able to recognize her son by conferring on him an Irish order, he
told a new lady friend, Lady Bradford, this 'was the son of a
grande dame who was kind to me when I was a youth, though she
was a tyrant in her way'.[10] Another time he had said of her that
she was 'half ruffian – half great lady'.[11] In short she was just the
sort of tough and determined, spirited and *soignée* woman that
sustained him through a long life. Lady Londonderry's grand-
daughter, in writing of Disraeli's attraction to women, saw that his
desire was symbolic and affectionate rather than sexual. 'For
Disraeli,' she wrote, 'Woman was the perfect companion, and it is
remarkable that the pleasure he experienced in female society
was largely intellectual and often quite independent of physical
attraction.'[12] He liked women with a powerful and dramatic sense
of themselves. This often overrode his physical attraction to them.
That someone could have recognized this about him so close to

his own generation is evidence that Disraeli's contemporaries knew that Disraeli's orientation to the opposite sex was out of the ordinary.

Edward Stanley remarked in his character of Disraeli that one of his most 'amiable' features was his domestic devotion to his wife.[13] Mary Anne was a constant presence and perhaps the most silently sustaining of all these women. She is silent in the historical record because they were so often together that there was little reason to write letters to one another. She went frequently to parties, while he sat long nights on the opposition front bench, or stayed home and studied goverment bluebooks. She was hiring and firing servants, planning the meals for their table, arranging the garden at Hughenden. With the death of Mrs Brydges Willyams and Lady Londonderry she comes back into a poignant focus.

In the 1850s the problem facing Disraeli was how to reunite the Conservative party, to find the necessary alliances that would bring the Tories back to power. He was always ambitious to be in office, whereas Derby's strategy was to wait and he was more conscious than Disraeli of the dangers of taking office prematurely. Disraeli counted on his genius and parliamentary manoeuvre to bring the party back together; Derby counted on time healing the party's old wounds.

In the 1860s much turned on Palmerston. Though technically a Whig, he was the most conservative politician imaginable. He was popular in the country. His age and personality conferred a prestige that made him nearly impossible to dislodge from the premiership. When he died in 1865, suddenly politics were dynamic and fluid again. While Palmerston lived, the question of expanding the provisions of the 1832 Reform Bill had been off the agenda. After his death, both Liberals and Conservatives jockeyed to introduce a new reform bill that would capture the post-Palmerston world and introduce new momentum in their favour.

Disraeli's political fortunes revived with the failure of his Liberal opponents to pass a satisfactory reform bill. This brought Derby and Disraeli back into office in 1866. Disraeli in the spring of 1867 brought in a reform bill of his own, which famously became much more radical than its author had originally intended. He accepted one radical amendment after another in order to keep the bill alive, and more importantly to undermine the Whigs and Liberals who regarded themselves as the natural party of reform. Mary Anne welcomed him home one late night after the first successful division in his bill's passage through Parliament. She had 'got him a raised pie from Fortnum and Mason's, and a bottle of champagne, and he ate half the pie and drank all the champagne, and then he said: "Why, my dear, you are more like a mistress than a wife."'[14] One would not necessarily need to sleep with such a man to appreciate his lines and enjoy his company.

Mary Anne was twelve years older than him and in her midseventies. At the very moment of his triumph with the Second Reform Bill she was struck down by a serious illness, possibly a precursor of the stomach cancer that killed her five years later. He had gout at the same time and they wrote notes to one another in their separate bedrooms at Grosvenor Gate. One of his to her reads,

Being on my back, pardon the pencil.

You have sent me the most amusing and charming letter I ever had. It beats Horace Walpole and Mme. de Sévigné.

Grosvenor Gate has become a hospital, but a hospital with you is worth a palace with anybody else. Your own D.[15]

Disraeli could write a wonderful love letter even when he was flat on his back.

Lord Derby resigned in February 1868, himself worn out by the gout that had stricken him off and on for decades. The passage of the Second Reform Bill meant that Disraeli had a new weight and standing. He had single-handedly passed an important reform of the constitution while he was in a minority of seventy in the House of Commons. This increased admiration for him in the country and it pleased the Queen, who had not thought such a difficult question could be settled so quickly. He was now not only the man who had led the Conservative party through nearly twenty years of wilderness and opposition, but also the man of the hour who had shown that Conservatives too had the capacity for progressive reform. When Derby resigned, the Queen had no hesitation in sending for Disraeli. Thus early in 1868 he kissed hands with the Queen for the first time as prime minister. He and Mary Anne decided to give a party in the Foreign Office to consolidate the party and celebrate his having been named to the premiership. After the Houses of Parliament themselves, the Foreign Office was one of the grandest of public buildings erected for official purposes during the nineteenth century. Although the building was not completely finished, the Disraelis staged a memorable party there. The Bishop of Oxford, no great fan of Disraeli's, wrote in his diary: 'Dizzy in his glory, leading about the Princess of Wales; the Prince of Wales, Mrs. Dizzy – she looking very ill and haggard.'[16] Ill, haggard, but what the Bishop of Oxford omitted, still in love with her husband after nearly thirty years of marriage, Mary Anne and Disraeli were still a great team.

This first premiership brought increased contact with the Queen and in September 1868 Disraeli made his first trip to Balmoral, the Queen's house in Scotland. These Victorian trips to Scotland were an ordeal because they involved spending long hours on the train, often overnight. Mary Anne packed him a picnic for his long train ride north: cold partridge, chicken, tongue, 'plenty of good wine!' His letter to her on his journey north continues,

Nothing but the gravity of public life sustains me under a great trial, which no one can understand except those who live on the terms of entire affection and companionship like ourselves: and, I believe, they are very few.

Write to me every day, if it is only a line to tell me how you are; but you, with your lively mind and life, will be able to tell me a great deal more.[17]

Disraeli was much changed from the giddy, hedonistic youth who wrote *Popanilla*. Now, the 'gravity of public life' was his stimulus; he had the sense that the spotlight was on him and he had to act up to certain standards of heavy Victorian decorum if he wanted the rewards of power, patronage, fame and deference. Only Mary Anne had known him in both incarnations. He paid tribute to the warmth and longevity of their marriage by saying that very few could live on the terms of 'entire affection and companionship' that they enjoyed together.

One of the things he loved about her was that she could appreciate a sly homoerotic joke. He wrote to her from Balmoral that one of the Queen's German sons-in-law wore a kilt for the first time. The custom was to wear nothing underneath. Disraeli told Mary Anne that the German son-in-law 'was an hour getting' the kilt 'right by the aid of his wife and his affectionate brother-in-law [the Duke of Edinburgh]'.[18] Nothing was more funny than Germans wearing kilts and young men struggling naked under their tartans.

Disraeli was not long in his coveted office. Gladstone, who through oratorical skills that rivalled his own had become Disraeli's chief antagonist, cleverly wrong-footed him on the issue of the Irish Church. Disraeli and his party lost an election in December 1868. Many of the new voters enfranchised by his Reform Bill voted against him. So in December he had to contemplate making his list of resignation honours, the traditional way in which an outgoing premier recognizes his supporters. He told the Queen that he would like to break with precedent. Rather than accept any honour for himself, he wanted Mary Anne to be raised to the peerage as Viscountess Beaconsfield in her own right. He was 64 years old; she was 76. He knew that she might not outlast another long period of opposition. Moreover, though he spoke often of his love for tradition and precedent, there was always something in him willing to crush the traditionary forces that had for so long held him at arm's length. The Queen accepted his proposal and Mary Anne was raised to the peerage. It was a tribute entirely typical of his loving radicalism and his devotion to the silly but iron-willed woman who had so effectively backed him up for many long years.

The future Lord Rosebery, aged eighteen, sat next to Mary Anne at dinner in a country house one evening in 1865. He stole away later to write down the conversation and he has left a vivid portrait of Mary Anne's absurd side. He asked her whether she was interested in politics. She replied, 'No I have no time, I have so many books and pamphlets to read and see if his [Disraeli's] name is in any of them!' When he told her he was going up to Oxford, she said, 'Oh yes, I love Oxford; they are all so fond of Mr. Dizzy there, they all applaud him so.' She also confessed to her young companion that she did not like it much when Disraeli was in office:

> 'for then I lose him altogether, and though I have many people who call themselves my friends, yet I have no friend like him. I have not been separated from him since we have been in the country, except when I have been in the woods, and I cannot lose him' (here her voice trembled touchingly) . . .

Rosebery thought this 'half crazy warm-hearted woman's talk',[19] but it conveys her utter and moving devotion to her husband.

Queen Victoria was never especially friendly to breaks with precedent, especially in raising people to the peerage, but she assented to Disraeli's request because she understood his loyalty to his wife. It is often written in error that Disraeli flattered the Queen and thus easily won her. That does injustice to the complexity of their relationship. Both of them admired at the same time as they manipulated one other.

The Queen presented a contrast with Mary Anne. Her husband, Prince Albert, to whom she was as utterly devoted as

Mary Anne was to Disraeli, had died young in 1861. Indeed, one of the key ways that Disraeli gained political stature in the 1860s was through court favour. The Queen, though stricken, was especially pleased at Disraeli's parliamentary eulogy of Prince Albert in 1862.[20] Throughout the 1860s, she retired from public life, mourning the death of her husband, a little selfishly, somewhat depressed, gaining weight and wearing black. It is what can happen if there are not powerful people to tell you what not to do when everyone sympathizes with you. The Queen complained constantly of her health, especially when she was asked to end her mourning and to appear in public. Whenever politicians saw her, however, she seemed to them redder, fatter and in ruder health than before her husband had died. This was certainly Disraeli's impression when he was invited to Windsor to dine and sleep the night in 1863. She seemed to him 'stouter' than before, but thought possibly it might have been her dress that was not slimming. She had invited him as a prominent member of the opposition. She also wanted him to speak and vote in favour of a grant to fund one of her pet projects, the erection of a statue of Prince Albert in Hyde Park, that was to become the Albert Memorial. She did not ask him to vote for it, but she was especially gracious to him on the morning before she sent him back to speak in the debate later that day. He did speak and the House of Commons voted the additional money.[21] She had not bribed him exactly, but the process had begun whereby they showed one another courtesy and got the political help they needed in return.

Disraeli's attraction to the monarchy was legendary even in his own time. He wrote pages in his unpublished reminiscences on the Prince of Wales's wedding to Alexandra of Denmark in 1863. Jonathan Parry remarks that it was Palmerston's cunning to get Disraeli invited to the wedding, thereby softening him up and making him a less spiky opponent of the government.[22] Disraeli told Sarah Brydges Willyams that it had been 'a perfect pageant'. He loved too the 'presence of the imperial and widowed mother in her Gothic pavilion, watching everything with intense interest, seeing everything, though herself almost unseen'.[23] He knew this because he had trained his opera glasses on the Queen sitting in her secret balcony above the altar at St George's and had been rewarded by a royal glare when she saw him looking at her. Buckle believed this showed Disraeli's strangely feminine sensibility. Whereas 'most British statesmen in the Victorian era regarded' such ceremonies 'as a necessary bore, whatever pleasure their wives may have taken in them', Disraeli entered into them 'with keen zest'.[24] To take such a female interest in the monarchy was odd in a man. It was another way of saying between the lines that Disraeli was sexually ambiguous, foreign, Jewish, oriental, not an ordinary Englishman.

Nevertheless, Disraeli would brook no nonsense from the Queen where his party interests were at stake. When it came to his great showdown with the Liberals over the Second Reform Bill, the Queen offered to mediate. She wanted the bill passed through Parliament with as little threat of revolution and as much consensus as possible. He, on the other hand, wanted to gain as great a party advantage as he could and if possible to slap Gladstone – rhetorically – in the face. So he wrote to a colleague of the Queen's desire to negotiate between the rival parties:

> The royal project of gracious interposition with our rivals is a mere phantom. It pleases the vanity of a Court deprived of substantial power, but we know, from the experience of similar sentimental schemes, that there is nothing practical in it, or, rather, that the only practical result is to convey to our rivals that we are at the same time feeble and perplexed.[25]

Power was a greater drug for him than royalty. So he coldly rejected the offer of royal mediation.

Thwarted in her desire to mediate, the Queen was still pleased with the outcome of the reform debates. She was ready to be better friends with Disraeli in the moment of his triumph than she had been before. The aristocratic Whigs saw this and disapproved. One of them, Lord Clarendon, had the news via one of the ladies-in-waiting that

> Dizzy writes daily letters to the Queen in his best novel style, telling her every scrap of political news dressed up to serve his own purpose, and every scrap of social gossip cooked to amuse her. She declares that she has never had such letters in her life, which is probably true, and that she never before knew *everything!*[26]

Disraeli did send gossip to her and that may have been one foundation of their relationship. Her sending flowers to him was another. In the spring of 1868 she sent him the first of many bouquets and received Mary Anne's thanks: 'Mr. Disraeli is passionately fond of flowers, and their lustre and perfume were enhanced by the condescending hand which has showered upon him all the treasures of spring.'[27] There is a passage in the Alan Clark diaries about his spending a morning in his ministerial office in the 1980s arranging flowers as if he were a 'quean', but few other British politicians can have been so secretly florists on the side as Disraeli was. Sarah Brydges Willyams had once discovered that a reliable way to please him was by sending flowers, and now the Queen discovered it anew.

Although he complained to Mary Anne about the strain of the long train journey to Balmoral in the autumn of 1868, once he got there he found that royal Deeside was not so bad. First of all, the Queen's courtiers, composed mainly of retired military officers and charming widowed ladies, often from distinguished though relatively impoverished families, went out of their way to put him at ease. Lord Bridport, the equerry who happened to be in waiting, told Disraeli that he 'need not wear frock coats' and then added a tiny joke flattering to Disraeli's vanity. Bridport said that he knew Disraeli 'as a country gentleman' would 'abominate' wearing formal dress in the country.[28]

His first dinner with the Queen was just like a fashionable dinner in town with an unmarried man. He told Mary Anne: 'We dined in the Library, a small, square room, with good books – very cosy; like dining with a bachelor in very good rooms in the Albany.'[29] He also liked the decoration of her rooms upstairs where she received him to go over business, and noted the garden details that he knew would interest his wife.

> Her rooms are upstairs: not on the ground floor. Nothing can
> be more exquisite, than the view from her window. An expanse
> of green and shaven lawn more extensive than that from the
> terrace of Clifden, and singularly striking in a land of moun-
> tains: but H. M. told me, that it was all artificial, and they had
> levelled a rugged and undulating soil. In short our garden at
> Hughenden on a great scale: except this was a broad, green
> glade, the flower garden being at the other side of the Castle.[30]

The Queen took trouble to entertain her guest. One day she ordered that there was to be a picnic beside the River Dee. 'The party was very merry,' Disraeli told his wife, 'all the courtiers had a holiday. Lady Churchill said that, when she asked the Queen, through the Princess Louise, whether she was wanted this morning, the Queen replied "No: all the ladies are to go, to make it amusing to Mr. Disraeli."'[31] If he had thwarted her desire to get involved in the reform debates, she now won several tricks from him. All that summer and autumn of 1868 Disraeli was sending her proposals for filling up vacant bishoprics; he even had to fill up the Archbishop of Canterbury's place as the incumbent had recently died. He did not take much interest in Church of England personnel. He saw these as opportunities to strengthen the Tory party in the House of Lords where bishops sat and voted. He cared much more about the bishops' political than their religious proclivities. The Queen would not hear of this. She wanted good Broad Churchmen, political moderates who would hold the balance in furious contests between Low Church Evangelicals and High Church Ritualists. She refused to allow their party political opinions to be a criterion in their selection. In every case she got her candidate appointed over the man whom Disraeli had originally proposed. It was the beginning of a genuine lovefest between the Queen and Disraeli, but neither one gave up pressing a political agenda at the same time.

19

Enamoured Sexagenarians

In the 1860s, as he lost two of his great lady friends in the deaths of Mrs Brydges Willyams and Lady Londonderry, while his relations with the Queen and Mary Anne prospered, Disraeli's rivalry with Gladstone also approached its peak. Although their hatred of one another and the stylistic differences between them are legendary, few have seen how similar the two men were. Much of their aversion to one another may have arisen from autobiographical parallels between them; and, at least on Disraeli's part, there may have been as strong an attraction to Gladstone underneath, as there was apparent aversion to him on the surface.

A decade earlier, in the 1850s, Disraeli and Derby were always hoping to lure the former adherents of Peel, like Gladstone, back into the folds of the Conservative party. It was also clear that of the younger generation in the House, Disraeli's and Gladstone's were the two greatest oratorical talents, but no one hated Disraeli more than the Peelites, who blamed him not only for Peel's fall from power but also his premature death in 1850. Nevertheless, when Disraeli and Derby had an opportunity of strengthening their minority government in 1858, Disraeli wrote to Gladstone asking that all personal questions between them be put aside. Disraeli told a colleague, 'I almost went on my knees' to

Gladstone. The exchange of letters was an echo of that between Disraeli and Lockhart when Disraeli accused Lockhart of pursuing a personal vendetta against him in *The Quarterly Review*. Like Lockhart, Gladstone wrote a cutting reply denying that 'relations between yourself and me' had ever affected a single decision he had made.[1] There was a good deal of emotion, metaphorical romance and desire to wound mixed up in this correspondence.

There was also a mixture of love and hate between them on religious questions. Gladstone knew much more about the affairs of the Church than Disraeli did, so he was much more effective in fighting with the Queen for the men he wanted to appoint as bishops. However, when it came to the Anglican High Church, there were certain telling affinities between Gladstone and Disraeli. During the nineteenth century there had been a significant Catholic-sympathizing movement within the Protestant Church of England. This had begun with the Oxford Movement, which emphasized the historical, medieval and pre-Reformation character of the Church of England. It survived at mid-century as 'Ritualist' clergymen and congregations who liked a more elaborate, more Roman service than was usual in Anglican churches. Buckle noted that: 'Gladstone's respect [for Disraeli] was combined with an alloy of deep moral disapprobation – a frame of mind which was fostered by what Disraeli had called the "finical and fastidious crew" of high Anglicans among whom Gladstone familiarly moved.'[2]

Gladstone had a popular reputation for sympathizing with Oxford and the Ritualists. Disraeli tried to exploit this by using the same words to describe the most prominent member of the Oxford Movement, John Henry Newman, who actually gave up Anglicanism and, much to the disapproval of ordinary Englishmen, became a Roman Catholic. If the Church were disestablished at the behest of Oxford converts – he implied that Gladstone was among them – it might, Disraeli warned, 'subside into a fastidious, not to say finical congregation'.[3] Disraeli meant to play upon popular prejudice against converts to Catholicism which labelled them 'effeminate' and to tar Gladstone with that brush. The Low Church response to Newman was Thomas Arnold's 'muscular Christianity'. It was an attempt to reassert masculinity and Englishness against the foreign, Romanizers in their elaborate cassocks and other fancy dress.

However, as effeminacy was something of which Disraeli himself had been accused, and as a defence of effeminate males is one of the most persistent themes in his fiction, it is ironic that he should choose to classify Gladstone with the 'finical and fastidious' Newman. Disraeli himself had been much attracted to the Roman Catholic Church on his first trip to the Continent. Young England too had been as sympathetic to the Oxford Movement as Gladstone had ever been. Even in the 1860s Disraeli admired the pope, 'an old man on a Semitic throne', for fighting off Garibaldi's nationalist barbarians, 'the modern Attilas'.[4] He liked the idea of history and ceremony fighting off liberalism, nationalism and modernity.

Nor had the comic weekly newspaper, *Punch*, forgotten his days of dressing up when he was a young man. He made a speech at Oxford, in November 1864, where he attacked Darwin's theory of evolution. 'The question is,' he had asked, 'is man an ape or an angel? Now, I am on the side of the angels.' His audience loved the line, but *Punch* took this opportunity to depict him as a cross-dressing angel, a man with his hair in flowers, wearing a lady's gown, admiring himself in a mirror as he prepares for a masked ball. [*See plate 16.*] This is surely one of the most explicit references that survives to mid-Victorian notions that still linked the Conservative leader with the effeminacy of Regency dandies and questioned his sexuality.

Another thing that Disraeli and Gladstone had in common was a perceived mental instability. Disraeli liked to capitalize on Whig rumours that Gladstone was mad by referring to his delicate 'nervous system', his 'eager mind' and his doubtful 'temperament'. In a parliamentary speech of 1860, where he claimed that the Tories had no wish to take office, he made a series of sly jokes at Gladstone's expense. He said that he would not recommend leading the House of Commons to anyone 'who has any regard for his nervous system. The important office which the Chancellor of the Exchequer [Gladstone] fills gives ample opportunity to his eager mind and his impetuous rhetoric . . . From what I have observed of the right hon. gentleman's temperament,' Disraeli continued, it was as well that Gladstone served under Palmerston and Lord John Russell. It was good that he did not lead the House for the time being, though he imagined he was ambitious for such a post.[5] Recall that Vivian Grey, the young Duke of St James and Contarini Fleming all worried about their sanity as young men. When juxtaposed with the pages in his early novels spent wondering about whether his own intractable depression was not a form of madness – passages which he suppressed as the novels came out in new editions – this suggests more parallels or affinities, even sympathies, between the two than differences.

They were also both great speakers. Usually, their oratorical styles sharply contrasted with one another. Gladstone's speaking relied on Evangelical zeal and pulpit earnestness, while Disraeli's was, at its best, provocative, devilish, easy and amusing. It is strange then to find Disraeli capitalizing on differences between Gladstone and Palmerston in the 1860s by suggesting that Gladstone had been forced to adopt his own oratorical style. Palmerston as prime minister was recommending an aggressive foreign policy which Gladstone at the Treasury was forced to fund, even though he disapproved of it. Disraeli told the House:

> We have a patriotic Prime Minister appealing to the spirit of the country; and . . . at the same time we find his Chancellor of the Exchequer, whose duty it is to supply the ways and means by which those exertions are to be supported, proposing votes with innuendo, and recommending expenditure in a whispered invective.[6]

'Innuendo' and 'whispered invective' were what Disraeli's admirers most enjoyed in his speeches; he was teasing Gladstone with having been forced to adopt a rhetorical mode at odds with his reputation for high moral character.

Disraeli switched back to his own native mode and effectively ridiculed Gladstone's objections to the Reform Bill of 1867. He was able through turns of phrase to capture Gladstone's style of speaking, as if Gladstone were a Jupiter hurling thunderbolts, and the House dissolved in laughter. Even a Gladstone-sympathizing journalist admired Disraeli's speech for the way it disarmed the leader of the opposition.

> Its bold caricature of Mr. Gladstone's cloud-compelling manner placed an obstacle such as ridicule can rarely raise in the path of the official Opposition. The whole House seemed tickled too much ever seriously to fall out with Mr. Disraeli on this subject again . . . Men who have heard Mr. Disraeli throughout his career agree that never did he show such mastery over his audience, such boundless histrionic resource.'[7]

Despite their oratorical rivalry on the floor of the House of Commons, there was an emotional bond between them that was channelled through Mary Anne. Disraeli's wife had always liked Gladstone and he returned her affectionate notice. When she fell seriously ill in the closing months of 1867, Gladstone stood up at the beginning of an extraordinary autumn session and expressed sympathy for Disraeli at a time of anxiety for his wife's health. Disraeli responded with tears in his eyes, one of the few, if perhaps the only time he ever showed such emotion on the floor of the House. He then wrote to Gladstone, saying that Mary Anne had always had 'a strong personal regard for you, and being of a vivid and original character, she could comprehend and value your great gifts and qualities'.[8]

Is it not then a possibility that there was a hint of subconscious *eros* in their attitude to each other? Harry Coningsby's best friend at Eton is Millbank, an earnest and rather humourless young man, the son of a northern manufacturer who could easily pass for

Gladstone, and whose sister Coningsby marries at the end of the novel. Similarly, the meticulously careful editor of Gladstone's diaries spoke of a schoolboy love of Gladstone's: 'The chief love of Gladstone's schooldays [at Eton] was Arthur Henry Hallam, son of the Whig historian and subject of Tennyson's great elegy, *In Memoriam*. This relationship with Arthur Hallam was certainly not the usual "crush" developed between boarding-school boys living in close proximity' because they were in different houses and it was unusual for such boys to meet often. 'None the less the relationship was intense, though not directly sexual, and prefigured several such relationships, with both sexes in Gladstone's later life.'[9] They both shared, thus, what most men of the Victorian upper classes had in common, a nostalgic memory of love for boys and a capacity for sublimated love for other men.

Gladstone gave as good as he got in parliamentary contest with Disraeli. He waited for the very moment of Disraeli's triumph, his rival's first cherished taste of the most powerful office in the land. Only weeks after Disraeli had become prime minister in 1868, Gladstone introduced resolutions on the Irish Church in the House of Commons. He meant to steal the initiative and the thunder from the new prime minister, who thought he had secured the alliance of English Catholics to the Tories by promising them an officially endowed Catholic university in Dublin. Gladstone offered Catholics something better: he promised to take away the official protection from the Protestant Church of Ireland altogether. Thereby he secured for the Liberals not only English and Irish Catholics, but also all Irishmen anxious to free themselves from the burdens of English rule. It was the issue on which Gladstone would win the election that autumn. Even the loyal Buckle described this as 'Gladstone's most brilliant and successful stroke as party leader'.[10] Disraeli and the Conservatives left office in December 1868 after a Liberal majority at the election that promised them another considerable exile in opposition. Gladstone was the only man who could bring tears to Disraeli's eyes in public; he was also the only man who could condemn him to more hated years of lounging on the opposition front benches.

Disraeli's charm and appeal is that setbacks never set him back for long. He took up his pen again for the first time in decades and started to write fiction. From a signal defeat, he once again wrought gold. His story's hero is a late adolescent boy, Lothair, 'a shapely youth', 'bronzed by a life of air and exercise', with 'a profusion of dark auburn hair'.[11] Lothair is rich, orphaned and heir to a great landed estate. Bertram, heir to another great estate, is Lothair's best friend. At their 'time of life', Disraeli says, 'the claims of friendship are paramount'. It is a high point when Lothair goes to visit Bertram's family in the country for the first time. Bertram's family is a revelation to him because 'hitherto [he had] passed through life rarely with pleasure, and never with joy'.[12] So in the very first pages we have a return to Disraeli's favourite themes: handsome but depressed boys whose lives look up when they find best friends and are invited to stately houses.

There is also Disraeli's usual coded reference to Graeco-Roman homosexuality. The work begins with a Latin tag from Terence, a Roman writer of comedies. It is from his play *Eunuchus*, a story whose chief male character dresses as a eunuch to woo a slave girl. According to one of *Lothair*'s modern editors, the tag is a warning to a young man to stay away from harlots, which seems a strange enough way for an ex-prime minister to begin a work of fiction in an age legendary for its strict morality.[13] Stranger still is that Terence was protected in his day by Laelius, described by Cicero as the 'intimate friend' of Scipio Aemilianus in his dialogue, *De Amicitia (On Friendship)*. Aemilianus was another protector of Terence. What was going on between these three men friends? It is significant that Disraeli signed himself 'Laelius' in his letters to *The Times* when he wrote attacking the Whigs as a young man. He must have been writing for an audience knowledgeable about the classics and aware of the sexually charged ambiguities in the word 'friend'.

Nevertheless, the novel's chief action is not between Lothair and Bertram, but in Lothair's choosing between the love of three different women. He admires Bertram's sister who is Protestant and another eligible young woman who is Catholic. A third, who is an older married lady, Lothair loves the best, probably because she is the least available of the three. Still, that warning against 'harlots' sticks out as extraordinarily odd as the preface to Lothair's perfectly usual attraction to three beautiful women.

Lothair's real temptation, the real 'harlot' or 'scarlet lady' of the novel, is the Roman Catholic Church. Disraeli loosely based the story of *Lothair* on the recent conversion of the Marquess of Bute, a rich and eligible young man, to the Roman Catholic Church. In the novel, Catholic priests and cardinals are always trying to snag Lothair, to dupe him into converting so as to promote their cause in England. When Lady Corisande, Bertram's sister, hears that Lothair may convert to Catholicism, she remarks, 'It seems so unpatriotic, so effeminate.'[14] This is not the sort of effeminacy Disraeli defended to his mother when he was wearing jewelled studs in Spain. This is one of the worst things a woman can say about a man.

One of Disraeli's purposes must have been to make another secret attack on Gladstone, whose sympathy for Ritualism and the High Church was well known. His Irish Church Bill of 1869 radically improved the prospects for Catholics to govern Ireland. The Queen and members of the Victorian middle classes could sometimes be led to believe that Gladstone so liked Roman ritual in the Anglican Church that he himself had 'gone over' to Rome. Disraeli's novel is his usual means of proceeding, via innuendo and 'whispered invective', to suggest that England was menaced by Catholics in the year 1870, that members of the aristocracy were vulnerable to the Roman Church's seductive appeal and that Gladstone was the pope's willing tool.

Disraeli often forgets, however, that he is making an attack. He draws characters with all the remembered zest and enjoyment of his younger days as a writer. One of the best characters in the book is a dandy, the heir to a rich dukedom, Bertram's brother-in-law, Lord St Aldegonde. Henry James, whose homosexuality was buried so deep that it has taken a recent novelist to bring it out,[15] especially praised St Aldegonde for his 'genuine plausibility' in his review of *Lothair* for the *Atlantic Monthly* in August 1870. James also saw Disraeli's essential gravity beneath his light-hearted portrait of a Regency dandy living a generation beyond his time in the middle of Queen Victoria's reign: 'Essentially light and superficial,' James wrote of *Lothair*, 'the author is never more so than when he is serious and profound.'[16] St Aldegonde is a light and superficial character whose very lightness and superficiality is itself a profound message of Disraeli's. St Aldegonde demonstrates once again a theme that is never far beneath the surface in Disraeli's biography: in life we must seek pleasure and enjoyment. Conventional morality is a waste of time. Dress up. Relish the bizarre.

Disraeli described St Aldegonde as 'listless and handsome' or 'listless and freakish'.[17] After dinner one evening at a house party the men are left alone at the table.

> The gentlemen lingered and looked at each other, as if they were an assembly of poachers gathering for an expedition, and then Lord St. Aldegonde, tall, fair, and languid, said to Lothair, 'Do you smoke?'
> 'No!'
> 'I should have thought Bertram would have seduced you by this time. Then let us try.'[18]

The novel may be about the seduction of Lothair by the Roman Catholics, but it is also about his seduction by the worldly wise St Aldegonde. '"I like Lothair," said St. Aldegonde dreamily, "He is a nice boy."'[19] The reader suspects he may not be a nice boy for long if St Aldegonde has his way.

St Aldegonde is very spoiled, but he knows it. He has odd views, in which Disraeli parodies his own radical Toryism.

Had he been an ordinary being, he would have merely subsided into selfishness and caprice, but having good abilities and a good disposition, he was eccentric, adventurous, and sentimental. Notwithstanding the apathy which had been engendered by premature experience, St. Aldegonde held extreme opinions, especially on political affairs, being a republican of the reddest dye. He was opposed to all privilege, and indeed to all orders of men, except dukes, who were a necessity. He was also strongly in favour of the equal division of all property, except land. Liberty depended on land, and the greater the landowners, the greater the liberty of the country . . . St. Aldegonde had married for love, and he loved his wife, but he was strongly in favour of woman's rights and their extremest consequences.[20]

Disraeli had just passed the Second Reform Bill, derided as 'a leap in the dark' by its critics. It had been considerably more generous than the Liberals had been willing to be in enfranchising the urban working classes. St Aldegonde is a variety of Disraeli himself, seeing nothing wrong with equality of property, but insisting that there should still be great landowners, and always dukes. It is also a measure of Disraeli's unconventionality that he makes his most sparkling character in the novel a proponent of women's rights. By implication he too had told the House of Commons that he was not an opponent in principle of female suffrage.[21] Perhaps he saw that in politics one proceeds first by imagining a compelling story of reform before one can legally enact it.

There are other touches of autobiography in St Aldegonde's character. He refuses all courses at dinner except some cold meats. Disraeli was troubled by his digestion in later life and the dinner parties he once loved became an ordeal. So he would come to the table, taking only biscuits or water or something cold so as not to miss the chatter and the entertainment. St Aldegonde and the narrator of the novel both say separately that they hate Sundays in the country. St Aldegonde and Disraeli both had Wildean personas long before the heyday of Oscar Wilde himself. This is St Aldegonde at Lothair's coming-of-age house party:

> St. Aldegonde loved to preside over the mysteries of the smoking-room. There, enveloped in his Egyptian robe, occasionally blurting out some careless or headstrong paradox to provoke discussion among the others, which would amuse himself, rioting in a Rabelaisian anecdote, and listening with critical delight to endless memoirs of horses and prima-donnas, St. Aldegonde was never bored.[22]

Just as Disraeli was proud of the fact that he got on well with the woodsmen at Hughenden, St Aldegonde is particularly good with the working classes, with whom he feels a natural affinity. Lothair receives all the guests from the neighbouring farms and towns at his coming-of-age 'down to the stokers of the trains from Grandchester, with whose presence St Aldegonde was much pleased, and whom he carefully addressed as they passed by'.[23]

Late in the novel Lothair and St Aldegonde meet in the Middle East. They have a frank discussion about the male beauty of a Syrian called Paraclete. '"That is a good-looking fellow, Lothair," said St. Aldegonde; "or is it the dress that turns them out such swells? I feel quite a lout by some of these fellows." "I think he would be good-looking in any dress," said Lothair.'[24] Almost the last thing we are told about St Aldegonde is that he 'had a taste for marriages and public executions'.[25] He is the best evidence there is that Disraeli's Byronism, his love of dressing up, his frank appreciation of handsome men that he associated with the freedom of the East, had not died, but simply gone underground.

Two other characters, portraits of people he knew, but also self-portraits, are worth noticing in *Lothair*. One is a wonderfully silly woman, a little like Mary Anne, the wife of Lothair's attorney: 'Mrs. Giles, or as she described herself Mrs. Putney Giles, taking advantage of a second and territorial Christian name of her husband, was a showy woman.' She wants 'to become acquainted with the aristocracy and to be herself surrounded by celebrities'.[26] She gives a dinner to Lothair and Cardinal Grandison, one of Lothair's guardians. It was 'a great day' for her 'not only to have Lothair on her right hand at dinner, but the prospect of receiving a Cardinal in the evening . . . The repast was sumptuous; Lothair thought the dinner would never end, there were so many dishes, and apparently all of the highest pretension.'[27] This is Disraeli the suave aficionado of dinner parties in later middle age recalling with a twinge of comic embarrassment how proud he had been to meet the aristocracy when he was just a budding novelist. *Lothair* is an affectionate retrospective as much as a way of dishing Gladstone and whiling away the longueurs of opposition.

Mr Phoebus is an established artist, sometimes said to be patterned on Lord Leighton, then an influential painter and president of the Royal Academy after 1878. He is also one side of Disraeli himself, just as Mrs Putney Giles and Lord St Aldegonde are. Phoebus speaks a pre-Nietzschean philosophy of admiration for 'Aryan' civilization, by which he means the ancient Greeks and Romans, ruined by 'Semitism', by which he means Christianity. Phoebus gives splendid parties in the novel. One is an outdoor banquet that could only be captured properly by one of the court painters of the reign of Louis XV. Everyone is well dressed. The soup is served in Sèvres cups, the wines in Venetian glass and there are ortolans on the menu.[28] This is the Disraeli *locus classicus*, a world painted by Fragonard, or Boucher, or Watteau in the middle of the eighteenth century. He had little sympathy for the moral narratives of the nineteenth-century Pre-Raphaelite painters and their followers.

Lothair also meets Phoebus in the Mediterranean, where he is sailing on his steam yacht, *Pan*. Phoebus gives a party on the yacht where the crew is dressed in Venetian costume.[29] Phoebus lives for some of the year on a Greek island where he 'pursued a life . . . partly feudal, partly oriental, partly Venetian and partly idiosyncratic'. Phoebus loves Greece because the natives

> make parties of pleasure; they go in procession to a fountain or a grove. They dance and eat fruit, and they return home singing songs. They have in fact, been performing unconsciously the religious ceremonies of their ancestors, and which they pursue, and will for ever, though they may have forgotten the name of the dryad or the nymph who presides over their water.[30]

In short Phoebus likes Greece for its memories of pagan religion and he sums up his own religion as a variety of Platonic philosophy: 'true religion is the worship of the beautiful. For the beautiful cannot be attained without virtue, if virtue consists, as I believe, in the control of the passions, in the sentiment of repose, and the avoidance of all things of excess.'[31] Disraeli had been recommending Plato to his readers ever since the discovery of 'PLATO' was a revelation to Vivian Grey in his father's library. Disraeli's return to such a theme shows how important a pagan appreciation of the beautiful was to his life's philosophy of pleasure and how he was still, Popanilla-like, trying to provide an alternative to an Evangelical Christian morality.

Phoebus sounds very much like the unreconstructed Disraeli of old, dwelling upon a pagan worship of pleasure and beauty. Just as Disraeli loved jewels, Phoebus buys them for his wife whenever he has spare money. He prefers carrying around a sack of jewels in his pocket because he dislikes paper money. Phoebus's yacht *Pan* refers to the Greek god of forests, and there is a prominent nude Pan in the garden at Hughenden, as well as a satyr [*See plates 18 and 19*] and a worshipper of the Greek god of wine. It is as if Disraeli's garden statuary matched Phoebus's love of nature and pleasurable abandon.

However, a remark by the wise Syrian, Paraclete, suggests that

Disraeli is not entirely the pleasure-lover of old, and that even he foresaw the disasters inherent in too complete an embrace of Wildean aestheticism. Paraclete, whose name means holy spirit, or helper, or comforter, warns Lothair that Phoebus's worship of the beautiful 'always ends in an orgy'.[32] As Disraeli got older, the sensualism of his youth, though it might have been nice to recall, was tempered with something higher, more disciplined, more spiritually fulfilling.

However, old age did not mean diminished expectations as a lover. Phoebus has an eye for male beauty. 'He liked youth, and good-looking youth; and youth that was intelligent and engaging and well-mannered. He also liked old men.' At seventy men attained their 'second childhood, the charm often returned. Age was frequently beautiful, wisdom appeared like an aftermath, and the heart which seemed dry and deadened suddenly put forth shoots of sympathy.'[33] When he wrote this Disraeli was himself approaching seventy and the narrator goes out of his way in the novel to say that sixty- and seventy-year-olds are still ardent lovers. 'Threescore and ten, at the present day, is the period of romantic passions. As for our enamoured sexagenarians, they avenge the theories of our cold-hearted youth.'[34] Disraeli had himself met a new 'good-looking youth' in the era he was writing *Lothair*. There is no evidence that this youth ever became Disraeli's lover in a physical sense, but Disraeli certainly ended his life loving this young man as passionately as he had ever loved anyone.

Disraeli met Montagu Corry at Raby Castle, the home of the Duke and Duchess of Cleveland, where the Disraelis were staying in 1865. There was a large house party, which included this young son of one of Disraeli's Tory colleagues. Disraeli was in his sixties, Corry in his twenties. On a rainy afternoon, some of the young women persuaded Corry to perform a comic song and dance. Disraeli happened to be passing the doorway of the drawing room and stopped to see the young man perform. Corry thought he had made a fool of himself in front of one of the most important politicians in the country. Not at all. Disraeli highly approved. In Buckle's account of their meeting:

> Disraeli, though his face had worn its usual mask, had been greatly attracted by the combination of youth, ability, good looks, good-nature, and social gifts, and, after dinner that evening, secured the lifelong devotion of a prince among private secretaries with the gracious words, 'I think you must be my impresario.'[35]

His metaphor is key. Disraeli wanted Corry to be the manager of his show, the producer of his performance. Politics and life were nothing more than theatre and entertainment. He wanted Corry to help him put on the final act.

Disraeli proceeded quickly to sideline Ralph Earle and put Corry in his place. Earle became an MP at the election of 1865 and Disraeli arranged for a salaried position for him on the Poor Law Board. Earle was dissatisfied and complained that he had been cut off from all the old confidential information to which he had been privy as Disraeli's private secretary. He even attacked his old chief in the debates over the Second Reform Bill, a performance considered embarrassing to both political parties as everyone knew how close Disraeli had been to his former secretary. It was like a fight between former lovers hung upon a political pretext. Interestingly, Earle resigned his post, left England and set up a business in the Middle East. He never married.[36]

Meanwhile, as Buckle remarked, 'In a very few weeks the relation between the Minister [Disraeli] and his principal secretary [Corry] had become of the most intimate and confidential character, and so remained till Disraeli's death, fifteen years later.'[37] Like Earle, Corry was himself a lifelong bachelor, though he apparently fathered several illegitimate children, one with Violet, wife of the eighth Duke of Rutland.[38] Later in life, he took up charitable good works and founded the Rowton Houses, inexpensive houses for unmarried working men in London.

However, when he first came to work for Disraeli, it was the statesman alone to whom he was devoted. Corry was not afraid to tell Mary Anne that in the opening salvos of the Reform Bill debates of 1867 that of all people, only he, Corry, sympathized with Disraeli as much as Mary Anne did. Disraeli famously compared a private secretary to a wife in his last novel, *Endymion*, but here was Corry identifying himself with Mary Anne when he had been working for Disraeli for less than a year.[39]

As the decade of the 1870s opened, Disraeli had a new novel, *Lothair*, a tremendous financial success. He also had a new secretary, who was as much a protégé and a friend as he was a political assistant. To top all, Disraeli sensed a change in the zeitgeist, which would ultimately be beneficial to the Tories. He told another former protégé, Lord Stanley, now become Earl of Derby, that the Franco-Prussian War was beginning to divert people's attention away from the domestic reforms which Gladstone, and the generation of Whigs and Liberals before him, had championed. Disraeli believed that it was well

> that the mind of the nation should be diverted from that morbid spirit of domestic change and criticism, which has ruled us too much for the last forty years, and that the reign of priggism should terminate. It has done its work, and in its generation very well, but there is another spirit abroad now, and it is time there should be.[40]

Disraeli, the canny politician, saw his opportunity coming and he was getting ready to jump.

20

Amidst Imperial Triumphs

In his last novel, published in 1880 when he was in his seventy-sixth year, Disraeli described a mock medieval tournament held at a Victorian country house. The opening of the tournament consisted of a grand procession of all the aristocratic competitors. Disraeli wrote, 'Every procession must end. It is a pity, for there is nothing so popular with mankind. The splendid part of the pageant had passed, but still the people gazed and looked as if they would have gazed forever.'[1] Processions, triumphs and parades had always interested him. Perhaps then it was no coincidence that the first sign of his reviving political fortunes nearly a decade earlier had come on the day of an unusual royal procession from Buckingham Palace to St Paul's Cathedral. In the autumn of 1871 the Prince of Wales nearly died of typhoid fever. Crowds gathered outside newspaper and telegraph offices for news. Expressions of public sympathy and interest in his recovery were marked. After the prince regained strength, he and the Queen were so touched by the popular interest that they agreed to go in an unusual procession to the City to hear a service of thanksgiving in February 1872. After the service, Disraeli, as leader of the opposition, was allowed to get away in his carriage unusually early from St Paul's. Although he was not a part of the official procession, he received an impromptu ovation from the crowds still assembled along the parade route as he drove back to the West End and the Carlton Club. The newspapers remarked that the applause for him along the line of the route was greater than for Gladstone, then in the midst of his first premiership. Afterwards, a famous diarist of the mid-century, Sir William Fraser, observed Disraeli at the Carlton.

> Disraeli was leaning against the table immediately opposite to the glass door, wearing the curious white coat which he had for years occasionally put on over his usual dress. Familiar as I was with his looks and expression, I never saw him with such a countenance as he had at that moment . . .

Fraser believed that Disraeli was looking into the future when he would be prime minister again.[2]

Disraeli had for the most part given up his extravagant dress in the later 1840s when he began to sit on the Conservative front bench. The white coat was a sign of the dandy's resurgence: he was old enough now not to give a damn what people thought. He was a wit and a celebrity in his own right, a proven parliamentary performer. Tory backbenchers had so often tried and failed to remove this extravagant outsider from the lead that he now had nothing to lose by flamboyance.

It was a season of sadness as well as one of ageing, confidence and political promise. In the final phases of her illness Mary Anne's poor body swelled up to uncomfortable proportions. She found it almost impossible to eat and when she did it was difficult to keep down her food. Disraeli, the young scoundrel who had married her for her money, had grown to love her surpassingly, and she him. To watch her die was misery. He invited a party to Hughenden to amuse her in her declining weeks. Among the guests was Lord Ronald Gower, a younger son of the Duke of Sutherland and an artist who spent much of his adult life living with a Venetian gondolier. He was as good company for Contarini Disraeli as for Mary Anne and he offers a glimpse of the

Disraeli who received the surprise ovation on the recovery of the Prince of Wales. Gower described his entrance to the house and being ushered into the library to meet his host.

> Passing through a small Gothic entrance-hall and corridor, in which is a bust of Mr. Disraeli when apparently about twenty, we were shown into the library, where our host welcomed us. He was dressed in a double-breasted tailless jacket, that made him look quite boyish.[3]

Like Proust who spent a lifetime writing and rewriting his hero's adolescence, Disraeli never got over his boyhood. It is the subject of all his novels, and as he neared one of the great crises of his life, he adopted the unusual dress that he had loved when he was a young man.

Mary Anne died in December 1872 less than a month after Gower's visit. This saddled Disraeli with a great unhappiness at the same time as it freed him for the most important romantic relationships of his later life. The loss of his wife meant that he looked forward to the resumption of political power without her important support. The backdrop of these personal and political dilemmas was the recovery of the monarchy's fortunes in the third quarter of the nineteenth century. The monarchy had always been an institution to which he was deeply attracted and in which he was very much interested. From a period of seclusion and popular ill will the Queen gradually emerged as the centrepiece of a popular, ceremonial and imperial monarchy: all this historians usually attribute to Disraeli. He was the minister, so the story goes, who rehabilitated the monarchy and discovered a pro-imperial message that not only stimulated his own party's electoral fortunes, but set the dominant tone of late nineteenth-century British politics.

The real story is more complicated than that. It is a story that must be modified if we take the pleasure principle of Disraeli's politics into account and if we pay attention to the centrality of his ambiguous sexuality. Disraeli's closeness to the Queen could be a liability as well as an asset. The gossip and insinuation about his unusually affectionate relations with younger men persisted in such a way that it became a part of the remarkably affectionate image of him disseminated in the press. An image of him leaning on the arm of Montagu Corry appeared in *Vanity Fair* and references to the pair were a regular feature of newspaper columns commenting on social life in London. What on the one hand seems a late Victorian tolerance, even celebration of male friendship, could be twisted by Gladstone into a condemnation of his rival for unnatural vice. These seemingly unrelated phenomena – monarchy, male friendship and the policy of Disraeli's last premiership – came together in discussion of empire.

Disraeli's two most famous speeches on the subject of empire were just after Easter 1872 in Manchester and again in June that year at the Crystal Palace. At the first of these speeches Mary Anne was well enough to be on the platform with him. He drank two bottles of white brandy, indistinguishable from water, during a speech of more than three hours. Although he had long ago given up the heavy drinking of his youth, he still seems to have been capable of magnificent feats of imbibing. As good a speaker as he was, one still wonders at the marvellous patience of Victorian audiences for political oratory. Both Disraeli's speeches emphasized that the British empire was itself a marvel, a magnificent thing of which Englishmen ought to be proud. He saw an opportunity to deride the cheeseparing, economical policies of the Liberals, to enhance popular disenchantment with the government's refusal to play a role while titanic events were in the process of happening on the Continent. An empire had been born in Germany and a new republic in France without England playing a part. Disraeli wanted to use the undeniable weight of England's imperial possessions both to stir up feelings of pride and patriotism as well as to return England to its proper weight in decision-making among the great powers in Europe. His emphasis on imperial grandeur as preferable to mean-spirited practicality, which he said was characteristic of his opponents, was a return to his attack on the utilitarians in *Popanilla* (1828). It was better to enjoy something magnificent than to make narrow and depressing calculations about what was sensible or affordable. At the Crystal Palace in June 1872, he said Liberal principles were foreign and 'Continental', while, in Buckle's summary of the speech, 'true English spirit was "Imperial" and "where your sons, when they rise, rise to paramount positions, and obtain not merely the esteem of their countrymen, but command the respect of the world".'[4]

The success of the two speeches helped him settle once and for all his title to the leadership of the Conservative party. Even after Disraeli's triumph with the Second Reform Bill in 1867, it was hard to keep his party in order, especially after a decisive electoral defeat in 1868. The publication of *Lothair* in 1870, according to Buckle, 'deepened doubts of statesmen about Disraeli's seriousness. Politicians out of office, it was thought then, should write classical, historical, or constitutional studies.' Even Buckle conceded, however, that *Lothair* made Disraeli 'more interesting as a man'.[5] Moreover, it was the enjoyment of aristocracy, the pleasure derived from a beautiful young marquess with a multitude of romantic choices, that had animated *Lothair*. These had their counterpart in Disraeli's imperial speeches in a love of England's grandeur and the prestige conferred by the empire. His oratory was born in the crucible of creating fictional characters, who operate in a mystic haze of greatness. The speeches led directly to a Conservative victory at the election of early 1874 and Disraeli's longest premiership. The public had grown tired of Gladstone's whirlwind of domestic changes – the Irish Church disendowed, the secret ballot introduced, the officer class of the Army reformed. They were ready for Disraeli's celebration of England's empire as it was.

For the first time in his entire career he held office with a strong parliamentary majority adequate to nearly any measure he decided to propose. He left the proposals for legislation mainly to his colleagues, however. He meant to enjoy himself. The victory had its downside, however. There were two new measures for which he had to take some personal responsibility, but which came from the palace. The Prince of Wales made a successful trip to India in 1875. This reminded the Queen that she had often been called 'Empress of India' on the subcontinent. She had recently bridled at the arrogance of some of her children's imperial in-laws who believed her offspring ranked lower than theirs did as the children of a mere Queen. She wanted to be called Empress of India to show that her rank was equal to the emperor of the recently unified German empire and the Russian tsar who also regarded his court as imperial. She asked and Disraeli agreed to bring in legislation to add this to her title as 'Queen of Great Britain and Ireland'.

This caused both of them a great deal more trouble than they had anticipated, as the bill ran into unusual difficulties in the House of Commons. Some of the attacks on the bill echoed the attacks on his personality that he had experienced throughout his career. A famous cartoon in *Punch* thus suggested parallels between the Queen's new title and the story of Aladdin and his magic lamp from the *Arabian Nights*. In the cartoon, subtitled 'Aladdin adapted', the Queen is pictured as Aladdin, tricked by a wizard, whom the cartoonist has pictured as Disraeli. [*See plate 17.*] Aladdin gives up his magic lamp for a worthless one, just as the wizard Disraeli appears to fool the Queen into taking a new, oriental crown, probably in the terms of the cartoon 'worthless', for a valuable crown she should not be giving up, her English crown as Queen of England. In the image Disraeli is showing elaborate, un-English deference to the sovereign. The image also emphasizes Disraeli in a skirt as an effeminate, oriental figure. Male effeminacy could be associated in the Victorian mind with many attributes: they believed it was characteristic of foreigners in general, for example the French. They also thought it was characteristic of male Muslims, whom they believed had given way to sensual excess and lived hedonistic lives with multiple wives in harems. Another association of effeminacy was with courts: the wide belief was that it was manly and virtuous to be an independent member of a debating chamber like the House of Commons, but debased and effeminate to bow down before kings and tyrants.[6] A final, though nearly unmentionable mental association of effeminacy in the mid-Victorian period was with sodomy. The *Punch* cartoon was meant through innuendo to take in all these associations and put them together with what many knew of his biography. He had lived regularly during the parliamentary recess in Paris and travelled through the Muslim Middle East. He was regarded as overly deferential, an unmanly courtier to Queen Victoria. Throughout his career there had been hints that he was a sodomite, whether from Benjamin Haydon or from Rosina Bulwer. It was possible to express much that was damning in a political cartoon by alluding without explicitly referring to unmentionable vice.

Liberals in the House of Commons said the titles 'emperor' and 'empress' had associations with the worst period of the Roman empire: it reminded some of Roman 'force, violence, and even debauchery' and thus put moral 'tarnish' on the old English title of Queen.[7] Disraeli responded mildly with reference to Gibbon's admiration of the Antonine emperors of Rome. Nevertheless, the opposition to the title ended the honeymoon of his election to the premiership and showed how difficult monarchical considerations could be. The Liberals perceived him to be vulnerable on the question of debauchery. They were hinting that there were links between his personal story and the history of corrupt Roman emperors, whose sexual debauchery had been detailed in Suetonius' *Lives of the Twelve Caesars*. When the Queen asked him to make her 'Empress of India' neither of them saw how his doing her wishes could damage his standing in the House.

Robert Lowe, a Liberal who was a longtime opponent of Disraeli, said in the House of Commons that the Queen had asked for the new title from previous governments but had been refused. In Disraeli she had found a 'more pliant' and 'servile' minister. Disraeli for once allowed his calm façade to crack. He read out a statement from the Queen denying Lowe's allegation that she had asked for the title before. One expert witness noticed that 'the words "pliant minister" . . . seemed literally to choke Disraeli'.[8] His unusual difficulty with the words showed that Lowe's charge had wounded him.

There was another way in which his opponents were able to connect his imperialism to hints of his moral, even sexual, impropriety. In 1876 it was discovered that a group of Christians had been murdered by Muslims in an outlying Bulgarian outpost of Turkey's empire. Europeans were shocked by this and used it as the basis for a demand that Turkey reform its empire and provide greater protection for Christian minorities within its borders. Disraeli remained aloof from what he regarded as a kind of popular panic about Christian safety. His inclination was to support the Turks, especially against the demands of Austria and Russia, who both wanted to annex Turkish territory bordering their own empires. Disraeli believed that Turkey was the key to the security of Britain's Indian empire. Only if the Turks would continue to serve as a bulwark against Russian ambitions for a Mediterranean port and along the Afghan frontier could Britain continue to defend its Indian interests.

In the autumn of 1876 Gladstone published a pamphlet to capitalize on public indignation against the Turks, and to exploit the potential political vulnerabilities of Disraeli's support for them. Gladstone accused the Turks, in allowing the Bulgarian 'atrocities', of 'fell Satanic orgies'. He meant they were guilty not only of having allowed the murder of Christians but of the sexual irregularity which was a common feature of Victorian prejudice against Muslims.

To his intimates Gladstone was even more explicit about connecting Disraeli's imperialism to what he deemed sexual immorality. Lord Acton was one of Gladstone's confidantes. Acton said to Gladstone's daughter at the time of Disraeli's death that her father believed Disraeli's '"doctrines false, but the man more false than his doctrine"; believed "that he demoralized public opinion, bargained with diseased appetites, stimulated passions, prejudices, and selfish desires, that they might maintain his influence"; and deemed him, in short, "the worst and most immoral Minister since Castlereagh".[9] Lord Castlereagh was a leading politician of the Napoleonic era who committed suicide believing himself about to be accused of sodomy.[10] Gladstone was making the point that Disraeli was guilty of the same crime. The frequency of words like 'desire', 'passion', and 'diseased appetite' in Gladstone's private attack on Disraeli all indicate that he intended some connotation of sexual irregularity. Thus, Gladstone and other critics used Disraeli's imperialism, his attachment to the throne, his ambition to control the destinies of Europe by using England's empire to give England's voice special weight in European councils, to suggest his policies were not only wrong, but morally unnatural. It was the old way of getting at Disraeli by suggesting sexual vice, but it also made use of a long-standing republican criticism of courts and thrones and empires as seats of corruption.

When Disraeli himself referred to empires and courts, he often used a Byronic tone of mock heroism. He loved grandeur, but he was always satirizing it at the same time. It could well be that the Conservative party and Gladstone took him much more seriously than he took himself. For example, he had made two new close friends in the aftermath of his wife's death. Lady Bradford and Lady Chesterfield were sisters and grandmothers. One was in her fifties and the other considerably older when he started to become friendly with them both in the mid-1870s. Lady Chesterfield was a widow. He proposed marriage to her. She rejected him, but they remained close friends. He was much closer to Selina Bradford, whose husband served as Master of the Horse in Disraeli's 1874 government. She was one of those aristocratic ladies who spurred his imagination and he developed a serious crush on her, although, as Buckle remarks, she was probably 'embarrassed by his septuagenarian ardour'.[11] His letters to Lady

Bradford are one of the best sources for his emotional and intellectual outlook late in life. One letter in particular, from August 1875, shows the jokey, irreverent side in his use of the word 'imperial'. He wrote to her saying that he would soon send her the government's official speech that would close the session. He was committing an enormous indiscretion and leaking a top-secret document to demonstrate his affection for her. He knew she did not entirely return his feelings. The speech, he wrote, 'will soon be in your hands – those hands that I may never touch. Amidst imperial triumphs the bitterness of my heart will still overtake me.' It was a histrionic display meant to entertain, amuse and make her feel guilty. It was at once a serious and a mock appeal to grandeur.[12]

European indignation with Turkish misrule ended in a war between Russia and Turkey, followed by a conference of the great powers in Berlin. Disraeli, though tired and ill, went personally to this conference to insist on Britain's interests in Europe, as well as to protect the Indian empire. His exchange with Queen Victoria on the eve of his departure in the summer of 1878 for Berlin echoed the kind of lightly ironic tone he had used a few years earlier with Lady Bradford. The Queen had sent him a big salmon, caught by her gamekeeper friend, John Brown, in Scotland. Disraeli joked with her that the fish was so big he was tempted to take it with him to Berlin as it would feed the entire conference. '[B]ut on soberer reflection,' he wrote to her that he had persuaded himself 'to dine on a small portion of it this evening.'[13] Juxtaposed with his letter about the fish was the letter he wrote her the very next day in which he inserted one of his flattering verbal constructions saying that the Queen's 'imperial courage' had sustained him through all his difficulties.[14] In one sense he meant it. He had made her an empress. She had supported him unwaveringly through immense difficulties with his cabinet and in the House of Commons. But in one other equally intended sense, her 'imperial courage' was on the same scale as the big fish: it was a lightly ironic courtesy, a rhetorical device, a gesture that made fun of his own grandiloquence at the same time as it praised a woman he genuinely admired. It was much more these than a distinct policy for expanding the empire or sending out more imperial governors.

When Disraeli got to Berlin, he delivered an ultimatum to the Russians. They must understand that England intended to stick by Turkey, and to support the weaker power against European threats in order to protect England's interests. Or else it meant war. That was one dimension of his 'imperial' policy, but another, underlying and fundamental source of the policy was his love of grandeur. He liked glitter and prestige and royalty and always had, ever since he had been a young man in Lady Londonderry's drawing rooms. An empire was grand; cheap government was paltry, utilitarian and uninspiring. Government ought to be, he thought, a matter of imagination as well as of practicality; it ought to inspire as well as keep the peace. No soldier was willing to sacrifice his all for a queen he could not imagine, but for a queen empress who was both visible and awe-inspiring – that was something different. Nowhere is this clearer than in the private letters he sent home from the Berlin conference. Were they about the defence of India, or the protection of the trade route? No. They were about interior decoration. He wrote to Lady Bradford from Potsdam, on a weekend visit to Queen Victoria's daughter, the Crown Princess of Germany,

I like Rococo for Palaces; this reminded me a little of the palace at Wurzburg which I always thought the model of the style. This one is covered externally with pilasters and crowned and niched in every part with statues. Its interior wonderful for tapestry and golden ceilings and carving and gilding, and amber and silver chairs and black and onyx and lapis luzuli cabinets

. . .

I have most beautiful apartments here, and in my bedroom, which is painted and gilt all over, the Crown Prince was born.

I have fires in every room; and there are strict orders that I am not to walk, or stand on the marble floors which abound. 'Mamma' has evidently given very strict orders, etc.[15]

Golden ceilings and marble floors. These were the rooms he had dreamed of inhabiting ever since he was a boy. His love of grandeur at Potsdam with all its royal associations was the counterpart of his recommending imperial grandeur to the electorate. Both were about a sense of self-respect and sensual pleasure that came from magnificence.

Just as Gladstone attacked Disraeli for supporting the Turks and their 'fell Satanic orgies', Disraeli's support of the Turks was not entirely based on their strategic importance in protecting the eastern Mediterranean. The Turks gave a banquet at the Berlin conference. 'There was a disposition,' he wrote to the Queen,

– too frequent on other occasions and in other things – to treat the Turkish invitation somewhat contemptuously, and to expect a not very satisfactory reception. It was just the reverse. It was impossible for anything to be better served than the dinner; there were a number of attendants in superb dresses, and one or two national dishes, especially a huge *pilaf*, created much interest.[16]

He remembered the hedonism of his eastern travels, the 'superb dresses', the lavish dinners, the Turkish baths. To defend the rights of Muslim Turks against Christian Europe was to strike a blow for sumptuousness against the moral hypocrisies of English Evangelicals who voted with the Liberals. It was to stand up, paradoxically, also for the Jews and Jerusalem and other Middle Eastern cultures against the dissenting Welsh chapels who usually supported Mr Gladstone. His imperialism then was of a piece with his persistent sense of difference, sexually, religiously, culturally, from his own countrymen and the mainstream of Europeans as well.

Disraeli came home having got his way in Berlin and enjoyed the peak of his popularity as prime minister. The Queen had raised

him to the peerage as Earl of Beaconsfield two years previously
and he happily put the coronet of his earldom on his writing
paper. Life in the House of Lords was easier as the hours were not
so late and debate was less demanding. But it did not last.
Unanticipated and badly managed wars on the Afghan frontier
and in southern Africa diminished his standing in the country. A
series of bad harvests further eroded the electorate's confidence in
the Conservative party. As he approached an election in the spring
of 1880, he suspected things might not go his way. He complained to the son of his late friend, Bulwer Lytton, whom he had
made viceroy of India: 'The spirit of England is yet so high, that
I believe, it would endure any amount of taxation if its imperial
position were at stake; but taxes, without that sentiment of glory
and patriotism, will pull down any Ministry.'[17] Emphasizing the
empire had been his way of getting the electorate to vote
Conservative by capturing 'glory and patriotism' for his party
and denying it to Gladstonian Liberals. His politics were always
more frankly selfish than Gladstone's and though his honesty is
appealing, there is nothing particularly admirable about what he
did. What is interesting, however, is the way that his idea about
manipulating the English public's love of empire came not from a
cynical sense of superiority to them, but by reference to his own
youthful love of social grandeur. To love the empire was not far
off loving the jasmine and the military band on the Londonderrys'
stairs at their coronation reception. Good government was a
matter of creating happiness and enjoyment. He knew of no
better happiness than the sort of enjoyment he had enjoyed when
climbing the steps of England's social ladder.

At the summit of his career, much of his enjoyment also came
from his epistolary relations with two ladies. He enjoyed himself
writing to them and struggled with ill health. Through his letters
to them, he returned to play the themes of a lifetime with mas-
terly strokes of his pen, like a violinist coaxing emotion from his
instrument as the performance nears the end.

Buckle went out of his way to say that Disraeli's relationship with Selina Bradford was not a physical one.[18] His love for her was to a degree unrequited, as she was in the midst of a successful marriage to one of his colleagues in the government. Therefore, his love was not unlike his love for younger men: it was based on an imaginative attraction to her high rank, an appreciation of her well-bred manner and, from a sexual point of view, probably chaste. Nevertheless, he enjoyed a lover's way of teasing her and one theme of their correspondence in the 1870s is a kind of emotional blackmail. He remarked early in 1874 that both of her sons were standing as Conservatives for parliamentary seats in the coming election. He always wanted her to write to him more often than she did. 'With two sons candidates you certainly ought to write to their chief every day.'[19] If she wanted any favours for her family from headquarters, she should be flirting with him more often.

More pointed is a letter a few weeks later. How could she have left London, he asked her, at the moment when he was taking office as prime minister? 'I shall always consider it most unfortunate, I would almost say unkind, that you quitted town at this conjuncture – the greatest of my life. I do not think I could have deserted you – but I will only say – Adieu!'[20] In the same vein is this letter from two years later:

> The only person whom you seem neither to care to see, nor to please, is myself. And when you come to town it will only, I fear, be to tell me, as you usually do, that you are going again into the country on some visit, or still more probably, even abroad. I fear our Romance is over, if indeed it ever existed except in my imagination – but still I sometimes dreamed that the dream might last until I slumbered for ever.[21]

He well knew that their 'Romance' was imaginary and that it required his superheated fancy to keep it going, but he did wish that she would play along a little more.

His correspondence with her was not always filled with reproaches. He was one of the best writers of love letters there ever was. When she wrote to him deprecating her abilities and wondering why he should give his affection to someone so unequal to him as her, he wrote:

> Your last letter was a darling letter and makes me feel doubly your absence. I do not know, or care to know, whether you are my equal or my superior. I know that your society charms me. A sweet simplicity, blended with high breeding; an intellect not over-drilled, but lively, acute and picturesque; a seraphic temper and a disposition infinitely sympathetic – these are some of the charms that make you loved by D.[22]

He was capable too of a little sexy flirtation with her. She wrote to him in the winter of 1879 about having fallen while ice skating. 'Your letter was very agreeable,' he told her, 'as your letters always are, but I should not have known about your skating fall had I not a little examined you.'[23] Though he was in his seventies and she in her fifties, he was not too tired to hint that he would like to play doctor with her.

If she mortified him by not entirely returning his affection, he was not above faintly malicious humour behind her back and at her expense. He told her sister in February 1874 when he was forming the government that he had given Selina's husband a high post in the Royal Household. 'Bradford is Master of the Horse, and Selina will ride in Royal carriages, head the line even in the entrée and gallop over all Her Majesty's lieges. I see a difference already in her demeanour.'[24] He was also capable of a sharp attack on her when she disagreed with his policy. In September 1877 he suddenly discovered that she was inclined to support the Russians when his policy was to back Turkey in the conflict that arose from the murder of Christians in Bulgaria. He was sorry about her position, but sorrier still

> that you concealed it from me, which indicates that insincerity with which you have, more than once, painfully impressed me.

I often ask myself what single point of sympathy there is
between us? Certainly not in literature, but I was sometimes
under a hesitating delusion that my political [career] might
interest you, beyond the narrow limit of places and appoint-
ments.[25]

She might disagree with him on policy, but it was a low blow to
accuse her of only being friendly to influence the patronage he
had to exercise. Still, she was an important friend and he knew it.
She was his muse. When she was in London, he could slip away
from Downing Street in the afternoon and discuss his problems
with her in Lowndes Square. When she was away, 'I have no one
to complain to and, in complaining, consult.'[26] He knew his own
psychology well enough to understand that her sympathetic ear
was a way towards helping him find solutions.

His other great lady friend and colleague – for he adored it
when the functions of lady friend and colleague were mixed
together – in the 1870s was the Queen. Unlike her policy and
practice with most of her previous premiers, the Queen
responded warmly to Disraeli's offer of friendship. In fact, when
Disraeli retired from office in 1880, the Queen's private secretary, Henry Ponsonby, wrote an unusual letter declaring how
much the Queen had been helped by her personal relationship
with him. Ponsonby distrusted Disraeli's policy, but wrote
asking whether he might be allowed to convey his 'deep sense
of the service of friendship you have rendered to the Queen
personally, which has undoubtedly softened her difficulties and
alleviated her troubles?'[27] Although Disraeli and the Queen
were ultimately less close than he and Lady Bradford, he still
understood her and appreciated her unusual gestures of friendship towards him. He told Lady Bradford of one extended chat
with the Queen at Windsor before dinner, formally called an
audience. They had been so wrapped up in their conversation
that the Queen's daughters had had to knock on the door at
half past nine to remind their mother that it was past time for

dinner. Disraeli heard afterwards from one of the Queen's ladies-in-waiting that

> I had never been so delightful; with your [Lady Bradford's] knowledge of human nature you can easily conceive who the delightful person really was. We are never so pleased as when we please others, and, in our gratified generosity, attribute to them the very results we have ourselves accomplished.[28]

In pleasing others we are ourselves pleased. This was key to his own success in society as well as central to his political philosophy that enjoyment – pleasing and being pleased – ought to be at the core of our social selves. His relationship with Queen Victoria was central to his enjoyment of his last premiership and if he has been famous for rehabilitating the monarchy, it was simply because he wanted to take his own pleasure in the presence of the royal court and make it more widely available to his countrymen.

He found that on a lonely evening, when he was dining by himself, writing to the Queen could cheer him up. 'I wrote a very long letter to Balmoral,' he told Lady Bradford, 'which made the evening less gloomy, and so roused me that I attacked my Despatch boxes, from which I had previously shrunk, with effect, so I have no arrears.'[29] However, just as he was capable of attacking Selina Bradford with some energy over political differences, so too could he menace the Queen when she threatened to disagree with him over an important policy point. The usual picture of him is that he had his way with the Queen because he flattered her, but he also reminded her what she owed him and got her agreement by raising the spectre of what might happen if they fell apart. In December 1877, when his cabinet was disunited over Turkey, he told her that the two of them must stick together. He had expended significant political capital on two bills which she had insisted on, the Public Worship Regulation Bill of 1874 and the Royal Titles Bill, which made her 'Empress of India' in January 1877. Now she had to support him in his cabinet disputes. If she did, he would certainly be able to keep his cabinet colleagues in line; if she did not, she would be ungrateful. 'All this is another proof,' he told the Queen, 'of what may be done when the Sovereign and the Minister act together. Witness the Public Worship Act. Witness your Majesty's Imperial Crown . . .'[30]

Though they had their disagreements, their relationship brightened his working days. One indication of how relaxed he had become with her was that when he went to Berlin in 1878, he proposed to write her a diary of what went on. She had become one of his devoted ideal readers, like Sarah, his sister, in former days, or Mrs Brydges Willyams, or Lady Londonderry. The 'diary' format showed that he could be utterly himself with her. He also aimed to please her by telling her all the gossip he knew she wanted to know. For example, he knew of her fascination with the powerful German Chancellor Otto von Bismarck. As soon as he got there he told her how he remembered Bismarck once, long ago, with 'a wasplike waist' but that now he had grown quite 'stout'.[31]

At a critical moment in the conference, Disraeli had to convince Bismarck that an ultimatum the British had given to the Russians was serious. 'After dinner,' he wrote in his diary for the Queen,

> we retired to another room, where he smoked and I followed his example. I believe I gave the last blow to my shattered constitution, but I felt it absolutely necessary . . . he was convinced that the ultimatum was not a sham, and before I went to bed, I had the satisfaction of knowing that St. Petersburg had surrendered.[32]

The smoking was homage to the youth he had once been, who had first learned to love a hookah somewhere in the eastern Mediterranean, but the vignette of the two most powerful men in Europe sizing one another up, looking at one another's poker faces through a cloud of smoke, was pure Disraeli, a mini-novel written for a particularly irresistible reader.

He told her about the personalities at the conference, including the wife of the Austrian envoy, Countess Karolyi. He thought her 'Remarkably unaffected'.

> I sate [*sic*] next to her at dinner, and as she had the menu in her hand, in order to say something, I asked her whether she was studying her campaign. She said quite innocently, 'Oh no – I never refuse a dish.'
>
> I watched her and it was literally true. I watched her with amazement, that so delicate and pretty a mouth could perform such awful feats.[33]

Nor was he afraid to share with her how much he appreciated the beauty of good-looking boys. He dined one night at the conference with the family of the German minister of state, von Bülow: 'two or three sons at table, who I really think were the best-looking, the best-dressed, and the best-mannered young gentlemen I ever met. They were all in the army, but she [B's wife] has 7 sons, equally engaging it is said.'[34] In fact, the Queen may have been just as good as Mary Anne had been about sensing the fascination of homoerotic attraction for him. Of course, she would not have thought of it that way. Nevertheless, she knew something was there and she thought it harmless. He certainly had told her a little about the ups and downs of his relations with Henry Lennox. When Lennox had to resign his government post in a scandal over a tram company of which he was one of the directors, Disraeli explained it to the Queen as a mere 'mischance'. He told her he had known Lennox 'intimately for 30 years', and that his 'very faults were not disagreeable'.[35] Further, the Queen understood instinctively that Disraeli's relationship to Montagu Corry was more than that of employer and employee. She accorded Corry what we would call 'spousal privileges', which she generally accorded neither to spouses nor to private secretaries in that era. When the Queen sent instructions in January 1875 that Disraeli was not only to bring Corry for a dine-and-sleep at her house on the Isle of Wight, but that they should both use the royal yacht, *Alberta*, Disraeli was flabbergasted. 'What do you think of this?' he wrote to Lady Bradford. 'Fancy Monty a recognized courtier! The first Private Secretary whose existence has been acknowledged by royal lips.'[36] At one point, Corry was even staying in the big house and given Disraeli's dressing room in which to sleep. This was the exact arrangement of most upper-class husbands and wives, where the wife occupied the main bedroom and her husband slept in a small antechamber, or 'dressing room', to one side. Disraeli understood and sympathized with the ambiguities in her relationship with John Brown; she did the same for him in his relationship with Corry. The Queen was a rare find, not only as a sovereign, but as a friend.

21

Every Procession Must End

Two relationships with younger men, one a comic and annoying reminder of past affection, the other perhaps the closest friend Disraeli ever had, made for a significant motif of what he would have called 'intimate friendship' in his last decade. However, there were as many disappointments as there were happily-ever-afters with these two. The relationships with Lady Bradford and Queen Victoria left him happier, more fulfilled and more satisfied. Nevertheless, his relationship to the two younger men was a significant and semi-public feature of his declining years. *Vanity Fair* had published a cartoon of Lennox in which he is a highly effeminate male with affected mannerisms, and although there was no direct association between effeminacy and homosexuality in the period, there was enough overlap for the suggestion to be made to readers that there was something peculiar about Disraeli's close friend. In the same era, *Vanity Fair* published 'Power and Place', an image of Disraeli leaning on Corry's arm. It was relatively unusual for *Vanity Fair* to publish two figures caricatured together and the effect was to suggest that there was an unusual relationship between the subjects. [*See plate 10.*] The point is that Disraeli's men friends were no secret.

The relationship between Disraeli and Lennox had diminished

after Lennox resigned from the 1866–8 government in protest at what he thought Disraeli's too radical reform bill. In the 1870s, however, he was still writing to his old chief and Disraeli gave him a post in the 1874 government as President of the Board of Public Works. It carried with it responsibility for exterior upkeep of the royal palaces as well as the interiors of public buildings. It was a job often given to men known for their decorating abilities. The second Lord Esher and LouLou Harcourt were both bisexual men who were appointed to similar posts in the same office in succeeding generations.[1] Disraeli told Lennox it was a place where he could exercise his notable 'taste'. Buckle described the position as above Lennox's 'deserts' but decidedly below his 'hopes' and said that he never forgave Disraeli for what he regarded as an 'indignity'.[2] Lennox was a tricky character and Disraeli's failure to pacify him, even when giving him a lucrative position that was more than he ought to have expected, had something to do with their personal as well as their political relations to one another.

Lennox caused Disraeli trouble almost from the beginning. He tangled with the Treasury and Disraeli chose an unusual metaphor to describe what was going on to Lady Bradford: 'The Henry Lennox business is not settled. He is an eel, but I do not think he will escape my grasp, which can be firm.'[3] To Lady Chesterfield he wrote a month later, returning to one of his favourite texts. 'Henry Lennox, they say, has a lucid interval and there is a prospect of our extricating him out of his scrape. His various accounts of his troubles and their causes equal, in number and invention, the Arabian nights. I have still a regard for him, although he worries and mortifies me.'[4] As 'Arabian nights' might well have been a code for unusual sexuality, either he thought Lady Chesterfield would not know, or that she knew very well what he meant and it did not bother her in the least.

Lennox held his job until 1876 when he resigned over trouble connected with the Lisbon Tramways Company, of which he was one of the directors. The two friends did not lose touch though. Lennox organized the popular reception to greet Disraeli when he returned victorious from the Berlin conference in 1878. Disraeli invited him to one of his official dinners in 1879, where he observed Lennox in a comic scene with the French ambassador. Disraeli told Lady Bradford that

> My dinner turned out very well yesterday; a success produced, probably, by the variety of elements and some new ones. Henry Lennox whispered to Monty 'who is that old buffer you have been talking to?' 'The French Ambassador.' Henry fell like a shot and in five minutes was cringing round his Excellency and chattering French like an ape.[5]

It is very like a sharp little pen portrait his critics would have drawn of Disraeli himself when he was a younger man and making his way up the greasy pole.

Still, Disraeli remained loyal and affectionate to Lennox. When the government fell in 1880, he tried to give Lennox a permanent place worth £1500 a year. His cabinet colleagues were appalled and had to persuade Disraeli that so generous a gift would look too much like an abuse of the patronage at their disposal. Buckle grouped this with the unusual peerage that Disraeli gave to Corry at the same time. He thought they were both examples of Disraeli having allowed excessive affection to cloud his judgement. Yet, there are areas of male friendship among the Victorian upper classes that we shall probably never fully understand. Lennox outlived Disraeli by six years. At his death, Lennox's friend, the fifteenth Earl of Derby, another of Disraeli's protégés, wrote of Lennox that he had never been popular with his own class, 'but he lived much among actors, speculators, and small hangers-on to newspapers: and in this Bohemian world he was much appreciated'.[6] That was Disraeli's world too, as it was Byron's or Bulwer Lytton's.

Montagu Corry was a much more reliable object of affection than Lennox: he was a good secretary, a gentleman who never grated on Disraeli's fine-tuned nerves, a companion, a son, a student, above all a longed-for friend when he was absent, as Corry often was when Disraeli wanted him most. Mary Anne very much approved of Corry and as she was dying, it was to Corry that Disraeli confided his misery. Disraeli told Corry 'it entirely unmans me'.[7] It took away his vital strength. It made him weak and vulnerable. Such a confession was also an appeal to the younger man's sympathy and affection. After she died, and in going through her things, he discovered she had kept envelopes full of his hair from all the different times she had cut it for him. Disraeli offered a packet of this hair to Corry, a reversal of the usual Victorian custom where one gave a lock of the dead person's hair as a memento.[8]

Disraeli had always been proud of his long curly hair and often gave his heroes, like Contarini, 'hyacinthine' hair. He noticed Corry's hair as well. When Lord Ronald Gower remarked upon a portrait of Corry in Disraeli's 'gallery of friendship' at Hughenden, Disraeli complained that the artist had 'not given the golden light in Monty's hair'. Gower remarked dryly in his diary, 'which light I had never seen'.[9]

After Mary Anne's death, Corry quickly took over some of the duties that would normally have been undertaken by a wife. He acted the part of spouse and co-host when Queen Victoria visited Hughenden in 1877. She brought her daughter, Princess Beatrice, and several members of her Household. He had only Corry. They greeted her on the platform at High Wycombe station and then took the party back to Hughenden alone.[10] Corry also acted as a sort of Eleanor Roosevelt for Disraeli, going out and taking 'the pulse of society' when Disraeli was incapacitated by gout or too tired to dine out in the evenings.[11]

The surviving letters show, though, how much time Disraeli spent missing Corry. Although Corry never married, he had, like Disraeli himself, many intense friendships with women, whom he frequently went off to see. He also had family who were unwell, including a sick sister who took him out of the country and far away from England at a time of crisis in Disraeli's own health. Also like Disraeli, Corry had a 'nervous complaint' brought on by

overwork and worry. Corry experienced some sort of nervous
breakdown in the autumn of 1877 and early in 1878. Disraeli told
Queen Victoria in January 1878:

> It is a great blow. Mr. Corry has broken down from over-work
> and over-anxiety. His nervous system has given way. His loss to
> Lord Beaconsfield cannot be estimated. He has fine talents, a
> sweet temper, wonderful energy, and a noble disposition.
> Besides, he understood, and appreciated, your Majesty's charac-
> ter, which was a bond of sympathy between them, and a source
> of constant consolation. Mr. Corry will have to travel abroad.[12]

Corry had recovered enough by the summer to accompany
Disraeli to Berlin. By December Disraeli was complaining to
Lady Bradford that Corry was well enough to write to a different
lady every day and was just off to visit his friend, Lady Ilchester,
at Melbury. 'What a Don Juan!'[13] It was Corry as the hero of
Byron's epic. On another occasion, he remarked half jealously, half
admiringly of Corry's relations to his women friends, 'What a
Lothario Monty is.'[14] So Corry was a libertine and a rake; or possibly he was 'Lothair' as well. He could not help but think of his
young friend as either a stylish Restoration womanizer, or one of
the handsome youths of his own fiction.

Corry was both an object of his affection and a mirror of the
young men Disraeli had imagined or had been at one time himself. When Disraeli fell from office, he told one of his other
secretaries, Lord Barrington: 'He chiefly deplored his fall from
power, on account of M. Corry, who in his opinion was fitted to
fill any *Cabinet* office. This was said with genuine warmth.'[15]
Although he could not appoint his young friend to the cabinet,
Disraeli could make him a peer, which he proposed to Queen
Victoria. She had suggested that Disraeli's nephew be given a
barony on his resignation. He wanted the barony, instead, for
Corry 'who was also his intimate friend'.[16] He wanted this
'unique distinction, which no private secretary had received

before' to signal publicly his high opinion of Corry's merits, as a thanks for his service, and to show the world with an unprecedented act that this man was to be his true heir. Although Disraeli's estate was entailed on the son of his younger brother, as many English agricultural estates were then, his valuable papers and the care for shaping his legacy went to Corry. Even the Queen, who was prepared to accept virtually anything her friend proposed on leaving office, was a little aghast at the grandeur of Disraeli's gesture towards Corry.

However, the peerage went through and Corry became Lord Rowton. He continued to act as Disraeli's secretary when his chief went into opposition. He also acted as agent when Disraeli produced the manuscript for his twelfth novel, *Endymion*, in the summer of 1880. Disraeli began writing it shortly after the publication of *Lothair* in 1870, but put it aside when he became busy again with political work. He finished it rapidly in the four months after leaving office. The old man clearly had some energy left for literary work and one loves Disraeli for going straight to his desk at Hughenden the moment the electorate had dismissed him from Downing Street. Rowton negotiated the largest advance that had been paid for a work of fiction during the nineteenth century. The publisher, Longman, agreed to pay Disraeli £10,000, with the first £2500 payable on receipt of the manuscript in September. Once he had handed over the manuscript and received a cheque, Disraeli wrote to Rowton: 'I know no magic of the Middle Ages equal to it! And you are the Magician, best and dearest of friends!'[17]

Endymion is the most authentic memoir Disraeli ever wrote. It summarizes and epitomizes a lifetime of love and politics. It provides a key to what he most valued in political life. What the novel does not say, but we must imagine, is the seventy-five-year-old Disraeli, crippled by gout and asthma and bronchitis, deeply disappointed at the electoral rejection of 1880, nevertheless getting up in the morning at Hughenden and committing a final work to paper.

The Archbishop of Canterbury confided to his diary on

completing Disraeli's novel, 'I have finished *Endymion* with a painful feeling that the writer considers all political life as mere play and gambling.'[18] Disraeli probably would not have minded if the novel caused some pain to those who regarded themselves as guardians of public morals. The book is about a young man named Endymion who rises from pennilessness and obscurity, receives indispensable help from his sister and high-born women, gives remarkable speeches in Parliament, marries a widow and becomes prime minister. It is of course about Disraeli himself. At one point, a French princess says to an Englishman that she found in some memoirs that her court was described as

> a corrupt and dissolute court. It was a court of pleasure, if you like; but of pleasure that animated and refined, and put the world in good humour, which, after all, is good government. The most corrupt and dissolute courts on the continent of Europe that I have known . . . have been outwardly the dullest and most decorous.[19]

This might well have been Disraeli's reply to the Archbishop. His aim in the novel was to amuse himself by looking back on a long career and to put 'the world in good humour' at the same time. He could not underrate play or pleasure; they were the purpose of life, not secondary to it. This was the transcendent theme of his political just as much as of his literary life.

To capture Disraeli's point about pleasure in a more attractive light, consider a gathering at Mr Vigo's suburban house in the country. Vigo is not grand, but he has style and imagination. He is a tailor who dresses both dandies and statesmen. Vigo helps Endymion on his path to the premiership by dressing him exquisitely and for free. He also throws a wonderful party. Mr Vigo's

> dinner was a banquet, – a choice bouquet before every guest, turtle and venison and piles of whitebait, and pine-apples of prodigious size, and bunches of grapes that had gained prizes.

The champagne seemed to flow in fountains, and was only interrupted that the guests might quaff Burgundy or taste Tokay. But what was more delightful than all this was the enjoyment of all present, and especially of their host. That is a rare sight. Banquets are not rare, nor choice guests, nor gracious hosts; but when do we ever see a person enjoying anything? But these gay children of art and whim, and successful labour and happy speculation, some of them very rich and some of them without a sou, seemed only to think of the festive hour and all its joys. Neither wealth nor poverty brought them cares.[20]

The pleasure of food combined with the pleasure of good company: this was the ultimate enjoyment for Disraeli. His last novel is a paean of praise to this peak of human existence. He had come to adulthood celebrating the Regency pleasures of dress and decoration; his last novel was published at the dawn of the era of Oscar Wilde and the *Yellow Book* where once again the pleasures of pure style were on the table. His genius was to survive mid-Victorian puritanism and serve as inspiration to a new generation of artists and politicians.

Endymion the young man 'pursued a life of enjoyment, but also of observation and much labour'.[21] When he is first appointed to a small civil service post, 'humble as was his lot, he began to feel the pride of public life'.[22] Further on, when he makes it into Parliament and even enjoys a spell in office with the government of the day, Endymion reflects on the sort of pleasure he derives from public service, just as he is about to lose his place.

The charms of office arrayed themselves before him. The social influence, the secret information, the danger, the dexterity, the ceaseless excitement, the delights of patronage which everybody affects to disregard, the power of benefiting others, and often the worthy and unknown which is real joy . . .[23]

Pleasure came from hard work and high office as well as from society and dining and drinking. Although these were different orders of pleasure, they had been treated side by side in every Disraelian work of fiction from *Popanilla* through *Endymion*. Hedonism and high society and social parties led seamlessly in his mind and in his experience to Parliament and office and political parties. Disraeli enjoyed the secret information, the danger and the patronage of office more than doing good to the worthy, but at least he was honest about what he enjoyed and dared to put it into print.

Corry said that Disraeli named the hero of *Endymion* after Endymion Porter, a royalist ancestor of Mary Anne's. Buckle thought it more likely that the book was a covert tribute to Selina Bradford. In Greek mythology, Endymion was a shepherd and lover of Selene, the goddess of the moon.[24] There are other necessary ways of understanding Disraeli's impulse in naming the book. Two images of Endymion that would have been available in the late Victorian period show a handsome youth lying naked in the moonlight. Unusually for a painting of that era, rather than a female, it is a nude male who invites the viewer to desire him. This suggests that for an educated Victorian audience there might well have been some homoerotic association with the name 'Endymion'. French novelists used Girodet's 'Endymion' as a way of hinting in code at a character's unusual sexuality.[25] [*See plate 21.*] The male nude in the British painter Atkinson Grimshaw's 'Endymion on Mount Latmos' is an equally sensual figure and was painted in the 1870s, the same era in which Disraeli wrote his book.[26] A final pertinent moon reference is from Disraeli's father's work. When Isaac D'Israeli had written of James I's attraction to Buckingham, he had made reference to Michael Drayton's satirical poem, 'The Moon-Calf', to show that homosexual vice had been common in that era.[27] So when Disraeli published his last book he was once more taking a risk and sending a message about his hero and himself.

John Keats's narrative poem *Endymion* (1818) dwelled on aesthetic ecstasy as a transcendent emotion. The poet's tribute to the emotion produced by art influenced Disraeli's contemporary, the art critic Walter Pater. Pater's argument was that the purpose of art was not moral teaching, but the moment of passing pleasure that an image gave the viewer, a philosophy often summed up since as 'art for art's sake'. Art need have no social purpose. The point of a beautiful verse or a nude in sculpture or a lovely painting was enjoyment for its own sake; the experience of art was itself worthwhile as a purifying and elevating emotion. Inspired by Keats, Pater had been himself an inspiration to Oscar Wilde at Oxford. Wilde later put Pater's aesthetic theory into his flippantly serious drama and criticism where he said, for example, that lying was the highest form of art, that pleasure was more important than earnestness and that what a man wore was more important than what he believed. All this is the counterpart in art of Disraeli's view of politics that pleasure or enjoyment was something worth aiming for in its own right. Just as Keats and Pater and Wilde warred against a moral vision of art that it had to have some sort of socially improving goal, Disraeli's whole life was devoted to a war on a utilitarian, or a Gladstonian, view of politics that its sole goal was future-oriented reform and improvement. Happiness in the present fleeting moment – even though probably this was a happiness mostly unalterable by parliamentary action – was Disraeli's idea of perfection. Among the descendants of this Disraelian philosophy in the twentieth century were the suave silliness of Noël Coward's plays and Michael Oakeshott's more sober statements defining a conservative disposition. The title of one of Coward's plays, *Present Laughter* (1943), made its way into a famous statement of conservatism by Michael Oakeshott: 'To be conservative, then, is to prefer . . . present laughter to utopian bliss.'[28] Disraeli's mind was itself one that tended to convey a serious political idea in the style of a light-hearted musical.

Endymion is shot through with parliamentary atmosphere and an expectation that his readers will catch sly references to legends surrounding old parliamentary hands. For example, Endymion's father is William Pitt Ferrars. This Ferrars made his way in

Parliament, occasionally speaking, until 'Lord Castlereagh, who liked young men, made him a Lord of the Treasury'.[29] Here Disraeli is not only claiming descent for his hero, Endymion, from the greatest Tory of all time, William Pitt the Younger, but also referring markedly to Castlereagh as someone who 'liked young men'. Castlereagh told George IV before he committed suicide that he was about to be arrested on the same charge as the Bishop of Clogher. Clogher was an Irish prelate who had been caught having sex with a guardsman and was about to be publicly charged before he fled to Scotland and changed his name.

References to Horace Walpole in Disraeli's fiction are also invariably allusions to Walpole having had male lovers. Endymion at one point meets the older boy to whom he had acted as 'fag' at Eton, the 'Count of Otranto'. *The Castle of Otranto* was one of Walpole's best-known novels. When these two young men meet, Otranto, who is in disguise as 'Colonel Albert', stares at Endymion with the hungry stare of a lover.

> Colonel Albert, who was silent, was watching all this time Endymion with intentness, who now looked up and encountered the gaze of the new comer. Their eyes met, their countenances were agitated, they seemed perplexed, and then it seemed that at the same time both extended their hands.[30]

Like his author, Endymion was perpetually troubled by such wordless exchanges with men either his superior or inferior in age. The wonder of Disraeli as a writer, and of his audience as readers, is that all were prepared to enjoy seeing these troublesome attractions of men to other men committed to print.

Endymion's closest relationships in the novel are, as Disraeli's were in life, to women. The women are always trying to persuade him to marry, but Endymion tells both his sister Myra, and another woman with whom he is flirting, that he is not 'a marrying man'.[31] Eventually, his sister persuades him that he has put off marriage too long and he agrees to marry Lady Montfort, a widow. He cannot get up the courage, so she proposes marriage to him by presenting him with an empty library at her new London house in Carlton Gardens. With this Disraeli came almost full circle. He had been born in a library, he liked to claim, now his hero finds a woman he can truly love through the gift of a library. Shortly thereafter, the circle is completely closed. Endymion becomes prime minister. On the last page of the novel his beloved sister asks him to come with her and revisit the nursery in the house where they both grew up. She tells him that everything she has desired and wished for has come to pass: 'let me give you my last embrace'. The last page of the novel then is a reunion with Sarah Disraeli. All the romances with men and with women, all the parliamentary triumphs, all the patient waiting for office, seemed to rank second to his love for the older sister whom he had lost over twenty years before.

Disraeli was unwell early in 1881. He became worse after he was caught in a blast of sleet and cold wind while coming home from a party in March: a combination of asthma, bronchitis and terrible weakness kept him in his bed or propped up on a sofa. He knew he was approaching the end and was troubled by Corry's leaving the country to take his sister for her health to Algiers. 'Your absence is a calamity', Disraeli wrote to him semi-reproachfully in December 1880.[32] Corry came back to England for a short spell but went out to Algiers again in February 1881. Disraeli wrote to him in March 1881: 'Barrington is very kind and sedulous, but I want you. My health has been very bad, and I have really been fit for nothing, but perhaps the spring, which commences in a week, may help me.'[33]

Queen Victoria knew exactly what he was thinking. 'Hoping to hear a good report of you tonight,' she wrote him, 'and that Lord Rowton will be back very soon. Ever yours very affectionately, V[ictoria] R[egina et] I[mperatrix].'[34] Rowton did start back from Algiers when he heard how ill Disraeli was. The strange thing was that Disraeli refused to see him. He claimed that the shock would be too much, but it is almost too as if he were a lover administering a final rebuke for Corry's having stayed away so long. "'I cannot see him" he kept saying. "Surely Monty, who is so fond of you – you would like to see him when he arrives" Barrington pleaded. "You and Rose must arrange it gradually; it would be too great a shock,'" Disraeli said.[35]

Corry arrived at Disraeli's house on 7 April. Three days later Disraeli still refused to see him. Corry wrote miserably to Selina Bradford:

> He still shrinks from seeing me! He knows I am always here, day and night, and I have begged him to give no thought to me till we can meet without effort to him. The doctors wish him to be as quiet as possible, and, I think, even were you here, would combat your seeing him! He does not try to read letters.
>
> I have seen *him* often, and do not see any bad change in his face. But the weakness! and how can we overcome it?
>
> . . . He talks of death without a shade of fear.[36]

A few days later Corry came in quietly, without permission, to read a parliamentary debate to his chief. Disraeli did not object. Corry was there for the final struggle, and perhaps Disraeli had wanted to save his friend the sight of that. Corry described the final days to Lady Bradford:

> Day and night was I with him trying to help him over all his pains and troubles, as each arose, or to dispel some of the confusions which came over his poor tired brain. It was weary work that sitting, with my hand in his, in the night watches, trying to guide that mighty mind, as a child's had to be led – that trying to be cheerful, when I could scarcely help weeping![37]

On 19 April 1881 Disraeli died. He and Corry were both released from their suffering.

Epilogue

Following the completion of *Endymion* Disraeli started work on a new novel. He wrote only nine chapters but the surviving fragment shows that as he neared death fiction remained alive and vital for him as a medium. The central character in this fragment is Joseph Toplady Falconet, a satirical portrait of Disraeli's old rival, Gladstone. Falconet, like Gladstone, is the younger son of a family that has grown rich in trade. The idea of Gladstone as a bird of prey, a falcon or a hawk, probably lodged in his mind from a letter he had written to Queen Victoria in March 1875. Gladstone had suddenly and unexpectedly returned to the House of Commons, having retired as Liberal leader, to comment on an Army bill. 'Mr. Gladstone,' Disraeli wrote, 'not only appeared but rushed into the debate. The House, very full, was breathless. The new members trembled and fluttered like small birds when a hawk is in the air.'[1] So his old metaphor was to hand when he christened his new Gladstone character 'Falconet'.

Augustus Toplady was an eighteenth-century hymn writer, a fierce controversialist, and a defender of the puritan streak in the Church of England, which Disraeli connected with what he thought of as Gladstone's moral 'humbug'. Blake speculated that Disraeli knew that Gladstone had once translated Toplady's hymn, 'Rock of Ages', into Latin.[2] Falconet lives up to all the negative stereotypes that surrounded Gladstone: he is 'disputatious', 'grave', 'austere' and has an 'eager and earnest temperament'.[3]

On first glance the author might seem to be a vindictive

Disraeli settling old political scores in his final months. Instead, on a closer look, the fragment of the novel shows that the young man who had dashed off *Vivian Grey* even in old age still had his former zest and exuberance.[4] Moreover, the work shows what part Disraeli's persistent inclination towards the homoerotic played in the whole man. It also shows what made him ruler of his country, and in what his greatness truly lay.

Young Falconet is first elected to Parliament, as Gladstone was, for an old-fashioned 'close borough' where a very few electors, often influenced by a single nobleman, controlled the return of an MP. The electors choose Falconet because of his denunciation of the slave trade, even though his own family and the local nobleman have both profited from it. Even more absurd, the revival of the slave trade in the Red Sea which Falconet denounces is actually based on a mistaken telegraph report 'manipulated by a functionary suffering from *coup de soleil* or *delirium tremens*'.[5]

This runs parallel not only to Gladstone's origins from a family that had grown rich off slave-grown sugar in the West Indies, but also to his ability in the later 1870s to arouse popular passions about the mistreatment of Bulgarian Christians. Disraeli distrusted such whipping up of popular indignation. He thought the Turkish slaughter of Bulgarian Christians had been exaggerated. He was one of the few in the 1850s who stood up in the House of Commons to denounce the popular hysteria arising from what he believed were inflated accounts of Englishmen being murdered in the Indian Mutiny. But more than this, the novel shows Disraeli's gift for cultivating the ridiculous; the *coup de soleil* or *delirium tremens* of the telegraph operator was the distinctive Disraelian touch. It was what made him different from Gladstone, who was celebrated for his energy, but also his humourlessness. It was the distinctive feature of Disraeli's oratory too: a pointed sarcasm meant to raise a laugh from what was a daring insult when he was young, which mellowed in his old age to a light-hearted irony. His was an approach to the world that was less concerned with moral crusades than with revelling in the joys and silliness of the here and now.

Falconet's parents ask the nobleman for whom they have always worked where their unmarried son, the new MP, might find lodgings in London. He tells them Falconet must have a set of rooms in Albany, the fashionable apartments off Piccadilly. They reply that they had hoped young Falconet might lodge 'with some serious family'. "'Ah!" said the Earl, "I fear that serious families are rarer than they were in Westminster . . ."[6] 'Serious families' is code for the earnest Evangelical Christians to whom Gladstone had always appealed in real life. Their influence in British politics was at its peak in the first three-quarters of the century, but it was definitely on the wane by the 1880s. Disraeli's achievement was that this poking fun at serious Christian families should seem entirely appropriate, even from a senior figure who was leader of one of the great political parties. Formerly, they were largely unchallenged as a force in politics. He had outlasted the Christian fundamentalists of his day and in outlasting them he had also vanquished them.

Blake supposed that the finished novel would have been called 'Falconet', but it is equally possible that Disraeli would have named it for the autobiographical character, Lord Gaston, who is in every way the opposite of Falconet.[7] All Disraeli's novels were deeply autobiographical and this was a key secret of his success. More than his policies, the selling point of his political career as well as of his fiction was a compelling theatre of his own personality. In twelve different novels he explored different corners of himself. He wrote and rewrote his own history. In politics what fascinated both the House of Commons and the public was the story of a Christianized Jew who dared to flout convention, to manage his party for decades in the face of overwhelming odds against him, to rise unexpectedly to a commanding position in Parliament, and to speak in an amusing manner as if 'oratory' were too grand a word for what he was doing. They loved him for this more than for his challenge to

Peel, or for the Second Reform Bill, or for the settlement at Berlin in 1878.

Gaston is the son of the earl who has advised the Falconets on London lodgings for their son. He is, like Disraeli, a mixture of nations. His name suggests Parisian sensuality; he is also 'handsome; the highest order of English beauty . . . and with hyacinthine locks of auburn hair'.[8] One of his intimates remembered Disraeli in later middle age wearing his dressing gown in the morning, a scarf tied around his wet hair to keep in place the signature curl which he always draped over his forehead.[9] Disraeli's greatness lay in this. He upended a creed that men ought not to be vain and made a system of ethics out of his own personal appearance. That curling hair was the emblem of his philosophy that we ought to devote ourselves to pleasing and being pleased.

The key difference, both stylistic and political, between Falconet and Gaston comes down to this. Falconet is devoted 'to the vindication and the triumph of religious truth', whereas Gaston remarks, 'I am also capable of devotion . . . and that is to the happiness of my species.'[10] This was Disraeli's politics of pleasure. This happiness was the equivalent of Disraeli's lifelong devotion to amusement, sensuality, an enjoyed life in the present for himself and his friends. This was not something which Parliament could provide; rather the government of the day created the conditions – safety, security, prosperity, pride, confidence – which allowed everyone to get on with whatever they enjoyed most. The writing of novels too was about enjoyment, not active instruction; and the contrast with Gladstone, who wrote about the proper relations between Church and state, or who analysed Homeric texts for the way they synchronized with Christian doctrine, could not be clearer. When he heard that the Queen was to ask him to form a government late in 1868, Gladstone, who was chopping down a tree, said, 'My mission is to pacify Ireland.'[11] Nothing could be further from Disraeli's sense of what politics was about than this Gladstonian missionary zeal. If Gladstone set out to teach and improve,

Disraeli's goal was to gain power and then, as a later Tory prime minister, Harold Macmillan, once remarked of his own policy, 'to wait upon events'. Many have pointed out that Disraeli's legislative achievement was spotty. The Second Reform Bill may have had a good end result, but it arose more from short-term political calculation than from a long-term assessment of the public good. Similarly, most of the domestic legislation enacted by the 1874–80 government came from quarters other than Number Ten, though Disraeli took responsibility for what the cabinet decided. Rather, as he told Lady Bradford, what he loved was the game, the play. 'I live for Power and the Affections,' he told her, and capitalized the nouns to emphasize it.[12] He did have consistent ideas, for example, about the necessity of a territorial aristocracy counterbalancing the power of the central government in London. But on the whole, the electorate must trust to what they knew of him in order to have confidence in his decisions on events as they arose. The electorate cared more about him than about the territorial aristocracy anyway.

And people knew quite a lot about him, as he had been telling them about himself for a very long time. The beginning of 'Falconet' was no exception, as it reworks familiar themes from his own adolescence. We learn that Gaston had been born with an odd temperament.

> Even as a child he was inquisitive, sceptical, and eccentric; doing things which were forbidden . . . He had the awkward habit of asking questions which could not be easily answered, and expressing opinions which perplexed and sometimes shocked.[13]

Gaston is also able to fix his contemporaries with a troubling stare: 'his first glance fascinated'.[14] The anticipated school romance, such a feature of *Contarini* or *Coningsby*, never happens to Gaston, however. Rather, he is sent away from his school because he circulates works, possibly like Plato's, which pretend to be philosophical but which the authorities find subversive.

> At a great public school he was soon idolized, but it ended by the authorities privately communicating with his father that they thought, on the whole, it would be advantageous that his son should be withdrawn from their control. Not that he ever did anything disgraceful, mean, or ignominious, or even committed violent or rebellious acts, but he was in the habit of circulating opinions which injuriously affected the discipline of the school; was in the habit of reading and advising others to read books which, while affecting to be philosophical, could not for a moment be tolerated, as tending, in the opinion of the masters, to the destruction of morals and religion.[15]

Gaston goes to university, but does not fit in there either. He engages 'in a controversy on the origin of evil which terminated by his somewhat abruptly quitting his Alma Mater'.[16] Gaston then enters the foreign service, but there too gets involved in a dubious affair. He has to be expelled from the service when his correspondence with a revolutionary leader is exposed: 'it was the interest of all parties that the affair should be hushed up'.[17] The shroud of mystery Disraeli throws over this allows some ambiguity about whether the matter was political or romantic. Whenever there is any discussion about the marriage of an heiress, Gaston's name 'was almost invariably dismissed as that of a man who had no thought of marriage'.[18] Gaston, like many of Disraeli's heroes, is not the marrying kind.

This flirting with the homoerotic is such a persistent theme of Disraeli's fiction that it has to be seen as an important part of his personality. It was one important way of many that he differed from the norm. His Mediterranean appearance, or what he called his 'Murillo face', was another. His religion was a third way. Rather than hiding these differences, he dramatized them. In his dandyism, both in dress and in speaking, he asserted his difference from the crowd. He espoused unpopular opinions on Christianity being a sort of perfected Judaism at the very moment when he most needed to woo truculent Tory backbenchers to his side. He dared to be dangerously, sometimes insultingly, different from others because he believed above all in his own genius. He believed that his difference equalled distinction. In the short term this annoyed his political friends and garnered hostile reviews, but ultimately this dwelling on his difference from the common order of men got him attention inside and outside the House of Commons. That attention was what he throve upon and was probably more important in his rise to power than the policies he adopted on his way there or once he arrived.

Disraeli enjoyed the company of young men and elderly women; but he also loved the House of Commons. In 'Falconet' he suggested that any member who had the ambition to rise there should romance the House as if it were a woman:

> the House of Commons is a jealous mistress and will not grant success without due attention. The greatest compliment you can pay to a woman is to give her your time, and it is the same with our Senate. A man who is always in his place becomes a sort of favourite.[19]

It is easy to be misled into thinking that Disraeli overcame or sub-dued his nature in order to win the House of Commons. Instead, he used the drama of his personality to woo and win the House. This drama came out in his speaking. The boy Lothair was a good speaker too. He made his first public speech to an informal gath-ering of his tenants and neighbours when he arrived at his estate in Staffordshire for his coming-of-age. 'What he [Lothair] said was said very well, and it was addressed to a people who, though the shyest in the world, have a passion for public speaking.'[20] Disraeli believed this 'passion for public speaking' was a distinctive trait of the English national character. He made it his goal to develop his natural gift for public speaking from the moment that he realized he could entertain his audience with an election speech given while holding on to the lion atop the portico of the Red Lion public house at High Wycombe in 1832.[21]

Sometimes Disraeli and his reporters were themselves a little misled about how he succeeded as a politician. Contarini Fleming, like Disraeli, was a depressed and lonesome child, but once he observed his power over his fellow schoolboys his 'ambition conquered . . . [his] nature'. Similarly, a reporter watching him address local Conservatives at Taunton noticed that Disraeli had begun speaking as a ridiculously affected fop, but as he warmed to his theme the 'dandy was transformed into the man of mind'.[22] Both Disraeli and his reporter got it wrong. He did not conquer his nature with his ambition, nor did he overcome his effeminate dandyism. Rather, his nature was his tool to realize his ambition. His would not have risen to the top if he had not used his persona to capture his audience's attention and forge a dandy-ish style of parliamentary oratory.

His oratorical style was composed of different elements. One famous diarist of the 1870s remembered Disraeli's ease and touch-ing on serious subjects in a way that nevertheless made men smile. The diarist called this Disraeli's 'serio-comicality'.[23] His oratory combined all the features that d'Orsay and Brummell themselves would have recognized. These were what Buckle called 'wit and humour . . . irony, sarcasm, and ridicule'.[24] When he was under attack by the opposite side, he would pull down his top hat and pretend to be asleep. He put four syllables into 'Parliament' and three into 'business'.[25] He approached the House as if he were an actor. Of a shipping bill which he had to steer through the House at the last minute, he told Lady Bradford that he only just got it ready before the sitting commenced. When he rose before the front bench, it was as if 'they were painting the scenes as the cur-tain drew up'.[26] His brilliance as both writer and speaker rested on precisely that sort of airy theatricality.

If Disraeli loved the House of Commons, he also worshipped in the same semi-grave, semi-comic way at the foot of the Queen.

The monarchy's appeal, like that of Disraeli himself, rested not on doing, or accomplishing, or proving, or teaching, but on being, presiding, appearing, and setting a tone or evoking an atmosphere. The monarchy recalled English history. It inspired confidence and the imagination. It provided much of the allure that brought him to Westminster in the first place. In Victorian terms this corresponded to a 'separate spheres' stereotype where royal 'being' was feminine, while parliamentary 'doing' was masculine. But neither Disraeli nor the Queen lived up to the stereotype. Disraeli combined the masculine and feminine in his own personality, while his novels dwelled on the powers of effeminate men. The Queen understood that in Disraeli she was dealing with something of a hybrid, like herself. She too had a role to play as the nation's first female, but another role to play as someone who was deeply interested and intent upon influencing the male world of politics.

Nor was it always the Queen of England who captured Disraeli's imagination. He also much enjoyed his contact with the court of Louis Philippe when he spent time in Paris in the 1840s. In *Endymion* too he imagined that his hero's sister became Queen of France at the very moment Endymion became prime minister. And even in an early short story, his favourite character was a royal figure in hell. In Disraeli's 'The Infernal Marriage', Tiresias warns Proserpine, wife of Pluto and queen of hell, that the way to the Elysian Fields is not easy. He tells her, 'the pleasant is generally difficult; let us be grateful that in our instance it is not, as usual, forbidden'. Proserpine replies, 'You say truly; I am sorry to confess how very often it appears to me that sin is enjoyment.'[27] Disraeli published this in 1834 at the very moment he was trying to get into Parliament and making it clear to future constituents, if they would have him, that he thoroughly sympathized with the queen of hell. His Elysium was almost always a sort of wicked intimacy with royal ladies. It is one of the most attractive ironies of his biography that this man, who regularly preferred the naughty to the nice, and committed his preference to print, should come to be prime minister of a serious-minded people.

Late in the spring of 1881 Disraeli was buried outside the east end of the church at Hughenden next to Mary Anne and Mrs Brydges Willyams, in death, as in life, making an odd but characteristic threesome with two older ladies. At the Christian burial service, with the Rothschilds, Britain's most prominent Jews, the Queen's private secretary and all the political world in attendance, his spirit was entrusted to heaven. But Disraeli had spent a long time thinking that hell must be a marvellous place too. Less than a year before he died he wrote to Lady Chesterfield about a series of Buckinghamshire thunderstorms. Peacocks were his favourite, showy birds and Hughenden was full of them, but they did shriek in a storm. 'Weather here consists of frequent thunderstorms and of great length,' he told her. 'At every crack the peacocks scream. I hardly know which sound is the most infernal. The mixture quite a day of judgment.'[28] You would never catch him fearing the underworld. A satirical play on words was more his style.

One of his very first autobiographical characters, Popanilla, went around wearing nothing but the skin of a serpent. He also had 'a devil of a tongue'. Disraeli had never spent very much of his imaginative life dwelling on Eden. He liked snakes and other references to Satan. Indeed, in 1843, he and Mary Anne had attended a masked ball at the Paris Opéra which was one of the best parties he could remember. His hosts had taken them to the Opéra after midnight, he told his sister, Sarah. They had

> an admirable box, the scene indescribable. Between three and four thousand *devils* dancing and masquerading beyond fancy. A thorough Carnival; the *salle* of the Grand Opera formed into one immense Belshazzar's hall with a hundred streaming lustres. The grand galoppe, five hundred figures whirling like a witches' sabbath, truly infernal. The contrast, too, between the bright fantastic scene below and the boxes filled with ladies in black dominoes and masks, very striking, and made the scene altogether Eblisian. Fancy me walking about in such a dissolute devilry . . .[29]

No doubt Sarah would have smiled at her brother walking about in such an Eblis that only a Beckford could have committed to print before him. That was why he loved her. Having imagined himself in the happy company of fallen angels all his life, it would not have worried him much to contemplate, on the brink of the grave, going to hell. He would probably enjoy himself.

Notes

Abbreviations

All places of publication London unless noted otherwise

Blake	Robert Blake, *Disraeli* (1966)
Bradford	Sarah Bradford, *Disraeli* (1982)
DL	*Benjamin Disraeli Letters, 1815–1859*, ed. M. G. Wiebe *et al.*, 7 vols. to date (Toronto, 1987–2004)
HP	Hughenden Papers on loan from the National Trust to the Bodleian Library, Oxford, Dep. Hughenden
M & B	William Flavelle Monypenny and George Earle Buckle, *The Life of Benjamin Disraeli, Earl of Beaconsfield*, 6 vols. (1910–20)
M & B, 1929	William Flavelle Monypenny and George Earle Buckle, *The Life of Benjamin Disraeli, Earl of Beaconsfield*, new and rev. edn in 2 vols., ed. G. E. Buckle (1929)
ODNB	*Oxford Dictionary of National Biography*
Ridley	Jane Ridley, *The Young Disraeli, 1804–1846* (1995)
Smith	Paul Smith, *Disraeli: A Brief Life* (Cambridge, 1996)
Vincent	John Vincent, *Disraeli* (Oxford, 1990)
Weintraub	Stanley Weintraub, *Disraeli* (1993)
Zetland	*The Letters of Disraeli to Lady Bradford and Lady Chesterfield*, ed. Marquess of Zetland, 2 vols. (1929)

Prologue

1 *DL*, 111, Disraeli to Sarah Disraeli, 28 May 1831; Blake, *Disraeli's Grand Tour* (1982), 81, 87.
2 Benjamin Disraeli, *Contarini Fleming* (1832; 1878), 168–70.

3 Ibid., 177.

4 Ibid., 186–7.

5 M & B.

6 Blake. In his recent essay on Disraeli for the *ODNB*, Jonathan Parry has suggested some of the book's faults.

7 Bradford; Ridley.

8 *DL*.

9 Vincent; Smith; Weintraub; Christopher Hibbert, *Disraeli* (2004).

10 Edgar Feuchtwanger, *Disraeli* (2000).

11 Michael Flavin's *Benjamin Disraeli* (Brighton, 2005) uses the novels as a way of examining the political ideas which would eventually become Disraeli's policy. See also Robert O'Kell, 'The Autobiographical Nature of Disraeli's Early Fiction', *Nineteenth-Century Fiction*, 31, (Dec. 1976), 253–84.

12 M & B, VI, 553, n. 1.

13 Ibid., 553.

14 Thom Braun, *Disraeli the Novelist* (1981), 23, makes a similar point, though, as a literary critic, his book is more concerned with setting Disraeli's work in its literary context than with using it to reconsider our understanding of Disraeli's life.

15 Blake liked some of the works better than others; but, more typically, he said the second part of *Vivian Grey* was 'trash' and described Disraeli's story, 'Popanilla', as 'slight', 53.

16 *Disraeli's Reminiscences*, ed. Helen M. Swartz and Marvin Swartz (1975), 95.

17 Quoted in Blake, 38.

18 Isaiah Berlin, 'Benjamin Disraeli, Karl Marx and the Search for Identity', in *Against the Current*, ed. with biblio. Henry Hardy, intro. Roger Hausheer (New York, 1980), 264.

19 Blake, 13–14.

20 Randolph Trumbach is the expert on this subject; see his *Sex and the Gender Revolution*, I (Chicago and London, 1998).

21 Shelley to Peacock, 16 Aug. 1818, *The Letters of Percy Bysshe Shelley*, ed. Frederick L. Jones, 2 vols. (Oxford, 1964), II, 475.

22 Blake, 51.

23 Ibid., 77.

24 Richard Ellmann, *Oscar Wilde* (New York, 1987), 311, suggests Wilhelm Meinhold's *Sidonia* as a possible source for *Dorian Gray*. There is another connection here as Sidonia is one of the autobiographical figures in Disraeli's novel *Coningsby*.

25 Matt Cook, *London and the Culture of Homosexuality, 1885–1914* (Cambridge, 2003), 12.

26 Graham Robb, *Strangers: Homosexual Love in the Nineteenth Century* (2003), 98–101.

27 H. G. Cocks, *Nameless Offences* (2003), 105, 107, 157.

28 Neil Bartlett, *Who Was That Man? A Present for Mr Oscar Wilde* (1988), 30.

29 Robb, 90.

30 Bradford, 218; Ridley, 22.

31 Blake, 74–5.

32 Oscar Wilde, *A Woman of No Importance*, in *The Best of Oscar Wilde: Selected Plays and Literary Criticism*, ed. with an updated intro. Sylvan Barnet (New York, 2004), 143.

33 On this theme see, most recently, David Gelernter, 'The Inventor of Modern Conservatism', *The Weekly Standard*, 7 Feb. 2005, cited in David Brooks, 'The Sidney Awards, 2005', *New York Times*, 28 Dec. 2005.

34 *Disraeli's Reminiscences*, 95.

35 James A. Notopoulos, *The Platonism of Shelley* (Durham, NC, 1949), 382–6.

36 Arthur Ponsonby, *Henry Ponsonby* (1942), 246.

37 Margot Asquith to Arthur Ponsonby, 6 Oct. 1940, Ponsonby MSS, Shulbrede Priory.

38 *Disraeli's Reminiscences*, 89.

1 – The Boys Will Laugh at Me

1 Bradford, 1; Barrington, *Notes & Queries*, 6th ser. (1884), X, 458.

2 M & B, I, 5.

3 Weintraub, 20. See also Bernard Glassman, *Benjamin Disraeli* (Lanham, MD, 2003).

4 Blake, 3.

5 Blake realized this; see ibid., 3–4.

6 Simon Bradley and Nikolaus Pevsner, *London 6: Westminster* (New Haven, CT and London, 2003), 326.

7 Isaac Disraeli, *Curiosities of Literature*, with a view of the life and writings of the author by his son, 14th edn, 3 vols. (1849), I, xx–xxi; the spelling of Disraeli in this edition is that adopted by the son, though not by his father in his lifetime. Disraeli had started leaving out the apostrophe in the family surname by about 1822.

8 Simon Bradley and Nikolaus Pevsner, *London 1: The City of London* (1997), 272–3.

9 Quoted in Christopher Hibbert, *Venice: The Biography of a City* (1988), 201.

10 Fiona MacCarthy, *Byron: Life and Legend* (2002), 341, 367.

11 Quoted in Hibbert, 286; on Venice's reputation for fewer legal restrictions on homosexuality, see also Jonathan Gross, "'One Half What I Should Say": Byron's Gay Narrator in *Don Juan*', in *Mapping Male Sexuality: Nineteenth–Century England,* ed. Jay Losey and William D. Brewer (Madison and Teaneck, NJ, 2000), 97.

12 M & B, I, 16.

13 Isaac D'Israeli, *Curiosities*, I, xxiv; Bradford, 5.

14 Isaac D'Israeli, *Curiosities*, xxiv–xxv.

15 Ibid., xxv.

16 M & B, I, 7–8.

17 Isaac D'Israeli, *Curiosities*, I, xxviii.

18 Ibid., xxix.

19 Ibid., xxxix.

20 Ibid., xlii.

21 Ibid., xli. Richard Hole, *Remarks on the Arabian Nights' Entertainments; in which the origin of Sinbad's Voyages, and other oriental fictions, is particularly considered* (1797).

22 George Rousseau, "'Homoplatonic, Homodepressed, Homomorbid": Some Further Genealogies of Same Sex Attraction in Western Civilization', in *Love, Sex, Intimacy, and Friendship Between Men 1550–1800*, ed. Katherine O'Donnell and Michael O'Rourke (Basingstoke, 2003), 12–52.

23 Gregory Woods, *A History of Gay Literature* (New Haven, CT, and London, 1998), 54–6.

24 Blake, 8.

25 Bridget Cherry and Nikolaus Pevsner, *London 4: North* (1998), 310.

26 Isaac D'Israeli, *Inquiry into the Literary and Political Character of James the First* (1816).

27 There is some question about whether his name was Potticary or Potticany. I have followed the spelling in *DL*, 1, Disraeli to Maria D'Israeli, 1815 [?]. Similarly, although most sources list it as Elliott Place (eg M & B, I, 19) only Eliot Place remains in modern Blackheath.

28 Blake, 12.

29 Bridget Cherry and Nikolaus Pevsner, *London 2: South* (Harmondsworth, 1983), 422.

30 Disraeli to Lady Bradford, 14 Aug. 1874, Zetland, I, 135.

31 *Vivian Grey*, 5 vols. bound as 2 (vols. I, II, 1826; vols. III–V, 1827), I, 3.

32 Ibid., 5.

33 Ibid., 7.

34 Ibid., 9.
35 Ibid., 9, 11.
36 M & B, I, 19–20.
37 *DL*, 2, Disraeli to Edward Jones, 2 Jan. 1818.
38 Todd M. Endelman, *The Jews of Britain, 1656–2000* (Berkeley, CA, 2002), 62.
39 M & B, I, 22–3.
40 Ibid., 23.
41 Ibid., 24; Blake, 12.
42 Nikolaus Pevsner, *Essex*, rev. Enid Radcliffe (Harmondsworth, 1979), 409 has 'Highams', though Disraeli's recollection was 'Higham', for which see M & B, I, 24.
43 Quoted in Weintraub, 36.
44 *Vivian Grey*, I, 7.
45 Ibid., 22.
46 Ibid., 30–31.

2 – Sublimity and Sangfroid

1 Benjamin Disraeli, *Contarini Fleming, A Psychological Romance*, vol. IV of the Bradenham edn, with an intro. Philip Guedalla (New York, 1927), 15, 16, 17. I have generally used first editions of the novels, but there are some exceptions, as here.
2 Ibid., 22, 24.
3 Ibid., 24.
4 Ibid., 25.
5 Ibid.
6 Ibid., 26–7.
7 Ibid., 27.
8 Ibid.
9 Ibid., 28.
10 Ibid., 30.
11 Louis Crompton, *Byron and Greek Love* (1985); Alcibiades and Socrates were also figures some homosexuals looked back to when they made lists of previous pairs of male lovers to legitimate their own love, see Gregory Woods, *A History of Gay Literature* (New Haven, CT, and London, 1998), 3.
12 *Contarini*, 31.
13 Fiona MacCarthy, *Byron: Life and Legend* (2002), 39; on 'Hyacinth' see also Neil Bartlett, *Who Was That Man? A Present for Mr Oscar Wilde*, (1988), 56; on reference to Graeco–Roman literature as a coded way of referring to homosexuality see Elizabeth Dell and Jay Losey,

'Introduction', *Mapping Male Sexuality, Nineteenth-Century England*, ed. J. Losey and William D. Brewer (Madison and Teaneck, NJ, 2000), 10.

14 See *Vivian Grey*, ed. Lucien Wolf, 2 vols., (1904) I, 1 and 373.

15 A word to the wise is sufficient.

16 *Don Juan*, in *Lord Byron: The Complete Poetical Works*, ed. Jerome J. McGann, 7 vols. (Oxford, 1980–93), V, 25, canto I, stanza 53.

17 Quoted in MacCarthy, 435.

18 M & B, I, 30.

19 Ibid., 32.

20 Todd M. Endelman, *The Jews of Britain, 1656–2000* (Berkeley, CA, 2002), 99.

21 M & B, I, 32–3; Blake, 19.

22 M & B, I, 32–3.

23 *DL*, 11, Disraeli to Sarah Disraeli, 2 Aug. 1824. The *Disraeli Letters* preserve Disraeli's spelling and punctuation as found in the original.

24 Ibid., 12, Disraeli to Sarah Disraeli, 6 Aug. 1824.

25 Ibid., 13, Disraeli to Sarah Disraeli, 14 Aug. 1824.

26 Ibid., 11, Disraeli to Sarah Disraeli, 2 Aug. 1824.

27 Ibid., 13, Disraeli to Sarah Disraeli, 14 Aug. 1824.

28 Ibid., 14, Disraeli to Sarah Disraeli, 19 Aug. 1824.

29 Ibid., 15, Disraeli to Sarah Disraeli, 23 Aug. 1824.

30 Sir Peter Paul Rubens, knighted by Charles I; *DL*, 12, Disraeli to Sarah Disraeli, 6 Aug. 1824.

31 Ibid., 11, Disraeli to Sarah Disraeli, 2 Aug. 1824.

32 M & B, I, 45.

33 *Contarini*, 46–7.

34 Ibid., 50.

35 Ibid., 51.

36 See also David Hilliard, 'Un–English and Unmanly', *Victorian Studies* 25 (1982), 181–210.

37 *DL*, 12, Disraeli to Sarah Disraeli, 6 Aug. 1824.

38 Ibid., 14, Disraeli to Sarah Disraeli, 19 Aug. 1824.

39 Ibid., 10, Disraeli to Sarah Disraeli, 29 July 1824.

40 Ibid., 11, Disraeli to Sarah Disraeli, 2 Aug. 1824.

41 Ibid.

42 M & B, I, 39.

43 Ibid., 33.

44 On Regency dandyism see most recently Ian Kelly, *Beau Brummell* (2005).

45 Benjamin Disraeli, *Vivian Grey*, 5 vols. bound in 2 (vols. I, II, 1826; vols. III–V, 1827), I, 65.

3 – Château Désir

1 Blake, 48.

2 Vincent, 61.

3 Blake, 25; most of the following is based on Blake, though with reference to Ridley, Bradford, Weintraub and M & B.

4 *DL*, 24, Disraeli to Isaac D'Israeli, 5 Aug. 1825.

5 Ibid., 27, Disraeli to John Murray, 18 Sept. 1825.

6 'Lockhart, John Gibson (1794–1854)', *ODNB*.

7 *DL*, 35, Disraeli to John Gibson Lockhart, 1 Nov. 1825.

8 Ibid., 37, Disraeli to John Gibson Lockhart, 21 Nov. 1825.

9 Ibid., 40, Disraeli to John Gibson Lockhart, 23 Nov. 1825.

10 Ibid., n. 1.

11 *The Satires of Decimus Junius Juvenalis*, trans. William Gifford (1802), satire I, verses 41–5, 10–11.

12 Ibid., satire IV, verse 5, 111.

13 Anna Clark, *Scandal: The Sexual Politics of the British Constitution* (Princeton, NJ, and Oxford, 2004), 14.

14 Ellen Moers, *The Dandy* (1960), 52.

15 Benjamin Disraeli, *Vivian Grey*, 5 vols. bound as 2 (vols. I, II, 1826; vols. III–V, 1827), I, 52.

16 Ibid., 53–4.

17 Ibid., 73, 117.

18 Ridley, 44.

19 *Vivian Grey* (1827), IV, 293.

20 Ibid., I, 96.

21 Ibid., 133.

22 Ibid., 144–5.

23 Ibid., 178.

24 Ibid., 226–7.

25 Ibid., 233.

26 Ibid., II, 4.

27 Ibid., 142.

28 Ibid., 17.

29 *Vivian Grey*, ed. Lucien Wolf, 2 vols. (1904), II, 371.

30 *Vivian Grey* (1826), II, 32.

31 Ibid., 33.

32 Ibid., 50; see also Ridley, 47.

33 *Vivian Grey* (1826), II, 135.

34 Ibid., 218.

4 – Quite a Love of a Man

1 *Vivian Grey*, ed. Lucien Wolf, 2 vols. (1904), I, l, lvi–lvii; see also Blake, 773–4.

2 Quoted in *Disraeli's Novels Reviewed, 1826–1968*, ed. R. W. Stewart (Metuchen, NJ, 1975), 115, 117.

3 Benjamin Disraeli, *Vivian Grey*, 5 vols. bound as 2 (vols. I, II, 1826; vols. III–V, 1827), III, 27.

4 Ibid., 33.

5 Ibid., V, 11.

6 Ibid., III, 44.

7 Ibid., 154.

8 *DL*, 49, Disraeli to Benjamin Austen, July 1826.

9 Ibid., 50, Disraeli to Isaac D'Israeli, 9 Aug. 1826.

10 Ibid., 52, Disraeli to Isaac D'Israeli, 2 Sept. 1826.

11 M & B, I, 96.

12 Blake, 51–2.

13 *DL*, 51, Disraeli to Isaac D'Israeli, 21 Aug. 1826.

14 Ibid.

15 Ibid.

16 Ibid.

17 Quoted in *Disraeli's Novels Reviewed*, 113.

18 *DL*, 52, Disraeli to Isaac D'Israeli, 2 Sept. 1826.

19 Ibid., 53, Disraeli to Isaac D'Israeli, 13 Sept. 1826.

20 Ibid.

21 HP, 12/1/96, Sara Austen to Maria D'Israeli, 24 Sept. 1826.

22 *DL*, 53, Disraeli to Isaac D'Israeli, 13 Sept. 1826.

23 Ibid., 54, Disraeli to Isaac D'Israeli, 26 Sept. 1826.

24 Ibid., 55, Disraeli to Isaac D'Israeli, 29 Sept. 1826.

25 Ibid.

26 Ibid., 57, Disraeli to Isaac D'Israeli, 10 Oct. 1826.

27 M & B, I, 111.

28 Ibid.

5 – A Treatise on Nonchalance

1 *DL*, 66, Disraeli to Sharon Turner, 10 Mar. 1828.

2 M & B, I, 116.

3 Benjamin Disraeli, *The Voyage of Captain Popanilla*, by the author of 'Vivian Grey' (1828), 8.

4 M & B, I, 124.

5 *Popanilla*, 17.

6 John Lindley, *Vegetable Physiology* (1827); Sir Charles Bell, *Animal*

Mechanics, or *Proofs of design in the animal frame* (1827); Thomas Flower Ellis, *Outline of General History* (1828).

7 *Popanilla*, 32.
8 Ibid., 33–4.
9 Ibid., 43.
10 Ibid., 91.
11 Ibid., 95.
12 Ibid., 102–3.
13 Ibid., 113–18.
14 Ibid., 138.
15 Ibid., 149–50.
16 Ibid., 151–2.
17 Ibid., 153.
18 Ibid., 155.
19 Ibid., 179.
20 *DL*, 75, Disraeli to Mrs Charles Gore, 14 Feb. 1830, n. 3.
21 Hermione Hobhouse, *Lost London: A Century of Demolition and Decay* (1971), 201.
22 'A Colloquy on the Progress and Prospects of the "Court Journal"', *The Court Journal*, 23 May 1829, 49.
23 Ibid.
24 'Second Edition! Terrible Non–Occurrence!! Flight of a Distinguished Individual!!! Etc. Etc.', *The Court Journal*, 30 May 1829, 65–6.
25 'The Trial of Mivartinos', *The Court Journal*, 6 June 1829, 81.
26 Ibid., 82.
27 'The Levee of Augustus Villeroy', *The Court Journal*, 20 June 1829, 114.
28 *Popanilla*, 11–12.
29 See Anna Clark, *Scandal: The Sexual Politics of the British Constitution* (Princeton, NJ, and Oxford, 2004), 9, 11 on eighteenth-century associations of effeminacy with both sodomy and aristocracy.
30 James Eli Adams, *Dandies and Desert Saints: Styles of Victorian Masculinity* (Ithaca, NY, and London, 1995), 98–9.
31 See the last chapter of Alan Bray, *The Friend* (Chicago and London, 2003).
32 'Levee', 116.
33 Leslie Mitchell, *Bulwer Lytton* (2003), 88; *DL*, 75, Disraeli to Mrs Charles Gore, 14 Feb. 1830, n. 3.
34 *Bulwer Lytton*, 99.
35 HP, Edward Lytton Bulwer to Disraeli, July 1829, 104/1/9–10.

6 – His Manner Was His Magic

1 *DL*, 56, Disraeli to Isaac D'Israeli, 29 Sept. 1826.

2 Ibid., 74, Disraeli to Benjamin Austen, 8 Dec. 1829.

3 Benjamin Disraeli, *The Young Duke*, '*A moral Tale, though gay*', by the author of 'Vivian Grey', 3 vols. (1831), I, iii.

4 Ibid., 1.

5 Ellen Moers, *The Dandy* (1960), 20.

6 *Young Duke*, I, 55–6.

7 Ibid., 58.

8 Ibid., 93.

9 Ibid., 34.

10 Ibid., 35–6.

11 Isaac D'Israeli, *Curiosities of Literature*, 14th edn., 3 vols. (1849), I, 519.

12 *Young Duke*, I, 76.

13 Ibid., 209.

14 HP, Edward Lytton Bulwer to Disraeli, 10 Apr. 1830, 104/1/11–12.

15 Moers, *The Dandy*, 81.

16 *Oxford English Dictionary.*

17 *Young Duke*, II, 28.

18 Ibid., III, 45.

19 Ibid., I, 173.

20 Ibid., II, 54.

21 On the nineteenth–century locations of these two Murillo canvases see Xanthe Brooke and Peter Cherry, *Murillo: Scenes of Childhood* (2001), 96, 114.

22 *Young Duke*, II, 70.

23 Ibid., 70, 71.

24 Ibid., 70–1.

25 Ibid., I, 294.

26 Ibid., II, 218.

27 Ibid., 219.

28 Ibid., 133.

29 Daniel R. Schwartz, *Disraeli's Fiction* (1979), 22–3.

30 *Young Duke*, III, 213.

31 Ibid., 214–15.

32 Ibid., 228.

33 Ibid., 215.

34 Richard Ellmann, *Oscar Wilde* (New York, 1987), 319.

35 *Young Duke*, III, 253.

36 *DL*, 76, Disraeli to Henry Colburn, 14 Feb. 1830.

37 HP, Henry Colburn to Disraeli, undated [1830]; copy of agreement

between Colburn and Disraeli, 17 May 1830, 235/3/15–16.
38 Disraeli, *Young Duke*, I, 97.

7 – This Is My Palace

1   M & B, I, 136.
2   Louis Crompton, *Byron and Greek Love* (1985), 112, n. 13.
3   Eve Kosofsky Sedgwick, *Between Men: English Literature and Male Homosocial Desire* (New York, 1985), 182; another commentator on Burton thinks he was 'sex obsessed' but concedes that discussions of homosexuality in the *Arabian Nights* are more common than in Western literature, see Robert Irwin, *The Arabian Nights: A Companion* (1994), 34, 169–71.
4   Lord Byron, *Childe Harold's Pilgrimage* in *The Complete Poetical Works*, ed. Jerome J. McGann, 7 vols. (Oxford, 1980–1993), II, lines 279–282.
5   Lord Byron, *Don Juan*, in McGann ed., V, lines 503–4.
6   Ibid., lines 945–52.
7   M & B, I, 124.
8   *DL*, 92, Disraeli to Isaac D'Israeli, 14 July 1830.
9   Ibid., 90, Disraeli to Isaac D'Israeli, 1 July 1830.
10 On the male lovers see Timothy Mowl, *Horace Walpole: The Great Outsider* (1996). George Hardinge perceived Walpole as effeminate himself and part of an effeminate circle; see *The Yale Edition of Horace Walpole's Correspondence*, ed. W. S. Lewis (New Haven, CT, 1973), XXXV, 647–8. I am grateful to Randolph Trumbach for this reference.
11 *DL*, 92, Disraeli to Isaac D'Israeli, 14 July 1830.
12 Ibid., 91, Disraeli to Isaac D'Israeli, 1 July 1830.
13 Ibid., 93, Disraeli to Isaac D'Israeli, 26 July 1830.
14 Ibid., 94, Disraeli to Maria D'Israeli, 1 Aug. 1830.
15 Ibid., 91, Disraeli to Isaac D'Israeli, 1 July 1830.
16 Ibid., 90, Disraeli to Isaac D'Israeli, 1 July 1830.
17 Ibid., 91, Disraeli to Isaac D'Israeli, 1 July 1830.
18 Ibid., 98, Disraeli to Benjamin Austen, 14 Sept. 1830.
19 M & B, I, 149.
20 *DL*, 103, Disraeli to Benjamin Austen, 18 Nov. 1830.
21 Ibid., 97, Disraeli to Isaac D'Israeli, 25 Aug. 1830.
22 Ibid., 94, Disraeli to Maria D'Israeli, 1 Aug. 1830.
23 Ibid., 97, Disraeli to Isaac D'Israeli, 25 Aug. 1830.
24 Ibid.; M & B, I, 154–5.
25 *DL*, 99, Disraeli to Ralph Disraeli, 17 Sept. 1830.
26 Jonathan Ned Katz, *Love Stories* (Chicago, 2001), 259; Graham Robb, *Strangers* (2003), 148.

27 Fiona MacCarthy, *Byron: Life and Legend* (2002), 372, 375.
28 *DL*, 99, Disraeli to Ralph Disraeli, 17 Sept. 1830.
29 Robert Blake, *Disraeli's Grand Tour* (1982), 57.
30 *DL*, 101, Disraeli to Isaac D'Israeli, 25 Oct. 1830.
31 Ibid., 103, Disraeli to Benjamin Austen, 18 Nov. 1830.
32 M & B, I, 168.
33 *DL*, 109, Disraeli to Isaac D'Israeli, 11 Jan. 1831.
34 Crompton, 142–3.
35 See also Edward W. Said, *Orientalism* (1978).
36 Peter Gay, *Schnitzler's Century* (2001) treats the sexual openness of a century once known for its prudery.
37 Benjamin Disraeli, *Contarini Fleming*, 4 vols. (1832), IV, 154.
38 On whom see James Knox, *Robert Byron* (2003).
39 M & B, I, 172–3.
40 Benjamin Disraeli, *The Wondrous Tale of Alroy* and *The Rise of Iskander*, 3 vols. (1833), I, 212.
41 *DL*, 111, Disraeli to Sarah Disraeli, 28 May 1831.
42 *Contarini*, IV, 199.
43 *DL*, 111, Disraeli to Sarah Disraeli, 28 May 1831.
44 M & B, I, 166–7.
45 Martin Bernal, *Black Athena: The Afroasiatic Roots of Classical Civilization*, I: *The Fabrication of Ancient Greece 1785–1985* (1987).

8 – Solitary Rides in the Desert

 1 'The Mutilated Diary', in *DL*, I, 1815–34, appendix III, p. 447.
 2 Timothy Mowl, *William Beckford, Composing for Mozart* (1998); Timothy Mowl, 'Disraeli's Novels and the Beckford Connection' in Benjamin Disraeli, *Earl of Beaconsfield: Scenes from an Extraordinary Life*, ed. Helen Langley (Oxford, 2003).
 3 Benjamin Disraeli, *Contarini Fleming*, 4 vols. (1832), I, 142.
 4 Ibid., 144.
 5 Ibid., II, 242.
 6 Ibid., 87–9.
 7 Ibid., III, 190, 192.
 8 Ibid., IV, 199, 'solitary rides'; I, 252, 'govern men'.
 9 Ibid., 255.
10 Ibid., 262.
11 Ibid., IV, 201.
12 Ibid., 205–7.
13 For a complete account of the ambiguities in same-sex friendship since the Middle Ages, see Alan Bray *The Friend* (Chicago, 2003).

14 Benjamin Disraeli, *The Wondrous Tale of Alroy* and *The Rise of Iskander*, 3 vols. (1833), I, 10.

15 Ibid., 11.

16 Ibid., 30.

17 Ibid., 91–2.

18 Ibid., 240.

19 Ibid., II, 102.

20 M & B, I, 179.

21 *Alroy*, III, 103.

22 Richard Dellamora notes the metaphorical analogy between sodomy and impalement in 'Benjamin Disraeli, Judaism, and the Legacy of William Beckford', in *Mapping Male Sexuality*, ed. Jay Losey and William D. Brewer (Madison and Teaneck, NJ, 2000), 166.

23 *DL*, 117, Disraeli to Isaac D'Israeli, 17–23 Oct. 1831.

24 Ibid.

25 *Alroy*, I, xii.

26 *DL*, 114, Disraeli to Sarah Disraeli, 20 July 1831; 117, Disraeli to Isaac Disraeli, 17–23 Oct. 1831.

9 – An Awful Ambition and Fiery Passions

1 M & B, I, 338.

2 Ibid., I, 257; *DL*, 345, Disraeli to Lady Blessington, 5 Aug. 1834.

3 *DL*, 173, Disraeli to Sarah Disraeli, 7 Apr. 1832.

4 Benjamin and Sarah Disraeli, *A Year at Hartlebury, or The Election*, with appendices by Ellen Henderson and John P. Matthews (1834; 1983).

5 Ibid., 6.

6 Ibid., 59.

7 Ibid., 29.

8 Ibid., 9.

9 Ibid., 88.

10 Ibid., 209.

11 On two men expressing their passion for one another through a woman, see Eve Kosofsky Sedgwick, *Between Men* (New York, 1985), esp. ch. 1.

12 Ridley, 134.

13 'The Mutilated Diary', in *DL*, I, appendix III, p. 445.

14 Benjamin Disraeli, *Henrietta Temple: A Love Story*, by the author of 'Vivian Grey', 3 vols. (1836, although the title page of the first edition in the British Library lists its publication as 1837), I, 147.

15 Ibid., 158–9, 219.

16 Ibid., 243.
17 See e.g. Jonathan Parry, 'Holborn at Heart', *London Review of Books*, 23 Jan. 1997, 22.
18 *Henrietta Temple,* II, 46.
19 Ibid., 105.
20 M & B, I, 232; *DL*, 276, Disraeli to Sarah Disraeli, 5 June 1833.
21 *Henrietta Temple*, III, 140.
22 'The Mutilated Diary', in *DL*, I, appendix III, p. 446.
23 Benjamin Disraeli, *The Wondrous Tale of Alroy* and *The Rise of Iskander*, 3 vols. (1833), III, 117–18.
24 M & B, I, 223; *DL*, 233, Disraeli to Sarah Disraeli, 7 Feb. 1833.
25 Leslie Mitchell, *Bulwer Lytton* (2003), 100.
26 Ibid., 101.
27 Ibid., 62.
28 Ibid., 101.
29 Ibid., 101–2.
30 Nick Foulkes, *Last of the Dandies: The Scandalous Life and Escapades of Count d'Orsay* (2003), 97.
31 Ibid., 242.
32 *DL*, 494, Disraeli to Sarah Disraeli, 4 Apr. 1836.
33 Ibid., 178, Disraeli to Sarah Disraeli, 12 Apr. 1832.
34 Foulkes, 250.
35 *DL*, 560, Disraeli to Sarah Disraeli, 23 Jan. 1837.
36 *Henrietta Temple*, III, 148.
37 Ibid., 159.
38 Ibid., I, 29.
39 Ibid., 86.
40 Benjamin Disraeli, *Venetia*, by the author of 'Vivian Grey' and 'Henrietta Temple', 3 vols. (1837), III, 211–12.
41 Ibid., I, 273.
42 Ibid., III, 226.

10 – A Singular Blending of the Daring and the Soft

1 *DL*, 224, Disraeli to John Gibson Lockhart, 22 Dec. 1832, and n. 2.
2 'The Mutilated Diary', in *DL*, I, appendix III, p. 446.
3 *DL*, 296, Disraeli to Benjamin Austen, 30 Nov. 1833.
4 Ibid., 299, Disraeli to Benjamin Austen, 1 Dec. 1833.
5 E.g., ibid., 513, Disraeli to Benjamin Austen, 8 July 1836.
6 Benjamin Disraeli, *Henrietta Temple*, 3 vols. (1836), I, 126–7.
7 Ibid., III, 157.
8 Disraeli, *Venetia*, 3 vols. (1837), III, 186.

9 Jessica R. Feldman, *Gender on the Divide* (Ithaca, NY, and London, 1993), 4.

10 George Walden, *Who Is a Dandy?* with Jules Barbey d'Aurevilly, *On Dandyism and George Brummell*, trans. George Walden (2002), 148.

11 Benjamin and Sarah Disraeli, *A Year at Hartlebury*, with appendices by Ellen Henderson and John P. Matthews (1834; 1983), 140.

12 Disraeli, *Venetia*, III, 226.

13 Graham Robb, *Strangers: Homosexual Love in the Nineteenth Century* (2003), 144.

14 M & B, I, 231–2.

15 Ibid., I, 281.

16 Ibid., I, 284.

17 *DL*, 641, Disraeli to Sarah Disraeli, 25 July 1837, n. 1.

18 Quoted in Ridley, 130–1.

19 M & B, I, 251; *DL*, 331, Disraeli to Sarah Disraeli, 19 June 1834.

20 *DL*, 269, Disraeli to Sarah Disraeli, 30 Apr. 1833.

21 *Henrietta Temple*, II, 135, 139–40.

22 Ibid., 143.

23 Ibid., 145.

24 Ibid., 146.

25 Ibid., 146–7.

26 Ibid., 158.

27 Ibid., III, 39.

28 Ibid., 251.

29 Blake, 114–19.

30 *Hartlebury*, 101.

31 Ibid., 113–14.

32 *DL*, 540, Disraeli to Sarah Disraeli, 15 Dec. 1836.

33 Ibid., 646, Disraeli to Sarah Disraeli, 8 Aug. 1837.

34 Ibid., 676, Disraeli to Sarah Disraeli, 21 Nov. 1837.

35 M & B, II, 11.

36 Ibid., 8.

37 *DL*, 686, Disraeli to Sarah Disraeli, 8 Dec. 1837, n. 4.

38 Ibid., 694, Disraeli to Lady Caroline Maxse, 31 Dec. 1837.

39 *Henrietta Temple*, I, 94.

40 'The Runnymede Letters', in *DL*, II, appendix II, p. 345.

41 Ibid., 365.

11 – I Love Fame

1 M & B, II, 14.

2 Ibid., 35; *DL*, 804, Disraeli to Sarah Disraeli, 29 July 1838.

3 M & B, II, 66.

4 Ibid., 85.

5 Ibid., 127–8; *DL*, 1224, Disraeli to Mary Anne Disraeli, 9 Mar. 1842.

6 M & B, II, 191.

7 Ibid., 229.

8 Ibid., 245–6.

9 Ibid., 316.

10 Matt Cook has suggested connections between interest in Greek sculpture, particularly male nudes, and homosexuality, especially in scholars like Johann Joachim Winckelmann and Walter Pater, in *London and the Culture of Homosexuality, 1885–1914* (Cambridge, 2003), e.g. 95–6.

11 David Barchard, 'On the Wrong Side of History', *Cornucopia*, 5 (2003), 90–5.

12 *Disraeli's Reminiscences*, ed. Helen M. Swartz and Marvin Swartz (1975), 33.

13 Charles Whibley, *Lord John Manners and His Friends*, 2 vols. (Edinburgh and London, 1925), I, 55–6.

14 George Strangford, *Angela Pisani: A Novel*, with a memoir by Emily Strangford, 3 vols. (1875), I, xi–xii.

15 M & B, II, 126.

16 Quoted in Ibid., 128.

17 Smith, 57; Ridley, 265.

18 *Sexual Heretics: Male Homosexuality in English Literature from 1850 to 1900, An Anthology*, selected and with an intro. by Brian Reade (1970), 4–5; Richard Faber, *Young England* (1987), 64–5, 68, 70, 72–5.

19 Strangford, I, xiii.

20 Edward Barrington de Fonblanque, *Lives of the Lords Strangford* (London, Paris and New York, 1877), 222.

21 M & B, II, 163.

12 – He Interests Me

1 Edgar Feuchtwanger, *Disraeli* (2000), 49.

2 Jonathan Parry, 'Disraeli, Benjamin, first Earl of Beaconsfield', *ODNB*, 278.

3 Quoted in M & B, II, 305.

4 Benjamin Disraeli, *Coningsby; or, The New Generation*, by B. Disraeli, Esq. M.P., author of 'Contarini Fleming', 3 vols. (1844), I, 36.

5 Ibid., 37.

6 Ibid., 39.

7 Ibid., 40.

8 Ibid., 96–7.

9 Ibid., 287.

10 Ibid., II, 98.

11 Ibid., I, 85.

12 Ibid., 248.

13 Ibid., III, 26; II, 170–1.

14 Ibid., II, 134.

15 Gregory Woods, *A History of Gay Male Literature* (New Haven, CT, and London, 1998), 3.

16 'Commonplace Book. 1842', in *DL*, IV, Appendix V, pp. 376–381, see esp. Disraeli-numbered pages 4, 5, 9, and ?56.

17 For many of these figures see Louis Crompton, *Homosexuality and Civilization* (Cambridge, MA, 2003); also *Gay Histories and Cultures: An Encyclopedia*, ed. George E. Haggerty (New York, 2000); and *ODNB*. On James I, Buckingham and Marlowe see Michael B. Young, *James VI and I and the History of Homosexuality* (Basingstoke, 2000), 44–5; Isaac D'Israeli's *An Inquiry into the Literary and Political Character of James the First* (1816), 186–9, tried to defend James I by pointing to the 'coarseness' of early seventeenth-century manners, including men engaging in 'infamous vices'.

18 *Coningsby*, I, 250.

19 Ibid., 254.

20 Ibid., 274.

21 Ibid., II, 148–9.

22 *DL*, 1342, Disraeli to Lord Lyndhurst, 10 May 1844, n. 2.

23 *Coningsby*, III, 220.

13 – I Poured into the Fictitious Scene My Actual Sensations

1 M & B, II, 17.

2 Ibid., 36.

3 *DL*, 771, Disraeli to Mary Anne Lewis, 9 May 1838.

4 M & B, II, 48.

5 Ibid., 40.

6 Vincent, 79, points out that the work is only ambiguously flattering to Mary Anne.

7 Blake, 155. See *DL*, 767, Disraeli to Mary Anne Lewis, 26 Apr. 1838, where he told her that Rosina Bulwer was 'vulgar' and 'heartless'.

8 *Ancient Spanish Ballads, Historical and Romantic*, trans. J. G. Lockhart (Edinburgh, 1823).

9 Benjamin Disraeli, *The Tragedy of Count Alarcos*, by the author of 'Vivian Grey', (1839), 17.

10 Ibid., 49–50.

11 M & B, II, 53.
12 *DL*, 997, Disraeli to Maria D'Israeli, 30 Aug. 1839; 999, Disraeli to Sarah Disraeli, 7 Sept. 1839, n. 4; Mary Anne Disraeli to Isaac D'Israeli, 5 Sept. 1839.
13 Ibid., 861, Disraeli to Mary Anne Lewis, 30 Dec. 1838.
14 Weintraub, 182.
15 *DL*, 1207, 1209, Disraeli to Mary Anne Disraeli, 17, 18 Feb. 1842.
16 Ibid., 1026, Disraeli to William Beckford, 6 Jan. 1839.
17 Ibid., 1170, Disraeli to Maria D'Israeli, 20 June 1841.
18 Ibid., 1370, Disraeli to Mary Anne Disraeli, 27 Aug. 1844.
19 M & B, II, 243–4; *DL*, 1371, Disraeli to Mary Anne Disraeli, 28 Aug. 1844.
20 *DL*, 1514, Disraeli to George Mathew, 28 Aug. 1846.
21 M & B, II, 31–3.
22 *DL*, 790, Disraeli to Sarah Disraeli, 29 June 1838.
23 Quoted in Ibid., 769, Disraeli to Mary Anne Lewis, 1 May 1838, n. 2.
24 See William Kuhn, *Democratic Royalism* (Basingstoke and New York, 1996), ch. 2.
25 M & B, II, 32–3; *DL*, 791, Disraeli to Sarah Disraeli, 2 July 1838.
26 *DL*, 790, Disraeli to Sarah Disraeli, 29 June 1838.
27 Ibid., 791, Disraeli to Sarah Disraeli, 2 July 1838.
28 Ibid., 796, Disraeli to Sarah Disraeli, 10 July 1838.
29 Ibid., 1043, Disraeli to Sarah Disraeli, 7 Feb. 1840.
30 Ibid., 1174, Disraeli to Sarah Disraeli, 24 July 1841, n. 1.

14 – So Many Gentlemen, So Little Gentleness

1   M & B, III, 40.
2   Benjamin Disraeli, *Sybil; Or, The Two Nations*, by B. Disraeli, M.P., author of 'Coningsby', 3 vols. (1845), I, 3.
3   Ibid., 3–5.
4   Ibid., 66; my emphasis.
5   Ibid., 24.
6   Ibid., 181.
7   Ibid., 32.
8   Ibid., 198.
9   Ibid., 200.
10 M & B, 1929, I, 520.
11 *DL*, 1428, Disraeli to Sarah Disraeli, 19 July 1845.
12 Benjamin Disraeli, *Tancred; Or, The New Crusade*, by B. Disraeli, M.P., author of 'Coningsby', 'Sybil', etc., 3 vols. (1847) I, 283.
13 Benjamin Disraeli, Member of Parliament for the County of

Buckingham, *Lord George Bentinck: A Political Biography* (1852), 7, 70.
14   *DL*, 1737, Disraeli to Prince Metternich, 30 Oct. 1848.

15 – Recklessness as a Principle of Action

1   M & B, III, 14.
2   Ibid., 34.
3   Colm Tóibín, *The Master* (2004), 305.
4   Benjamin Disraeli, *Tancred; Or, The New Crusade*, by B. Disraeli, M.P., author of 'Coningsby', 'Sybil', etc., 3 vols. (1847), I, 6–7.
5   Benjamin Disraeli, *Sybil; Or, The Two Nations*, by B. Disraeli, M.P., author of 'Coningsby', 3 vols. (1845), I, 234.
6   Stanley Wells, *Looking for Sex in Shakespeare* (Cambridge, 2004), 43.
7   *Tancred*, I, 77.
8   Ibid., 79.
9   Ibid., 286; M & B, III, 38.
10   *Tancred*, I, 191.
11   Ibid, 79.
12   Neil Bartlett, *Who Was That Man? A Present for Mr Oscar Wilde* (1988), 56; Louis Crompton, *Byron and Greek Love* (1985), 127–8.
13   Linda Dowling's *Hellenism and Homosexuality in Victorian Oxford* (Ithaca, NY, 1994) is interesting here; but she does not think it was possible to make use of this combined Hellenism and homosexuality until after Benjamin Jowett's mid-Victorian mastership of Balliol and Walter Pater's work on the Renaissance of the mid 1870s. Disraeli's novels suggest otherwise.
14   *Tancred*, I, 103.
15   Ibid., 135.
16   Ibid., 254.
17   Ibid., II, 15–16.
18   Ibid., 20, 22.
19   Ibid., 92.
20   Ibid., 93–5.
21   Ibid., III, 59.
22   Ibid., II, 158–9.
23   Ibid., 177.
24   Ibid., 192.
25   Ibid., 100, 106.
26   Ibid., 234.
27   Ibid., 193, 194–5.
28   Ibid., 334.
29   Ibid., 340.

30 Ibid., III, 2.
31 Louis Crompton, *Homosexuality and Civilization* (Cambridge, MA, 2004), 124.
32 *Tancred*, III, 4.
33 Ibid., 165.
34 Ibid., II, 58.
35 Edward W. Said, *Orientalism* (1978), 190.
36 *The Phoenix of Sodom, or The Vere Street Coterie* (1813), 25–6; cited in Matt Cook, *London and the Culture of Homosexuality, 1885–1914* (Cambridge, 2003).
37 Quoted in Jonathan Ned Katz, *Love Stories* (Chicago, 2001), 207.
38 *DL*, 301, Disraeli to Benjamin Austen, 1 Jan. 1834.
39 Vincent, 98. Vincent also suggests in a highly elliptical way that Sidonia, the Jewish figure in *Coningsby*, 'embodies repression' and 'sublimation for a psychological tendency'. Vincent argues that Sidonia's pose is 'more Byronic than Judaic', by which he appears to mean that Disraeli's Jewishness and his homosexuality were linked via the figure of Sidonia; 86–7.
40 See also, Richard Dellamora, 'Benjamin Disraeli, Judaism, and the Legacy of William Beckford', in *Mapping Male Sexuality: Nineteenth–Century England*, ed. Jay Losey and William D. Brewer (Madison and Teaneck, NJ, 2000).
41 M & B, III, 136.
42 Ibid., 86.
43 Vincent, 14.
44 M & B, III, 14.
45 Quoted in ibid., II, 316.
46 Ibid.
47 *DL*, 1700, Disraeli to Sarah Disraeli, 30 Aug. 1848, n. 1, 2.
48 Quoted in M & B, III, 191.
49 Ibid., 152.
50 *DL*, 1721, Disraeli to Lord John Manners, 30 Sept. 1848.
51 Ibid., 1730, Disraeli to Mary Anne Disraeli, 18 Oct. 1848; M & B, III, 151–2.
52 M & B, III, 162; *DL*, 1867, Disraeli to Sarah Disraeli, 19 Aug. 1849.
53 Ibid., 190 has 'lovely Bucks château' but see *DL*, 1725, Disraeli to Prince Metternich, 12 Oct. 1848.
54 Quoted in M & B, II, 306.
55 Ibid., III, 328.
56 *DL*, 1542, Disraeli to Mary Anne Disraeli , 26 Dec. 1847.
57 Ibid., 2110, Disraeli to Sarah Disraeli, 22 Mar. 1851.
58 Ibid., 2216, Disraeli to Lord Henry Lennox, 29 Dec. 1851.

16 – That Fine Tall Room

1   *DL*, 2340, Disraeli to Sarah Disraeli, 27 July 1852, n. 2, letter of Sarah Disraeli to Disraeli, 27 May 1852.

2   'Disraeli, Benjamin, first Earl of Beaconsfield', *ODNB*.

3   M & B, 1929, I, 1402.

4   Ibid., 1162.

5   Blake, 325, 327, 714.

6   *DL*, VI, xxiv.

7   Bradford, 215–18.

8   M & B, 1929, I, 1198.

9   'Lord Henry G. C. Gordon-Lennox', *Vanity Fair*, 30 July 1870, 47.

10 *DL*, 2335, Disraeli to Lord Henry Lennox, 18 July 1852; see for Lennox's earlier letter to Disraeli, n. 7.

11 Blake, 326–7.

12 HP, 102/1, Lord Henry Lennox to Disraeli, ?1852, folio 18.

13 M & B, 1929, I, 1200; *DL*, 2346, Disraeli to Lord Henry Lennox, 7 Aug. 1852.

14 M & B, 1929, I, 1203; *DL*, 2364, Disraeli to Lord Henry Lennox, 16 Aug. 1852.

15 *Disraeli's Reminiscences*, ed. Helen M. Swartz and Marvin Swartz (1975), 22.

16 HP, 102/1, Lord Henry Lennox to Disraeli, ?1852, folio 33.

17 Ibid., Lord Henry Lennox to Disraeli, 21 Aug. 1852, folio 36.

18 M & B, 1929, I, 1203–4; *DL*, 2382, Disraeli to Lord Henry Lennox, 1 Sept. 1852, n. 1 says *DL*, 2364, provoked Lennox's response in the train.

19 *DL*, 2417, Disraeli to Mary Anne Disraeli, 8 Oct. 1852.

20 M & B, 1929, I, 1250.

21 Excerpt from *The Leader*, 25 Sept. 1852, quoted in M & B, 1929, I, 1192.

22 HP, 102/1, Lord Henry Lennox to Disraeli, 17 Jan. 1853, folio 64; emphasis in the original.

23 Andrew Elfenbein, *Byron and the Victorians* (Cambridge, 1995), ch. 6, argues that Disraeli and Bulwer Lytton had 'performed' Byron's homosexuality in their youth as an attention-getting device. The persistence of Byron as a topic in private correspondence between Disraeli and Lennox suggests there was something more there than simply performance, as Elfenbein concedes, p. 216.

24 HP, 102/1, Lord Henry Lennox to Disraeli, Sept. 1853, folios 74–5; *DL*, 2560, Disraeli to Sarah Brydges Willyams, 29 Sept. 1853, n. 4.

25 HP, 102/1, Lord Henry Lennox to Disraeli, ?6 Oct. 1853, folio 80.

26 M & B, 1929, I, 1274–5; *DL*, 2560, Disraeli to Mrs Brydges Willyams,

29 Sept. 1853.

27 *DL*, 2560, Disraeli to Mrs Brydges Willyams, 29 Sept. 1853, n. 5.

28 Ibid., 2699, Disraeli to Lord Henry Lennox, ?27 Nov. 1854, n. 4.

29 Ibid., 3027, Disraeli to Sir William Jolliffe, 24 Feb. 1858, n. 3.

30 HP, 96/1, Ralph Earle to Disraeli, 1 June 1858, folios 190–1.

31 *DL*, 3204, Disraeli to Lord Malmesbury, 29 Sept. 1858, n. 1, 3.

32 Ibid., 3257, Disraeli to Lord Salisbury, 22 Dec. 1858.

33 Ibid., 3302, Disraeli to Lord Henry Lennox, 1 Mar. 1859, n. 1, 2.

34 HP, 96/3, Ralph Earle to Disraeli, ?1859, folio 80.

35 *DL*, 3356, Disraeli to Lord Henry Lennox, 27 May 1859, n. 1, 2.

36 M & B, 1929, I, 1600, n. 1.

37 Blake, 370–1.

38 HP, 96/1, Ralph Earle to Disraeli, 23 Jan. 1857, folios 19, 12.

39 Ibid., 4 Mar. 1857, folio 81.

40 Blake, 372.

41 M & B, 1929, I, 1468.

42 Ibid., 1633–4; *DL*, 3352, Disraeli to Mrs Brydges Willyams, 20 May 1859.

43 Blake, 372.

44 Ibid., 306–7.

45 *DL*, vol. VI, appendix 1A, Edward Stanley's jottings of Disraeli's habits and conversation, 534, 535.

46 Ibid., 2490, Disraeli to Lady Galway, 22 Feb. 1853, n. 3.

47 Ibid., 2596, Disraeli to Mary Anne Disraeli, 12 Dec. 1853; *Disraeli's Reminiscences*, 123.

48 *DL*, 2669, Disraeli to Lady Londonderry, 7 Aug. 1854; M & B, 1929, I, 1362–3.

49 *DL.*, 2894, Disraeli to Lord Stanley, 23 Jan. 1857.

50 M & B, 1929, I, 1537; *DL*, 3106, Disraeli to Lord Derby, 30 Apr. 1858, n. 1.

51 *DL*, 3138, Disraeli to Sir Edward Bulwer Lytton, 8 June 1858? (dating conjectural), n. 1.

52 M & B, 1929, I, 1592, 1593, n. 2.

53 Ibid., 1606.

17 – More Valuable than Parks and Palaces

1 M & B, 1929, I, 1423; *DL*, 2792, Disraeli to Mrs Brydges Willyams, 18 Nov. 1855.

2 M & B, 1929, I, 1607, n. 1; *DL*, 3304, Disraeli to Mrs Brydges Willyams, 5 Mar. 1859.

3 M & B, 1929, I, 1276, n. 1.

4   *DL*, 2651, Disraeli to Mrs Brydges Willyams, 23 Apr. 1854.
5   Weintraub, 307; M & B, 1929, I, 1283. For 'emerald isle' see M & B, 1929, I, 1278; *DL*, 2845, Disraeli to Sarah Brydges Willyams, 17 May 1856.
6   M & B, 1929, I, 1279.
7   Bradford, 85.
8   M & B, 1929, I, 1362–3; *DL*, 2669, Disraeli to Lady Londonderry, 7 Aug. 1854, n. 7.
9   *DL*, 2691, Disraeli to Lady Londonderry, 21 Oct. 1854.
10 Ibid., 2775, Disraeli to Lady Londonderry, 2 Sept. 1855.
11 M & B, 1929, I, 1494; *DL*, 2964, Disraeli to Lady Londonderry, 31 July 1857.
12 M & B, 1929, I, 1511; *DL*, 3015, Disraeli to Lady Londonderry, 7 Jan. 1858. For 'endless polkas' see *DL*, 3240, Disraeli to Lady Londonderry, 27 Nov. 1858.
13 Quoted in Blake, 143.
14 M & B, 1929, I, 1362.
15 Ibid., 1365.
16 *DL*, 2322X, Disraeli to Lady Londonderry, 26 June 1852; in vol. VII outside the main sequence of letters.
17 M & B, 1929, I, 1429; *DL*, 2835, Disraeli to Mrs Brydges Willyams, 24 Mar. 1856.
18 M & B, 1929, I, 1405; *DL*, 2747, Disraeli to Mrs Brydges Willyams, 1 May 1855.
19 M & B, 1929, I, 1508–9; *DL*, 3018, Disraeli to Lady Londonderry, 23 Jan. 1858.
20 M & B, 1929, I, 1169.
21 Ibid., 1170, 1525.
22 Ibid., 1524–5.
23 *DL*, 3089, Disraeli to Queen Victoria, 13 Apr. 1858.
24 Ibid., 3337, Disraeli to Queen Victoria, 19 Apr. 1859.
25 Ibid., 3425, Disraeli to Ralph Disraeli, 9 Dec. 1859.
26 Ibid., 3427, Disraeli to Sir William Jolliffe, 10 Dec. 1859.
27 Ibid., 3434, Disraeli to Lord Henry Lennox, 25 Dec. 1859.

18 – Pearls Are Like Girls, My Lord

1   *Disraeli, Derby and the Conservative Party: Journals and Memoirs of Edward Henry, Lord Stanley, 1849–1869*, ed. John Vincent (New York, 1978), 31.
2   Ibid., 33, and see n. 8.
3   Benjamin Disraeli, *Lothair* ed. with an intro. Vernon Bogdanor (1870;

1975), 134.

4 M & B, IV, 295.
5 Benjamin Disraeli, *Contarini Fleming*, vol. IV of the Bradenham edn., with intro. Philip Guedalla (New York, 1927), 24.
6 Ibid., 26.
7 M & B, IV, 302.
8 Ibid., 340.
9 Ibid., 304.
10 *Letters from Benjamin Disraeli to Frances Anne Marchioness of Londonderry 1837–1861*, ed. with an intro. the Marchioness of Londonderry (1938), 193.
11 Ibid., 194.
12 Ibid., vii.
13 *Disraeli, Derby and the Conservative Party*, 33.
14 M & B, IV, 533.
15 Ibid., 572.
16 Ibid., 600.
17 Ibid., V, 52.
18 Ibid., 53.
19 Quoted in Blake, 412.
20 M & B, IV, 384.
21 Ibid., 391–2.
22 See 'Disraeli, Benjamin, first Earl of Beaconsfield', *ODNB*, 282.
23 M & B, IV, 397.
24 Ibid., 396.
25 Ibid., 457.
26 Ibid., V, 47.
27 Ibid., 47–8.
28 Ibid., 52.
29 Ibid., 53.
30 Ibid.
31 Ibid., 53–4.

19 – Enamoured Sexagenarians

1 M & B, 1929, I, 1558–9.
2 M & B, V, 3.
3 Ibid., IV, 362.
4 Ibid., 325.
5 Ibid., 277.
6 Ibid., 307–8.
7 Quoted in ibid., 527.

8 Ibid., 570.
9 H. C. G. Matthew, *Gladstone, 1809–1874* (Oxford, 1988), 11.
10 M & B, V, 11.
11 Benjamin Disraeli, *Lothair*, ed. with intro. Vernon Bogdanor (1870; 1975), 21.
12 Ibid., 10.
13 Ibid., xii, n. 6.
14 Ibid., 41.
15 Colm Tóibín, *The Master* (2004).
16 *Disraeli's Novels Reviewed*, 1826–1968, ed. R. W. Stewart (Metuchen, NJ, 1975), 257–8.
17 *Lothair*, 7, 113.
18 Ibid., 8.
19 Ibid., 96.
20 Ibid., 71.
21 Edgar Feuchtwanger, *Disraeli* (2000), 75.
22 *Lothair*, 170.
23 Ibid., 194–5.
24 Ibid., 311.
25 Ibid., 362.
26 Ibid., 20.
27 Ibid., 24.
28 Ibid., 142.
29 Ibid., 292, 295.
30 Ibid., 297.
31 Ibid., 298.
32 Ibid., 315.
33 Ibid., 294.
34 Ibid., 141.
35 M & B, IV, 419.
36 Ibid., 528–9.
37 Ibid., 447.
38 'Corry, Montagu William Lowry, Baron Rowton, 1838–1903', *ODNB*.
39 M & B, IV, 502.
40 Ibid., V, 132.

20 – Amidst Imperial Triumphs

1 Benjamin Disraeli, *Endymion* (1880; 1881), 265.
2 M & B, V, 182–3.
3 Lord Ronald Gower, *My Reminiscences* (1882; 1895), 275.

4 M & B, V, 194–5.
5 Ibid., 169–70.
6 Anna Clark, *Scandal: The Sexual Politics of the British Constitution* (Princeton, NJ and Oxford, 2004), 11.
7 M & B, V, 464.
8 Ibid., 478–9.
9 Ibid., VI, 59–60.
10 See John W. Derry, *Castlereagh* (New York, 1976), 227; H. Montgomery Hyde, *The Strange Death of Lord Castlereagh* (1959), 179. Castlereagh, who became 2nd Marquess of Londonderry, is also on Disraeli's list of men who loved other men, which he had written down in the 1840s.
11 M & B, V, 242.
12 Zetland, I, 273.
13 Disraeli to Queen Victoria, 7 June 1878, quoted in M & B, VI, 308–9.
14 Disraeli to Queen Victoria, 8 June 1878, quoted in Ibid., 309.
15 Zetland, II, 172.
16 M & B, VI, 330, diary entry 1 July 1878.
17 Ibid., 476.
18 Ibid., V, 242.
19 Zetland, I, 50–1.
20 Ibid., 56.
21 Ibid., II, 42.
22 Ibid., I, 81.
23 Ibid., II, 203.
24 Ibid., I, 54.
25 Ibid., II, 138.
26 Ibid., I, 261.
27 M & B, VI, 474.
28 Zetland, II, 253.
29 Ibid., I, 93.
30 M & B, VI, 207.
31 Ibid., 314.
32 Ibid., 324.
33 Ibid., 327.
34 Ibid., 331.
35 Ibid., V, 483.
36 Zetland, I, 194.

21 – Every Procession Must End

1 Esher, as Reginald Brett, was Permanent Secretary of the Office of

Works from 1895 to 1902; Harcourt was First Commissioner of the Office of Works from 1905 to 1910. Esher's bisexuality is well known; see James Lees-Milne's biography, *Enigmatic Edwardian* (1986). Harcourt died in mysterious circumstances, possibly a suicide like Castlereagh's, after accusations made against him by a young man who had just left Eton. See also both their entries in the *ODNB*.

2 M & B, V, 291.

3 Zetland, I, 183.

4 Ibid., 193.

5 Ibid., II, 211.

6 Quoted in 'Lord Henry Charles George Gordon-Lennox (1821–1886)' under entry for his father, 'Lennox, Charles Gordon, fifth duke of Richmond and fifth duke of Lennox (1791–1860)', *ODNB*.

7 M & B, V, 222.

8 Ibid., 256.

9 Lord Ronald Gower, *Reminiscences*, (1882; 1895), 509.

10 M & B, VI, 202.

11 Ibid., 282.

12 Ibid., 237.

13 Zetland, II, 197.

14 Quoted in 'Corry, Montagu William Lowry, Baron Rowton', *ODNB*.

15 M & B, VI, 524.

16 Ibid., 528–9.

17 Ibid., 552.

18 Ibid., 568.

19 Earl of Beaconsfield, *Endymion* (1880; 1881), 19.

20 Ibid., 101.

21 Ibid., 288.

22 Ibid., 96.

23 Ibid., 292.

24 M & B, VI, 566.

25 Graham Robb, *Strangers* (2003), 90. Art historians agree that Girodet's 'Endymion' 'exudes eroticism' and emphasizes the androgyny of the male figure. It was painted late in 1791 and first exhibited in Paris in 1793. See Stephanie Nevison Brown, 'Girodet (de Roussy-Trioson), Anne-Louis', in *Grove Dictionary of Art* (1996), XII, 730; and James Smalls, 'Girodet-Trioson, Anne-Louis (1767–1824)', *An Encyclopedia of Gay, Lesbian, Bisexual, Transgender & Queer Culture* (online), accessed 22 June 2005, www.glbtq.com/arts/girodet_trioson_al.html. See also Abigail Solomon-Godeau, 'Endymion était–il gay? Interprétation historique, histoire de l'art homosexuelle et historiographie queer', in

Sylvain Bellenger, *Girodet, 1767–1824* (Paris, 2005), 81–95.

26 Alexander Robertson, *Atkinson Grimshaw* (1988), 59.

27 Isaac D'Israeli, *An Inquiry into the Literary and Political Character of James the First* (1816), 188–9.

28 See Oakeshott's 'On Being Conservative', in *Rationalism and Politics* (1962), 169.

29 *Endymion*, 10.

30 Ibid., 149. Otranto/Albert is a thinly veiled portrait of Napoleon III, whom Disraeli knew from his days in the circle of d'Orsay and Lady Blessington.

31 Ibid., 344; see also 314.

32 M & B, VI, 592.

33 Ibid., 609.

34 Ibid., 613.

35 Ibid., 614.

36 Ibid.

37 Ibid., 617–18.

Epilogue

1 M & B, V, 375–6.

2 Blake, 739.

3 The fragment, 'Falconet', is in the appendix of M & B, V, 534.

4 Blake, 739.

5 M & B, V, 536.

6 Ibid., 538–9.

7 Blake, 739.

8 M & B, V, 544–5.

9 Ibid., VI, 635.

10 Ibid., V, 546.

11 John Morley, *The Life of William Ewart Gladstone*, 3 vols. (1903), II, 252.

12 M & B, V, 308.

13 Ibid., 546.

14 Ibid., 547.

15 Ibid.

16 Ibid., 548.

17 Ibid.

18 Ibid., 550.

19 Ibid.

20 Benjamin Disraeli, *Lothair*, ed. with an intro. Vernon Bogdanor (1870; 1975), 148.

21 Ridley, 118.
22 M & B, I, 284.
23 Ibid., V, 338.
24 Ibid., 513.
25 Ibid., 503, 506, 508.
26 Ibid., 382.
27 Benjamin Disraeli, 'The Infernal Marriage', in *Popanilla and Other Tales*, ed. and intro. Philip Guedalla, vol. III of the Bradenham edn (1926), 179.
28 Zetland, II, 279.
29 *DL*, 1272, Disraeli to Sarah Disraeli, 16 Jan. 1843.

Selected Bibliography

Primary Sources

Ancient Spanish Ballads, Historical and Romantic, trans. J. G. Lockhart (Edinburgh, 1823).

Benjamin Disraeli Letters, 1815–1859, ed. M.G. Wiebe, *et al.*, 7 vols. (in progress), (Toronto, 1987–2004).

Byron, Lord, *Childe Harold's Pilgrimage* in *The Complete Poetical Works*, ed. Jerome J. McGann, 7 vols. (Oxford, 1980–93), II.

——, *Don Juan* in *The Complete Poetical Works*, ed. Jerome J. McGann, 7 vols. (Oxford, 1980–93), V.

D'Israeli, Isaac, *An Inquiry into the Literary and Political Character of James the First* (1816).

——, *Curiosities of Literature*, with a view of the life and writings of the author by his son, 14th edn, 3 vols. (1849).

Disraeli, Benjamin, 'A Colloquy on the Progress and Prospect of the 'Court Journal'', *The Court Journal*, 23 May 1829.

——, 'Second Edition! Terrible Non-Occurrence!! Flight of a Distinguished Individual!!! Etc. Etc.', *The Court Journal*, 30 May 1829.

——, 'The Trial of Mivartinos', *The Court Journal*, 6 June 1829.

——, 'The Levee of Augustus Villeroy', *The Court Journal*, 20 June 1829.

——, *Coningsby; or, The New Generation*, by B. Disraeli, Esq. M.P., author of 'Contarini Fleming', 3 vols. (1844).

——, *Contarini Fleming: A Psychological Autobiography*, 4 vols., (1832). Another edn, subtitled *A Psychological Romance* (1878), vol. IV of the Bradenham edn, ed. and intro. Philip Guedalla (New York, 1927).

——, *Endymion*, by the Earl of Beaconsfield (1880; 1881).

——, *Henrietta Temple: A Love Story*, by the author of 'Vivian Grey', 3 vols. (1836).

——, *Lord George Bentinck: A Political Biography*, by B. Disraeli, Member of

Parliament for the County of Buckingham (1852).

——, *Lothair*, ed. and intro. Vernon Bogdanor (1870; 1975).

——, 'The Infernal Marriage', in *Popanilla and Other Tales*, ed. and intro. Philip Guedalla, vol. III of the Bradenham edn (1926).

——, *Sybil; or, The Two Nations*, by B. Disraeli, M.P., author of 'Coningsby', 3 vols. (1845).

——, *Tancred; or, The New Crusade*, by B. Disraeli, M.P., author of 'Coningsby', 'Sybil', etc., 3 vols. (1847).

——, *The Tragedy of Count Alarcos*, by the author of 'Vivian Grey' (1839).

——, *The Wondrous Tale of Alroy* and *The Rise of Iskander*, 3 vols. (1833).

——, *The Young Duke, 'A moral Tale, though gay'*, by the author of 'Vivian Grey', 3 vols. (1831).

——, *Venetia*, by the author of 'Vivian Grey' and 'Henrietta Temple', 3 vols. (1837).

——, *Vivian Grey*, 5 vols. bound in 2, vols. I–II (1826), vols. III–V (1827). Another edn, ed. Lucien Wolf, 2 vols. (1904).

——, *The Voyage of Captain Popanilla*, by the author of 'Vivian Grey' (1828).

Disraeli, Benjamin and Sarah Disraeli, *A Year at Hartlebury, or The Election*, with appendices by Ellen Henderson and John P. Matthews (1834; 1983).

Disraeli, Derby and the Conservative Party: Journals and Memoirs of Edward Henry, Lord Stanley, 1849–1869, ed. John Vincent (New York, 1978).

Disraeli's Novels Reviewed, 1826–1968, ed. R. W. Stewart (Metuchen, NJ, 1975).

Disraeli's Reminiscences, ed. Helen M. Swartz and Marvin Swartz (1975).

Fonblanque, Edward Barrington de., *Lives of the Lords Strangford* (London, Paris and New York, 1877).

Fraser's Magazine.

Gower, Lord Ronald, *My Reminiscences* (1882; 1895).

Hole, Richard, *Remarks on the Arabian Nights' Entertainments; in which the origin of Sinbad's Voyages, and other oriental fictions, is particularly considered* (1797).

Hughenden Papers. The papers of Benjamin Disraeli on loan from the National Trust to the Bodleian Library, Oxford, Dep. Hughenden.

Illustrated London News.

Juvenal, Decimus Junius, *The Satires of Decimus Junius Juvenal*, trans. William Gifford (1802).

Letters from Benjamin Disraeli to Frances Anne Marchioness of Londonderry 1837–1861, ed. and intro. Marchioness of Londonderry (1938).

Letters of Disraeli to Lady Bradford and Lady Chesterfield, ed. Marquess of Zetland, 2 vols. (1929).

Phoenix of Sodom, or The Vere Street Coterie (1813).

Ponsonby Papers. Shulbrede Priory.

Punch.

Smythe, George, 7th Viscount Strangford, *Angela Pisani: A Novel*, with a brief memoir of the author by Emily Strangford, 3 vols. (1875).

Vanity Fair.

Secondary Sources

Ackerman, Gerald M., *The Life and Work of Jean-Léon Gérôme* (1986).

Adams, James Eli, *Dandies and Desert Saints: Styles of Victorian Masculinity* (Ithaca, NY and London, 1995).

Barchard, David, 'On the Wrong Side of History', *Cornucopia*, issue 29, vol. V. (2003).

Bartlett, Neil, *Who Was That Man? A Present for Mr Oscar Wilde* (1988).

Berlin, Isaiah, 'Benjamin Disraeli, Karl Marx and the Search for Identity', in *Against the Current: Essays in the History of Ideas*, ed. and bibliography Henry Hardy; intro. Roger Hausheer (New York, 1980).

Bernal, Martin, *Black Athena: The Afroasiatic Roots of Classical Civilization*, vol. I., *The Fabrication of Ancient Greece, 1785–1985* (1987).

Blake, Robert, *Disraeli* (1966).

Blake, Robert, *Disraeli's Grand Tour: Benjamin Disraeli and the Holy Land, 1830–1831* (1982).

Bradford, Sarah, *Disraeli* (1982).

Bradley, Simon and Nikolaus Pevsner, *London 1: The City of London* (1997).

——, *London 6: Westminster*, (New Haven, CT and London, 2003).

Braun, Thom, *Disraeli the Novelist* (1981).

Bray, Alan, *The Friend* (Chicago and London, 2003).

Brooke, Xanthe and Peter Cherry, *Murillo: Scenes of Childhood* (2001).

Cherry, Bridget and Nikolaus Pevsner, *London 2: South* (Harmondsworth, 1983).

——, *London 4: North* (1998).

Clark, Anna, *Scandal: The Sexual Politics of the British Constitution* (Princteton, NJ and Oxford, 2004).

Clarke, Kenneth, 'Disraeli as Chancellor', in *Benjamin Disraeli, Earl of Beaconsfield: Scenes from an Extraordinary Life*, ed. Helen Langley (Oxford, 2003).

Cocks, H. G., *Nameless Offences: Homosexual Desire in the Nineteenth Century* (2003).

Cook, Matt, *London and the Culture of Homosexuality, 1885–1914* (Cambridge, 2003).

Crompton, Louis, *Byron and Greek Love* (1985).

386 *The Politics of Pleasure*

——, *Homosexuality and Civilization* (Cambridge, MA, 2003).

Dell, Elizabeth and Jay Losey, 'Introduction', in *Mapping Male Sexuality: Nineteenth-Century England,* ed. Jay Losey and William D. Brewer (Madison and Teaneck, NJ, 2000).

Dellamora, Richard, 'Benjamin Disraeli, Judaism, and the Legacy of William Beckford', in *Mapping Male Sexuality: Nineteenth-Century England,* ed. Jay Losey and William D. Brewer (Madison and Teaneck, NJ, 2000).

Derry, John W., *Castlereagh* (New York, 1976).

Dowling, Linda, *Hellenism and Homosexuality in Victorian Oxford* (Ithaca, NY and London, 1994).

Elfenbein, Andrew, *Byron and the Victorians* (Cambridge, 1995).

Ellmann, Richard, *Oscar Wilde* (1987).

Endelman, Todd M., *The Jews of Britain, 1656–2000* (Berkeley, CA, 2002).

Faber, Richard, *Young England* (1987).

Feldman, Jessica R., *Gender on the Divide: The Dandy in Modernist Literature* (Ithaca, NY and London, 1993).

Feuchtwanger, Edgar, *Disraeli* (2000).

Flavin, Michael, *Benjamin Disraeli: The Novel as Political Discourse* (Brighton and Portland, OR, 2005).

Foulkes, Nick, *Last of the Dandies: The Scandalous Life and Escapades of Count d'Orsay* (2003).

Gay, Peter, *Schnitzler's Century: The Making of Middle-Class Culture, 1815–1914* (2001).

Glassman, Bernard, *Benjamin Disraeli: The Fabricated Jew in Myth and Memory* (Lanham, MD, 2003).

Gross, Jonathan, '"One Half What I Should Say": Byron's Gay Narrator in *Don Juan*', in *Mapping Male Sexuality: Nineteenth-Century England,* ed. Jay Losey and William D. Brewer (Madison and Teaneck, NJ, 2000).

Haggerty, George, ed., *Gay Histories and Cultures: An Encyclopedia* (2000).

Hibbert, Christopher, *Venice: The Biography of a City* (1988).

——, *Disraeli: A Personal History* (2004).

Hilliard, David, 'Un-English and Unmanly', *Victorian Studies,* 25 (1982).

Hobhouse, Hermione, *Lost London: A Century of Demolition and Decay* (1971).

Hughenden Manor, Buckinghamshire (1997).

Hyde, H. Montgomery, *The Strange Death of Lord Castlereagh* (1959).

Irwin, Robert, *The Arabian Nights: A Companion* (1994).

Katz, Jonathan Ned, *Love Stories: Sex Between Men before Homosexuality* (Chicago, 2001).

Kelly, Ian, *Beau Brummell: The Ultimate Dandy* (2005).

Knox, James, *Robert Byron* (2003).

Kuhn, William, *Democratic Royalism: The Transformation of the British Monarchy, 1861–1914* (Basingstoke and New York, 1996).

——, *Henry and Mary Ponsonby: Life at the Court of Queen Victoria* (2002).

Langley, Helen, ed., *Benjamin Disraeli, Earl of Beaconsfield: Scenes from an Extraordinary Life* (Oxford, 2003).

Lochhead, Marion, *John Gibson Lockhart* (1954).

Lytton, Earl of, *The Life of Edward, First Lord Lytton*, by his grandson, 2 vols. (1913).

MacCarthy, Fiona, *Byron: Life and Legend* (2002).

Matthew, H. C. G., *Gladstone, 1809–1874* (Oxford, 1988).

Mitchell, Leslie, *Bulwer Lytton: The Rise and Fall of a Victorian Man of Letters* (2003).

Moers, Ellen, *The Dandy. Brummell to Beerbohm* (1960).

Monypenny, William Flavelle, and George Earle Buckle, *The Life of Benjamin Disraeli, Earl of Beaconsfield*, 6 vols. (1910–1920).

——, *The Life of Benjamin Disraeli, Earl of Beaconsfield*, ed. George Earle Buckle, 2 vols. (1929).

Mowl, Timothy, *Horace Walpole: The Great Outsider* (1996).

——, 'Disraeli's Novels and the Beckford Connection', in *Benjamin Disraeli, Earl of Beaconsfield: Scenes from an Extraordinary Life*, ed. Helen Langley (Oxford, 2003).

——, *William Beckford: Composing for Mozart* (1998).

Notopoulos, James A., *The Platonism of Shelley* (Durham, NC, 1949).

Oakeshott, Michael, *Rationalism and Politics* (New York, 1962).

Ogden, James, *Isaac D'Israeli* (Oxford, 1969).

O'Kell, Robert, 'The Autobiographical Nature of Disraeli's Early Fiction', *Nineteenth-Century Fiction*, 31 (1976).

Parry, Jonathan, 'Disraeli, Benjamin, first earl of Beaconsfield', *ODNB*.

——, 'Holborn at Heart', *London Review of Books*, 23 Jan. 1997.

Pevsner, Nikolaus, *Essex*, rev. Enid Radcliffe (Harmondsworth, 1979).

Ponsonby, Arthur, *Henry Ponsonby, Queen Victoria's Private Secretary. His Life from his Letters* (1942).

Reade, Brian, *Sexual Heretics. Male Homosexuality in English Literature from 1850 to 1900. An Anthology*, intro. Brian Reade (1970).

Ridley, Jane, *The Young Disraeli, 1804–1846* (1995).

Robb, Graham, *Strangers: Homosexual Love in the Nineteenth Century* (2003).

Robertson, Alexander, *Atkinson Grimshaw* (1988).

Rousseau, George. '"Homoplatonic, Homodepressed, Homomorbid": Some Further Genealogies of Same Sex Attraction in Western Civilization', in *Love, Sex, Intimacy and Friendship Between Men 1550–1800*, ed. Katherine O'Donnell and Michael O'Rourke (Basingstoke, 2003).

Said, Edward W., *Orientalism* (1978).

Schwartz, Daniel R., *Disraeli's Fiction* (1979).

Sedgwick, Eve Kosofsky, *Between Men: English Literature and Male Homosocial Desire* (New York, 1985).

Smith, Paul, *Disraeli: A Brief Life* (Cambridge, 1996).

Solomon-Godeau, Abigail, 'Endymion était-il gay? Interprétation historique, histoire de l'art homosexuelle et historiographie queer', in Sylvain Bellenger, *Girodet, 1767–1824* (Paris, 2005).

Survey of London (1960).

Tóibín, Colm, *The Master* (2004).

Trumbach, Randolph, *Sex and the Gender Revolution,* vol. I, *Heterosexuality and the Third Gender in Enlightenment London* (Chicago and London, 1998).

Vincent, John, *Disraeli* (Oxford, 1990).

Walden, George, *Who Is a Dandy?* with Jules Barbey d'Aurevilly, *On Dandyism and George Brummell,* trans. George Walden (2002).

Weintraub, Stanley, *Disraeli* (1993).

Wells, Stanley, *Looking for Sex in Shakespeare* (Cambridge, 2004).

Whibley, Charles, *Lord John Manners and His Friends,* 2 vols. (1925).

Wilde, Oscar, *A Woman of No Importance* in *The Best of Oscar Wilde: Selected Plays and Literary Criticism,* ed. and intro. Sylvan Barnet, (New York, 2004).

Woods, Gregory, *A History of Gay Literature* (New Haven, CT and London, 1998).

Young, James B., *James VI and I and the History of Homosexuality* (Basingstoke, 2000).

Index